MUNICH:
BEFORE AND AFTER

MUNICH:
BEFORE AND AFTER

A fully documented Czechoslovak account
of the crises of September 1938 and March
1939 with a detailed analysis of the repercussions of the Munich Agreement on the
situation of Europe as a whole and of Central Europe in particular, together with an
essay on the reconstruction of a free Europe

by

DR. HUBERT RIPKA

Translated from the manuscript

by

IDA ŠINDELKOVÁ

and

Comdr. EDGAR P. YOUNG

NEW YORK

Howard Fertig

1969

First published in 1939 by Victor Gollancz Ltd.

HOWARD FERTIG, INC. EDITION 1969
Published by arrangement with Victor Gollancz, Ltd.

Library of Congress Catalog Card Number: 68-9630

PRINTED IN THE UNITED STATES OF AMERICA
BY NOBLE OFFSET PRINTERS, INC.

56608

CONTENTS

CONTENTS

MAPS

NOTE

I WISH to acknowledge the kind permission of His Majesty's Stationery Office to reproduce extracts taken from Cmd. Papers 5847 and 5848 and from certain Parliamentary Debates, House of Commons Official Reports.

Certain documents which are reproduced here belong to the collection of Czechoslovak State Documents, and at the time when I obtained access to them were the property of the First Czechoslovak Republic. Though in several cases the documents quoted are notes sent by the British or French Governments to the Czechoslovak Government, these notes have not been published officially either in English or in French. These documents are, therefore, retranslations from the Czech.

Preface

THIS book is an attempt to tell the dramatic story of the European crisis from September, 1938, to March, 1939. It is not only because the author is a Czechoslovak that the fate of Czechoslovakia is the centre of this history. This place is sufficiently justified by the fact that events in Europe and in the world took a revolutionary turn the moment the external, and subsequently the internal, independence of Czechoslovakia was destroyed. The geographical position of this country in the very heart of Europe inexorably determines the unalterable fact that the whole face of Europe changes according to the fate of the Czechoslovak people. This assertion does not mean that the Czechoslovak nation determines the fate of Europe. To say so would be absurd and extravagant. But it cannot be denied that the Czech nation was always—in the Middle Ages as well as in modern times—a very important factor in European politics. Its importance has always been out of all proportion to its numerical strength. This is due not only to its geographical situation at the crossroads of conflicting European interests, tendencies and movements, but also to its creative genius, which drove it to take its place in culture and politics beside the greatest nations of Europe. As the fate of this nation was insolubly bound up with the general development and state of Europe, so everything that happened to it did not remain confined to its immediate vicinity, but has always had a far-reaching influence on the course of European history as a whole. All attempts to neglect, or to ignore, its importance, not only for Central Europe, but the entire continent, will always entail the gravest consequences.

After the war an independent, democratic Czechoslovakia was one of the main pillars on which the new order in Europe was built. The order established by the Peace Treaties of 1919–20 was based on certain principles, which in international politics were best expressed by the tendencies represented by the League of Nations. They could be summarised quite briefly as: respect for international law and for all treaties; the recognition of the equality of all nations without distinction of size; respect for the integrity, independence and freedom of all nations, both large and small; the condemnation of war as an instrument for the settlement of disputes between nations; the peaceful adjustment of such conflicts by means of voluntary agreement or arbitration; the collective guarantee for the security of every country against threatened aggression. Against these principles, which were, on the whole, an application of democratic doctrine to the sphere of international relations, there arose the opposition of Italian Fascism and German National Socialism, which reject with passionate consistency the whole democratic conception of equal rights for all nations, exalt the power of the strong over the weak above all international law and systematically encourage the cult of brute force and war. The democratic countries were driven on to the defensive by these "dynamic" Powers, to whom they lost one position after another. The armed occupation of Manchuria by Japan in 1931 was the beginning of a sequence which continued with the conquest of Abyssinia by Italy, the remilitarisation of the Rhineland and the annexation of Austria by Germany, the Italian and German intervention in Spain and culminated in March, 1939, in the occupation of Czechoslovakia by the Third Reich, speedily followed by the invasion of Albania by Italy. Though all these events exerted a profound influence on international relations, it was only the destruction of Czechoslovakia which overthrew the whole structure of the post-war European order. The balance of power of the post-war period was upset and the political relations between nations radically changed.

But even more has happened: Europe has been thrown into a warlike ferment, a new world war can break out at any moment and the enormous tension between individual states is accompanied by a strong social tension, which is discharged in the increased " ideological " conflicts between the nations and between the individuals who compose them.

It is really unbelievable, how insufficiently the importance of an independent Czechoslovakia in the interplay of European forces was understood and appreciated. Only the Nazi imperialists fully realised the difference which its destruction would make in the scales of Europe. They knew that the fundamental condition of their success was the destruction of a strong Czechoslovakia. As long as they had not removed this obstacle all their plans for expansion, whether they were directed to the east or to the west, remained very hazardous gambles, without substantial hope of success. The Nazis were more practical and more earnest than their opponents among the great Powers: they studied the map of Europe and its history with characteristic thoroughness. From all such studies the European importance of Czechoslovakia emerged more and more clearly. Czechoslovakia held a strategic position of first-class importance. This position was the key to the whole Danube Basin, the first-line defence of the Balkans. Even after the invasion of Austria, Germany could not hope to dominate the Danube Basin and the Balkans, so long as an independent Czechoslovakia was in existence. Her destruction was a necessary condition of the success of a Pan-German *Mitteleuropa.* Her weakening as an effective political power lowered the power of resistance of all other Danubian nations. When, after Munich, Czechoslovakia was forced to become the vassal of Germany, the doors of the whole Danubian region were thrown open to expansionist Pan-Germanism. Not only were Hungary, Yugoslavia and Rumania endangered, but Poland in the north and Turkey and Greece in the extreme south were threatened by Germany and also by Italy. Prague had been one pole of an axis, whose second pole was in Ankara. If this axis was broken at one end, it was inevitably weakened at the other. But Prague lay also on another axis—the axis running between Paris and Moscow, which connected eastern and western Europe. The democratic system of Czechoslovakia was internally so balanced and strong that it had no political or social reasons to fear even close collaboration with the Soviet Union. As Czechoslovakia knew that there was no other state in Eastern Europe which could take the place of Soviet Russia—as the only single Power which can balance Germany—she worked systematically for the establishment of the friendliest collaboration between the Western Powers and the Soviet Union. For Western Europe, Czechoslovakia represented not only a link of vital strategic importance, but the only link which was politically sound. After the destruction of Czechoslovakia, collaboration between the west and Moscow can be realised only through the medium of Poland—and there is no need to stress the difficulties which arise from the unsatisfactory nature of Polish-Soviet relations.

Thus the Pan-Germans fully realised what Czechoslovakia meant on the European chess-board. They were also well aware of the military potential of this state, which was out of all proportion to the number of its inhabitants. Of all Central European states Czechoslovakia alone had an army equipped with modern technical weapons, an army which in every respect, technical and moral, was on the same level as the armies of the European Great Powers. Her air force was two thirds the strength of the French. Furthermore, she was enormously strong in economic resources, both in industrial production and in agriculture. For her extensive armaments and metal industries she was called by the Germans the " Arsenal of Europe." Czechoslovakia was the most important and the strongest of the opponents of the Third Reich in the whole of Central Europe. It was for this reason that the Pan-Germans had to work for her destruction before they could embark on their long-term plan for the domination of Europe.

The tragedy of the Czechoslovak nation was the fact that this destructive work of the Third Reich found support among its own allies and friends. Czechoslovakia was the only state in Central Europe which had with unshakable consistency preserved her loyalty to the two Western democracies. The Czechoslovak Government had invariably resisted the policy of time-serving opportunism which was followed by Colonel Beck in Warsaw and M. Stojadinović in Belgrade. When, however, Nazi agression centred on the Czechoslovak nation, its appeal for help went unheard by those in whom it had trusted and towards whom it had fulfilled all its obligations.

In September, 1938, Czechoslovakia yielded not so much to the pressure of the Third Reich, but, first and foremost to the pressure of France and Great Britain. This pressure took the form, not only of informing the Czechoslovak Government that failure to accept their terms would result in the complete international isolation of Czechoslovakia; but also the threat, in so many words, that Czechoslovakia would alone be responsible for the outbreak of war and would therefore have to take the consequences of refusing to yield to Germany. It is a unique occurrence in history that the Great Powers should deliberately prevent a small nation from defending itself, though it was ready to fight with all its forces. The threats and warlike preparations of the Germans were insufficient to break the readiness of the Czechoslovak people to defend themselves. That resistance was finally broken when they were not only deserted but ordered to conform to the German wishes by their former friends.

But Hitler was not content with the great successes he had gained at Munich. He wanted to make them completely sure, in order to continue in greater security his drive towards German hegemony over Europe and the world. When the work of internal disruption in subjugated Czechoslovakia had sufficiently advanced, he threw himself on the defenceless nation in order to bring it under the direct rule of Greater Germany. Thus in March, 1939, Germany completed the work which had been begun in September, 1938: Czechoslovakia was completely destroyed. The sacrifice, to which she had been forced at Munich, in the name of European peace and the promise of the guarantee of its frontiers, had been in vain. Not only was peace not saved or even secured for some time, but, on the contrary, Europe found itself on the very brink of war. The military occupation of Czechoslovakia was a clear signal that the Third Reich had decided to enforce its plans for world domination even at the cost of European war. Everything that happened afterwards confirmed this: whether it was the immediately increased pressure on Rumania by Germany or preparations against Poland or the occupation of Albania by Italy—the Rome-Berlin Axis continues its programme of aggression and is on the war-path against the rest of Europe.

This book describes the main events which happened between September 19, 1938, and the end of March, 1939. The story begins with the journey of Mr. Chamberlain to Berchtesgaden, the decisive turn in the politics of the Western Powers, a turn the consequence of which was Munich. It is, of course, necessary to explain quite briefly what appeared on the surface to be the nature of the conflict between Germany and Czechoslovakia. I therefore explain first the real essence of the Sudeten German problem, then describe in detail the September crisis, in which I took part in Prague as a direct and active witness. I then explain the consequences of Munich, as they appeared in Czechoslovakia and the whole of Central Europe, and finally close the whole history with an account of the occupation of Czechoslovakia in March, 1939. I have thought it necessary to add in conclusion some political reflections which defend the conception of an independent Czechoslovakia as established by Masaryk, and express the creed of a Czechoslovak democrat. I wish to contribute by this book to a better understanding of the European importance of the Czechoslovak nation, and to the strengthening of confidence in the ultimate victory of truth and right over the dark forces of evil and brutal violence. The actual struggle is still to come. Enormously important positions have been lost, but the final result has not yet been decided.

The chapter on the German occupation of Bohemia and Moravia was written immediately after it took place. The later development of those provinces has followed the Nazi model of political, economic and intellectual repression enforced by a growing terror. For the first time, however, the Nazis have come up against a non-German population and are faced, not only with a foreign language, but with a foreign psychology. The Czechs have a will to freedom, not only as individuals, but as a nation, and the experience of our national liberation is too recent for its lessons to have been forgotten. There has been no need to foster the spirit of resistance, but rather to organise it and control it until the moment at which it will, even now, prove a decisive factor in the European situation. Our country has been taken from us, but our people remain, and the coat of arms of the Republic is the conviction of the people: " Truth will prevail."

The greater part of this book was written in the winter of 1938–39. Though much has happened since the last lines were written, subsequent events have but confirmed its main thesis— that a calamity for Europe was not avoided, but in fact precipitated, by the destruction of an independent Czechoslovakia.

CHAPTER I

*Self-determination for the Sudeten Germans or the Destruction of
Czechoslovakia?*

THE decisive turn in the tension which existed between Germany
and Czechoslovakia in the autumn of 1938 came at the moment
when Mr. Neville Chamberlain, the British Prime Minister,
decided to fly to Berchtesgaden to seek an interview with the
German Chancellor, Adolf Hitler.

News of this projected visit reached Prague on the night of
September 14. It was just after 9 o'clock, I remember, when I
received from the offices of my paper, the *Lidové Noviny*, a telephone message saying that a news agency had reported that Mr.
Chamberlain was going to Berchtesgaden to see Herr Hitler.
Several friends of mine, politicians of various parties and a few
diplomats, had come in to see me that evening and were there
when this message arrived. All of them, without exception, dismissed the story as a wild bit of sensational reporting, and we
continued our discussion of the probability of a happy sequel to
the collapse of Henlein's *Putsch*—for by that time his attempted
revolt had already been virtually suppressed. A few minutes
later, however, the report about Mr. Chamberlain was officially
confirmed. Consternation is the only word which correctly describes our reaction to this shock. We rang up the Government
departments concerned to find out what they thought about it,
and from all quarters came replies that it was " very serious,"
" very bad," " extremely dangerous."

It should be explained, perhaps, for the benefit of the British
reader why it was that the news of Mr. Chamberlain's visit to
Herr Hitler should have caused us so much anxiety and alarm.
It was because we realised at once, only too clearly, that such a
gesture on the part of the Western Powers would encourage
Hitler in his defiance, that he would interpret it as an indication
of their weakness and become, therefore, more obstinate in his
exaggerated demands and dangerous implacability. We rightly
feared that we alone would have to foot the bill. When I write
this, I am not being wise after the event, for I describe what
was the feeling throughout Prague. Nor was this feeling

confined to political circles; on the night of September 14, even the general public was alarmed. Heaven knows how many people there were—some of them strangers to me—who rang me up that night expressing excitement and fear lest we should be asked to concede everything that was demanded in order to satisfy Germany. Events justified their fears more even, alas! than we then imagined possible.

Mr. Chamberlain's decision to fly to Berchtesgaden was the explanation, in my opinion, of the sudden improvement in the situation for the Nazis which immediately ensued. We in Prague were at a loss to understand why it was that the further fulfilment of Germany's expansionist plans should thus be facilitated just at the moment when the complete collapse, within two or three days of its outbreak, of the Henleinist *Putsch*, which took place immediately after Herr Hitler's speech at Nürnberg on September 12, had radically transformed the situation with regard to the so-called Sudeten-German problem. It seemed to us that the far-reaching effects of that collapse were perhaps not fully recognised. Yet we knew that ample evidence was in the hands of the Prague authorities to prove beyond doubt that this *Putsch*, far from being a " spontaneous " revolt of the " oppressed Sudeten-Germans," had been deliberately prepared. As early as the morning of September 12—that is to say, before Hitler had made his Nürnberg speech—suspicious telephone conversations between Henleinist party officials and Germany had been intercepted; it was obvious from the fact that these officials had been reporting, " We are ready," that something was afoot. It is probable that it was this evidence which convinced even Lord Runciman that the revolt had been deliberately planned beforehand. In his Report of September 21 he stated that " incidents were provoked and instigated on the 11th September and, with greater effect, after Herr Hitler's speech on the 12th September."

The detailed story of the result falls outside the intended scope of this book, but I would stress the fact that the revolt was suppressed within two or three days by ordinary police measures, military aid being invoked only in a few exceptional instances. If the Czechoslovak Government had adopted more drastic measures, the revolt could have been suppressed within twenty-four hours. But this might have meant heavier civilian casualties, though the losses suffered by the Czech police in applying their milder methods would certainly have been fewer. I would underline, moreover, the fact that the revolt, although it was intended by its instigators to be a general one, was by no means universal throughout the Sudeten-German territory. A great part of the territory remained completely inactive, and in several places Henlein's extremist agitators were driven away by actual members of the Sudeten-German Party.

Two important facts must therefore be borne in mind: firstly, that the revolt was rapidly and comparatively easily suppressed, although the rebels were amply provided with arms, mostly of German origin, and secondly that it received no active support from the majority of the Sudeten Germans. This is surely proof—lamentable, because it led to the loss of seventy human lives, most of them Czechs who had been attacked—that the majority of the Sudeten Germans were not in sympathy with revolutionary National Socialism. It may be argued against this that Henlein's Sudeten-German Party received the majority of the German votes in the parliamentary elections of 1935 and even more in the municipal elections held in the spring of 1938, but the results on both occasions would certainly have been less favourable for Henlein if the Czechoslovak authorities had taken more effective measures against the physical and psychological terrorisation of the Sudeten-German masses which was exercised by Henlein's agitators, vigorously supported in every way by propaganda from Germany. The Czechoslovak authorities could, and should, have countered this, not only by enforcing the law against any kind of terrorisation, but also by widespread and effective support of the anti-Nazi elements, who always constituted at least one-third of the Sudeten-German population. Czechoslovak democracy deserves blame for having failed in the main to do these things. If it had been true that the majority of the Sudeten Germans really regarded Hitler, represented among them in the person of Henlein, as their leader, one might have expected them to grasp eagerly at this opportunity to revolt and free themselves from the Czech yoke. In actual fact, however, it was only a minority, composed mainly of inexperienced youths, which showed enthusiasm for the Pan-German slogan of the Nazis for the unification of all Germans, " *Ein Volk, Ein Reich, Ein Führer.*" Most of the supporters of the Sudeten-German Party wanted " autonomy," but without any clear conception of what they meant by the word. The so-called " Fourth Plan " presented by the Czechoslovak Government on September 5 offered them a wider degree of autonomy than they had ever dreamed of, satisfying in principle, it would seem, all the main demands of Henlein's well-known Karlsbad Programme. Such, at any rate, was the view adopted by Lord Runciman, for in his Report already quoted he wrote about the " Fourth Plan " thus : " In my opinion—and, I believe, in the opinion of the more responsible Sudeten leaders—this plan embodies almost all the requirements of the Karlsbad eight points, and with a little clarification and extension could have been made to cover them in their entirety. But little doubt remains in my mind," continues the Report, " that the very fact that they [the Czech terms] were so favourable operated against their chances with the more extreme members of the Sudeten-German Party." It is indeed a fact that these extremists, incited by Germany, took care that the " Fourth Plan " should not be put into execution. The German Nazis were as opposed to " autonomy " as to any other system which might lead to a satisfactory solution of the Sudeten-German problem. Instead, they demanded a " totalitarian " solution in accordance with Pan-German principles. Afraid that reconciliation between the Czechs and Germans might be effected within the framework of the Czechoslovak Republic, they provoked one bloody incident after another and finished by organising widespread revolt. In this way they prepared the ground for declaring that events had superseded the Karlsbad Programme and, finally, encouraged by the news of Mr. Chamberlain's visit to Berchtesgaden, they demanded union with the Reich.

One cannot overstress the fact that the demand for union with the Reich was no spontaneous expression of the desire of the majority of the Sudeten-German people. This demand was imposed upon the Sudeten Germans by a minority of Pan-German extremists among them, who were working in close collaboration with and following the instructions of Hitler's political General Staff. This was revealed by the passivity of the greater part of the Sudeten Germans during the days of the revolt. As soon, moreover, as the revolt had been completely suppressed, it came in for criticism by important members of the Sudeten-German Party. These men disowned their radical leaders, who had meanwhile fled into Germany, and declared their loyalty to Czechoslovakia. A large proportion of Henlein's supporters were incredibly quick in ostentatiously discarding their membership cards and badges, while many of them even went so far as to ask German Socialists and Democrats to speak in their favour with the Czech authorities.

These developments did not surprise us particularly, since we had long been well aware of the situation among the Sudeten Germans. It was known that only a minority were active in the support of Pan-German National Socialism, while the majority, carried along with the stream, were merely being made use of in order to bring pressure to bear on the Czech authorities. When Henlein's revolt was so rapidly and easily suppressed, it was clear to us that, if only time could be gained, the whole movement would disintegrate and sane judgment would begin to pre-dominate over passion among the Sudeten Germans. If this were to happen, it was absolutely necessary that decisive action by the Western Powers should hold up Hitler's expansionist plans. If the British and French had shown firmness at this point, we should have been able, on the basis of the " Fourth Plan," to come to a satisfactory settlement of the Sudeten-German prob-lem—indeed of the whole problem of our minorities—without disrupting the integrity or the Constitution of Czechoslovakia. This is exactly what Mr. Chamberlain himself had advocated in his memorable declaration of March 24, which had been expli-citly confirmed by Sir John Simon in his speech on August 27— scarcely two weeks previously.

But the possibility of this solution was exactly what was feared in Germany. The Nazis realised that as soon as Czechoslovakia settled the Sudeten-German problem, Nazi Germany would have lost a powerful instrument for the furtherance of her aggressive expansionism. The " liberation " of the Sudeten Germans was not an end in itself, but merely a means for the elimination of an independent Czechoslovakia, which the Nazis quite correctly— and, it must be admitted, with more foresight than the politicians and diplomats of Western Europe—regarded as the keystone of the balance of power in post-war Europe. It is unfortunate that what was really at stake at that time was not well understood, either in Britain or in France. Astute German propagandists used the great complexity of the Sudeten-German problem, which was naturally remote and strange to the majority of the English and French, to disguise its fundamental nature. The Nazis deliberately created the impression that it was a matter merely of a dispute between Czechs and Germans as to whether the Sudeten Germans should be granted the right of self-determination in a wider sense (union with the Reich) or in a narrower sense (autonomy within the Czechoslovak Republic). One can note the influence of this point of view in the British Prime Minister's speech of March 24.

The insufficient understanding in London and in Paris of the real significance of the Sudeten-German question proved fatal to us. We understood very well, and indeed shared, the desire of the allied Western Powers that this problem should be settled as quickly as possible and thus removed from the scene of international politics. If there was agreement, however, between London and Paris, on the one hand, and Prague, on the other, as to the end to be pursued, it was more difficult to come to such an agreement as regards ways and means of attaining it. The view which prevailed in London and Paris was that Hitler's aggressiveness should be toned down by " concessions," and it was considered that a " just " solution of the Sudeten-German problem on a basis of autonomy would satisfy Hitler. It was therefore thought wise—always with an eye on Hitler—to exert " friendly pressure " on Prague in order to make the Czechoslovak Government go " to the utmost limit " of concessions to the Sudeten Germans. Doubt prevailed in Prague whether this tactic of making " concessions " would serve to reduce the rapacity of the Nazis; it was feared, rather, that it would encourage them to put forward increasingly pressing and presumptuous demands. This fear was strengthened by the consciousness that Berlin was not concerned with the fate of the Sudeten Germans, but rather with the elimination of an independent Czechoslovakia which would be able to oppose successfully German expansion in Central Europe.

Konrad Henlein was a powerful agent of the Nazis in confusing in the British mind the real issues at stake. His moderate behaviour while he was in London created a good impression on the politicians he met. It inspired confidence and tended to refute the allegations that he was no more than the mere puppet of Berlin. We, in Prague, had no such confidence in him. The Czechoslovak Government realised that Henlein could not be considered as a leader who could come to decisions on his own, for he had neither the force nor the ability sufficient to make him independent of orders from Berlin. Furthermore, we had in our possession evidence to convince us that the policy of the Sudeten-German Party was controlled from Berlin. It was necessary only to read the Henlein Press to see that in everything, down to the very smallest details, it was following orders and instructions from the Nazi centres in the German Reich.

Under these circumstances, it is understandable that the Czechoslovak Government only made concessions reluctantly and often even with embarrassment to the " friendly advice " which came from London and Paris. There were often just grounds for criticism of this attitude, for there is no doubt that much time was wasted—to our cost—and many opportunities were missed. I myself consider, and many other Czech politicians have thought the same, that immediately after May 21, at the moment when our partial mobilisation and the firm decision of Britain and France had forced Hitler to retreat and when his prestige was considerably diminished even among the Sudeten Germans themselves, we should have proposed a broad-minded solution of our nationality problem. This solution should have been carried through quickly—by the end of July at the latest. It should have been carried through preferably in agreement with the Sudeten-German Party, but otherwise without it, and in any case, of course, in agreement with the loyal, democratic Sudeten Germans. It was undoubtedly a great mistake that we did not do this, for we gave the Nazis time to recover themselves and to become even more intransigent. By failing to take a firm and constructive line, we gave many people in the West, even those well-disposed towards us, the impression that we did not take seriously the settlement of our nationality problem.

In this context I feel it absolutely necessary to contradict most strongly the campaign which misrepresents President Beneš as having been the main obstacle to an agreement with the Sudeten-German Party. When I visited London and Paris last July, I heard it said on many occasions that our Prime Minister, Dr. Hodža, was in favour of a quick agreement, but that President Beneš was preventing it. In actual fact, however, nothing could be further from the truth. It is possible that on certain specific occasions, Dr. Beneš and Dr. Hodža, men very different in temperament, may have adopted different tactics, but they were both agreed that it was essential—absolutely essential —to solve the nationality problem as quickly and as thoroughly as possible. It was in this direction that each of them, in entire agreement with the other, exerted his influence in all political circles. Between April and the end of September President Beneš invited the political editors of the Czechoslovak newspapers on no less than ten occasions, in order to explain to them with the greatest urgency and with his full authority all the reasons in favour of a rapid and broad settlement of nationality questions. Latterly, because greater and greater concessions were being made to the Sudeten Germans, while at the same time the Nazi and Henleinist propaganda was becoming more and more aggressive, it became necessary for the President to exercise his authority in order to persuade the Czechoslovak public to accept the ever-increasing sacrifices which were demanded of it in connection with nationality questions. President Beneš, careless of his personal popularity, which necessarily suffered under these circumstances, never shrank from exerting himself to the point of self-sacrifice. There was no other Czechoslovak politician who would have dared to support, so utterly and so openly as he did, the nationality concessions which were made. Those Agrarian politicians who, for various reasons, had advocated compromise with the Sudeten-German Party, retired into the background during the decisive months of last summer, only too glad that the full weight of responsibility was assumed by President Beneš. From the middle of August onwards all negotiations on nationality matters were handled by his office.

One cannot but realise that the task which President Beneš undertook was no easy one and that he ran great risks in attempting its achievement. He himself was well aware of the risks which he was incurring, especially of those involved in the so-called " Fourth Plan," which threatened to impair the internal cohesion of the State. He hoped, however, that the nation would be able to withstand this danger, and he kept his word, once he had given it and accepted full responsibility. It was not his fault that the period after May 21 was not used as it should have been—and as he himself would have desired—for he was not a dictator, and, as a democratic President, he had to respect the Constitution and the views of other political elements. He had in his support only the weight of his arguments and the force of his moral authority, which were greater than his constitutional powers. It is sheer injustice and a disgraceful calumny to say that he prevented the settlement of the nationality question with the Sudeten German and other minorities. It would be more true to say that sometimes—notably in the " Fourth Plan "—he went too far with his concessions, confident always that the Czechoslovak nation would show sufficient creative power and ability to overcome new difficulties even in an increasingly dangerous international situation. It is true, of course, that President Beneš was anxious that the new nationality agreement should not disrupt the integrity of the Republic or impair its independence, because he regarded these as being of the utmost importance, not merely for Czechoslovakia, but for the whole of Europe. Even if his firmness be deemed unpardonable in the eyes of the Nazis and their allies, what honest man would reproach him for having tried to act as a Czechoslovak patriot and as a good European ?

Every mistake of tactics or of principle which was committed by Prague or by the Western Powers in seeking a " just and reasonable " settlement of the Sudeten-German question was due to one and the same fundamental misconception : they were looking for reconciliation with a partner who desired, not reconciliation, but domination. London and Paris, and to a certain extent Prague also, though less consistently, hoped that it would be possible to come to an agreement with the Sudeten-German Party. This hope presupposed, of course, that such an agreement was within the bounds of possibility. Such a supposition implied, moreover, the assumption or hope that the Sudeten-German

Party would be able to come to an independent decision, or that, even if it looked to Germany for guidance, which would be understandable, it would at least be free to adopt an attitude in accordance with the needs and interests of those whom it professed to represent. That would have meant, of course, that it would be prepared, if necessary, even to oppose the wishes of Berlin. Such ideas and hopes were, however, without foundation. There is no doubt that even within the Sudeten-German Party there were influential people who did not agree with the disastrous ideas of their extremists, and who followed with increasing alarm the development of the warlike, adventurous policy of German National Socialism. Influential groups of industrialists, having heard from their friends in Germany angry complaints against " Nazi Bolshevism," regarded with anxiety the State capitalist system of the National Socialists. The Austro-German *Anschluss* had intimidated the Sudeten-German Catholics and Agrarians into seeking safety by hastily merging into Henlein's party, but subsequent developments in Austria (with which country the Sudeten Germans had far more direct relations than with Germany), and especially the persecution of the Austrian Catholics, again alienated these new adherents of Henlein, as well as many of the older members of his party. The enthusiasm for the Nazi Reich was not increasing. The majority of Henlein's supporters were undoubtedly in favour of a larger degree of autonomy, but they scarcely desired union with Germany. In a party like the Sudeten-German Party, however, it is not the moderate elements, but rather the radicals and extremists, who decide policy, and with the latter no agreement was possible unless it granted the full 100 per cent. of the Nazi demands.

Many misunderstandings, and consequently many grave political errors, are due to the fact that the revolutionary character of National Socialism has not yet been widely appreciated. Hitler himself has always stressed the fact that his National Socialism is not a party, but a movement; and its character, aims and methods are all those of a revolutionary movement. It is true that he proclaims " order " as one of the highest laws, but he arrives at this " order " by upsetting and overriding the existing political, economic, social and international order. National Socialism, in no less a degree than

Bolshevism, aims at a complete re-creation of all existing values (" *Umwertung aller Werte* "), revealing thereby its extremist and revolutionary character. Its more moderate elements necessarily fall more and more into the background, while the real leadership passes into the hands of the extreme radicals.

This process took place within the Sudeten-German Party: the radical elements always overpowered the more moderate, and whenever it has seemed possible that the latter might succeed in their policy, the extremists immediately provoked incidents which rendered further compromise impossible, just at the moment when such compromise seemed within reach. One of my friends, who belonged to the more moderate wings of Henlein's party, told me: " Whenever Kundt [who was the leading negotiator of the Sudeten-German Party in the summer of 1938] speaks reasonably at party meetings, he is met with ice-cold silence in his audience. What can he do, then, but adopt the tone of wild radicalism, even though that may be contrary to his original intention ? " Only in this way could he win " unanimous and enthusiastic approval."[1]

In June and July, when the Nationalities Statute and certain administrative reforms which would grant increased local autonomy within the framework of the State were being drawn up, there were certain Henleinist politicians who considered this satisfactory, but dared not say so publicly for fear of their radicals. The sending of Lord Runciman to Prague as mediator at the beginning of August, 1938, stiffened the intransigence of the Henleinists, for they hoped from the very first that his mediation would help their cause. They manœuvred in such a way as to convince the Runciman Mission of the " ill-will " of the Czechs and to persuade them that nothing short of the acceptance of the eight points of their Karlsbad Programme would constitute a satisfactory agreement. The mediation of the Runciman Mission was deliberately disturbed by the provocation of minor and major incidents, and it was no mere coincidence that such incidents should have become more numerous from the second half of August onwards. After August 20, when such important progress had been achieved in the negotiations that

[1] It should be noted in passing that Kundt, when he became leader of the Germans in the post-Munich Republic, adopted a tone which fully deserved the " unanimous and enthusiastic approval " of the Nazis.

even the Henleinist politicians dared not fail to admit it, especially when they were in the presence of and under the control of the Runciman Mission, the leading extremist of the Sudeten-German Party, a deputy named Frank, took steps to counter it. On August 26 Henlein's paper, *Rundschau*, published a notice advising party members " to defend themselves " against " acts of aggression or provocation " by their opponents. This was nothing more nor less than an exhortation to individual acts of violence. Such action, of course, drastically prejudiced the success of further negotiation.

While all this was taking place in Czechoslovakia, Britain and France, alarmed by the increasing threat of a Germany already mobilised for war, urged Prague expressly to " go immediately and unconditionally to the utmost limit of concession." The British and French Ministers in Prague urged the concessions should be made before the National Socialist Congress opened at Nürnberg. It was thus that, on September 5, the so-called "Fourth Plan" was published. As has already been stated, this plan was considered by Lord Runciman to be a very favourable basis for renewed negotiation, since it satisfied nearly all the Karlsbad demands. A similar view was held by many of the leading men in Henlein's party, some of whom even went so far as to welcome the plan as a happy way out of a complicated situation. Certain Henlein leaders made no secret of their opinions to President Beneš, with whom they had already been in confidential contact before the plan was published. I could without difficulty name the persons of whom I write, but, although they broke faith later on in order to secure posts for themselves under their new ruler, Hitler, I should not like to burden my conscience with responsibility for the consequences which they would probably suffer, if I were to write openly of their activities during those days. Suffice to say, then, that the " Fourth Plan " satisfied even the more prominent elements of the Sudeten-German Party, and that this itself was displeasing to the extremists. On September 7, the very day on which an affirmative answer to the Government's proposals (the " Fourth Plan ") was expected from Henlein's negotiators, a violent disturbance was provoked in Moravskà Ostrava [Mährisch Ostrau] between Henleinist rioters and the local police. Although the incident was not of a grave character, the negotiators, evidently through fear of their extremists, announced that they could not continue discussions with the Government until the incident had been settled to their satisfaction. Satisfaction was granted them, though at no small sacrifice of authority by the Czechoslovak administration—a fact which naturally roused strong resentment among the Czech public. Nevertheless, the plot of the extremists was frustrated and on September 10 Henlein's negotiators said that they were willing to resume discussions. They insisted, however, that this should not be until September 13, i.e. only after Hitler had made his speech at Nürnberg, which was announced for the evening of September 12. The delay permitted the extremists, acting on instructions from Germany, to renew their agitation, and immediately after Hitler's speech they provoked the attempt at widespread rebellion of which we have spoken above. The comparatively easy suppression of this attempt and the consequent discredit which it brought on the extremists, who immediately left the country, opened, it is true, the possibility of renewing negotiations in a more favourable atmosphere. However, it was just at that moment that the Western Great Powers intervened by Mr. Chamberlain's flight to Berchtesgaden.

I mention the foregoing in order to show how the extremists always overcame the more moderate elements, and how the radical nature of the Henleinist movement rendered final agreement impossible except on the basis of the total capitulation of their opponents. The same was found to be true on a much larger scale, in the second half of September, during the negotiations between the Western Powers and Hitler; the Munich Agreement was not a compromise in which all parties, including, of course, Germany, made concessions, but a total acceptance of the most radical demands of Pan-German National Socialism.

I am well aware that my contention that an agreement was not possible with Henlein's party will inevitably raise the question, " Since that party undoubtedly represented the majority of the Sudeten-Germans, does that mean that the Sudeten-German problem was absolutely insoluble within the framework of the Czechoslovak State ? " Such, of course, was the final conclusion at which Lord Runciman arrived, but it was a most unfortunate conclusion, since it can have been reached only by a process of unreal and one-sided simplification of the issues. Our capital mistake, in my opinion, was in not attempting to come to terms with the Sudeten-German people, rather than with Henlein. By which I mean that it was absolutely essential to give the widest possible satisfaction to all *reasonable* demands of the Sudeten Germans (I quote the words used by Mr. Chamberlain in his statement of March 24), and *only* those which were reasonable. In practice this meant extending the degree of provincial and departmental autonomy, and carrying this programme through without reference to Henlein's extremist movement, which was irrevocably committed to seeking a totalitarian Pan-German solution of the problem. It is possible, and indeed probable, that the whole of Henlein's party would have begun by opposing this programme; but it is certain that sooner or later that party would have disintegrated, for the internal conflicts within any totalitarian party are and can be suppressed only by the determined and violent enforcement of the leader's authority. It is unnecessary to repeat here what has already been written in many other places about the different groups and currents within the Sudeten-German Party: great industrialists, bankers, business men and working people, including the poorest working men and women; Catholics and people who admired the pagan myths of Rosenberg; Conservatives and extreme revolutionaries with a leaning to Bolshevism; Pan-German fanatics and nationalists with their roots in the tradition of a centuries-old " Bohemia "; all these incongruous and conflicting elements were assembled together in an artificial unity. In a totalitarian State it is possible, though only by force, to keep up the fiction of the " unity " of a single party which rules alone, without any rival to criticise or check it; but in a democratic State like Czechoslovakia it was impossible to do that for any great length of time. It may be argued with truth that Henlein's party had existed since 1934–5 and that, despite internal crises and minor setbacks, it had not become weakened during that period, but had, on the contrary, increased in strength in the spring of 1938. The correct explanation of this, however, is that the party received support from Germany; it did not grow on its own, but rather shared in the increasing strength of German National Socialism as a whole. Whenever the

Third Reich suffered from internal or external difficulties, there was a wane in the Henleinists' enthusiasm; whenever the Third Reich scored a victory, the Nazi wing of every German community in the world was strengthened.

The problem with which we were concerned was, therefore, more than a mere domestic problem of the Czechoslovak Republic, for it was at the same time a matter of international importance. If the Great Powers in Europe had worked towards checking the spectacular and aggressive policy of the Third Reich, the Henleinists, or rather the radical leaders who decided their policy, would have lost their dominating supremacy among the Sudeten Germans. The problem could have been solved justly and to the satisfaction of all except the extreme radicals; but only if a solution could have been sought without regard to those radicals—which would, of course, also have meant without regard to the expansionist plans of the Third Reich. The radicals inside Czechoslovakia, like those who rule the Third Reich, were aiming finally at the destruction of the existing Central European system, which was based essentially on the integrity and independence of the Czechoslovak Republic, and therefore no agreed solution was possible with them except that which was dictated to us at Munich.

An agreed and moderate solution was always openly advocated by the anti-Nazi Sudeten Germans, who never numbered less than one-third of the whole, and was secretly desired also by a large proportion of the Sudeten Germans who, while belonging for various reasons to Henlein's party, did not agree with its extremists or else did not realise where those extremists were leading them.

Thus, were a compromise impossible with the Sudeten-German Party (simply because of the revolutionary character of its extremist leaders), it would, nevertheless, have been possible to come to terms with the Sudeten-German people themselves. Practical co-operation would have been possible at once with the democrats among them and, sooner or later, also with the Henleinist elements who decided to dissociate themselves from their extremists. The success of such a policy would have depended, of course, on the adoption by the European Powers, especially by those of Western Europe, of a united and resolute attitude towards Nazi Germany. Instead, however, they preferred to adopt a policy of " concessions," which led to Munich and to its aftermath, with which I shall deal later.

The policy of the British Government was clearly not dictated by an analysis of the Sudeten-German problem, but rather by the international outlook, political view-point and wider aims which the British Government envisaged for Europe. The essential miscalculation of the British was not understood until the following March. At the time Lord Runciman had come to the conclusion that those frontier districts which were inhabited by a mostly Sudeten-German population should at once be transferred to Germany. Yet he adds, in his Report of September 21: " The transfer of these frontier districts does not, however, dispose finally of the question how Germans and Czechs are to live together peacefully in the future. Even if all the areas where the Germans have a majority were transferred to Germany, there would remain in Czechoslovakia a large number of Germans, and in the areas transferred to Germany a certain number of Czechs. Economic connections are so close that an absolute separation is not only undesirable, but inconceivable; and I repeat my conviction that history has proved that in terms of peace the two peoples can live together on friendly terms."

He recommended, therefore, that an effort be made to find a basis for local autonomy on the modified lines of the " Fourth Plan " for those Sudeten Germans who would remain in Czechoslovakia even after the territorial cessions, but his Report continues: " As I have already said, there is always a danger that agreement reached in principle may lead to further divergencies in practice. But I think that in a more peaceful future this risk can be minimised."

The remarks which I have quoted do not, in my opinion, support Lord Runciman's principal point that the cession of the frontier districts was essential. Lord Runciman admitted that it would be impossible to draw a purely ethnographical frontier through the districts in which the nationalities are very mixed, that in any case there would always remain larger or smaller minorities of Germans in Czechoslovakia and of Czechs in Germany, and that there would always be numerous causes of friction and conflict so that minorities must be afforded a certain degree of autonomy. It may be mentioned, in passing, that Lord Runciman did not mention how to secure the interests of the Czech minority in Germany ! Lord Runciman's Report will be an important record that even the man responsible for proposing the transfer of Sudeten-German territory was conscious that it did not represent a complete solution of the problem. Lord Runciman's solution did not do away with minorities; though it was dealing with the rights of the German minority in Czechoslovakia, it had to be admitted that " an absolute separation is not only undesirable, but inconceivable." Munich subsequently proved quite clearly that it was not a question of satisfying the German minority in Czechoslovakia, but of satisfying the Third Reich, which, bent on expansion, used the Sudeten Germans as a lever to disrupt Czechoslovakia and to smash the balance of power, not only in Central Europe, but throughout Europe.

Since this chapter deals with the Sudeten-German problem, there are two further matters which should be mentioned. Certain Czechoslovak politicians, especially those of the Agrarian Party, contended that it would be wise to establish collaboration with the Sudeten-German Party, even at the cost of pushing the German democratic parties into the opposition. I will not here go into the question whether Czechoslovak public opinion would have tolerated the inclusion in the Governmental coalition of a party whose loyalty to the State was more and more questionable every day, and whose doctrine, and, even more, whose practice, was in direct conflict with the democratic laws and customs of the country. Nor do I wish here to discuss to what extent the Czechoslovak politicians referred to were inspired by a desire to help the State towards a solution of the problem of the German minority, and to what extent by sectarian hope that, with the help of Henlein's " anti-Marxists," they would be able to dispense with the co-operation in the Government of the Czechoslovak parties of the Left. Supposing, however, that this political combination had been successfully brought about, it requires no imagination to see what would have been the logical and necessary outcome. Henlein would have played in the Czechoslovak Government the same role which Seyss-Inquart played in Austria, and the Trojan Horse of Pan-German National

Socialism would have been admitted inside the defences of independent Czechoslovak democracy. The Czechoslovak political *bloc*, which, despite all party differences, had until then remained united and a model of discipline, would inevitably have been disrupted. Nationality conflicts, far from being allayed, would have become more acute, and to them would have been added bitter internal dissension among the Czechs: each concession made to Henlein by his Czechoslovak colleagues in the Government would have been condemned by the Czech opposition as a crime against the interests of the nation and of the State, and by the German opposition as furthering the cause and interests of National Socialism. A new nationality settlement, based on a wide degree of autonomy, would have been possible only with the concurrence of all the principal Czechoslovak parties, so that all would have borne the same responsibility for it. Only in such conditions could one count on its durability, for neither the Left nor the Right alone could have successfully achieved such a settlement, since each would certainly have rejected the settlement reached by the other. There can be no possible doubt, therefore, that the inclusion in the Government of the Sudeten-German Party, which would have become increasingly importunate in its demands, would have led to the disintegration of Czechoslovak unity, in addition to the total demoralisation of the German democrats which would have naturally followed. The Czechoslovak State would thus have been so fatally weakened that it would have been completely at the mercy of Germany. We should have become vassals of the Third Reich and Hitler would have as assuredly taken possession of the country on the day it suited him as he did after Munich. The final result for Czechoslovakia would have been the same as that which resulted from Munich, but our situation would have been infinitely and irreparably worse; for whereas the Munich terms were brutally forced upon us, in the case of collaboration with Henlein we should ourselves have brought about the destruction of our Republic and the loss of our freedom and independence. There is a fundamental difference between being hurled to destruction and hurling oneself there !

I should perhaps explain why we did not propose the " Fourth Plan " much sooner, instead of waiting till September. I have already made it clear that in my opinion we lost much by missing the favourable opportunity which presented itself after May 21, and I would stress the fact that this was not the fault of President Beneš. It was our ponderous political system, based on a coalition of bureaucratic parties, which let us down. The advantage of this system was that it had considerable political and social stability; it prevented sudden and spasmodic political changes and subjected the parties and the whole of our political life to a strict discipline. Dr. Hodža defined Czechoslovak democracy as " an authoritative democracy based on voluntary self-discipline." But it also had grave drawbacks; it was clumsy and exceedingly slow at reaching a decision, which was, in any case only possible when all parties were in agreement. Furthermore, it automatically treated any new impulse, any original or daring proposal or idea, with grumbling suspicion. Finally, we must add to these drawbacks the deplorable fact that the leadership of every party, and thus of the State executive, was composed—with a few exceptions—of politicians who were worn out with old age or by long years of exhausting public activity. We had neither sufficient elasticity nor sufficient imagination to adapt ourselves to an age of rapid and revolutionary changes, which called for ready initiative and for quick and bold decisions. Many people were anxious for radical changes, and more especially for changes of the leading statesmen, which would lead, if not immediately to a new régime, at least to a new working procedure. President Beneš could not do everything by himself, and had no constitutional authority to make vital decisions. But he was afraid that changes in leadership and working procedure might lead to serious crises in the political parties and in the State executive—crises which might have had unfortunate consequences when our State was the centre of grave international tension. This explanation, though not sufficient to excuse our having missed the favourable opportunity after May 21, may help the reader to understand what was happening in our country and why it happened.

It would, nevertheless, be wrong to suppose that it would have been possible to make such far-reaching proposals as those embodied in the " Fourth Plan " earlier than in September. Political and social ideas which will be acceptable to-morrow are generally unacceptable to-day. Ideas need time to ripen in the public mind and there is always trouble if they are prematurely enforced. If the British and French Governments are compelled to pay attention to public opinion, the Czechoslovak Government could not afford to overlook it, and the Czechoslovak public only grudgingly accepted the making of concessions to the Sudeten Germans. One may justly reproach Czechoslovak politicians and journalists for having paid too little heed to the constant reproaches and reminders of Presidents Masaryk and Beneš. Both men constantly spoke of the necessity for finding a completely satisfactory settlement of the nationalities question; their colleagues were to blame that they did not educate and prepare the public in time for this settlement. But, despite all the mistakes which we undoubtedly made in this respect, and even if I accept without challenge all the criticisms of our minority policy made by Lord Runciman in his Report—though it would be easy for me to add such limiting qualifications and comments on them as would reveal the real situation in a very different light—I maintain that the grossest errors on our part would not justify the injustice of our virtual subordination to Germany at Munich and the terrible consequences which it has entailed. I make this claim fully conscious of my responsibility, although—or, perhaps, rather because— from the very earliest post-war days I have repeatedly criticised, in the spirit of Masaryk's policy, the shortcomings and errors of our treatment of the minorities. Yet the fact remains that there was no nation in Europe which treated its minorities more justly and more liberally than we did. Switzerland has no minorities, being composed of three equal nationalities; Belgium is similarly composed of two equal nationalities. Whereas in Germany, Poland and Italy, or in any of the states which lie between us and the Ægean, the minorities are literally oppressed and are struggling against great difficulties to obtain the primitive right to their own language and culture, in Czechoslovakia—and I must underline the fact that it was only in Czechoslovakia—the minorities enjoyed not only the right to their own language and culture, but also full civic and political rights. The struggle of the Sudeten Germans was not for their nationality rights, but for political supremacy. For this reason it was not to be wondered at that Czechoslovak public opinion showed little enthusiasm in making concessions whereby the political position of the Sudeten Germans was gradually strengthened. It should not be forgotten that the Sudeten Germans themselves greeted each concession with fiercer and more insolent attacks on the State.

The Czechoslovak people as a whole are not chauvinistic nationalists, and their few chauvinists have never had great influence among them. From 1926 to the spring of 1938 the participation of German representatives in the Government was recognised by the vast majority of them as a natural and desirable phenomenon. But Czechs are profound patriots, and their uneasiness at the concessions which were being made sprang, not from national ill-feeling or ill-will to the Germans, but from anxiety lest the Henleinists would abuse all concessions for the furtherance of the Pan-German Nazi aim of disrupting the Republic. The Czechs are, however, politically mature to a quite exceptional degree, even as compared with the peoples of much larger nations, and, despite their uneasiness—for which there was more than ample justification—they understood during the summer that it was in the interest of their State, for international reasons, to make concessions in the nationality question. I would not attempt, nevertheless, to pretend that our public received the " Fourth Plan " without unconcealed disapproval and misgiving. It would take me too long to analyse these sentiments in detail, but it must be obvious that if the Karlsbad Programme was considered very dangerous at the time of its publication, in April, 1938, a plan which would satisfy its main demands must seem no less dangerous five months later. We accepted the " Fourth Plan " because it was known that it had been extorted from our Government under urgent pressure from Britain and France, upon whose help we counted and whose wishes we therefore fulfilled, and because President Beneš, in whom the people had absolute confidence, had endorsed it with the full weight of his authority. The Czechoslovak Government was obliged, however, to give an assurance that it was " final " and that, in the words of the Deputy Prime Minister, M. Bechyně, they would not go " one millimetre further " in their concessions. But this Government declaration, which was demanded by Czechoslovak public opinion, was not well received by the British and French diplomatic representatives in Prague, who expressed fears that it might " provoke " the Germans. There seemed to us a certain disproportion in their concern for the feelings of the Germans as compared with the absence of concern for the feelings of the Czechoslovak public.

It would really have been impossible, therefore, to produce the " Fourth Plan " earlier than at the beginning of September, and it was possible then only because of the circumstances which obtained at the time and without which it would have met with insuperable obstacles. It speaks well, moreover, for the sound political judgment and broad-mindedness of the Czecho-slovak people that they should have gone so far in accepting such a daring and even dangerous plan, in order to provide a basis upon which, as even Lord Runciman quite rightly agreed, it would be possible to reach a completely satisfactory solution of the Sudeten-German problem and of the whole question of nationalities within the country.

International considerations, however, proved decisive and prevented further satisfactory progress. The Sudeten-German problem obviously had an important international aspect, since Germany had interested herself in it, and ever since February, 1938, the Chancellor of the Third Reich had with increasing emphasis declared himself the protector of the Sudeten Germans. It would have been possible, by negotiation between the Czecho-slovak Government and the Sudeten Germans, to find a solution of the problem which would take into consideration also its international political consequences—and that within the framework of the Republic—but this would no longer have satis-fied the Third Reich. Germany, I repeat, wished to make use of the Sudeten Germans for the disruption of Czechoslovakia, and thus to open the road for her expansion into Central and Eastern Europe. That, as subsequent events have proved, was the only real reason for Germany's interest in the Sudeten-German pro-blem, and the Western Powers undeniably assisted Germany in the achievement of the goal which she so ardently desired. The first open step in this direction was taken on September 14, when Mr. Chamberlain decided to visit the German Chancellor in his home at Berchtesgaden.

Chapter II

Berchtesgaden

1. *Hitler's Threats and the Danger of War.*

IT is obvious, therefore, that a profound difference existed between the Czech and the Anglo-French estimate, not only of the Sudeten-German problem, but of the whole European situation. This alone explains why Mr. Chamberlain's trip to Berchtesgaden was welcomed in the Western countries and regarded as most ominous in Prague.

How can this difference have come about ? Undoubtedly, at the last moment Hitler's threat to make war had more effect in the Western capitals than in Prague. That does not mean that the Czechs underestimated the gravity of the German menace, but rather that they took it seriously from the beginning. This was not so in England and France. In August, for instance, when we were seriously alarmed by German war preparations and by the vast scale of German mobilisation, we were surprised that the Western Powers did not attribute (or pretended not to attribute) to them as much importance as we would have expected. It was a matter of grave concern in Prague, in the face of the ever-increasing concentration of German forces along our frontiers, that both of the Western Powers continually advised us not to increase our military preparedness, on the score that such action might " provoke reaction " on Germany's part. Until August, this Anglo-French attitude was comprehensible, and the Czechoslovak Government was prepared, therefore, (though unwillingly) to obey M. Daladier's urgent warning not to carry out the intention, which we had had in mind since the spring, of prolonging the period of our military service from two to three years. By the end of August, however, it was already evident that Germany had not been deterred, either by Sir John Simon's speech at Lanark or by the diplomatic conversations of Sir Neville Henderson, British Ambassador in Berlin. On September 5 the French Government decided to call up certain classes of specialists. Yet even after that Paris and London continued to warn Prague against taking any further precautionary measures, and this, I would add, was the attitude

which was maintained right up to September 23—that is, until
Mr. Chamberlain's disappointment at the result of the Godesberg
meeting.

The Czechs, on the other hand—both people and Government
—realised the danger somewhat earlier. We were perfectly
aware, moreover, as Mr. Chamberlain himself had stated in
March, that the German threat to us represented a danger to
the whole of Europe. We differed from England and France in
our opinion that a firm attitude, so far from provoking, would
in fact deter German aggression. We steadily maintained that
if the European Powers would unite and exhibit just the spirit
of self-defence from which they were restraining us, Hitler would
be obliged to give way, even after the Nuremberg Rally. The
adoption of a decided attitude by the Western Powers would
have reduced the risk of war to a minimum. At Nuremberg Hitler
still left open the possibility of retreat.

We felt justified, therefore, in hoping that pressure at this
juncture from the Western Powers would force Hitler to adapt
his policy to the changed situation and announce, as his great
success, that Prague had been " forced " to grant the widest
degree of autonomy to the Sudeten Germans, in accordance
with the Karlsbad Programme. By this means a more realistic
" negotiated " agreement might have been reached, since the
" Fourth Plan " substantially satisfied the Sudeten Germans,
was approved by the Runciman Mission and could have been
accepted by Hitler as the only peaceful alternative. Hitler's
speech at Nuremberg on September 12 was certainly most
bellicose, but it left this loophole. Of course as Lord Runciman
wrote in his Report, " I felt that any such arrangement [i.e. a
settlement within the existing framework of the Czechoslovak
State] would have been temporary, not lasting." So far as
Germany is concerned, that was probably true. Hitler Germany
was unlikely in the long run to consent to any permanent
arrangement which would meet the " reasonable " and " justified " claims of the Sudeten Germans and therefore deprive her
of the means by which she hoped to establish her mastery over
Czechoslovakia. Time, however, would have been gained till the
spring or summer of 1939 and, as the statesmen of Great Britain
have since learned, it was bought very dearly in September.

The Munich Agreement, so far from reducing the necessity of taking drastic measures if peace is to be preserved in 1939, has substantially increased that necessity by immense additions, at the expense of Czechoslovakia, to the war potential of Germany. A forced retreat in September would have meant for Hitler a grave loss of prestige, which he would not have born so easily as that which he had already suffered after May 21. Even if one could not have hoped for his immediate collapse, there can be no doubt that if it had not been for his spectacular victory in Czechoslovakia, the Nazi régime would have been faced with serious difficulties in the winter of 1938–9. It may be argued that he would therefore have preferred war on any terms—even those terms which most military experts are now agreed would have meant the certain defeat of Germany by the combination Britain–France–Czechoslovakia–Russia. There certainly was danger that war might break out in September, but I am still convinced—even more now than I was at that time—that it was not so great as was imagined by the Western Powers. The internal situation in Germany was far from being so calm and satisfactory as was described by Dr. Goebbels in his propaganda.

The hasty conscription of German labour for forced work on the Rhineland defences had created a considerable amount of discontent, especially among the men coming from the country districts and from Austria, who disliked the harsh routine to which they were subjected. It had been found necessary to take drastic steps to prevent the spread of this " revolutionary " discontent among those of their fellow-workers who, unlike the Austrians, had become accustomed to their conditions by five years of Hitler's military discipline. The diversion of labour to work on fortifications caused dissatisfaction among the industrialists also, for it adversely affected their production. Persecution of the Catholics still continued, while the situation of the Protestants had not yet been completely " settled " (*gleichgeschaltet*). One way and another, therefore, the increasing military preparations had, especially since the mobilisation in August, aroused widespread feelings of anxiety and fear of war among the people of Germany. The Government's propaganda, designed to create a war spirit among them, had had exactly the opposite effect; instead of making the people enthusiastic for war, it had merely deepened their dejection. The general fear of war was clearly perceptible during the latter part of September by the total absence of public enthusiasm and by the occasional shouting of anti-war slogans when troops in full war equipment passed through Berlin—an experience which was repeated in other German towns. The German military authorities must have been well aware of this anti-war spirit. It was well known that, in spite of all the tales of the terrible and barbarous oppression of the Sudeten Germans by " Bolshevik hordes of Czech soldiery," a war, even against Czechoslovakia, would find little popular support.

The military authorities were more conscious, moreover, than were the Nazi agitators of the material and technical deficiencies of the German Army. Considerable concern was felt at the shortage of trained reservists, and more especially of officers and N.C.Os. It is common knowledge that in the autumn of 1938 Germany had at most 2,000,000 trained soldiers—a number approximately equal to that of the Czechoslovak Army when fully mobilised—but she had not enough officers and N.C.Os. to lead an army of that size in a successful offensive. It is known also that, in spite of the feverish efforts which had been made since June to complete the fortifications along Germany's western frontier, those fortifications were still far from being in a condition to withstand prolonged and concentrated attack by artillery and aircraft. The moment the crisis was over, Czechoslovakia dismembered and France demobilised, Hitler himself admitted this. In his speech at Nuremberg on September 12, he referred to the western " front of iron and concrete—with three, and sometimes four lines of defence—and with a depth of 50 kilometres." At Saarbrücken on October 9, this " front " had become incomplete and imperfect. Hitler declared his decision to continue, with increased energy, the construction of the fortifications and to extend them into two more (frontier) districts, Aix-la-Chapelle and Saarbrücken, which had hitherto been neglected !

The German General Staff was perfectly well aware of Germany's inability (owing primarily to her limited supplies of foodstuffs and raw materials, of which she had not accumulated enough to withstand a serious blockade) to sustain a prolonged war or a war waged on two fronts, i.e. in the east and in the west. It was informed of the war potential of Czechoslovakia, and its own estimate was that she would be able to hold out on her own for at least three months. Above all, the German General Staff fully realised the strategic importance of Czechoslovakia to Germany's opponents. In the event of attack, Czechoslovakia could immediately become, according to the German description, an " aircraft carrier," from which air attacks could easily be launched against Germany's eastern bases while meantime the Czechoslovak Army could withstand German assault until such time as the Russian Army could come over the Carpathians to her aid, while at the same time diverting against her some fifty to seventy German divisions which might otherwise be used on the western front. For all these reasons, the German General Staff was opposed to Hitler's foreign policy, which it regarded as far too dangerous. Early in September, General Beck, Chief of the German General Staff, handed in his resignation. The resignation of a German General, let alone the Chief of Staff, on the eve of war, was absolutely unprecedented. Hitler was faced, not only with civil discontent, but with an ugly temper in the German Army.[1]

General Beck's resignation was, of course, officially denied at the moment when it took place. It was essential for Hitler to hide the disagreement between him and his chief military adviser at the moment of his great diplomatic offensive. It may legitimately be asked, however, why this essential fact was hidden from their own public by the Governments of Britain and France. The governments and general staffs of all the countries concerned were not only informed of General Beck's request to be relieved of his duties as Chief of the German General Staff, but they had in their possession detailed information regarding the split between the political and the military leadership of Germany. If it were not for the risk that by doing so I might help Herr Himmler in his task and that some Germans might pay for it with their lives, I could write much which would surprise the public about how the Nazi régime was tottering at the time of the September crisis, and could show how Hitler

[1] See memorandum, p. 212.

inflated himself more and more as he felt the ground slipping from beneath his feet. Paris and London were certainly as well informed as, and were probably even better informed than, Prague about this state of affairs. Yet one can find no indication that the knowledge of Germany's weakness had any effect upon them, and their behaviour would appear to indicate that they never questioned the supremacy of Germany or the invincibility of her armed forces ! Only in October, after everything had gone according to plan and when there was therefore no object in keeping the matter secret, was General Beck's resignation made public.

I have no doubt that the future will reveal many facts which will confirm the foregoing allegation that in September, 1938, Germany was far from being so strong that Herr Hitler's declaration to Mr. Chamberlain at Berchtesgaden (i.e. that he would risk world war rather than postpone helping the Sudeten Germans) had to be accepted at its face value. Hitler's threats, however, were taken seriously and Germany's power was over-estimated in the west. This, it must be assumed, was evidently the main reason why the two Western Powers took the road which led first to Berchtesgaden and then to Munich.

2. *The Visit to Berchtesgaden.*

It is not yet possible to ascertain, from the documents and reports which have been published, the origin of the idea of Mr. Chamberlain's first flight to Berchtesgaden on September 15. Both Mr. Chamberlain and M. Daladier take the credit for the idea upon themselves. The immediate impulse was given, it seems, by the Henleinist revolt, which caused very great excitement in Paris and London—far more, in fact, than in Prague. This revolt was probably considered the immediate prelude to German aggression, and not much importance was attached, therefore, to the assurances from Prague that it would be successfully suppressed. A very strong impression must have been created in Paris and London by the report of Henlein's ultimatum, sent from Cheb (Eger) to the Czechoslovak Government on the evening of September 13. This ultimatum demanded that the martial law (which had been proclaimed that day in certain Sudeten-German districts) should be suspended within six hours and the Czech police should be withdrawn from the Sudeten-German territories. Henlein suggested that otherwise he would not hold himself responsible for further developments. The Czechoslovak Government made no reply, of course, to this boast, but made it understood that the exceptional measures they had taken would be relaxed as soon as order had been restored. They would then be prepared to resume negotiations on the basis of their " Fourth Plan." But on the night of September 13–14, while the Czechoslovak Government were thus successfully handling the revolt, the fatal decision was taken: it was agreed between Mr. Chamberlain and M. Daladier by telephone that the former should visit Herr Hitler.

When, on the evening of September 14, news of this decision leaked out, M. Daladier published the following statement:

" Late yesterday afternoon [i.e. on September 13], in view of the rapid development of events in Czechoslovakia, which made it difficult to continue the local negotiations, on my own initiative I established personal and direct contact with the British Prime Minister, in order to discuss with him the possibility of devising some special procedure which would enable us to examine with Germany the most effective means whereby the dispute between the Sudeten Germans and their Government might be amicably settled, and European peace might be thus preserved. I am particularly happy, therefore, that our two Governments should have reached the same conclusion on this question."

In the speech which he delivered in the Chamber of Deputies on October 4, M. Daladier amended his original statement:

" During the night of September 13–14 I got in touch with Mr. Chamberlain and suggested to him that it would be a good idea to replace diplomatic representations and notes by direct contact between the principals concerned. The British Prime Minister, for his part, felt exactly as I did, and went to Berchtesgaden."

Mr. Chamberlain, in his report to the House of Commons on

September 28, made no mention, however, of M. Daladier's suggestion, but spoke as though he had made the visit to Berchtesgaden entirely on his own initiative:

" In those circumstances I decided that the time had come to put into operation a plan which I had had in my mind for a considerable period as a last resort. One of the principal difficulties in dealing with totalitarian Governments is the lack of any means of establishing contact with the personalities in whose hands lie the final decisions for the country. So I resolved to go to Germany myself to interview Herr Hitler and find out in personal conversation whether there was yet any hope of saving the peace. I knew very well that in taking such an unprecedented course I was laying myself open to criticism on the ground that I was detracting from the dignity of a British Prime Minister and to disappointment, and perhaps even resentment, if I failed to bring back a satisfactory agreement. But I felt that in such a crisis, where the issues at stake were so vital for millions of human beings, such considerations could not be allowed to count.

" Herr Hitler responded to my suggestion with cordiality, and on 15th September I made my first flight to Munich."

It is possible that M. Daladier originally intended to be present at Berchtesgaden, and that he abandoned this project in order to avoid complicating matters by having to invite representatives of Italy and Russia (and perhaps even of Poland also) to attend the discussions. But in any case, whether it was Mr. Chamberlain's own idea or one inspired by M. Daladier that he should meet Herr Hitler, the fact remains that the representative of the French Government associated himself with the proposal of that first meeting. It is also a fact beyond question that M. Daladier did not consider it necessary to inform the Government of his Czechoslovak allies beforehand about this matter of such far-reaching importance. Neither in Paris, nor in London, was the Czechoslovak Minister given any prior intimation of Mr. Chamberlain's intention of going to see Herr Hitler personally and of negotiating with him about the Sudeten Germans. Just as previously, when it had been decided to send Lord Runciman to Czechoslovakia as " mediator," so now, although matters of vital importance to Czechoslovakia were going to be discussed, Prague was presented by Paris and, of course, by London also, with a *fait accompli*.

While this audacious decision received in England,[1] according to Mr. Chamberlain, a warm reception (which, he confessed, surprised him), it was received in Prague with unconcealed apprehension. We continued to hope, however, that no fundamental interest of ours would be betrayed by our Western friends and allies, although we knew that they would be urged to make new and serious sacrifices. We had grave fears, but we did not suspect that the Western Powers, of whom one (France) was bound to us by the most clear treaty obligations that could exist, and the other (Great Britain) had on several occasions expressed her interest in the maintenance of Czechoslovak independence, would be capable of demanding the unmitigated terms which Herr Hitler had attempted to extort from us through the agency of Henlein. In spite of profound misgiving, we still had confidence in the Western Powers. We therefore did not attribute any special importance at first to Henlein's violent proclamation of September 15, in which he demanded the German annexation of the Sudeten Germans.

" Fellow-countrymen !

" As bearer of your confidence and conscious of my responsibility, I state firmly before world public opinion, that with the employment of machine guns, armoured cars and tanks against the unarmed Sudeten Germans, the system of oppression by the Czech nation has reached the highest point. By this the Czech nation has shown to the whole world that it has at last become quite impossible for us to live together with it in one State. Our experience of domination by force and more especially the heavy sacrifice of our blood during these last days oblige me to declare:

" 1. In the year 1919 we were denied the right of self-determination which had been solemnly assured us and were forced against our will into the Czech State.

" 2. Without ever having renounced our right of self-determination, we have tried, by making very great sacrifices,

---

[1] As it did also in France.

to safeguard for ourselves our existence within the Czech State.

" 3. All our efforts to bring the Czech nation and those responsible for it to an honest and just compromise have wrecked themselves against their implacable desire to destroy us.

" In this hour of distress for the Sudeten Germans, I stand before you, the German nation, and before the entire civilised world and proclaim: We wish to live as a free German people ! We desire peace and work in our Fatherland ! We want to go back to Germany ! God bless us and our just fight.

" KONRAD HENLEIN."

It is not only the wording of this proclamation which is of importance, but also the time and date of its publication: it was broadcast from the German radio stations and distributed by the German Press Bureau shortly after 1 p.m. on September 15. Mr. Chamberlain had landed at the Munich airport at 12.30 p.m. on that same day, and the first news which awaited him in Germany after his landing was Henlein's announcement that the Sudeten Germans desired annexation by Germany. The German Government was anxious that Mr. Chamberlain should be faced with this fact before he started his conversation with Hitler, for which he arrived at Obersalzburg at 4.55 p.m. on that day. This created, of course, an entirely new situation, because the question of German annexation had never previously been raised either by Henlein or by Hitler and on September 7 a Foreign Office communiqué had officially stated that this was not the policy of the British Government. It is true that Herr Hitler, in his Nuremberg speech, had demanded the right of self-determination for the Sudeten Germans, but he had not in any way defined how he imagined it might actually be realised, and had terminated that part of his speech with the words:

" After all, it is the business of the Czechoslovak Government to make an agreement with the Sudeten-German representatives whom it has invited to negotiate and somehow or another to come to understanding with them. My task, and the task of all of us here, is to take care that justice shall not be perverted into injustice."

These words could equally be interpreted to mean that Herr Hitler admitted the possibility of a Czech-German settlement within the framework of the Czechoslovak State. Herr Hitler simply prepared himself for all eventualities, intending to decide according to the circumstances of the international political situation. On one point, however, he was very careful, for all the ferocity and militancy of his declaration. Knowing the opposition of his military advisers to any warlike adventure, he contented himself with rattling his sabre, but did not dare to unsheath it. He acted in precisely the same way after he had provoked the Henleinists to revolt: although the Czechoslovak Government took severe measures against the rioters, and although shooting took place in the Sudeten-German districts, from the Reich only " blank rounds " of propaganda were fired against Czechoslovakia. Herr Hitler was in no haste to afford military assistance to his " oppressed " and " slaughtered " Sudeten-German brethren; he stirred them to revolt, but at the same time looked round cautiously to see what were the international reactions, especially on the part of the Western Powers, of which he could be by no means certain. We know to-day that there were cheers in Berlin when it was proposed from London that Mr. Chamberlain should visit the Chancellor of the Reich. This proposal was received with an enthusiasm which it was difficult to suppress, for it was immediately understood as an indication that the West was afraid of war and was ready to make far-reaching concessions. Herr von Ribbentrop realised at once that he need not take very seriously the official disclaimer of the article which appeared in *The Times* of September 7 suggesting the cession of the Sudeten-German territory to Germany. He was already in possession of reliable information about the real intentions of the French Foreign Minister, for his agents had informed him that in the most influential banking circles in Paris large-scale transactions were being made on the assurance that France would not go to war " for the sake of the Czechs " or " on account of a few German frontier districts." Under such circumstances, the German politicians acted rapidly. Before Mr. Chamberlain could begin his conversations with Herr Hitler, Henlein's demand for the annexation of the Sudeten Germans to the Reich was announced. It was only after it had been decided in the West that Mr. Chamberlain should go to Berchtesgaden that Germany dared to interpret the principle of self-determination claimed for the Sudeten Germans as meaning their annexation by the Reich. This was the first result of the decision made by Mr. Chamberlain and M. Daladier on the night of September 13–14 in their desire to "preserve the peace of Europe."

One must admit that Herr Hitler, perceiving the excellent opportunity offered to him by the West, knew how to make use of it very quickly. In this way he neutralised to a certain extent and prevented the development of the unfavourable effects which might otherwise have made themselves felt in Germany when the Henleinist *Putsch* completely collapsed. This ignominious collapse was, of course, one of the main reasons for the immediate demand for the annexation of the Sudeten Germans. For the same reason, it became absolutely necessary for German propaganda to keep up the impression that fighting and bloodshed were continual in the Sudeten-German districts. If on September 15 Mr. Chamberlain possessed no other information than those he was able to secure at Munich and Berchtesgaden, he must have imagined that the Henleinist revolt was in full blast whereas in reality it had been dying down since September 14. On September 15–16, the last isolated cinders were being quenched. On September 15 martial law had been extended into more districts,[1] but this was done to forestall and prevent possible disorder and violence rather than to suppress any actual revolt.

By September 16 only one fatal incident was reported, involving the loss of one human life, and three or four minor skirmishes; apart from these, order had everywhere been restored. On the same day the dissolution of Henlein's party was officially decreed; this was the natural sequel to the illegal action of Henlein and other leading members of the party, who, having fled to Germany to save themselves, used the German broadcasting stations in their efforts to instigate the Sudeten-German people to further revolt. The Sudeten Germans, however, did not respond to their appeal; on the contrary, indeed, many members

---

Only sixteen districts out of forty-nine were affected, which indicates that the revolt was far from being universal throughout the Sudeten-German territory.

and even party officials resigned from Henlein's party, denounced their fugitive leaders, handed in their arms and declared their loyalty to Czechoslovakia. Panic began to run through the ranks of the Henleinists, and the activities of the Sudeten-German democrats were revived. On September 17 the German Social-Democrats issued a public declaration announcing the foundation of a united " German National Council."

It made an enormous impression on the Sudeten Germans when they learned with what great sympathy the people of Prague received the refugees from the Sudeten-German districts, who had been assaulted by the German storm-troopers and who had been obliged to fly into the interior of Bohemia to escape their brutality. Although Czech people also were being killed in the border districts, the German refugees, 2,000 of whom reached Prague on September 17, were made welcome and cared for by the population of that city without national discrimination. This spontaneous action by the people of Prague, who are well known for their keen patriotism and their excitable temperament, was an expressive and persuasive proof that for the Czechs and Germans to live together in peace and friendship and to co-operate together was not a Utopian dream, but a practical possibility, and that the solution of the Sudeten-German problem did not demand the separation of the two races. On September 17 complete calm and order reigned everywhere throughout the Republic. On that day also some of the Sudeten Germans who had fled into Germany returned to their homes, because they did not want to be included in the labour corps which were sent to work on the fortifications. All that we lived through during those days, all our experience as regards Germans and Czechs alike, the whole development of the unsuccessful Henleinist *Putsch*, the speedy recovery of sanity, even by the members of Henlein's party, the new activity of the democratic Germans, all these strengthened us in our belief that we would soon reach a satisfactory solution of the nationality problem, if only we could have a few months of peace and quietness. All depended on whether Hitler's aggressive attitude against Czecho-slovakia could be countered by the firmness of the European Powers united together.

During the week of September 12–19, the internal situation in our state developed in a very satisfactory manner. After the collapse of the Henleinist *Putsch* a new grouping was apparent in the German camp, while the Czechoslovaks, in the face of increased danger, united together for the common cause of national preparedness and defence. At the end of that week, moreover, a favourable change began even in Hlinka's Slovak Catholic Party, which started in the face of national danger to reconsider a *rapprochement* with the Government coalition and to make preparations for participation in the Government. On September 19 the Slovak Catholic Party held a Conference at Bratislava, at which it was decided to insist upon the immediate recognition and realisation of Slovak autonomy " for the interior and exterior strengthening of the Czechoslovak State." A delegation of three was sent from this Conference to Prague, in order to negotiate with the President of the Republic and the other Czechoslovak political leaders. The same day (September 19), the Slovak representatives in the Government declared in Bratislava that it was now necessary to put aside all partisan interests and to " bring about the unity of all Slovaks for the safety and defence of the Republic, which would promote the maintenance of the national freedom of the Slovaks." They also asked the Slovak population to rally together more closely than ever round the President of the Republic and their Government. On September 17 a delegation of the Czech nobility made a solemn pronouncement to the President of the Republic in favour of the " old frontiers of the state." " Our wish," ran this declaration, " that the old frontiers of the Czech Crown may remain inviolate arises out of our anxiety for the future of those who come after us and *from our feeling of responsibility for the liberty and prosperity of the Czech Germans*. Our forefathers always insisted upon friendly relations between the two nations which are settled in our country and we likewise desire that our countrymen of the German language also may share with us our love for our indivisible Country." Thus the advent of danger for our state united all the estates, all classes and all parties of the Czechoslovak nation, and together with them a great part of the national minorities: from the nobleman to the communist, all were ready to defend their homes and their rights against a threatened attack.

While the situation was developing in so satisfactory a manner within the Czechoslovak Republic, the danger from without was increasing. The negotiations between Mr. Chamberlain and Herr Hitler at Berchtesgaden still remained secret. They had ended on Thursday, September 15, and Mr. Chamberlain hurried back to London the next day and immediately summoned a full Cabinet meeting on the Saturday. It was evident that the Berchtesgaden meeting had a very serious effect. It was announced that MM. Daladier and Bonnet would come to London on September 18. Although it was impossible to learn anything that was positively certain about all these meetings, it was quite obvious from the reports which came separately from London and Paris that, in some way or other, the question of our frontiers had been raised, and means were being considered to satisfy the Sudeten-German claim for the " right of self-determination." In some western European newspapers the question of a plebiscite was suggested, and therefore from September 15 onwards we concentrated our attention on that question. Our Press published lengthy proofs of the inacceptability of this demand.

On Saturday, September 17, the Deputy Prime Minister, M. Bechyně, in an interview with the Editor of the *Lidové Noviny*, was asked what he thought of the news that the idea of holding a plebiscite in the Sudeten-German districts had been discussed at Berchtesgaden. He answered:

" It is nonsense. I do not believe it. A plebiscite would be a short cut to war and for that reason no government could be found in Czechoslovakia which would accept the proposal of a plebiscite. And even if such a government could be found, it would fall within an hour, owing to the dissatisfaction of the whole nation."

On the following day, September 18, the Prime Minister, Dr. Hodža, spoke directly in the name of the whole Government:

" The settlement of Czech-German relations should not and must not be the source of new conflicts; nor must it create a psychological barrier which would render impossible the future co-operation of the two nations just precisely in those spheres in

Europe where peace, progress and happiness depend on their pacific and constructive collaboration. A *so-called* plebiscite *could* not *bring about any sort of a solution* which would harmonise with that great aim. Upon this are unanimous not only all those who hold responsible positions here at home, but also all objective experts who have studied the complicated racial and territorial situation in Czechoslovakia and Central Europe. In those places where a plebiscite was able to facilitate the settlement of a nationality dispute, it has already been carried out. If it had been considered that a plebiscite was a suitable means for settling the nationality problems of Czechoslovakia, it would have been welcomed as an instrument for that purpose by the Peace Conference. A plebiscite in Czechoslovakia is therefore unacceptable, not only from the subjective point of view of the State, but also objectively, if only for that reason that it would create a whole series of new problems."

And, in order that there should be not the slightest doubts about the intentions of the Government after the liquidation of the Henleinist *Putsch*, the Prime Minister continued:

" Czechoslovakia is willing to pursue her work for peace even during the period of tension. In the name of all the constitutional authorities, I proclaim that, in spite of Henlein's refusal to come to an agreement with the Czechoslovak Government about the settlement of nationality problems, and in spite of his attempted revolt, our Government, which is defending the absolute integrity of the State, *will make no changes in its present policy of agreement with the national minorities and especially with the Sudeten Germans*; but insists upon its last proposals as a basis. To-day, *it is not with Herr Henlein and the others who have fled with him* that the Government should *negotiate*. Internal events and the fiasco of the revolt will show clearly that the vast majority of the masses of the Sudeten-German people with whom it now must deal desires agreement and national appeasement. The Government *will not adopt any policy of revenge and persecution*, but it must take care that law, peace and order shall be preserved and respected. Where it is a question of peace and order, it can make no concessions, because only in conditions of peace and order will it be possible to ensure a complete and reasonable agreement."

This speech, which was delivered at noon on Sunday, September 18, was intended not only for the Czechoslovak public, but also for London, where the British and French statesmen were in conference; but those in conference were already deaf to any voice coming from Czechoslovakia, because they were deafened by the voice which came from Berchtesgaden, delivering the ultimatum: Hitler would rather risk world war than wait for the liberation of the Sudeten Germans.

3. *The London Conference of September* 18.

It is not intended that this book, which deliberately limits itself, as far as possible, to the detailed description of events in Czechoslovakia, should describe what went on in other countries during the month of September. In order, however, to preserve the continuity of the whole account and to facilitate a better understanding of the Czechoslovak attitude, it is necessary to give a brief outline at least of the main events of these fatal days.

Mr. Chamberlain, in his speech in the House of Commons on September 28, described the trend of the negotiations at Berchtesgaden. Hitler had demanded the right of self-determination for the Sudeten Germans, in the sense that it should be possible for them, if they so wished, to return to the Reich. Hitler threatened that, if they could not achieve this by their own efforts, he would assist them to do so. He also declared categorically that, rather than wait, he would be prepared to risk a world war. He gave Mr. Chamberlain the impression that he was contemplating an immediate invasion of Czechoslovakia. Mr. Chamberlain therefore asked Hitler why he had allowed him to travel all that way. Thereupon Herr Hitler said that if Mr. Chamberlain could give him an assurance that the British Government accepted the principle of self-determination he would be quite ready to discuss ways and means of carrying it out, but that otherwise it was of no use to continue the conversations. Mr. Chamberlain then promised that he would consult his

Government, and asked Herr Hitler to postpone the opening of his attack until he received the British reply. Herr Hitler promised to do that, on condition that nothing happened in Czechoslovakia of such a nature as to force his hand. Mr. Chamberlain was so persuaded that a German invasion of Czechoslovakia was intended that he had no doubt whatever, even as late as September 28 (when he made this report in the House of Commons), that his visit alone had prevented the invasion, for which everything was prepared. On Saturday, September 17, the British Cabinet had meetings which lasted throughout the day, and which were attended also by Lord Runciman, who had travelled by air from Prague to London on the previous day. The opinion which he expressed during these discussions was, according to Mr. Chamberlain, that the cession of the frontier territory to Germany was inevitable. The result of the British Government's discussion on September 17 was the acceptance, in principle, of Hitler's demands at Berchtesgaden. This decision was agreed to by MM. Daladier and Bonnet on the following day (September 18), when they arrived in London. M. Daladier managed to obtain from Great Britain—not, it is stated, without some difficulty—an undertaking that, in return for the sacrifice demanded of Czechoslovakia, she also would bind herself to guarantee the new boundaries of that state against unprovoked aggression.

The vital question, as Mr. Chamberlain said in his speech in the House of Commons on September 28, was not the independence of a small nation, nor the future stability of Europe, but to prevent immediate danger:

" During these conversations the representatives of the two Governments were guided by a desire to find a solution which would not bring about a European war, and, therefore, a solution which would not automatically compel France to take action in accordance with her obligations."

The next day, September 20, the British and French Governments agreed to accept the decisions of the London Conference, and at 2 p.m. they were officially announced to the Czechoslovak Government.

Before describing the reaction in Prague to this terrible decision, I would add some critical remarks regarding these negotiations. In the first place, it is not yet known whether Herr Hitler
at Berchtesgaden defined his territorial demands or whether he
spoke generally about the right of the Sudeten Germans to be
annexed by the Reich. The second is more probably what
occurred, for he personally did not wish to commit himself at the
very beginning of the conversations nor did he want to provoke
the resistance of Britain and France by premature demands,
which might have seemed unacceptable in practice, as happened
at Godesberg. One may presume, therefore, that it was the
British and French Governments who suggested the cession of
territory containing more than 50 per cent. of Sudeten Germans.
Both Mr. Chamberlain and M. Daladier, in attempting to
explain and justify their decision of September 19, laid emphasis
on Lord Runciman's advice, but Lord Runciman's written
Report, which he sent to the British Prime Minister,[1] was dated
September 21, and therefore three days after the decisions of the
Franco-British Conference. In it there is no mention of any
exact percentage of population. Lord Runciman refers only to
territory in which the Sudeten Germans have " an important
majority."

" It has become self-evident to me," he writes, " that those
frontier districts between Czechoslovakia and Germany where
the Sudeten population is in an important majority should be
given full right of self-determination at once." It is obvious
from Lord Runciman's Report which has also been quoted
above (page 32) that Lord Runciman did not contemplate the
creation of a Czech minority in Germany far larger than the
German minority in Czechoslovakia. This is what happened at
Munich.

It is probably therefore no mis-statement to say that the proposal for the cession of territory with more than 50 per cent. of
Sudeten-German population was not made by Lord Runciman,
and that he had in mind a much higher percentage. It is known,
at any rate, that he was very much taken aback when he heard
the percentage upon which the London Conference had decided.
As soon as it had become known that a simple majority of over

[1] And also, in exactly the same wording, to President Beneš.

one-half had been suggested, many politicians and diplomats supposed that 75 per cent. was intended—which is probably nearer to Lord Runciman's conception. Why, in spite of this, did the London Conference adopt the standard of 50 per cent. ? Who made this proposal ? Or who inspired it ? Was it the influence of the Berchtesgaden conversations, about which up to now no more is known than what was recounted by Mr. Chamberlain ? As yet we can obtain no reliable answers to all these questions, and until they are available we cannot correctly determine who made this decision or who had an active influence upon it.

M. Daladier, referring to the London Conference in his Report to the Chamber on October 4, said: " We bent over the maps." If that is true, our surprise at their decisions cannot but be greater, for how was it possible that M. Daladier, who was not only Prime Minister, but also Minister of War, could agree to the cession of territory which, if he looked at the map, he must have noticed would effectively deprive Czechoslovakia of all practical possibility of military defence ? The decision handed over to Germany not only the mountainous and wooded frontier districts, whose natural structure itself offers useful support for defence, but at the same time all the Czechoslovak fortifications. These were not, it is true, built with French money, as was often argued, but were built by agreement with and at the wish (certainly quite well-founded) of our French allies ! But when M. Daladier agreed to this proposal, the obvious consequence of which was that Czechoslovakia would no longer be able to defend herself, one should ask oneself of what practical importance it could be to insist upon Great Britain guaranteeing a new frontier which would be very difficult to defend. One may also ask the question: How is it that Great Britain, who had previously refused to accept any obligation with regard to a Czechoslovakia that was militarily strong and that was capable of a long resistance, should all at once have agreed to guarantee the boundaries of a state which was crippled and weakened in every way ? There are so many glaring contradictions in connection with this whole affair that it defies anyone, even the most subtle sophist, to explain them— except on the assumption that the promise of a new guarantee, which was supposed to replace Czechoslovakia's then-existing system of alliances, was not taken with the seriousness which it merits. It is not impossible, of course, that those who accepted the idea of ceding the territory with more than 50 per cent. Sudeten Germans did not realise quite clearly what it was that they had agreed to cede to Germany, and that they did not realise the inevitable consequences of that territorial upheaval. When I was in Paris at the end of September (i.e. just after Godesberg), I was asked by a leading French politician whether it was not possible for us to build fortifications on our new boundaries. And when I showed him—not only on the nationality, but even more on the physical map, what it really was that had been proposed at the London Conference, he held his head nervously and sighed: " I never realised that ! " If it were really true that those responsible for the London proposals were not fully aware of the consequences of their demands, it would be easier to understand the unbelievably far-reaching effect of their proposals. But even if that were the explanation, it would nevertheless be no justification for what was done.

4. *Britain and France desert Czechoslovakia.*

The worst part of this story, especially for us Czechoslovaks, was the attitude and outlook of the French Ministers. M. Daladier on September 18 did not resemble at all the M. Daladier of April 29, who, while conducting negotiations for the closest co-operation between France and Britain, even in military matters, had nevertheless so firmly maintained his opinion that France would under all circumstances fulfil her obligations towards Czechoslovakia that the British Government, whatever its feelings may have been, took that opinion into account. M. Daladier's attitude was entirely different, however, on September 18, when he accepted the proposals made by the British representatives, and M. Daladier must share with M. Bonnet the responsibility before history for the consent of the French Government, without which it would never have been possible to extort from Czechoslovakia the cession of the Sudeten-German territories, with the fatal consequence that Czechoslovakia became a vassal and, finally, a province of the Third Reich. The French negotiators adopted in London a policy which was described by Mr. Chamberlain as one of trying " to find a solution which would not automatically compel France to take action in accordance with her obligations towards Czechoslovakia." They had already pursued this policy for a longish period, actually since July. From the moment that Lord Runciman had been sent to Prague on the initiative of the British Government, the French had surrendered to Britain all leadership with regard to policy in the German-Czechoslovak dispute. Yet it was clear that that dispute was to an infinitely greater degree a matter of French rather than British interest. A certain change in the attitude of Paris towards Prague had been perceptible even after April 29; when the French Government assured itself of the alliance of Britain, her interest in her Allies in Eastern and Central Europe began to diminish. On May 21 her attitude was still firm, but the attitude of London at that time was no less firm ! But from then onwards Paris had adopted an increasingly passive attitude towards her Czechoslovak ally, and from July onwards the French had simply followed the actions of the British, on whose policy they modelled their own without any modification whatsoever. We well understood that France was obliged, in her own interest, to consider first of all how her attitude might affect her alliance with Britain—for, quite apart from other important reasons, the mere fact of the geographical proximity of these two Powers necessitated and gave vital importance to their collaboration and alliance—but at the same time we realised that, if France could not do without Britain, no more could Britain do without France, whose excellent Army represented one of the main defences of Britain, as well as of France. We imagined also that, quite regardless of Germany, France had need of her Eastern allies as a make-weight in her favour when dealing with Britain, unless she was prepared to weaken her status as a Great Power on an equality with the British Empire. I had occasion to speak with M. Daladier in March, 1938, a few days after the annexation of Austria, and I think I am committing no indiscretion when I say that I was very much pleased with his realistic appreciation of the role in European politics of Franco-British co-operation, whether in Central Europe or in the Mediterranean. M. Daladier must have changed his ideas very much since then, for otherwise he would have opposed more strongly the British proposals which were made to him in

London on September 18. He would have opposed these proposals, whatever may have been at that time the views of his Foreign Minister M. Bonnet. There can be no doubt, moreover, especially when it is remembered that he was Minister of War as well as Prime Minister, that his opposition to those proposals would have been sufficient to force Britain to compromise.

I would not wish to minimise in any way the responsibility of the British statesmen for what occurred, and in my account of the consequences of Munich I will try to show that even fundamental British interests have been gravely prejudiced, but there is no doubt that the responsibility of the representatives of France is the greater. In the first place, France had a definite treaty of guarantee with Czechoslovakia and MM. Daladier and Bonnet proclaimed until the last moment that her contractual obligations under that Treaty were " sacred," whereas Britain had no such special obligations. Quite apart, however, from the question of legal obligations, the political interest of France in Czechoslovakia was much more immediate and concrete than that of Britain: Czechoslovakia was the keystone of the system which prevented Germany from dominating Central Europe, and on which depended the security of France. That being so, it was really unbelievable that France could permit Czechoslovakia to be placed at the mercy of Germany; thereby France weakened herself and sacrificed all the fruits of her victory in 1918.

For Britain, on the other hand, Czechoslovakia and the Danube Basin were areas of secondary interest and importance. Britain would, of course, have been obliged to interest herself in their integrity if France had been consistent and maintained her attitude of April 29, but ever since the summer of 1938 the attitude of France had been such as must have created in London an impression that the maintenance of a strong and independent Czechoslovakia had ceased to be an essential condition for France. Therein lies the special responsibility of M. Georges Bonnet and those French circles which supported him, agreed with him or otherwise influenced him in his policy. Even if the London proposals, which were simply the concrete expression of Hitler's requirements at Berchtesgaden, were " Made in Britain," their manufacture there was faciliated by the attitude already adopted by France. Under the guidance of M. Bonnet, the

impression had been deliberately created in England that the
Chamberlain group must have had every reason to suppose that
its proposals would be acceptable for France and that France
would insist upon their acceptance by Prague.

Once the British Government realised what was the attitude
of M. Bonnet, it soon became generally assumed in Great Britain
that France would hesitate to fulfil her treaty obligations towards Czechoslovakia. The fact that French diplomacy in
London did not support the claims of Czechoslovakia in her conflict with Germany can only have strengthened this impression.
It is admittedly true that M. Corbin, the French Ambassador
in London, acting on instructions received from the Quai
d'Orsay, very strenuously took the part of Czechoslovakia, and
that in doing so he expressed also his personal sympathies, but
it is also true that his emphatic assurances that France would
consistently stand beside Czechoslovakia did not create any
great impression in British circles. Thus, for example, Lord
Halifax was not much impressed by the fact that, before the
Nuremberg speech, M. Corbin explained to him that, in the
opinion of France, the Sudeten-German dispute could not be
solved by a plebiscite or in any other reasonable way, since it was
a pretext for expansionist aggression by Germany, which would be
answered immediately by French intervention. On September
14 and 15 there was much discussion in official circles in London
of the report which had been made by Sir Eric Phipps, the
British Ambassador in Paris, after a conversation which he had
had on September 13 with M. Bonnet. This report conveyed the
impression that the policy of France was to preserve peace,
even if necessary, at the price of sacrificing Czechoslovakia. The
main argument in favour of this view was that France was unable
to go to war, because she was insufficiently prepared for it. Thus,
just at the moment when Mr. Chamberlain's trip to Berchtesgaden was decided, the British politicians were strengthened in
their belief that France would desert Czechoslovakia and that
she would accept any solution in order not to be obliged to risk
a war. It is less surprising, therefore, than it might be that
shortly before going to Berchtesgaden Mr. Chamberlain should
have expressed in private his opinion that he did not believe that
France would help Czechoslovakia, and that consequently he

did not wish, and indeed was unable, to commit Britain to a policy of possibly isolated action.

It is worth quoting, in this connection, the following extract from an article, which there is reason to believe is authentic, published under the pseudonym of " Le Guet d'Orsay " in *L'Europe Nouvelle* of November 19, 1938.[1]

" At the present time the director of our diplomacy is wooing certain Deputies whom he does not consider sufficiently moved by the act of grace at Munich. He is buzzing round the Moderates, the Radicals and even the Socialists, and is assuring all of them that it is the fault of England. But we may be sure that he forgets to tell them that his declaration of fidelity to our obligations towards Czechoslovakia, which occurred in his speech at la Pointe de Graves [on September 4], was only included at the request of Great Britain and not without hesitation on his part."

In *L'Europe Nouvelle* of October 8, 1938,[2] we find, from the same anonymous author:

" Some day we shall certainly be able to prove that the Minister of Foreign Affairs spared no effort to create the impression in England that France was not at all in a position to embark on a war on account of Czechoslovakia, and, furthermore, that she had no intention of doing so. Moreover, the remarks made on a certain occasion by M. Bonnet at the meeting of the Cabinet were, to say the least, strange, for did he not explain that there was an ' exterior ' policy and an ' interior ' policy as regards the Czechoslovak affair ? In other words, that if it were useful, or even necessary, to make Germany and the rest of the world believe that we would respect our engagements, that did not, by any means, imply necessarily that henceforth the French Cabinet was irrevocably bound to that decision. . . . While we kept England under the impression that under no circumstances would we go to war, everything possible was done to inspire the minds of the French with grave doubts regarding Great Britain's intentions. On Sunday, September 11, when Mr. Chamberlain's

[1] P. 1,252.　　　[2] P. 1,087.

declaration was published, promising, in very definite terms, England's support for France, we did our best to minimise the importance of the news. There were strange telephone calls from the office of the Foreign Minister to certain journalists. And anyhow, as is proved by an article by the Paris correspondent of *The Times*, M. Georges Bonnet was not afraid, during the last days of September, even to put the blame for the weak policy pursued on the British Cabinet. It is true that *The Times* correspondent, by referring to ' the spokesman of the Quai d'Orsay,' tried to pretend that it had nothing to do with M. Bonnet personally, but actually he was misusing the word ' spokesman ' to deceive the public just as the French people were deceived with regard to the Foreign Office declaration of September 26—about which everything is known to-day."

In its issue of October 29, also,[1] *L'Europe Nouvelle* published the following information:

" On August 24, Mr. Neville Chamberlain, Lord Halifax and Sir John Simon held a Conference at the Foreign Office. Mr. Neville Chamberlain was about to leave London for a few days, and he discussed with his collaborators the necessity of publishing a statement which would be in the nature of a warning to Germany before the Nuremberg Congress. Several newspapers made this clearly understood. Even the *Daily Mail* wrote: ' The declaration will take the form of an extremely clear assurance which will allow France to count on our support if she is involved in hostilities on account of her obligations towards Czechoslovakia.'

"But, on the evening of August 25, the *Deutsches Nachrichtenbüro* [*D.N.B.*] published a telegram from London, contradicting ' from an official source ' this information. No such official contradiction had, of course, reached Hitler's news agency. What is curious, however, is that at the same time the Havas Agency published a ' special ' (that is to say a report intended for the newspapers in the provinces and abroad) of a very unofficial appearance, which, in effect, confirmed the German contradiction. ' Much surprise is felt

[1] P. 1,168.

in well-informed circles,' said the Havas Agency, ' at the news published this morning in the British Press. It was alleged that at a meeting which took place yesterday Mr. Neville Chamberlain, Lord Halifax and Sir John Simon decided that the British Government would shortly make a statement, renewing the British assurances to France, in the event of the latter being drawn into a conflict on account of her obligations towards Czechoslovakia. M. Georges Bonnet was in communication by telephone during the day with M. Roger Cambon, the French Chargé d'Affaires in London, who met Lord Halifax this morning. The Minister of Foreign Affairs has not received the confirmation of the news, which would appear to be incorrect.'

" Elsewhere in the same report it is suggested that Mr. Chamberlain's departure seemed to discourage ' the supposition that any British initiative of such importance is impending.'

" This Havas Agency ' special ' was very strange, and when I refer to its ' very unofficial appearance,' I am using a mild euphemism, for although no mention is made of M. Georges Bonnet, it could only have been published with his consent —and when I write ' consent,' I am guilty of another euphemism.

" . . . We all know what followed. M. Georges Bonnet's efforts were not crowned with success. It is possible that it was the ' special ' which induced the British Government not to entrust Lord Halifax with the task of making a speech re-affirming Great Britain's assurances to France. We know, at any rate, that the task was conferred on Sir John Simon, who spoke less vigorously than the head of the Foreign Office would undoubtedly have done. But, all the same, the speech made by the Chancellor of the Exchequer at Lanark on August 27 repeated without ambiguity the declaration made by Mr. Chamberlain in the House of Commons on March 24."

I will quote in conclusion, though chronologically it belongs elsewhere, one more extract from the article already quoted in *L'Europe Nouvelle* of November 19:[1]

[1] P. 1,252.

" On September 25, after Godesberg, MM. Daladier and
Bonnet went to London. On the morning of September 26,
M. Daladier alone went to see Mr. Chamberlain, who confirmed
the previous declarations regarding British support. M.
Bonnet had quarrelled with M. Daladier, who therefore did
not speak to him, and, consequently, did not tell him about
his conversation with the British Prime Minister.

" Meanwhile our Minister of Foreign Affairs was uneasy.
He had a presentiment of something. So, on the evening
of September 26, he sent instructions to our Ambassador
in London . . . instructions which go beyond anything
that we can imagine, for he tells our Ambassador that if
Great Britain associates herself with us, she must satisfy
two conditions:

" (1) That she will bear half the financial and economic
costs of the war, and

" (2) That she will introduce conscription.

" Anyone who knows the English will know how the making
of such conditions in advance must have been received.

" It should be added, moreover, that, as regards conscription, Mr. Chamberlain had already made a statement to the
effect that if war broke out, conscription would immediately
be decreed."

If we seek an explanation of the policy pursued by the British
and French statesmen on September 18 in London, we are
forced to the conclusion that they wished to avoid war with
Germany, even at the price of sacrificing the independence of
Czechoslovak democracy. They probably had not the slightest
doubt that Hitler would really risk a world war, rather than
forgo the annexation of the Sudeten Germans to the Reich.
They yielded to that threat without trying to find out more
exactly in what measure Hitler actually desired war and *was
able* to carry his threat into effect. In British circles, where,
unfortunately, the Sudeten-German problem was never well
understood, the view was already widely held that the best
solution would be the cession of the Sudeten-German territory to
Germany. The British were sceptical, moreover, as to whether in
fact Czechoslovakia would be able to preserve her independence.

Incorrectly appreciating the situation, they hastily concluded that Czechoslovakia was doomed to the same fate which Austria had suffered in March. As early as May, Mr. Chamberlain had expressed himself to some American journalists in that sense. Although, in fact, he had made the statement in confidence, it immediately became known in well-informed political and diplomatic circles and, of course, to the Germans also. Mr. Garvin's bitterly anti-Czechoslovak articles in the *Observer* expressed the opinion, not only of influential, but to a large extent even of official British circles. The British underestimated the military potential of Czechoslovakia. They exaggerated the disadvantages of her strategical position and the weaknesses and deficiencies of her defences. Studiously and prominently, they reiterated the argument that it would be difficult to ensure military help to Czechoslovakia. The politicians expressed their opinions on military matters without making a careful or detailed analysis of the military problems of Czechoslovakia.

In such circumstances, British policy throughout the Czechoslovak crisis was necessarily disunited and confused. It would be incorrect to suppose that the British were anxious for Germany to seize Czechoslovakia. They wanted rather to adopt an attitude which would be able to force the Czechoslovak Government to make far-reaching concessions to Henlein. They hoped that Herr Hitler might perhaps be satisfied with this. From the very beginning official British circles maintained a censorious attitude towards the Czechs, and were predisposed to consider the possibility of a solution whereby the Sudeten-German districts would be given to Germany and Czechoslovakia would be sacrificed. The German propaganda was successful in making people believe that the question at issue was that of the right of the Sudeten Germans to self-determination, a right which British democracy could not, of course, deny. British policy would have had to follow very different lines, however, if the French had consistently supported Czechoslovakia, as they had done during the London Conferences of April 29 and May 21, but this did not happen. Attention has already been drawn to the fact that, especially in August, 1938, people in touch with the British Government became more and more certain that France would not go to the help of Czechoslovakia. The publication of the article which appeared in *The Times* on September 7, was made possible by this attitude of the French. The policy, however, which inspired it was that outlined by Mr. Chamberlain in May to the American journalists. Although it was officially stated later that this article did not express the views of the British Government, it soon became known—and notably to Herr von Ribbentrop—that certain highly placed people were responsible for its publication.

All this, of course, encouraged the Germans to press forward their demands. If Herr Hitler had not known how vacillating were the policies of Britain and France, if he had not been informed that the most influential British and French circles considered it better to sacrifice Czechoslovakia than to risk war, he would not have dared speak to Mr. Chamberlain in Berchtesgaden in a provocative and threatening manner. As it was, however, Herr Hitler insisted that if he did not obtain satisfaction in the Sudeten-German, or, more correctly, in the Czechoslovak and Central European affair, Germany was willing to embark on a world war. The Berchtesgaden meeting gave the fatal impetus to the performance of that operation already contemplated by certain English politicians. It became more easy for the British Government to adopt this policy when, shortly afterwards, Lord Runciman, who must by this time have been considered as an expert, himself advised the cession to Germany of the Sudeten-German districts along the frontier. It seems that Lord Runciman considered it of little importance that the Henleinist revolt was comparatively quickly suppressed and that a change was taking place amongst the Sudeten Germans themselves. This was because, whenever he thought of the Sudeten-German problem, Lord Runciman considered only, or primarily, Herr Henlein. Thus, though the decisive factor was Berchtesgaden, the written approval of Lord Runciman greatly contributed to the London decisions. Britain's readiness to satisfy Herr Hitler by making territorial concessions at Czechoslovakia's expense was encouraged in advance by the diplomacy of M. Bonnet. When M. Daladier offered no resistance, British readiness expressed itself in the form of a definite proposition. On September 18, in London, Great Britain and France capitulated before the threats of Herr Hitler.

5. *Prague refuses the Anglo-French Proposals.*

More detailed information about the results of the London Conference first reached Prague during the night of September 18–19, and on the morning of September 19 our Government knew what was proposed for us by our Western allies. It was not, however, until the afternoon of the next day that the general public learned about it. The full text of the London proposals was never published at all. Although it was impossible to conceal the basic facts, the Government, nevertheless, were afraid to let the public know the full extent of what was demanded of us. The British and French Governments also found it advisable to exercise a certain discretion. Therefore, even in the Western countries, a week elapsed before the full contents of the London proposals were published on September 26. While our people were passing through hours of anxious uncertainty, grasping desperately at every indication of sympathy from the Western countries, in the shape of articles, speeches or resolutions, our Government discussed with the President of the Republic how to answer the London proposals, which had been officially delivered on September 19 in a Note which read as follows:

" The representatives of the French and British Governments have been in consultation to-day on the general situation, and have considered the British Prime Minister's report of his conversation with Herr Hitler. British Ministers also placed before their French colleagues their conclusions derived from the account furnished to them of the work of his mission by Lord Runciman. We are both convinced that, after recent events, the point has now been reached where the further maintenance within the boundaries of the Czechoslovak state of the districts mainly inhabited by Sudeten Germans cannot, in fact, continue any longer without imperilling the interests of Czechoslovakia herself and of European peace.

" In the light of these considerations, both Governments have been compelled to the conclusion that the maintenance of peace and the safety of Czechoslovakia's vital interests cannot effectively be assured unless these areas are now transferred to the Reich.

" 2. This could be done either by direct transfer or as the result of a plebiscite. We realise the difficulties involved in a plebiscite, and we are aware of your objections already expressed to this course, particularly the possibility of far-reaching repercussions if the matter were treated on the basis of so wide a principle. For this reason, we anticipate, in the absence of indication to the contrary, that you may prefer to deal with the Sudeten-German problem by the method of direct transfer, and as a case by itself.

" 3. The area for transfer would probably have to include areas with over 50 per cent. of German inhabitants, but we should hope to arrange by negotiations provisions for adjustment of frontiers, where circumstances render it necessary, by some international body, including a Czech representative. We are satisfied that the transfer of smaller areas based on a higher percentage would not meet the case.

" 4. The international body referred to might also be charged with questions of possible exchange of population on the basis of right to opt within some specified time limit.

" 5. We recognise that, if the Czechoslovak Government is prepared to concur in the measures proposed, involving material changes in the conditions of the State, they are entitled to ask for some assurance of their future security.

" 6. Accordingly, His Majesty's Government in the United Kingdom would be prepared, as a contribution to the pacification of Europe, to join in an international guarantee of the new boundaries of the Czechoslovak state against unprovoked aggression. One of the principal conditions of such a guarantee would be the safeguarding of the independence of Czechoslovakia by the substitution of a general guarantee against unprovoked aggression in place of existing treaties which involve reciprocal obligations of a military character.

" 7. Both the French and British Governments recognise how great is the sacrifice thus required of the Czechoslovak Government in the cause of peace. But because that cause is common both to Europe in general and in particular to Czechoslovakia herself, they have felt it their duty jointly to set forth frankly the conditions essential to secure it.

" 8. The Prime Minister must resume conversations with

Herr Hitler not later than Wednesday, and earlier if possible. We therefore feel we must ask for your reply at the earliest possible moment." [Cmd. 5847.]

When the Czechoslovak Ministers, assembled at the President's Palace, were informed of these incredible proposals, they were all—and, I would emphasise, all without exception—unanimously in favour of rejecting them. To answer France and England with a rejection of their proposals was not easy, for it was necessary to take into consideration all the possible consequences which might arise from such a rejection. It was not out of the question that Germany, who already knew, of course, the basis of the London proposals, might take advantage of the new attitude of France and England to attack Czechoslovakia. The Government immediately consulted the military authorities, and invited General Syrový, the Inspector-General of the Czechoslovak armed forces, and General Krejčí, Chief of the General Staff, to attend its discussions. The generals thought that it would be extremely dangerous to risk measuring our forces with those of Germany, unless the help of France were assured.

Our situation was now exceedingly critical because, although Germany calmly continued to concentrate her forces in ever-increasing numbers along our frontiers, we were prevented from taking important defensive measures by England and France. We were warned continually not to " provoke " Germany—not to disturb the " peaceful negotiations " of the British Prime Minister. Though Germany had called to the colours 2,000,000 men, we had, at that time, only 450,000 at our disposal. Certain sectors on our frontier were practically unoccupied. In spite of this, however, the Czechoslovak Government, after long and detailed discussion, presided over by the President of the Republic in person, decided to reject the London proposals. We were fortified in our decision by the inconceivability of a French breach of faith. We knew, moreover, that certain members of the British Government were far from convinced of the advisability of these proposals, and that in the French Cabinet, which had passed them on September 19, there were strong differences of opinion. We were informed, in particular, that certain French Ministers had voted for the proposals only on condition that the

French obligation to go to the help of Czechoslovakia would remain valid even in the event of a Czech rejection. It was evident also, even if only from articles which appeared in the British and French Press of September 19 and 20, that public opinion was by no means unanimously behind the attitude adopted by the Governments. In these circumstances, there was always hope that the British and French Governments would revise their decisions of September 18 and that they would not insist upon their unconditional acceptance. Therefore, while not refusing to give consideration to the principle embodied in the London proposals, we suggested that the conflict should be settled in accordance with the German-Czechoslovak Treaty of Arbitration, which had been reaffirmed in a categorical statement by Germany as recently as March, 1938. The Czechoslovak Government was obliged, when coming to its decision, to take into consideration Czech public opinion. There was no doubt that the Czechoslovak Government would have met with passionate resistance if it had accepted outright the London proposals. Although our Press maintained an exemplary discipline and reserve, desiring not to make more difficult the already difficult decisions of the Government, nevertheless on September 19 and 20 it expressed itself clearly and unanimously against the immense sacrifices which were required of us. In this I did not differ from my colleagues, and when, on September 19, I wrote an article in the *Lidové Noviny* entitled " Unacceptable," I was speaking not only for the immense majority of my countrymen, but I was outlining what we all knew would be the consequences of surrender to Germany. The views which I now profess are not derived solely from the post-Munich experience. We consistently warned our Western friends of the dangers inherent for them also in the German attack on Czechoslovakia:

" However one may look at the London proposals, *it is clear that no Czechoslovak Government could have accepted them.* We have already rejected the proposal of a plebiscite precisely because it would have entailed the risk of territorial changes, so why should we now accept such changes as are now definitely proposed ?

" What is it hoped to achieve by these proposals ? It is difficult to believe that it is seriously imagined that ' peace ' can be preserved by the cession of the Sudeten-German districts to Germany. Such cession would, at most, merely postpone the final decision. For the real issue at stake is not ' the Sudeten-German problem,' but the relations of Germany with the rest of the world. Germany is endeavouring to seize the Sudeten Germans, because *she is convinced that thereby she will achieve the disruption of Czechoslovakia and thus become mistress of the Danube Basin. What, then, will be the position of the Western Powers ? Are they unable to see what is at stake ? In the face of such ignorance, whether it be real or pretended, we can only express profound astonishment.*

" If once the Western Powers start to revise the frontier between Germany and Czechoslovakia, Germany will naturally demand that the new frontier be one which it will be impossible for Czechoslovakia to maintain. If Germany succeeds in this, Czechosolvakia will become incapable of any resistance whatsoever in defence of her independence. Of what conceivable value will be promises to guarantee the integrity of such a frontier ? Our existing frontier has been guaranteed in the most solemn and binding fashion, and we have faith in the signature of France. The French guarantee of the integrity of our country was given unconditionally and with the full knowledge of its possible consequences. *Moreover, Mr. Chamberlain himself has spoken of the necessity of maintaining the integrity of Czechoslovakia,* Does that which was valid yesterday no longer hold good to-day ? If this is so, why should our guarantors be accepting obligations for to-morrow ?

" The statesmen of the Western Powers are incurring a terrible responsibility indeed if they themselves uproot faith in the sanctity of treaties. They are summoning anarchy which will not halt at the frontiers of their own countries nor of their possessions, for why should the German-Czechoslovak frontier alone be revised ? Why should not other frontiers also be subject to revision ? Can ' peace ' always be saved, whenever Germany rattles the sabre, by some new revision ? If they are willing to wipe out a frontier made by Nature

to endure, such as that which separates Germany from
Czechoslovakia, how can it be hoped that others, less stable,
should survive ?

" Furthermore, not even the proposed revision of the
frontier will rid Czechoslovakia of all her Germany minority.
Is the story to be repeated periodically whenever it pleases
Germany to demand it ? Not thus can peace be preserved,
but rather will chaos and international friction be let loose
upon the world.

" The solution proposed is one which would lead to the
strategic, political, economic and social disruption of Czechoslovakia. Either its consequences are not thought out or the
issues at stake have not been appreciated. This alone can account for the presentation of such proposals. Let me still believe
that it is in the interest of Great Britain and France that Czechoslovakia should maintain itself as an independent state. The
question of Frenchmen and Englishmen fighting ' for the
Czechoslovaks ' does not arise. The issue at stake is to *arrest the
imperialist expansion of Germany*, whose declared aim, according
to Hitler's programme, is the domination of Europe as a whole.
The maintenance of the independence of our country is primarily our own affair. If for others it is a diplomatic question of
power politics, for us it is a matter of *life and death*. Only yesterday our Prime Minister, Dr. Hodža, said ' not merely peace, but
also the future dignity of our whole Republic, is at stake.'
His words can be interpreted only as meaning that we will
defend the integrity of our State and will not tolerate its
disruption."

After discussions which lasted nearly two days, the President,
our Government and the representatives of all Czechoslovak
political parties approved and forwarded to the Governments of
France and Britain the following answer to their proposals:

" The Czechoslovak Government thank the British and
French Governments for the report transmitted, in which they
express their opinion on a solution of the present international
difficulties concerning Czechoslovakia. Conscious of the
responsibility they bear in the interests of Czechoslovakia, her
friends and allies and in the interest of general peace, they

express their conviction that the proposals contained in the report are incapable of attaining the aims which the British and French Governments expect from them in their great effort to preserve peace.

" These proposals were made without consultation with the representatives of Czechoslovakia. They were negotiated against Czechoslovakia, without hearing her case, though the Czechoslovak Government has pointed out that they cannot take responsibility for a declaration made without their consent. It is hence understandable that the proposals mentioned could not be such as to be acceptable to Czechoslovakia.

" The Czechoslovak Government cannot for constitutional reasons take a decision which would affect their frontiers. Such a decision would not be possible without violating the democratic régime and juridical order of the Czechoslovak state. In any case it would be necessary to consult Parliament.

" In the view of the Government, the acceptance of such a proposal would amount to a voluntary and complete mutilation of the state in every respect. Czechoslovakia would be completely paralysed in regard to economics and communications and, from a strategic point of view, her position would become extremely difficult. Sooner or later she would fall under the complete domination of Germany.

" Even if Czechoslovakia should make the sacrifices proposed, the question of peace would by no means be solved.

" (a) Many Sudeten Germans would, for well-known reasons, prefer to leave the Reich and would settle in the democratic atmosphere of the Czechoslovak state. New difficulties and new nationality conflicts would be the result.

" (b) The mutilation of Czechoslovakia would lead to a profound political change in the whole of Central and South-Eastern Europe. The balance of forces in Central Europe and in Europe as a whole would be completely destroyed: it would have the most far-reaching consequences for all other states and especially for France.

" (c) The Czechoslovak Government are sincerely grateful to the Great Powers for their intention of guaranteeing the integrity of Czechoslovakia; they appreciate it and value it

highly. Such a guarantee would certainly open the way to an
agreement between all interested Powers, if the present
nationality conflicts were settled amicably and in such a
manner as not to impose unacceptable sacrifices on Czechoslovakia.

" Czechoslovakia has during recent years given many proofs
of her unshakable devotion to peace. At the instance of her
friends, the Czechoslovak Government have gone so far in the
negotiations about the Sudeten-German question that it has
been acknowledged with gratitude by the whole world—also
a British government pronouncement stressed that it is
necessary not to exceed the bounds of the Czechoslovak
Constitution—and even the Sudeten-German Party did not
reject the last proposals of the Government but publicly
expressed its conviction that the intentions of the Government
were serious and sincere. In spite of the fact that a revolt has
just broken out among a part of the Sudeten population which
has been instigated from abroad, the Government have again
declared solemnly that they still adhere to the proposals which
had met the wishes of the Sudeten-German minority. Even
to-day they consider this solution as realisable as far as the
nationality questions of the republic are concerned.

" Czechoslovakia has always remained faithful to her
treaties and fulfilled her obligations resulting from them,
whether in the interests of her friends or the League of Nations
and its members or the other nations. She was resolved and is
still resolved to fulfil them under any circumstances. If she
now resists the possibility of the application of force, she does
so on the basis of recent obligations and declarations of her
neighbour and also on the basis of the arbitration treaty of
October 16, 1936, which the present German Government
have recognised as valid in several pronouncements. The
Czechoslovak Government emphasise that this treaty can be
applied and ask that this should be done. As they respect their
signature, they are prepared to accept any sentence of arbitration which might be pronounced. This would limit any conflict. It would make possible a quick, honourable solution
which would be worthy of all interested states.

" Czechoslovakia has been always bound to France by

respect and most devoted friendship and an alliance which no Czechoslovak Government and no Czechoslovak will ever violate. She has lived and still lives in the belief in the great French nation, whose Government have so frequently assured her of the firmness of their friendship. She is bound to Great Britain by traditional friendship and respect with which Czechoslovakia will always be inspired, by the undissoluble co-operation between the two countries and thus also by the common effort for peace, whatever conditions in Europe prevail.

" The Czechoslovak Government appreciate that the effort of the British and French Governments have their source in real sympathy. They thank them for it sincerely. Nevertheless, for reasons already stated, they appeal to them again and for the last time and ask them to reconsider their opinion. They do so in the conviction that they are defending, not only their own interests, but also the interest of their friends, the cause of peace and the cause of healthy development in Europe. At this decisive moment, it is not only a question of the fate of Czechoslovakia, but also the fate of other countries and especially of France.

" PRAGUE.

" *September* 20, 1938." [1]

The text of this Note was not published—for a long while it was unknown to the general public in the Western countries—but its basic contents became known to our own people on the night of September 20, and the decision thus taken was accepted by them with understandable relief and with general approval. The gravity of the situation was known to everyone.

[1] Czechoslovak State Document.

Chapter III

The Anglo-French Ultimatum

1. *The Night of September* 21.

OUR answer was, however, received in a very different manner by our Western friends. On the evening of September 20, when our Foreign Secretary, Dr. Krofta, presented the Czechoslovak Note to the British and French Ministers, the former told him immediately that if Czechoslovakia persisted in her rejection of the Anglo-French proposals the British Government would declare itself disinterested in her fate. The French Minister associated himself with this attitude. Dr. Krofta, of course, could only carry out the task with which he had been entrusted— namely, the presentation to the two diplomatic representatives of the Note in which the Czechoslovak Government rejected their Governments' proposals. Dr. Krofta naturally informed the President of the Republic and the Cabinet of the views which had been expressed to him by the British and French Ministers. On receipt of this information, the Cabinet decided to await the official reaction of London and Paris to their Note.

London and Paris responded more rapidly than might have been expected, and that very same night, shortly after 1 a.m. (Central European time) the British and French Ministers made urgent requests by telephone for an immediate interview with President Beneš. They were received by the President at 2 a.m., and informed him that both Britain and France urged the immediate acceptance by Czechoslovakia of their proposals. They declared that if Czechoslovakia persisted in her rejection of those proposals she must know that she could not count on help from either of those countries in the event of an attack by Germany. During this conversation, the British Minister, Mr. Newton, handed President Beneš the instructions which he had received from his Government:

" In the opinion of His Majesty's Government, the reply of the Czechoslovak Government does not meet the critical situation which the Anglo-French proposals were designed to remove and, if it should be adhered to, would lead, after publication, in the opinion of His Majesty's Government, to an immediate German invasion. His Majesty's Government therefore appeals to the Czechoslovak Government to retract their answer and to consider speedily an alternative which would take account of realities. On the basis of the answer submitted, His Majesty's Government would not have any hope in a useful result of the proposed second visit to Herr Hitler and the Prime Minister would be forced to abandon the necessary preparations for it. His Majesty's Government therefore asks the Czechoslovak Government for a speedy and earnest reconsideration before they create a situation for which His Majesty's Government could not take responsibility.

" His Majesty's Government would certainly be ready to submit the Czechoslovak proposal for arbitration to the German Government if they thought that under given circumstances there was any hope of it being favourably considered. But His Majesty's Government cannot believe for a moment that this proposal would be now acceptable and also do not think that the German Government would consider the situation as one which can be repaired by arbitration, as proposed by the Czechoslovak Government.

" If the Czechoslovak Government, after reconsideration, would still feel compelled to reject this advice, it must have, of course, complete freedom for any action which it considers appropriate in view of the situation which might develop later.

" *September* 21, 1938." [1]

The French Minister, M. de Lacroix, had been authorised by his Government only to make a verbal communication. He explained, therefore, to President Beneš that if, as a result of the negative attitude adopted towards the Anglo-French proposals by the Czechoslovak Government, hostilities were to break out, France would not take action (*ne s'y associera pas*). He went on to point out that, in circumstances such as he had described, Britain would not in any case come to the assistance of France even if she did move, but that Czechoslovakia, having rejected the Anglo-French proposals, would be held entirely responsible for having provoked a war. Therefore his Government urgently

[1] Czechoslovak State Document.

advised the Czechoslovak Government to accept unconditionally the terms which had been proposed. President Beneš, in the presence of the two Ministers, wrote down this verbal communication, but he nevertheless asked afterwards that it should be presented to him in writing—*litera scripta manet*. The message was presented in writing in the form of a Note during the day of September 21. The written version was milder in its expression and form, but the actual contents were unchanged. The French Government repeated its previous declaration that it would not come to the help of Czechoslovakia if, following on the rejection by her Government of the Anglo-French proposals, war broke out between her and Germany.

Professor Dominois, one of the best-informed French experts on Czechoslovakia, revealed in the October 1–15 issue of *Les Cahiers des Droits de l'Homme* (p. 587) that M. de Lacroix made the following declaration to President Beneš:

> " If the Czechoslovak Government does not accept unconditionally the Anglo-French plan, it will be held solely responsible for any war which may ensue, and France will take no part in it [*ne s'y associera pas*]."

In this one sentence, both the content and the meaning of M. de Lacroix's communication have been rendered exactly. The words: " *La France ne s'y associera pas* " are authentic— the very words originally used. We need not be afraid that M. de Lacroix himself would deny them. The *written* French note which was presented later—on the afternoon of September 21, only after the insistence of the Czechoslovak Government, states (as Professor Seton-Watson published for the first time in his book, *Munich and the Dictators*, p. 68):

> " *En repoussant la proposition franco-britannique, le government tchécoslovaque prend la responsabilité de determiner le recours à la force de l'Allemagne. Il rompt par la même la solidarité franco-britannique qui vient d'être établie et il enlève ainsi toute efficacité pratique à une assistance de la France.*"

(" In rejecting the Franco-British proposals, the Czechoslovak Government is taking upon itself the responsibility of making Germany decide to use force. At the same time, it is severing the Franco-British solidarity which has just been established and thus it deprives French assistance of any practical efficacy.")

The meaning of these words was perfectly clear and, according to the communications and explanations of M. de Lacroix, it was impossible to have the slightest doubt that the French Government was denouncing clearly and precisely its obligations to come to the help of Czechoslovakia.

It is hardly necessary to add the words of Viscount Cecil of Chelwood, spoken in the House of Lords debate in the first week of October:

" According to my information, the following is what was said to the Czech Government:

" Britain and France have the duty to prevent a European war, if humanly possible, and thus an invasion of Czechoslovakia. They wish the Czechoslovak Government to realise that if it does not unconditionally and at once accept the Anglo-French plan, it will stand before the world as solely responsible for the ensuing war.

" By refusing, Czechoslovakia will also be guilty of destroying Anglo-French solidarity, since, in that event, Britain will under no circumstances march, even if France went to the aid of Czechoslovakia. If the refusal should provoke a war, France gives official notice that she will not fulfil her treaty obligation."

Viscount Cecil added:

" I am quite aware that those terms I have read will not be found in the White Paper, and they were not referred to either by the Secretary of State or by the Prime Minister. They said merely that they had advised the Czech Government to agree."

It is true that the sentences which Viscount Cecil quoted in the House of Lords will not be found in any volume of official records, nor even do they appear, strictly speaking, in the written text of the British and French Notes. Yet Viscount Cecil was repeating faithfully and correctly both the contents and the meaning of what the British and French Ministers actually said to President Beneš during their joint *démarche*. There is in existence a verbatim report of this conversation, which lasted for over an hour, taken down by President Beneš in the presence of both Ministers. The correctness of the statements made above would certainly be admitted by the British and French Ministers, who, as we believe, would not suppress or pervert the truth. If, nevertheless, the testimony of the three men present at the interview in question is considered unimportant as evidence, the meaning of the British and French Note is perfectly clear and unambiguous, despite the deliberate carefulness of the expressions and forms which were used. Both Notes insisted upon the immediate acceptance of the Anglo-French proposals and declared that neither Britain nor France would come to the assistance of Czechoslovakia, if, having rejected those proposals, she were attacked by Germany. Both of them presented the Czechoslovak Government with two alternatives: either they must accept immediately the London proposals for the cession of the Sudeten-German territories to Germany or, in the event of war with Germany, they would find themselves isolated and unable to count on any help either from Britain or from France.

The unbelievable and incomprehensible had become a terrible fact. France was revoking and breaking her oath of alliance. France was not only deserting us, but was also herself actively insisting that we should consent to the cession of vast territories to Germany and thus lay ourselves open to the mercy of an enemy. It was indeed a terrible blow which France had dealt us, for by it our whole system of sure alliances, based essentially on France, came crumbling to the ground. By that one blow alone, we were instantly isolated, for if France deserted us it was evident that we could expect no help from Britain. It is true that our treaties of alliance with Rumania and Yugoslavia were in no way linked up with France, but, apart from the fact that they related only to Hungarian aggression against any state-member of the Little Entente, it was obvious that Rumania and Yugoslavia would remain strictly neutral if France and Britain were to leave us to our fate. As for Soviet Russia, she was bound to come to our aid only after France has already done so. As a result of France's defection, her help became uncertain and even unlikely. Soviet Russia was willing to come to our aid and, as will be shown in another connection, had given us proof of unlimited loyalty throughout the whole period of international crisis since the annexation of Austria. It would have been futile, of course, to appeal to the League of Nations, since it is Britain and France who decide what attitude shall be adopted at Geneva. Britain and France already informed us what this would be, and it was unlikely to be changed as a result of discussions at Geneva. It was therefore impossible to hope for early and effective help from Soviet Russia, even indirectly through the League of Nations. (The Czechoslovak-Soviet Treaty could become operative only after a certain procedure, stipulated in the Treaty itself, had been carried out by the League of Nations.) It would have been more than dangerous to ask Russia to help us independently of France and the League of Nations, for Britain and France, who were supporting German claims in the dispute, and who were therefore opposing us, would have considered such Russian intervention on our behalf as a dangerous expansion of " Bolshevism " in Europe. In the " ideological war " which might have ensued—for that is how it would immediately have been described in the German propaganda—the Great Powers of the West would undoubtedly have sympathised with the Berlin-Rome Axis, as the defenders of " order and European civilisation " against " Bolshevik disruption and decay." To ask for help from Soviet Russia alone would have been dangerous for internal Czechoslovak reasons also, for, although all our political parties were united in favour of seeking help from France and Russia combined, the parties of the Right would certainly have protested against accepting help from Russia alone. The resultant internal dissension would have dangerously weakened our national resistance. National unity, combined with iron discipline, was imperative and could not be endangered.

The Anglo-French *démarche* of that unhappy night meant, therefore, that we became internationally isolated. It meant also that Poland and Hungary would join Germany in attacking us. Poland's foreign policy was designed to suit all eventualities. With a completely cynical opportunism of which her representatives made no secret, the Poles had frankly declared: if Czechoslovakia is isolated, we shall march against her; if she is helped by France, we shall remain neutral and wait; but if Britain joins France we shall immediately march against Germany. Hungary,

on the other hand, was afraid of German expansion, but in the
event of an attack upon an isolated Czechoslovakia for the
" liberation " of the German and Polish minorities, Hungary
was forced to take part, in order to " liberate " the Hungarian minority. I draw attention particularly to this fact; the
Anglo-French ultimatum of the night of September 21 exposed
Czechoslovakia to attack, not only from Germany, but also from
Poland and Hungary—that was the worst feature of this intervention, and was also the main cause of our capitulation. Some
of our military authorities were of opinion that even if the worst
came to the worst, i.e. if we were completely isolated, we might
face a war with Germany, hoping to hold out successfully for
long enough to arouse the conscience of Europe and to gain its
support. A simultaneous attack by Germany, Poland and
Hungary on an isolated Czechoslovakia would have meant our
disastrous defeat within a few weeks.

All these considerations led President Beneš and the Cabinet,
after a meeting which began on the night of September 20 and
lasted into the following forenoon, to yield to the Anglo-French
ultimatum and to accept the London proposals. A Note to that
effect was handed in on the afternoon of September 21:

" The Czechoslovak Government, forced by circumstances,
yielding to unheard of pressure and drawing the consequences from the communication of the French and British
Governments of September 21, 1938, in which both Governments expressed their point of view as to help for Czechoslovakia in case she should refuse to accept the Franco-
British proposals and should be attacked by Germany, accepts
the Anglo-French proposals with feelings of pain, assuming
that both Governments will do everything in order to safeguard the vital interests of the Czechoslovak state in their
application. It notes with regret that these proposals were
elaborated without previous consultation with the Czechoslovak Government.

" Deeply regretting that their proposal of arbitration has
not been accepted, the Czechoslovak Government accept these
proposals as a whole, from which the principle of a guarantee,
as formulated in the note, cannot be detached, and accept

them with the further assumption that both Governments will not permit a German invasion of Czechoslovak territory, which will remain Czechoslovak up to the moment when it will be possible to carry its transfer after the determination of the new frontier by the International Commission referred to in the proposals.

" In the opinion of the Czechoslovak Government, the Franco-British proposals imply that all details of the practical realisation of the Franco-British proposals will be determined in agreement with the Czechoslovak Government.

" PRAGUE.

" *September* 21, 1938." [1]

2. *The Mysterious Telegram.*

Just as the chief responsibility for the presentation of the London Proposals rests with France, so also was she responsible for the exertion of unprecedented pressure on the Czechoslovak Government to make it accept them. In both cases it was evident that France was breaking her solemn obligations and had adopted the conception of " the scrap of paper." Previously this policy, since the phrase was coined by Bethman-Hollweg, had been attributed to Germany alone. One can understand, therefore, that the French statesmen directly responsible for these decisions should have endeavoured to shirk the blame. Thus it came about that an attempt was made to shift the blame on to Prague ! I should perhaps, therefore, say a few words here about the strange story of how this was done.

Let me begin with a brief contradiction of the story that President Beneš agreed that the salients of our frontiers should be ceded to Germany. It has been said that M. Daladier took to London on September 18 Dr. Beneš's consent to this cession. From this it has been deduced that President Beneš himself approved in principle the transfer of our territory to Germany. If the story were true, there is, nevertheless, a considerable difference between ceding our frontier salients and ceding those of our territories in which nearly half the population was Czech; for in the first case the natural and artificial defences of Czechoslovakia would have been preserved, while in the

[1] Czechoslovak State Document.

second the State was deprived of all possibility of successful resistance, and therefore of its independence. It is completely wrong, however, to suppose that President Beneš would have agreed to, or even have suggested, such an idea, and the story probably originated from a conversation which took place between President Beneš and M. de Lacroix before the London Conference of September 18. This conversation arose out of the receipt by M. de Lacroix of information that France would honour her treaty obligations towards Czechoslovakia, in spite of the difficulties she would experience in rendering effective military aid to that country. At that time the two men discussed the consequences of the fact that Mr. Chamberlain, by visiting Hitler in connection with the Sudeten-German dispute, had formally shifted that dispute from the sphere of Czechoslovak domestic politics into the international arena, thus changing it into a dispute between Germany and Czechoslovakia. President Beneš reminded M. de Lacroix that the questions under dispute had been discussed and decided at the Peace Conference, and he recalled in particular the fact which is generally known that he himself had at that time been in favour of the transfer to Germany of certain Sudeten-German districts on the frontier—in exchange, of course, for corresponding districts in Germany. President Beneš emphasised his opinion, however, that such transfers of territory were unthinkable in the present circumstances and could not even be considered. He was careful to point out to his visitor that what he said was not intended as a message to the French Government. It is indeed strange how it was possible to construe such remarks, made in the course of an informal conversation, as meaning that President Beneš agreed with the cession to Germany of the frontier salients, especially when he had expressly said the contrary. It is hardly possible, therefore, to believe that at the London Conference M. Daladier quoted President Beneš in the sense described. This explanation should suffice, I think, to refute a story which was designed for the purpose of saddling Prague with a share of the blame for what happened on September 18.

There is another story that calls for contradiction which is of a more serious nature. After Godesberg, when French public opinion was beginning to oppose the outrageous German demands,

it was put about in political circles in Paris that President
Beneš himself had " asked " the French Government to deliver
the ultimatum of the night of September 20–21. It was alleged
that President Beneš wanted to be able to explain to his public
that he was forced, by pressure from Britain and France, to
accept the London Proposals. I first heard this story on September 27 in the course of a conversation with one of the French
Ministers, in which I frankly said how amazed we had been that
the French Government could have consented to the London
Proposals and even have tried to force us to accept them. The
Minister with whom I was speaking pointed out, in the first
place, that at the meeting of the French Cabinet which was held
on September 19 it had been specifically agreed that no pressure
of any sort should be exerted upon us and that the Treaty of
Guarantee should remain valid, even if we rejected the proposals.
He went on to say that there had been no meeting of the French
Cabinet on September 20 at which it could have been decided to
exert pressure on us. He thus clearly hinted that the instructions
for the *démarche* made on the night of September 21 had been
issued by the Quai d'Orsay on its own, without informing all
members of the French Cabinet, although those instructions
were directly contrary to the decision arrived at by the whole
Cabinet on the previous day. "But, after all," he added, " if
you were surprised, we were no less so, for why did President
Beneš ask for that ultimatum ? " I was completely at a loss to
understand this last remark, so he explained to me that it had
been stated that President Beneš, through the French Minister
in Prague, had asked the French Government to send him an
ultimatum, as otherwise he could not justify in the eyes of the
Czechoslovak public his acceptance of the London proposals.
With considerable heat I replied: " That's a disgusting lie ! "
after which I described to my friend in detail the dramatic
course of events on September 20 and 21. I told him how
President Beneš had been more shattered than anyone else
at that incredible French communication—that we could
not count on help from France. I pointed out especially that
our President had to the last been unable to believe France
capable of such treachery. I heard the same story again on
the following day, this time from another important French

politician, who told me not only that President Beneš was reputed to have asked for the ultimatum, but also that the Quai d'Orsay had in its possession a telegram from M. de Lacroix to that effect. I remarked that the best thing would be to publish the telegram of which he spoke, so that we could defend ourselves against this shameless rumour. I have since heard that some French politicians have in fact asked for the publication of this telegram, because, if the story about it is a true one, the blame attributable to France would naturally be less. It appears that M. Daladier has refused their request, on the ground that it would be " embarrassing for Dr. Beneš."

Dr. Osuský, the Czechoslovak Minister in Paris, was, of course, informed of all this in detail and transmitted the information to Dr. Beneš, who immediately authorised him to issue a categorical denial of the truth of the story. Later on, however, in the middle of October, M. Emile Roche, director of the newspaper *La République*, repeated the story in public. His statement was answered by an official *démenti* from the Czechoslovak Legation in Paris, but he refused, nevertheless, to withdraw it. This led to the publication in *L'Europe Nouvelle* (p. 1,167) of October 29 by Professor Hubert Beuve-Méry[1] of a letter which he had received from " one of the Czechoslovak figures most closely involved in the drama." Although the name of his correspondent was not divulged, it is obvious that the letter came from Dr. Hodža, formerly Prime Minister of Czechoslovakia. This letter described the meeting on the afternoon of September 20, between the British and French Ministers in Prague and the Czechoslovak Foreign Minister, Dr. Krofta. Dr. Krofta had been charged with the handing of the Czechoslovak Government's reply rejecting the London Proposals. The letter describes how, on receiving this reply, the two representatives of the Western Powers informed the Czechoslovak Foreign Minister, Dr. Krofta, that in that case Britain and France would declare themselves disinterested in Czechoslovakia, and how Dr. Krofta immediately reported this to the Czechoslovak Cabinet, which was in session at the President's Palace from 5–8 p.m.

---

[1] Professor Hubert Beuve-Méry had been Prague correspondent of *Le Temps* until the end of September and had then, as a mark of his disapproval of its policy, relinquished his appointment.

" After this session," continued the letter, " the Prime Minister, Dr. Hodža, had a conversation with M. de Lacroix. Referring to the fact that the latter [M. de Lacroix] had made no protest against the declaration made by Mr. Newton to Dr. Krofta that afternoon regarding the possibility of his indifference to the fate of Czechoslovakia, Dr. Hodža asked, in most definite terms, whether Czechoslovakia could, or could not, count on French help. M. de Lacroix, deeply moved, was unable to give an immediate answer. He stated subsequently that, although he had no official instructions on the subject, he knew, nevertheless, that the answer was in the negative. Dr. Hodža asked M. de Lacroix to convey his information to the Czechoslovak Government as frankly as possible, as it concerned a matter which was of vital importance to the State. M. de Lacroix replied that he would need official instructions from his Government before doing that, so Dr. Hodža asked him to obtain such instructions in the most definite terms, so that he might be in a position to inform Prague precisely what attitude would be adopted by the French Government with regard to its treaty obligations, in the event of German aggression against Czechoslovakia consequent on the rejection by the Czechoslovak Government of the Anglo-French proposals. It was obviously essential that the Czechoslovak Government and Army should know for certain what that attitude would be. In the course of that night, M. de Lacroix delivered a verbal communication to the effect that France could not grant military aid to Czechoslovakia: this communication was later, at the request of the Czechoslovak Government, delivered again in writing."

Professor Beuve-Méry appended to this letter a few personal observations, from among which the following is especially worth quoting: " The Czechoslovak Government proclaimed a general mobilisation on the evening of September 23. Two hours before that, Mr. Newton and M. de Lacroix had informed Dr. Krofta that their respective Governments could no longer accept responsibility for the advice which they had given to Prague before, namely, that Czechoslovakia should not embarrass Mr. Chamberlain's negotiations by taking military precautions. This was, in the customary guarded terms used in diplomacy, tantamount to an approval in advance of the mobilisation.

Now, the Czechoslovak Government, and still more the Czechoslovak General Staff, had only with the deepest regret resigned themselves to waiting such a long time for this approval; on several occasions, and particularly on September 18, Prague had insisted on the offensive character of the German preparations, but had always been advised to take no military countermeasures. If the Government and General Staff alike were anxious to take action on September 18, and actually did take action as soon as they had the chance to do so on September 23, how could they have become advocates of surrender, unless it was under the influence of an Anglo-French threat ? "

The foregoing quotations provide clear evidence that President Beneš can have had nothing to do with the matter of the Anglo-French ultimatum, yet at the end of September, as has already been stated, his name was mentioned in this connection in Paris. It is evident also, from Dr. Hodža's account of his conversation with M. de Lacroix, that he (Dr. Hodža) did not ask that the Czechoslovak Government should be presented with an ultimatum as a means whereby it might justify, in the eyes of the Czechoslovak public, its acceptance of the London Proposals. It is quite understandable that Dr. Hodža should have insisted upon the French Government formally informing us in the most definite terms whether it would, or would not, fulfil its treaty obligations in the event of German aggression against us, consequent on our rejection of the Anglo-French proposals. It is important to note that, in spite of all the growing doubts about France's attitude, we did not until the very last moment believe that she could really desert us. We interpreted the pressure which she joined in exerting upon us on September 19 and 20 as being merely a grave warning, which we duly noted. We did not even then imagine that she would go so far as to repudiate the oath of alliance which she had given us. Such action was entirely out of keeping with all the past history of France ! *Moreover, even as late as the middle of September, the French Government had assured us of its faithfulness as an ally.* How could we then believe, not a week later, that she had decided to break faith with us ?

It is most unfortunate that M. de Lacroix's telegram, on which is based the story that Prague asked Paris for an ultimatum, has not yet been published. So far as is known, it contained a statement that our Prime Minister, with the approval of our President, of our Government and of our General Staff, asked that pressure should be exerted upon Prague from Paris, because only in that way could they justify before the Czechoslovak public their acceptance of the Anglo-French proposals, which, under the existing circumstances, they themselves, as well as the British and French Governments, considered an essential condition for the prevention of armed conflict. The very fact that our General Staff was dragged into the story is sufficient indication of its absurdity. President Beneš has denied the truth of it with a deep resentment, which he makes no attempt to conceal, at what he rightly considers a personally insulting and scandalous piece of gossip. Dr. Hodža's explanation was given in his letter published by Professor Beuve-Méry.

I must explain also that the story contains another fundamental misconception, either conscious or unconscious. It was not during the incident which we are now discussing, i.e. not while the Czechoslovak Government was supposed to have been asking Paris to exert pressure upon it, but during M. de Lacroix's night *démarche*, when he informed us verbally that France would not help us in the event of German aggression, that President Beneš requested that this declaration of historical importance should be given to him in writing, so that he might have it exactly in black and white. The story is thus contradicted by President Beneš, who spoke neither to Mr. Newton nor to M. de Lacroix, after they had been handed the rejection of their terms on the morning of September 20. M. de Lacroix has a reputation for honesty, so that it is out of the question that he should have been capable of telling a deliberate lie. It is just possible that M. de Lacroix did not understand correctly the real meaning of what Dr. Hodža said to him, and that he interpreted their conversation together in a manner which Dr. Hodža did not intend; but even so, if we exclude this possibility, we are still faced with a mystery.

At all events, it was strange that M. de Lacroix did not verify directly with President Beneš his conversation with M. Hodža. It should be noted that all diplomatic Ministers in Prague went directly to President Beneš in matters of urgent or primary importance. Thus it was, in the case of the ultimatum which demanded the acceptance of the Anglo-French proposals, the British and French Ministers did not apply either to M. Hodža nor to M. Krofta, but to President Beneš himself.

I gather from reliable sources of information in Paris that the Quai d'Orsay version of what took place is roughly as follows: On the evening of September 20 M. de Lacroix telephoned from Prague to the French Foreign Minister, M. Bonnet, and informed him that he had some important information for him. As soon as he intimated what it was about, M. Bonnet, fearing lest their telephone conversation might be intercepted, asked him not to go on speaking, but to telegraph his information in cypher immediately. M. de Lacroix's telegram, which reached Paris late that night, contained the request (already mentioned above) from Prague that pressure should be exerted, in order to justify the acceptance of the Anglo-French proposals. M. Bonnet considered this information of such great importance that he wanted the Prime Minister to call a meeting of the whole Cabinet. But this would have been impossible, for the practical reason that at that late hour (about midnight) it was impossible to get in touch with and summon all the Ministers. Immediate action was called for, however, so M. Bonnet, together with the President of the Republic, M. Lebrun, and M. Daladier, decided to send M. de Lacroix instructions to make the necessary *démarche* before President Beneš immediately on that same night.

This account certainly fails to explain all that took place. We must assume, for example, that either M. Bonnet or M. Daladier consulted London about the matter, since it will be recalled that the night *démarche* to President Beneš was made by the French and British Ministers together. It makes it easier for us, nevertheless, despite its incompleteness, to estimate correctly the part played by M. Bonnet.

When Bonnet received at 8 p.m. on September 20 the complete text of the Czechoslovak Note refusing the Anglo-French proposals, he immediately gave instructions to the Quai d'Orsay to prepare an ultimatum which would force Prague to accept these proposals by threatening that France would not fulfil her obligation to give assistance to Czechoslovakia. These instructions were given by Bonnet *before* he had received de Lacroix's telegram which reached him only about 10 p.m. M. Bonnet seized this telegram as a pretext for immediate action, hoping that if the Czechoslovak Government could no longer count on help from either Britain or France, it would give in to and accept the Anglo-French proposals. There was a risk, however, that not all the members of the French Cabinet would agree with this refusal of help. Only the previous day, September 19, some of them had insisted that France's treaty obligations should remain valid even if the Czechoslovak Government were to reject the Anglo-French proposals. It was necessary, therefore, to act quickly, and the late hour at which M. de Lacroix's report was received made it easier to explain away a change of policy and provided an excuse for not having summoned a meeting of the whole Cabinet. Thus it came about that France's decision to dishonour her treaty obligations towards Czechoslovakia was taken by only three people. They were admittedly competent and important people, but it may nevertheless be asked whether such a far-reaching decision, and one of which the consequences, not only for Czechoslovakia but also for the whole French system of alliances, were so disastrous, should not have been considered by the whole French Cabinet.

3. *The Czechs lose Confidence in France.*

The mysterious story of M. de Lacroix's telegram will certainly be properly cleared up sooner or later. But it may already be safely stated that the powers-that-be in Paris had decided to break the Franco-Czechoslovak alliance in the event of German aggression, quite irrespective of any reports which might have been received during the night of M. de Lacroix's conversation with Dr. Hodža. On the afternoon of September 20, when Dr. Krofta delivered to the British and French Ministers his Government's answer rejecting the Anglo-French proposals, M. de Lacroix had already joined Mr. Newton in threatening that in that case they would declare themselves disinterested in Czechoslovakia, and on the same evening, during his conversation with Dr. Hodža, he had said with emotion that he knew that the French Government's answer to the

Czechoslovak enquiry would be a negative one. He could not have spoken in such a way with the Czechoslovak Foreign Minister and Prime Minister if he had been in any doubt regarding the intentions of the Minister who decided his country's foreign policy. From what we already know of those intentions, though our knowledge is but fragmentary, we can fairly assume that France would, in collaboration with Britain, and without any compunction, have exerted pressure upon Czechoslovakia and would have categorically renounced her treaty obligations in any case, even if there had been no request made by the Czechoslovak Prime Minister—such a request, I repeat, Dr. Hodža absolutely denies ever having made—that pressure should be exerted.

I must here draw attention also to another serious matter. In his speech of September 28, Mr. Chamberlain said that during the discussions in London on September 18 the British and French statesmen had tried to find a solution which would not automatically force France to fulfil her treaty obligations. In other words, Britain and France tried to act in such a way that France would not be obliged to help Czechoslovakia in accordance with her treaty of guarantee, but that at the same time it would be impossible to accuse France of having broken her word. The fact, however, that the French statesmen gave their consent in London to proposals which destroyed the integrity of Czechoslovakia, which the Franco-Czechoslovak Treaty had specifically guaranteed, is sufficient to discredit this interpretation, while the *démarche* made by France to President Beneš on the night of September 20–21 was an express denunciation of her promise to her ally. This promise had been made by France to Czechoslovakia in a perfectly formal manner and was publicly reaffirmed to the Czechoslovak Government by French statesmen on numerous occasions right up to the end of the diplomatic negotiations.

It may perhaps be useful if I refresh my readers' memory by recalling some, at least, of these occasions. The Blum-Paul Boncour Government, in its Note of March 14, 1938, to the British Government, categorically declared its fidelity to its alliance with Czechoslovakia. This Note had considerable influence on the attitude which the British Government adopted at that time—it was immediately after the annexation of Austria, when the threat to Czechoslovakia first came to the fore —with regard to Czechoslovakia. Evidence of this was given in Mr. Chamberlain's famous speech of March 24.

Shortly after that, the Daladier-Bonnet Government was formed, and M. Bonnet, on assuming office as Foreign Minister, assured the Czechoslovak Minister in Paris that " no French Government could permit any loosening of the bonds which unite Prague and Paris, since that would encourage adventures directed against the existing balance of power in Europe—a balance which precludes any kind of hegemony."

On April 8, 1938, M. Bonnet authorised the French diplomatic representatives in Moscow, Warsaw, Bucarest and Prague to inform the Governments to which they were accredited that " France would fulfil her obligations towards Czechoslovakia." Only a few days later, on April 12, the French Prime Minister, M. Daladier, in the Government statement of policy, declared that he was " determined to tighten up his country's friendships and to demonstrate his fidelity to all the pacts and treaties which France had concluded."

Later, again, M. Daladier, in a speech delivered on July 12 at the dinner of the Société Provençale, recognised " the absolute loyalty of the Czechoslovak Government," proclaimed that " our solemn engagements towards Czechoslovakia are eternal and sacred to us," and stressed " the desire never to have to fulfil these obligations and the determination never to break our word if, by misfortune, this desire is not fulfilled."

As late even as September 4, M. Bonnet, on the occasion of the unveiling of the Memorial at La Pointe de Graves, said: " France will remain faithful in all circumstances to the pacts and treaties which she has concluded. She will remain faithful to the engagements which she has undertaken." And later still, when M. Daladier had already arranged with Mr. Chamberlain his visit to Herr Hitler, and when, therefore, it was clear that serious concessions were about to be demanded, Czechoslovakia received a new and quite formal reassurance from her French ally, given in answer to a direct and urgent request from President Beneš. M. de Lacroix handed President Beneš a reply, in which France declared her determination to stand by her oath of alliance. It is

true that this reply drew attention to the French Government's
Note of June 17, in which it was explained to the Czechoslovak
Government why France's assistance might not prove sufficiently
effective, but this reminder could at worst be considered only as
a warning, and certainly not as a refusal of assistance; on the
contrary, in spite of this warning, the French Government expressly recognised its obligations as an ally under the Treaty.
Is there cause for surprise, then, that, in spite of our doubts, we
should still have believed in the intention of France as an ally,
should occasion to fulfil her obligations arise in definitive and
drastic form ?

The following personal experience may perhaps be of some
interest in this connection. In the latter part of June, 1938, I was
given the opportunity of having a conversation with Mr. Winston
Churchill. Among the questions which we discussed was that of
Franco-Czechoslovak relations. I explained to him our reasons
for believing in the firmness of our alliance with France, and the
argument which seemed to impress him especially strongly was
that France, throughout her history, had never yet been un-
faithful to any formal treaty of alliance. I mention this, in order
to show that it was not only we, the francophil Czechoslovaks, but
also such realistic British politicians as Mr. Winston Churchill,
who were unable to imagine that France would disown her treaty
obligation. After that, I left London and went to Paris, where I
was naturally interested to assess the influence of M. Flandin's
campaign for the abandonment of the allies of France in Central
Europe, in return for a Franco-German *entente*. I received assurances from the Left and from the Right that M. Flandin's
influence was being exaggerated abroad and that in France his
attitude was quite exceptional. I heard, from many politicians
in varying versions, the judgment expressed by one of the more
important and influential Senators as follows: " Don't waste
your time on M. Flandin; he is not worth it. Everyone knows
what to think about him. You must not imagine that the
rumours which you hear in the *salons* of Paris are typical of the
attitude of politicians who are conscious of their responsibility
for the interests of France. The interests of France, after all, run
parallel with those of your country."

Professor Joseph Barthélémy had written a juridical analysis,

published in *Le Temps* in the spring, in which he tried to prove
that the Franco-Czechoslovak Treaty no longer entailed legal
obligations for France. Knowing that this article had been
written with the approval of, and in collusion with, certain very
highly placed political people, I made no attempt to conceal from
some of my French friends my doubt whether we could still
really safely rely upon the solidity of our French alliance. On one
occasion, when I expressed this doubt to a French Minister, he
was rather irritated and replied: " To entertain even a shadow of
such a suspicion is an insult to every Frenchman." Another
politician assured me that any French Government which hesitated, even for a moment, to go to the aid of Czechoslovakia,
would fall immediately. That same politician voted, on October 4,
in favour of the Munich Agreement. This was, mark you, in
June, 1938 ! All this reassured me, though it did not entirely
banish my doubts, but I would not be speaking the truth were I
to attempt now, after the lesson of September, to pretend that I
was not amazed when France deserted us. *Venkov*, the official organ
of our Agrarian Party, wrote on September 22: " It should be
clearly stated that nobody in Czechoslovakia ever doubted but
that France would come to our aid in a time of crisis." M. Osuský
was not the only one whose voice broke with emotion and whose
eyes were filled with tears on September 19, when, on leaving
M. Bonnet's office after being handed the London proposals, he
said to the assembled journalists: " You have come to see the
exit of a man who has been condemned without a hearing."

How, indeed, could we feel otherwise than crushed ? We had
been condemned by the ally in whom we had placed the utmost
confidence, and to whom we had remained faithful in her hour of
adversity, when other nations were forsaking her to win the
favour of the rising Third Reich. We had refused to follow the
example set by Colonel Beck and Dr. Stojadinovitch, whose
policies had fostered to a remarkable degree the expansionist
aims of Nazi Germany and had, at the same time, weakened the
position of France relative to Italy, as well as to Germany.

Whenever Germany had attempted a *rapprochement* with our
country, we had not only loyally informed our French ally, but
had also made it a rigid condition that such a *rapprochement* must
not be achieved at the cost of any weakening of our alliance with

France. We had always taken into account not only our own interests, but also the maintenance of France's position as a Great Power in Europe. If latterly we were being reproached —even by some Frenchmen—for not having been able to establish more friendly and tolerable relations with Germany, it would not be difficult for us to produce documentary evidence to show that it was very often primarily the unsettled and sometimes tense relations existing between France and Germany which had prevented us from doing so. If we had acted as Colonel Beck did in January, 1934, when, without the knowledge of his French ally, he concluded his famous alliance with Germany, we also could have won the " friendship " of the Third Reich. The price we would have had to pay would, of course, have made us eventually the vassal of Germany. So far as Poland is concerned, it remains to be seen what will be the fruits of Colonel Beck's " realism."

In December, 1936, confidential negotiations between President Beneš and certain persons in Herr Hitler's confidence had made such progress that it was considered certain that an agreement would be concluded in January, 1937. This agreement did not materialise for several reasons. The decisive reason was, perhaps, the hope held in Berlin that Stalin's oponents, of whom the most important was Marshal Tuchachevsky, would succeed in overthrowing his régime and in constituting a new government which would come to terms with Germany. The German Government considered it advisable to wait for this radical change in the balance of power in Eastern Europe. Our French friends were, of course, kept informed about these confidential negotiations. But they did not conceal their apprehension, and were anxious that various conditions should be made. I can myself recall how M. de Lacroix did not conceal his annoyance at that time, and President Beneš and Dr. Krofta could certainly make several interesting revelations concerning the French Minister's attitude. That there may be no misunderstanding, I should explain that we perfectly understood the anxiety of our French friends. We regarded it as the natural corollary of our treaty of alliance and our bonds of friendship. But in these circumstances we consider it unfitting for the French to reproach us because we did not succeed in coming to an agreement with Germany. Do we deserve reproach for not having achieved what the Great Powers of Western Europe, with infinitely greater possibilities at their disposal than were enjoyed by a small country, have still—even after Munich—failed to achieve ?

We can at any rate say with a perfectly clear conscience that nowhere in Europe (nowhere, in fact, in the world) did France have a more faithful, a more devoted or a more reliable friend than in Czechoslovakia. It was our consciousness of that fact which made our disappointment the more terrible at the attitude which she adopted on the night of September 20–21, 1938.

4. *Prague Surrenders.*

When Czechoslovak citizens picked up their newspapers on the morning of September 21, they did not yet learn what had taken place on the previous night. The articles and news items had all been written early on the previous evening under the influence of the Czechoslovak Government's answer which had been handed to the diplomatic representatives of Britain and France, rejecting their proposals. It was still unknown how the West would react to it. The Czechoslovak Press was trying, therefore, to remind their Western friends that the fate, not merely of Czechoslovakia, but of the whole of Europe, was at stake.

The editorial comment of Mr. Jan Scheinost, Editor-in-chief of *Lidové Listy*, the official organ of the Czech Catholic Party, was especially interesting:

"If France does not realise that what is at stake now, are her position as a Great Power, the value of her word, and her prestige among her allies and among the nations of the world, who have always regarded her as the hub, the foundation and the main pillar of international law and order, then she is on the downward slope.

" We need hardly mention what a blow her policy has dealt to world democracy, which will everywhere have to beat a retreat. If the democracies do not know how to defend themselves and how to triumph over the forces which are so brutally, and even cynically, threatening and ruining them, then they are consciously choosing death in preference to a fight for their survival. . . . England, as we have often said, fears the victory of Russia and the Bolshevisation of Germany which it would entail; but the English, just like the French, should ask themselves whether their present policy will not actually lead to the Bolshevisation of Britain and France. There is no doubt that the mass of the working classes in England and in France do not agree with the policy of their Governments, even if their leaders, for opportunist reasons, approve it. This dissatisfaction, heightened by the strong feeling that both countries will pay for it in loss of weight and prestige, with all its resultant consequences, must in the end find expression, either in the Fascisation or in the Bolshevisation of the English and French working classes—that is to say, in the disappearance of the régime responsible for the policy of to-day. This danger seems not to have been fully appreciated either in France or in England—the proverb says that even under big chandeliers there are shadows.

" The Great Powers of the West have therefore placed the future of their respective countries, and even that of democracy throughout the world, in a most vulnerable position. Do they realise at all that they themselves—the strongest pillars, excepting America, of world democracy—have opened the way to its capitulation ? Is it clear to them that by their policy they will certainly persuade Germany that ' the decay of the West,' of which Spengler wrote, has actually begun ? Will they recognise in time that their passivity renders them at worst an easy prey, and at best undesirable (because useless) allies for the dynamic countries ? Cannot even the more clever among them see that the bad example which they are setting to the whole world may ruin the good manners even of the better nations ? Do they understand—and this is the most important point—that their policy will create in Europe an entirely different situation which will soon reveal itself in their own weakening ? That they themselves will suffer for it ? "

The well-known military specialist, Colonel E. Moravec, of the General Staff, wrote in the *Lidové Noviny*:

" We imagine that treaties and friendship have the same meaning in other countries as they have in ours. Those who betrayed us, will be betrayed. . . . What to-day might still be achieved by vigorous diplomacy will to-morrow have become impossible to regain, even with the strongest army. . . . One thing must surely be clear to the West: if there should be a conflict between the Third Reich and the West, the West will be far weaker without Czechoslovakia on its side. Another thing must be clear. The crippling of Czechoslovakia cannot avert the clash between the Third Reich and the West, but will rather hurry it forward, because it will increase the power of the Third Reich. To-day it is not a matter of the Czechoslovak question, as in 1908 there was the question of Bosnia-Herzegovina, and in 1914 that of Serbia. The question at issue is who will dominate Europe."

The *Sozialdemokrat*—the organ of the Sudeten-German Social-Democrats, those heroes who, together with the German Communists and other democratic elements, have for years stood up, with unparalleled courage, to the Nazi terror of the Henlein Party—urged us to stand firm.

As though already anticipating (i.e. on the morning of September 21) the final result, the Agrarian paper *Večer* published a particularly gloomy article entitled " Betrayed," by Rudolf Halík, its Editor-in-chief. In this article, which created a great sensation, the author wrote:

" We have fought for our independence and we shall defend it. We have always had confidence in ourselves in the first place, but we also believed in our allies and friends. We believed also in our treaties and obligations. How many of us would love to-day to give our lives, if it were not true, as I am obliged to write, that we have been betrayed, and are deserted ? Strong words cannot express our pain and sorrow. How many of us have given way to our tears in some corner, and have not been ashamed ? . . . They are not tears of cowards or weaklings, but of people betrayed, robbed of their faith in the honesty of the world, robbed of their belief in anything that is right.

" We have been betrayed by those to whom for decades all our vital faith has been consecrated. Because we are a nation of Slav race we have been deserted by those who gave us their promise in which the great majority of our nation believed.

" Deserted by all, we stand alone in this world, forced to accept humiliation.

" We shall bear this humiliation. We became accustomed to it during our history. Only the dishonour of our nation we could not bear. Not one of us and nobody in the whole world can call the Czechoslovak nation a nation without honour—not even when the nation has decided through its representatives that it does not wish to be annihilated in a desperate, but a vain and lonely fight, but that it wants to live, in order to reconstruct its national altar; in order to believe that once again in this world right will be restored and honesty will return where it has been abandoned. We have been deprived of everything except our honour. If we have preserved and can preserve that, nothing is lost. Somewhere in the fog of future ages, vengeance is shaping itself. Vengeance will come, peoples of Czechoslovakia. Have faith and do not despair !

" Cling closer to each other; gather nearer to the Country ! A strong belief in future life ! Faith in ourselves and in our leaders ! Calm, iron calm and careful order ! Nerves like steel cables ! An honest nation will not perish, though it has been betrayed. God will allow neither us nor our descendants to perish ! "

I myself still believed there was hope and wrote in the *Lidové Noviny:*

" We are solid and united in our decision to defend, under all circumstances and regardless of the consequences, the heritage of our fathers. We wait for the attitude taken by our Government to be understood especially in France, but also in England. This hope is rightly strengthened when we observe that not only among the public, but even in the Governments of these countries, the dissatisfaction with the London proposals is growing every hour. We still believe that the far-sighted politicians of Britain and France will understand that the independence and integrity of Czechoslovakia are matters of vital interest to their respective countries."

I am quoting these articles and editorials so fully in order to show what our public opinion was like on the evening of September 20—after our rejection of the Anglo-French proposals. These quotations are, moreover, a proof of the accuracy with which our political authorities estimated the consequences of the Anglo-French policy of capitulation. For that reason also, they deserve to be remembered. But all these articles—except the one in the Agrarian paper *Večer*—were forestalled by the developments which took place that night. Hope perished at the very moment when it was being expressed.

That night and on the morning of September 21 which followed, the fate of Czechoslovakia was sealed. The British and French Ministers, Mr. Newton and M. de Lacroix, called on President Beneš just after 2 a.m. and remained with him until 3.30 a.m. It was decided to yield to the Franco-British pressure and to adopt the London proposals. The Prime Minister, Dr. Hodža, immediately summoned all the Ministers to the Kolovrat Palace, and there the Cabinet, after a session lasting from 6.30 a.m. to 9 a.m. ratified the decisions which had been reached by the political Cabinet in a meeting at the Castle of the President of the Republic. At 9 a.m. the Coalition Twenty (the parliamentary representatives of the Governmental parties) met at the Prime Minister's house, under the chairmanship of the President of the Chamber of Deputies, M. Malypetr, and the President of the Senate, M. Soukup. After a detailed report by the Prime Minister, this body also, after a session lasting till 1 p.m., took note of the decision made by the President of the Republic and the Government. The depression which prevailed at all these meetings defies description, and it was only with the greatest self-sacrifice and internal revulsion that the fatal decision was accepted. It was generally felt that it would be an inadmissible adventure to embark on a struggle with Germany in the state of absolute isolation, to which we had been reduced by the defection of our Western friends and allies. This opinion was shared also in competent military circles.

It is true that a certain group of politicians and soldiers did not agree with the capitulation and insisted that the honour and interest of the nation, especially with regard to its future, demanded that we should fight Germany if she attacked us, even if we had to fight alone. These people always sustained a small spark of hope that such a struggle would move the Western countries. We knew that public opinion was divided, and hoped therefore that in the end Britain and France would act in our favour; and, of course, we also counted on help from Russia. After what we have seen take place during the weeks which followed,[1] it is perhaps doubtful whether the hopes which were entertained by some of us at that time were justified. It is more probable that we would have shared a fate similar to that of Republican Spain, to whose help neither France nor England came, even though their vital interests were evidently at stake. In any case, whether they were right or wrong, the Czechoslovak politicians who were ready to risk war, even in isolation, were in an absolute minority. It was evident that the policy of resistance which they advised would entail mortal danger for the nation, because, after being deserted by France, we were not only isolated, but almost completely surrounded. For, side by side with Germany, as I shall presently describe, Poland and Hungary were preparing to act against us.

In the afternoon of September 21, when all the competent constitutional and political bodies had given their consent to the Cabinet decision of that night, a Note was presented to the French and British Ministers capitulating to their ultimatum.

5. *Popular Demonstrations in Prague and the Government of General Syrový.*

During the morning of September 21, however, the news leaked out that the Government had yielded and had accepted the London proposals, of which the public knew no more than that they meant capitulation to Germany. By noon this was generally known and had even spread to the provinces.

At first people refused to believe it; when the truth could no longer be denied, you could read horror in their faces. Men with iron nerves broke down in utter despair. People left their offices, their shops, their workshops, their apartments—all work came

---

[1] Especially in France, where even those who openly disagreed with the policy of capitulation (or, as it was euphemistically called, the policy of " appeasement ") remained quite passive, limiting themselves to more or less sharp criticism.

to a standstill; nobody had the heart to continue. Everyone, regardless of his or her social position or political beliefs, was heart-broken by the terrible shock to a degree which it is doubtful whether a foreigner could understand. The same questions were in every mouth: " What have we done to deserve this ? " and " How can it be that we have been deserted by an ally to whom we were so faithful ? "—and the fact that there were no satisfactory answers to these questions served to aggravate their grief.

I went, together with a few friends, to visit President Beneš. Though he was a man accustomed to stand fatigue without showing signs of it, he was quite unrecognisable. For several nights he had not slept, and the events of the previous night had been a most terrible blow for him. He had based his whole policy on the assumption of European co-operation, above all between the democracies of France and Britain. He had clung to that policy even when it was being discarded everywhere else in Central Europe, because he was convinced that in political, as in private affairs, faith must be kept—and now he had lived to see the day when he was abandoned by the representatives of the Western democracies. We saw before us a man who was physically worn out and morally crucified, and who could only with the greatest difficulty conceal from us his overwhelming despair. In a voice which could scarcely be heard, he said to us, " We have been disgracefully betrayed "—and yet, even at that time, he tried to encourage us not to lose our faith.

It was not until after seven o'clock that evening that the Government revealed the whole truth to the people in an official broadcast:

" The British and French Governments, during a common *démarche* made last night before the President of the Republic by their diplomatic representatives, intimated to the Czecho-slovak Government that this solution [i.e. negotiations in accordance with the Czech-German Treaty of Arbitration] would not prevent a conflict, and that Great Britain and France would be unable to afford any help to Czechoslovakia in the event of her being attacked by Germany, which would happen if Czechoslovakia did not immediately agree in

principle to the cession of the territories with German population to the Reich.

" Since the Soviet Union could afford us military help only
in company with France or, alternatively, if France would not
act, until Germany had been declared an aggressor by the
League of Nations, we found ourselves faced with the threat
of a war, which would endanger, not merely the present
boundaries of our State, but even the very existence of the
Czechs and Slovaks as one indivisible nation. The Government
is quite decided to maintain order with all the means at its
disposal and protect in every way the independence and
freedom of the nation under the new conditions which will
consequently obtain. The President of the Republic, therefore, together with the Government, could not do anything
but accept the plan of the two Great Powers as the basis of
further negotiations.

" We had no other choice, because we were left alone.

" The Government will guide and direct the State in the
new conditions, and believes that the National Assembly,
when it is assembled, and even after considering the inevitable
consequences of this painful decision, will confirm it. The
Government well understands and shares deeply the feelings
of the nation, its sorrow and its grief. It is, however, convinced
that, with the aid of all the moral and defensive forces of the
people, it will be able to strengthen the new Czechoslovak
State, which will represent even in the future the legacy of
our famous past as a nation. It will unite the whole nation
to defend the freedom and independence, within its new
framework, of our cherished Fatherland, which is just to all,
and will be strengthened in its resistance by the love of all
its citizens.

" We are all still completely ready and constantly prepared,
if necessary, to sacrifice our lives and property for our nation
and for our State.

" We have not allowed, and we shall not allow ourselves
and our successors to perish."

Immediately afterwards a statement by the Minister of
Propaganda, M. Hugo Vavrečka, was given out over the wireless.

This statement will be regarded in years to come as one of the most moving documents of the period, and deserves, therefore, to be quoted in full:

" Fellow-countrymen and fellow-countrywomen, our nation has, in the course of its history, been stricken by many calamities and sorrows. Terrible storms have often passed over our country, devastating the land and destroying thousands of our population. It has often seemed that our nation was wiped out and annihilated. Our history is written in our blood, and we read it with a tightening of the heart and with tears in our eyes, but in spite of that our people have stood up and recovered, and after the years of sorrow came years of prosperity when the peasant and the craftsman were able to return peacefully to their work, when science and the arts have flourished, and when our nation has produced new fruits of culture which have become the pride of future generations. Always, during periods of misfortune, memories of our glorious past have strengthened our nation. It has survived even the worst periods of slavery, when it seemed that never, never more would it be able to recover.

" In spite of everything the nation has always risen up again, thanks to its invincible vital force.

" You have heard the official news of the *démarche* of the Great Powers to our Government, and you have heard how in a manner without parallel in history, our allies and friends are dictating to us those sacrifices, which are imposed on a defeated nation. But we are not defeated, and if nevertheless our Government, headed by its President, has been obliged in the end unanimously to accept these cruel conditions, it has done so only because it wanted to save the people from vain sacrifices, from useless bloodshed, and from infinite suffering and sorrow. It is not lack of courage which has brought us to this decision, which is grieving us all inwardly. Even the bravest person may find himself in a situation where courage, honour and sentiment alike advise retreat before a huge boulder which rolls forward under the pressure of blind forces. God knows that at certain times one needs greater strength to live than to commit suicide; God knows that there is no honest person in the world who could say that we were afraid or cowardly this afternoon when we authorised our Minister of Foreign Affairs to tell Great Britain and France that we would sacrifice ourselves for the salvation of Europe. Ages ago, the Son of God sacrificed himself for the salvation of humanity—the Holy One who was crowned with thorns and nailed to the Cross.

" Dear brethren, sisters, fathers, mothers, children, we shall not to-day reproach those who left us alone and unsupported. History will pronounce its judgment on the events of these days. It is our duty to look ahead, and to build up and unite the nation which lives to-day and which will live to-morrow. We shall now be quite alone, we shall be strong, and it will depend on you, whether out of the darkness which enshrouds us for a time the rays of a new dawn will shine upon us.

" Let us have confidence in ourselves; let us believe in the genius of our nation. We shall not surrender, we shall hold the land of our fathers."

It was intended that such statements should calm the nation, prevent acts of desperation or popular resistance; but in the meantime spontaneous and huge-scale demonstrations started to take place all over Prague.

Already in the afternoon of September 21, groups of people had assembled in the streets and formed small processions; by evening the streets were crowded with tens of thousands of demonstrators. Insufficiently informed of what had really happened during the last few days and hours, the man in the street turned his justified anger against the Government and the President of the Republic, reproaching them for their capitulation. From the very beginning there were voices in the mob directed against the Government. Many were demanding a military dictatorship headed by General Syrový, the popular hero of the Czechoslovak Legions in Siberia during the World War. In the evening huge crowds marched up to the Castle, the seat of the President of the Republic, and there, after 10 p.m., General Syrový addressed them:

" I love our Republic just as much as you do. I am conscious of my responsibility. Have confidence in me. Military dictatorship would be of no help to us. You do not know the causes which forced the Government to make its decisions. We cannot lead the nation to suicide."

Here his speech was interrupted by cries of " Better death than surrender," " We want to fight," " We will not surrender our frontiers," " Mobilise ! " Only when General Syrový proclaimed that discipline and order must at all costs be maintained and that demonstrations of this sort were only helping Hitler did the crowds march off, singing the National Anthem. In the city the demonstrations continued, and it was in vain that the Mayor, Dr. Zenkl, appealed to the people to calm down and go home. But nevertheless, during all this period there was not a single riot calling for police intervention—the discipline of the crowds was unbroken. Demonstrations continued throughout the night, uninterruptedly, and it was necessary to give them a certain direction, otherwise there was danger that order could not be maintained. Demonstrations were reported also from the provincial towns.

On the morning of the following day, September 22, organised workers marched into the streets and to a certain extent led the demonstrations. They assembled partly in the Václavské Náměstí, partly before the Houses of Parliament, and by noon they numbered more than 100,000. Deputies of all political parties, from the Fascists to the Communists, addressed them. All spoke in the same terms: preserve your discipline or we are lost. A great impression was made on the crowd when the young Deputy, Ladislav Rašín, whose father[1] died as the result of an outrage committed by a fanatical young Communist, said:

" At this fatal hour I recognise no parties and I am ready to work with everybody, even with the Communists, for the defence of our endangered Country. Those who are not ready to fight and die for it are not worthy of freedom."

It had become obvious by this time that Dr. Hodža's Government could not remain in office any longer. The Government itself recognised this situation and resigned in the morning of

[1] Alois Rašín, Minister of Finance, one of the leaders of the Czechoslovak Liberation Revolution and the founder of the Czechoslovak monetary system.

September 22. Not until then, and until representatives of the Army had appealed to them to be calm and united, did the crowds consent to disperse quietly to their homes. It should be known that, in spite of the treachery of their Western " friends," only a few isolated voices were raised against them.

The demonstrations which took place simultaneously in Plzeň, Moravská Ostrava, Brno, Hradec Králové, Nová Paka, Turnov, Slaný and other provincial centres were marked by the same discipline—but the up-surge of popular resistance swept the Government of capitulation from power.

In the evening of September 22 a new Government assumed office, including from the former Government only Dr. Krofta, Minister of Foreign Affairs, Dr. Kalfus, Minister of Finance, and M. Vavrečka, Minister of Propaganda, none of whom was a Member of Parliament. The other ministerial posts were filled by officials and experts, while two popular figures, Dr. Zenkl, Mayor of Prague, and Dr. Bukovský, Head of the *Sokol* Movement, were appointed Ministers without portfolio. Two days later, on September 24, two Slovaks, Imrich Karvaš and Matuš Černák, were included in the Government. Both of these were professors, and the latter was on very close terms with the Slovak Autonomists. Parliamentary politicians were excluded from General Syrový's new Government, but the composition of the Government was agreed upon by the representatives of all parties. Actually, the members of Dr. Hodža's political Cabinet continued to function in the role of an " Advisory Council " for the new Government, and important political decisions were arrived at only after consultation with this body, the President of the Republic, and the leaders of the Governmental parties. Thus the political leadership of the State remained in fact in the same hands as before the appointment of the new Government. Therefore the latter felt itself bound by the decision taken on September 21 to accept the London proposals. The only importance of the change of Government lay in its psychological influence on the public. That, in itself, meant a great deal, but it could not undo the harm which had been done. The acceptance remained.

In the evening of September 22 President Beneš broadcast to the nation :

" We have had to act in accordance with existing circumstances of which we are all of us well aware.

" What will happen in the future remains to be seen. I am watching every development calmly and without fear. I have already told you that never in my life have I known fear—and I have no fear now for the future of our State. I have made plans for all eventualities, and I cannot be surprised, whatever may occur. I desire an understanding such as is being worked upon—an understanding between the greater nations of the world. If such an understanding is achieved, provided that it is an honourable one, it will be to the advantage also of our nation. It will mean a general appeasement between England and France and Germany, and between our country and Germany. It will mean also our co-operation with other countries, especially with those of Eastern Europe.

" Let us be patient then, and wait, with our strength unweakened and undisturbed by internal conflict, by lack of confidence, or by excitement and passion. We are a capable and realistic people, which has always understood a dangerous situation when it has arisen, and which knows when to act and when to fight. If it should be necessary to fight, we will know how to do so to the last breath. If it is necessary to negotiate, we will negotiate. If we have given way during these difficult days, it is to our honour, and history will prove, some day, that we have given way inevitably and in a progressive spirit, as good Europeans, and that our attitude and actions have been calm, brave, public-spirited and dignified.

" I repeat: I see things clearly and I have my plan. I have confidence in our people, in our nation and in our State. Our line of policy is firm, and we are trying to act in a thoughtful manner suited to the circumstances and events, which are now changing so rapidly. I fully understand the expression of your feelings and your patriotic demonstrations, and I appreciate them, because in their dignified form they are of benefit to the State; but be calm and manly in this crisis, and do not lose your feeling of optimism and that healthy common sense which is so characteristic of us Czechoslovaks.

" Our adversaries are expecting our disintegration and would take advantage of disorder or unrest, so it is essential, especially now, during the coming international negotiations, that order shall be maintained. And, above all, let us save our strength. We shall need it. Let us preserve our mental equilibrium. To-day we need it more than ever before. Europe is passing through a great crisis, and we—if we remain true to ourselves, firm in the unity of all our parties and movements, and steadfast in our wisdom and preparedness—we shall pass through it successfully and with honour. I repeat: Have no fear for the future of your Fatherland. There have been worse times than these, and we have survived to see better ones again."

Dr. Beneš' words " I have plans for all eventualities " were especially effective in restoring public confidence, and after the final catastrophe of Munich it was for these words in particular that he was strongly reproached. They were used extensively by his political opponents in their contemptible campaign against him. In well-informed political quarters, it was known what plan President Beneš intended. He hoped that negotiations concerning the realisation of the London proposals would last for several weeks, and thus give us time to come to an agreement with Poland,[1] even at the price of territorial concessions, and perhaps also with Hungary. It was especially this matter which President Beneš discussed with the leaders of the Army. They regarded it as of first-rate importance that at least our frontier with Poland should be covered. President Beneš intended thus to strengthen the position of Czechoslovakia, deserted by the Western Great Powers. Even in the event of our being forced to make territorial concessions to Germany, he believed that, together with Poland, and if necessary even with Hungary, Czechoslovakia would be able to maintain her independence and defensive power and to exist independently side by side with Germany. He realised that this was a risk, but he was prepared to take the full consequences. At the very moment at which President Beneš was speaking, news reached us that Herr Hitler had increased his demands at Godesberg and that he would go much further than he had dared to go at Berchtesgaden. This gave us grounds for hoping

[1] It was particularly important at that time that Poland should be diverted from a concerted German-Polish-Hungarian attack on Czechoslovakia.

that the Western Powers would resist these new German demands and that France would more definitely renew her alliance with Czechoslovakia with all that that entailed. The whole basis of such a policy was, of course, utterly destroyed by the Munich settlement.

Dr. Beneš' speech and the announcement of General Syrový's Government somewhat calmed the Czechoslovak people, who now awaited further developments—anxiously, it is true, but not completely without hope.

6. *Poland and Hungary announce their Claims.*

While these painful and dramatic events were taking place within Czechoslovakia, the international situation was steadily deteriorating. As soon as England and France approved in principle the adjustment of the Germano-Czechoslovak frontier, Poland and Hungary felt encouraged to demand the further dismemberment of the Republic. An inspired article in the Warsaw newspaper, the *Kurier Poranny*, declared as early as September 20: " There is no Power which can prevent the union of the Polish districts of Silesian Těšín with their Motherland in the same irrevocable manner as that in which the Germano-Czechoslovak problem is going to be solved." On September 20 the Polish Government authorised its Ambassadors in London, Paris, Rome and Berlin to announce to the Governments to which they were accredited the Polish claims regarding the Polish minority in Czechoslovakia. From that day onwards large demonstrations were organised in different parts of Poland, at which the demand for the cession of Těšín was vehemently expressed. Simultaneously the Polish Government threatened to take military measures against Czechoslovakia unless their claims were immediately satisfied. Nor was this boast unsupported by military action. By September 19 Polish military contingents were already moving up to the Těšín frontier, and within a few days of that date several divisions of Polish troops were concentrated, not only in the Těšín district, but also along the frontiers of Slovakia and Ruthenia.

On September 21 the Polish Minister in Prague handed to Dr. Krofta, the Czechoslovak Foreign Minister, a Note, denouncing the Polish-Czechoslovak Treaty of 1925 regarding their respective minorities and demanding that the Polish minority should be granted the same conditions as had been granted to the Sudeten-German minority. This demand was announced also, in very definite terms, in Paris and in London, and was justified by reference to the London proposals of September 18 regarding the Sudeten Germans. Poland just ruthlessly took advantage of the difficult situation into which Czechoslovakia had been forced by her Western friends, in order to seize the Těšín district and certain districts in Northern Slovakia. It has since become known that even then Poland was already negotiating with Italy and Hungary to establish a common Polish-Hungarian frontier.

The scale of the military preparations indicated that Poland was prepared to enforce her claims by military measures if that proved necessary, and even in conjunction with a German attack. The Polish Ambassador in Germany, M. Lipski, was at that very moment discussing it with Herr Hitler at Berchtesgaden. When it was somewhat feebly suggested in France that Poland should not take such measures against Czechoslovakia, the Polish Press reacted ironically and angrily. On September 22 the official *Gazeta Polska* wrote: " The attitude adopted by France occasions very considerable surprise in Poland. . . . The French public would do well to bear in mind the fact that Poland is a state of the same order and class as France." And the *Kurier Warzsavski* noted: " Does France not understand that it is not in her interest to strengthen Germany at the expense of Czechoslovakia, unless Poland is strengthened at the same time ? She reproaches us in her Press for taking advantage of a time when Czechoslovakia is deserted, in order to present our claims. We may say in answer, however, that our claim for frontier rectification is being made only after we have ascertained that France and England have considered such rectification in favour of Germany to be possible." On September 22 there was a mass demonstration in Warsaw in favour of the annexation of the Těšín district, and the demonstrators were addressed in a friendly manner by Marshal Rydz-Smygly, who assured them that the expression of their feelings of patriotism was universally respected. At these demonstrations there were shouts of " Long live Hitler ! " " Hurrah for a common

Polish-Hungarian frontier ! " " Hurrah for the greater Poland ! "

A similar attitude was adopted also by Hungary, though, even as late as August, the Hungarian statesmen who visited Germany had maintained an attitude of reserve towards the appeals of their hosts that Hungary should side with Germany against Czechoslovakia. The Hungarian Government had reason to fear the destruction of a strong, independent Czechoslovakia, for it realised that this would render Hungary incapable of resisting the pressure of a Germany, already enormously increased by the annexation of Austria, and would render her a vassal of the Third Reich. The Hungarian Government tried, therefore, to manœuvre in such a way that, should hostilities occur, Hungary would at first be able to remain neutral, and only later adapt its subsequent attitude to the circumstances which would arise. It is undeniable that Hungary hoped this policy would enable her, nevertheless, to realise certain revisionist claims. To anyone acquainted with the views prevalent in Budapest during August and September, it was evident that this fact of utmost importance was not taken into consideration by the statesmen either of Britain or of France when they were considering the vital decisions taken by them just prior to Berchtesgaden. It is important to realise, in this connection, that until it was clear that Britain and France were afraid of Hitler, the situation in the Danube Basin had been developing more and more to the disadvantage of Germany, for all the states in that area were afraid of German domination. This hostile reserve was particularly evident at the moment when the Henleinist *Putsch* had been comparatively easily suppressed by the Czechoslovak Government without Germany coming to the aid of her " slaughtered Sudeten-German brethren." Demonstrations in favour of Czechoslovakia multiplied, not only in Rumania (who, as a matter of fact, maintained throughout the crisis an exemplary attitude of fidelity as an ally), but also in Yugoslavia, where M. Stojadino-vitch's régime was showing signs of growing instability. Even in Poland, considerable uncertainty was noticeable: it was suddenly announced that new elections would be held, and there were serious indications that President Moscicki was seeking a *rapprochement* with the Polish opposition, which has always been profoundly pro-French and pro-Czech in character.

If the Western Powers had stood together and maintained a firm attitude, there is little reason to doubt that all the Central European states, including Poland and Hungary, would have stood by them. The situation completely altered, however, as soon as it was announced that Mr. Chamberlain was prepared to negotiate with Hitler. In the whole of Central Europe, Mr. Chamberlain's visit was taken to mean that the West was retreating before Nazi Germany and would sacrifice Czechoslovakia.

In such circumstances, Hungary, of course, was bound to change her attitude. On September 20, MM. Imrédy and Kanya hurriedly flew to Berchtesgaden to see Herr Hitler and remove the unfavourable impression which they had made on Germany during their visit in August, and in order to assure themselves of the support of the powerful dictator for their territorial claims in Slovakia. In return for such support, they now found it easy to promise that, in the event of a conflict, they would side with Germany and allow the German Army to move freely over Hungarian territory. The Germans took good care that the Hungarians should thoroughly realise that " he who risks nothing, gains nothing." Hungary's subsequent diplomatic action followed the same lines as that of Poland. She announced to the Great Powers her claims with regard to the Hungarian minority in Czechoslovakia. In Prague, the Hungarian Minister delivered a Note to this effect on September 22, and, just as now in Poland, mass demonstrations took place in Hungary, demanding the liberation of Hungarians from Czechoslovak rule.

The Polish and Hungarian claims were fully and ostentatiously supported by Italy. Signor Mussolini, since September 18 had made one speech after another in various Italian towns, in an effort to make the greatest possible impression on France and England. It was with the fire of his oratory that the Duce supported the Führer. On September 18, i.e. on the day of the Franco-British discussions in London, in a speech delivered at Trieste, he extended the Sudeten-German problem to include the problem of the Polish and Hungarian minorities. It is not yet clear to what extent this pleased Herr Hitler, but it certainly complicated the action of England and France, who had intended to confine themselves to the German-Czechoslovak conflict.

Signor Mussolini's Trieste speech should have warned the Western World that, by preparing the revision of the frontiers between Germany and Czechoslovakia, they were setting in motion a dangerous avalanche. Signor Mussolini said:

" What I am about to say is not dictated merely by the policy of the Rome-Berlin Axis, but finds a historical justification and precedent in the feelings of friendship which bind us to the Magyars and Poles and to the other nations of what one might describe as the ' Mosaic State No. 2.' . . . In regard to the problem which is disturbing Europe at the present time, there can be only one solution: a plebiscite—a plebiscite, that is to say, for every nationality which asks for it—for each nationality which was forced to remain in what aspired to be Great Czechoslovakia and what to-day is revealing its basic absurdity. . . . Should there come into being a ' United Front,' whether it be for or against Prague, let it be known that Italy has already decided on which side she will range herself."

Three days later, speaking at Treviso, he said:

" If Czechoslovakia finds herself to-day in what might be called a ' delicate situation,' it is because she was—one may already say ' was,' and I shall tell you why directly—not just Czechoslovakia, but was ' Czecho-Germano-Polono-Magyaro-Rutheno-Rumano-Slovakia,' and I would emphasise, now that this problem is faced up to, it is essential that it should be solved in a general manner."

It was in the sense of this declaration that Italian diplomacy was exercised. Italy supported the Hungarian and Polish claims and favoured the idea of a common Polish-Hungarian frontier. At that time the German Government had not yet pronounced itself openly against it. Though in March, 1939, it appeared to be accepted, in October, 1938, a stern German veto was opposed.

This immense change of attitude in Central Europe served to strengthen Germany's position very substantially. It was thus Mr. Chamberlain's trip to Berchtesgaden which was the decisive turning point of the situation in Germany's favour. The London Conference of September 18 proved an initial success on a scale far beyond anything that had been expected at Berchtesgaden, and Herr Hitler told Mr. Chamberlain with provocative frankness that he had not supposed for a moment that the British Government would accept the principle of self-determination which he had claimed at Berchtesgaden.[1] The previous misgiving of Herr Hitler was not to be wondered at, of course, for how could the Nazi leader have expected that the Western Powers would themselves assist him to gain the Czechoslovak bastion, which guarded the entrance to the Danube Basin, the Balkans and Eastern Europe ?

The Anglo-French attitude naturally increased Herr Hitler's temerity. Terrorist activities on the Czechoslovak frontiers were immediately increased, and on September 17 the Henleinist leaders, who had fled to Germany, announced the formation of a *Sudetendeutscher Freikorps*. On September 19, Herren Sebekowsky and Sandner, two of Henlein's leading men, made threatening speeches in Dresden, in which they announced that this *Freikorps* would fight for the liberation of the Sudeten Germans. From that time onwards bands of men, armed with German arms and hand-grenades, attacked nightly the Czechoslovak frontier guards, Customs houses and official buildings, and tried to penetrate into the Sudeten-German districts.

These attacks were still comparatively easily repulsed. The skirmishes being confined, as a rule, to the frontiers, and, excepting in the Aš (Asch) and Cheb (Eger) districts, the raiders were unable to penetrate into Czechoslovak territory. In order to provide no pretext for German intervention, the Czechoslovak patrols took care, when defending themselves, that their bullets should not fall in Germany, although this rendered their task more difficult. The raiders, on the other hand, did not hesitate to use women and children as a screen for their attacks. This was done, for instance, during the storming of the Customs house at Úpice. If any harm had befallen these women, deliberately exposed by the Nazis, the German propaganda would have made good use of the fact. Instead, Czech gendarmes, holding fire, were murdered from behind their skirts. Owing to the

---

[1] " He [i.e. Herr Hitler] told me afterwards that he never for one moment supposed that I should be able to come back and say that the principle was accepted." Mr. Chamberlain, House of Commons, September 28, 1938. *Hansard*, Vol. 339, No. 160, Column 20.

extreme care which was exercised by the Czechoslovak authorities, we lost numbers of our undefended men and the Germans were reduced to fabricating lying allegations and rumours about the " atrocities " which were perpetuated by the " Bolshevik hordes of Czech soldiery." It is doubtful whether more cowardly lies have ever been invented or such hatred stimulated against any nation, as was done during those September days by the German Ministry of Propaganda—inspired by the German Chancellor himself, who declares in *Mein Kampf* that lies are a legitimate and useful weapon.

The campaign of lies and threats became more and more intensified in proportion as the Sudeten-German population remained passive, and it is interesting to note that, even after September 18, when it became known that the Western Powers had proposed the cession of the Sudeten-German districts, the vast majority of the local population—with the exception of some fanatical youths, and only a few at that—preserved a calm behind which lay a secret dread lest their territory might in the near future become the scene of all the horrors of war.

The continual attacks imposed unusually great demands on the discipline and courage of the Czechoslovak defence forces, and served generally to increase the danger of German aggression. The Western Powers refused, nevertheless, to sanction any increased preparedness on the part of Czechoslovakia—on the ground that it might prejudice their " pacific efforts."[1]

---

[1] An excellent, impartial and eye-witness account of the September fighting has been given by a British journalist in *I saw the Crucifixion*, by Sydney Morrell.

1. *Hitler's Ultimatum.*

IN such circumstances, it was hardly surprising that Germany's
audacity increased. The Western Powers, by pressure for which
it would be difficult to find a parallel in history, had forced the
capitulation of Germany's most serious and strongest antagonist
in Central Europe. Poland and Hungary had turned definitely
against Czechoslovakia; both Rumania and Yugoslavia were
thoroughly disconcerted by the attitude of France and Britain;
and even Russia was obliged to act very warily. In addition,
Mussolini's aggressive speeches were proving a happy asset to
Hitler. What was the result?

On September 22, Mr. Chamberlain was able to go once more
to see the Chancellor of the Reich—this time at Godesberg—
taking with him the Czechoslovak acceptance of the London
proposals. But even before he stepped into his aeroplane in
London, the German Press was already writing that " the
settlement which had been possible a week ago was no longer
suitable." The *Westdeutscher Beobachter*, for instance, described
with brutal candour that morning what Germany was really
after: " The Czechs do not yet understand that the question at
issue is not the solution of the Sudeten-German problem, but
whether Europe shall be relieved of their bloodthirsty existence." The *Westfälische Landeszeitung* suggested that all equivo-
cation or doubt must be removed from any future Czechoslovak
foreign policy, and the paper quite openly demanded the removal
of the existing political leaders in Czechoslovakia, on the ground
that otherwise Czechoslovakia would always " weigh upon
Europe." It is of some interest to note that both these passages
were quoted in *Le Temps* of September 23—in other words, the
Western European public was quite well informed at the time of
the details, plans and intentions of the Third Reich which were
openly expounded by the German Press. Any doubt which one
might have had on this score would be removed by the message,
in the same issue of *Le Temps*,[1] of their Berlin correspondent,

---

[1] *Le Temps* was throughout the crisis 100 per cent. in favour of M. Bonnet.

writing from Godesberg before the opening of the conversations between Mr. Chamberlain and Herr Hitler: " The Germans declare that the agenda of the Conference will be nothing less than the final liquidation of the Peace Treaties in Central Europe. . . . German opinion seems to be . . . that France and England will abandon Czechoslovakia to her fate, which will therefore become a *foregone conclusion.* . . . It is stated openly in German quarters that the new Czechoslovakia must pass into the orbit of Germany, and will be nothing more than a tool in German hands."

As a matter of fact, these German hopes were a trifle premature, because Herr Hitler went too far at Godesberg. Mr. Chamberlain met him in the afternoon of September 22, and their conversation is best and most completely described in the speech delivered by Mr. Chamberlain himself in the House of Commons on September 28.[1]

"However, on the 22nd I went back to Germany to Godesberg on the Rhine, where the Chancellor had appointed a meeting place as being more convenient for me than the remote Berchtesgaden. Once again I had a very warm welcome in the streets and villages through which I passed, demonstrating to me the desire of the German people for peace, and on the afternoon of my arrival I had my second meeting with the Chancellor. During my stay in London the Government had worked out with the French Government arrangements for effecting the transfer of the territory proposed, and also for delimiting the final frontier. I explained these to Herr Hitler—he was not previously aware of them—and I also told him about the proposed guarantee against unprovoked aggression.

" On that point of a guarantee he made no objection, but said he could not enter into a guarantee unless other Powers, including Italy, were also guarantors. I said, I had not asked him to enter into a guarantee, but I had intended to ask him whether he was prepared to conclude a pact of non-aggression with the new Czechoslovakia. He said he could not enter into such a pact while other minorities in Czechoslovakia were still unsatisfied; but hon. Members will see that he has since put

[1] *Parliamentary Debates*, Vol. 339, No. 160, pp. 19–22.

his views in a more positive form, and said that when they are satisfied he will then be prepared to join in an international guarantee. At this particular time, however, no further discussion took place between us on the subject of a guarantee. Herr Hitler said he could not accept the other proposals I had described to him, on the ground that they were too dilatory and offered too many opportunities for further evasion on the part of the Czechs. He insisted that speedy solution was essential, on account of the oppression and terrorism to which the Sudeten Germans were being subjected, and he proceeded to give me the main outlines of the proposal which he subsequently embodied in a memorandum—except that he did not in this conversation actually name any time limit.

" Hon. Members will realise the perplexity in which I found myself, faced with this totally unexpected situation. I had been told at Berchtesgaden that if the principle of self-determination were accepted Herr Hitler would discuss with me the ways and means of carrying it out. He told me afterwards that he never for one moment supposed that I should be able to come back and say that the principle was accepted. I do not want hon. Members to think that he was deliberately deceiving me—I do not think so for one moment—but, for me, I expected that when I got back to Godesberg I had only to discuss quietly with him the proposals that I had brought with me; and it was a profound shock to me when I was told at the beginning of the conversation that these proposals were not acceptable, and that they were to be replaced by other proposals of a kind which I had not contemplated at all.

" I felt that I must have a little time to consider what I was to do. Consequently, I withdrew, my mind full of foreboding as to the success of my mission. I first, however, obtained from Herr Hitler an extension of his previous assurance, that he would not move his troops pending the results of the negotiations. I, on my side, undertook to appeal to the Czech Government to avoid any action which might provoke incidents. I have seen speculative accounts of what happened on the next day, which have suggested that long hours passed whilst I remained on one side of the Rhine and Herr Hitler on the other because I had difficulty in obtaining this assurance from

him about the moving of his troops. I want to say at once that
that is purely imaginary. There was no such difficulty. I will
explain in a moment what did cause the delay; but the assurance was given readily, and it has been, as I have said before,
abided by right up to the present time.

" We had arranged to resume our conversation at half-past
eleven the next morning, but, in view of the difficulties of
talking with a man through an interpreter and of the fact that
I could not feel sure that what I had said to Herr Hitler had
always been completely understood and appreciated by him,
I thought it would be wise to put down on paper some comments upon these new proposals of his and let him have them
some time before the talks began. Accordingly, I wrote him a
letter—which is No. 3 in the White Paper—which I sent to
him. I sent that soon after breakfast. It will be seen that in it
I declared my readiness to convey the proposals to the Czechoslovak Government, but I pointed out what seemed to me to
be grave difficulties in the way of their acceptance. On the
receipt of this letter, the Chancellor intimated that he would
like to send a written reply. Accordingly, the conversations
were postponed. The reply was not received until well into the
afternoon.

" I had hoped that this delay might mean that some modification was being worked out, but when I received the letter—
which is No. 4—I found, to my disappointment, that, although
it contained some explanation, it offered no modification at all
of the proposals which had been described to me the night
before. Accordingly, I replied as in document No. 5, asking for
a memorandum of the proposals and a copy of the map for
transmission to Prague, and intimating my intention to return
to England. The memorandum and the map were handed to
me at my final interview with the Chancellor, which began at
half-past ten that night and lasted into the small hours of the
morning, an interview at which the German Foreign Secretary
was present, as well as Sir Nevile Henderson and Sir Horace
Wilson; and, for the first time, I found in the memorandum a
time limit. Accordingly, on this occasion I spoke very frankly.
I dwelt with all the emphasis at my command on the risks
which would be incurred by insisting on such terms, and on the

terrible consequences of a war, if war ensued. I declared that the language and the manner of the document, which I described as an ultimatum rather than a memorandum, would profoundly shock public opinion in neutral countries, and I bitterly reproached the Chancellor for his failure to respond in any way to the efforts which I had made to secure peace. In spite of these plain words, this conversation was carried on on more friendly terms than any that had yet preceded it, and Herr Hitler informed me that he appreciated and was grateful for my efforts, but that he considered that he had made a response since he had held back the operations which he had planned and that he had offered in his proposal to Czechoslovakia a frontier very different from the one which he would have taken as the result of military conquest.

" I think I should add that before saying farewell to Herr Hitler I had a few words with him in private, which I do not think are without importance. In the first place he repeated to me with great earnestness what he had said already at Berchtesgaden, namely, that this was the last of his territorial ambitions in Europe and that he had no wish to include in the Reich people of other races than Germans. In the second place, he said, again very earnestly, that he wanted to be friends with England and that if only this Sudeten question could be got out of the way in peace he would gladly resume conversations. It is true he said, ' There is one awkward question, the Colonies.' [Hon. Members: ' Spain.'] [*Laughter.*] I really think that at a time like this these are not subjects for idle laughter. They are words which count in the long run and ought to be fully weighed. He said, ' There is one awkward question, the Colonies, but that is not a matter for war,' and, alluding to the mobilisation of the Czechoslovakian Army, which had been announced to us in the middle of our conversations and had given rise to some disturbance, he said, about the Colonies, ' There will be no mobilisation about that.' "

The Memorandum which Herr Hitler delivered to Mr. Chamberlain demanded the immediate Czech evacuation and German occupation of the Sudeten-German districts by October 1. On a map annexed to the Memorandum further areas were indicated over and above those which were to be occupied by Germany immediately. In these a plebiscite was to be held at a later date. The text of this Memorandum is as follows:[1]

" Reports which are increasing in number from hour to hour regarding incidents in the Sudetenland show that the situation has become completely intolerable for the Sudeten-German people and, in consequence, a danger to the peace of Europe. It is therefore essential that the separation of the Sudetenland agreed to by Czechoslovakia should be effected without any further delay. On the attached map the Sudeten-German area which is to be ceded is shaded red. The areas in which, over and above the areas which are to be occupied, a plebiscite is also to be held are drawn in and shaded green.

" The final delimitation of the frontier must correspond to the wishes of those concerned. In order to determine these wishes, a certain period is necessary for the preparation of the voting, during which disturbances must in all circumstances be prevented. A situation of parity must be created. The area designated on the attached map as a German area will be occupied by German troops without taking account as to whether in the plebiscite there may prove to be in this or that part of the area a Czech majority. On the other hand, the Czech territory is occupied by Czech troops without regard to the question whether, within this area, there lie large German language islands, the majority of which will without doubt avow their German nationality in the plebiscite.

"With a view to bringing about an immediate and final solution of the Sudeten-German problem, the following proposals are now made by the German Government:

" 1. Withdrawal of the whole Czech armed forces, the police, the gendarmerie, the customs officials and the frontier guards from the area to be evacuated as designated on the attached map, this area to be handed over to Germany on the 1st October.

" 2. The evacuated territory is to be handed over in its present condition (see further details in appendix). The German Government agree that a plenipotentiary representative of

[1] Correspondence respecting Czechoslovakia, No. 7/1938/Cmd. 5847, pp. 14–16.

Sketch Map based on the Map annexed to the Memorandum handed to the Prime Minister by the Reichschancellor on September 23, 1938.

(Red) To be handed over on October 1.

(Green) Additional plebiscite area.

the Czech Government or of the Czech Army should be attached to the headquarters of the German military forces to settle the details of the modalities of the evacuation.

" 3. The Czech Government discharges at once to their homes all Sudeten Germans serving in the military forces or the police anywhere in Czech State territory.

" 4. The Czech Government liberates all political prisoners of German race.

" 5. The German Government agrees to permit a plebiscite to take place in those areas, which will be more definitely defined, before at latest the 25th November. Alterations to the new frontier arising out of the plebiscite will be settled by a German-Czech or an international commission. The plebiscite itself will be carried out under the control of an international commission. All persons who were residing in the areas in question on the 28th October, 1918, or were born there prior to this date will be eligible to vote. A simple majority of all eligible male and female voters will determine the desire of the population to belong to either the German Reich or to the Czech State. During the plebiscite both parties will withdraw their military forces out of areas which will be defined more precisely. The date and duration will be settled by the German and Czech Governments together.

" 6. The German Government proposes that an authoritative German-Czech commission should be set up to settle all further details."

Although Mr. Chamberlain's speech gave, of course, only a summary of events during the dramatic days of Godesberg (September 22 and 23), it is quite sufficient to enable us to form a pretty comprehensive picture of all that went on. I am inclined to believe that Mr. Chamberlain was genuinely surprised by what he was told by Herr Hitler. He would have been very much less surprised if he had understood better the psychology of the man with whom he had to deal. One cannot understand the behaviour of the British and French politicians during the crisis unless one bears in mind the fact that the democratic statesmen appeared completely to misjudge the psychology of Herr Hitler and of Hitlerism. It would seem that they were unable to understand those who think and act in a manner to which they themselves were not accustomed. Unable to comprehend the wholly different mentality of the Nazis, they were naturally surprised to see that the concessions which they offered, far-reaching though they were, did not satisfy the latter, and that, on the contrary, the Nazis demanded, with even greater stubbornness and intransigence the absolute fulfilment of their maximum requirements. It must be admitted that Herr Hitler held a tactical and psychological supremacy over his Western visitor which gave him a great advantage in playing, as he did, a risky game. Whereas Mr. Chamberlain, after the Czech acceptance of the London proposals (which did, after all, fulfil the wishes expressed by Herr Hitler at Berchtesgaden), was expecting to have to discuss with the Chancellor only their " peaceful " implementation, Hitler immediately presented him with new, and more far-reaching, demands. The German Chancellor had already gained so much that he thought that he could afford to show his cards, so he came forward with his ultimatum. During the next few days, when public opinion in France and England was tending to react against this latest ultimatum, the German propagandists, and with them the uncompromising pacifists in Paris and London, pretended that the Godesberg demands were only an expression in concrete terms of the Anglo-French proposals. In fact, Mr. Chamberlain was very well aware at Godesberg that Herr Hitler was asking for infinitely more than had been offered by those proposals, which he himself had declared were his last word. Mr. Chamberlain openly declared that the new German demands were unacceptable. It is evident that on September 23, at Godesberg, Mr. Chamberlain believed that his conciliatory and mediatory mission had been completely wrecked. The same opinion prevailed also in Paris. Thus the first reaction of both the British and the French Governments was one of frank opposition to Hitler's ultimatum.

2. *The Czechoslovak Mobilisation.*

It thus came about that on the afternoon of September 23, while Mr. Chamberlain was still at Godesberg, and before even the Godesberg ultimatum had been delivered in Prague, that both London and Paris sent messages to the Czechoslovak

Government saying that they could no longer advise Czechoslovakia not to mobilise. These important messages were delivered by the British and French Ministers in Prague to Dr. Krno, the head of the political section of the Ministry of Foreign Affairs. Dr. Krno's notes about the incident are of interest:

" The Minister of Great Britain gave me, at 5 p.m. on September 23, 1938, the following message, received by telephone from London at 4.30 p.m., according to the statement of Mr. Troutbeck [the Secretary of the British Legation in Prague]:

" ' We have agreed with the French Government that the Czechoslovak Government should be informed that the French and British Governments can no longer continue to take the responsibility of advising them not to mobilise.'

" The British Minister, consulting his dossier read out the following:

" ' It must be emphasised that such action may very easily accelerate other action, and therefore the Czechoslovak Government may consider it advisable to avoid unnecessary publicity.'

" Mr. Newton added that he did not yet dismiss the possibility of agreement being reached at Godesberg, but that, nevertheless, the situation was ' very serious.'

" *(Signed)* DR. KRNO." [1]

Dr. Krno's notes concerning the French message read:

" The French Minister gave me, at 6.15 p.m. on September 23, 1938, the following message:

" ' The French Government can no longer take the responsibility of continuing the advice which they gave to the Czechoslovak Government covering the period of the Franco-British negotiations. From this moment, therefore, the Czechoslovak Government is free to decide for itself what measures it may consider necessary should the situation again become more serious.' "

[1] Czechoslovak State Document.

Dr. Krno added that M. Léger had made the following remarks to M. de Lacroix:

" 1. The French Government has no information that is particularly disturbing from the military point of view.

" 2. It advises the utmost discretion in taking any measures which might be considered necessary.

" (*Signed*) DR. KRNO."

During the evening of September 23 the British Minister informed the head of the Diplomatic Section, M. Smutný, of the news which he had received from Godesberg.

" Mr. Newton, the British Minister," wrote M. Smutný, in his official report, " asked me at 8.30 p.m. this evening, September 23, to see him, as he had received important despatches from Godesberg.

" In his first letter, of which Mr. Newton gave me a copy, Herr Hitler expresses the opinion that Czechoslovakia is provoking trouble, and that the occupation of the Sudeten-German territory by the German Army represents the only possible means of maintaining peace. Herr Hitler describes this proposal as being pacific. If his proposal is not accepted, he gives it to be understood, a military solution will be sought, and that there will be no question of a nationality frontier, but merely of a military and strategic one.

" Herr Hitler brought to the first conversation a map of Czechoslovakia, on which the new boundaries were indicated. Mr. Chamberlain objected that these new boundaries would give too much territory to Germany, whereupon Herr Hitler declared that he was ready to accept a plebiscite for those parts of the territory which might not be recognised as entirely German. This plebiscite would be conducted two or three months hence under international control, on the model of the plebiscite in the Saar. Any territory which should declare itself in favour of Germany would be occupied immediately by German troops.

" Mr. Chamberlain intended to raise certain objections to this second plan of Herr Hitler's at the second conversation, but it seems that this second conversation did not take place, since Mr. Chamberlain informed Herr Hitler of his objections by letter. He said in this letter that he was prepared to submit to the Czechoslovak Government Herr Hitler's proposals regarding the territories in which a plebiscite would be necessary and those in which it would not be necessary. But, Mr. Chamberlain wrote, there was a difficulty in the fact that Herr Hitler was proposing that all the territories should be occupied immediately.

" Under these circumstances, it was difficult to continue negotiations, and Mr. Chamberlain expressed doubts whether the plans, worked out by Herr Hitler, would diminish the tension, even if they were accepted. Herr Hitler does not quite understand that Mr. Chamberlain could not propose a plan which would be disapproved by public opinion in England and in France. He is sure that the proposed occupation of these territories by German troops—an action by which these territories would become, for practical purposes, a part of the Reich—would be considered as symbolic. Mr. Chamberlain believes that the Czechoslovak Government would reject a plan of this nature. It would be necessary that Herr Hitler's plan should contain alternatives, to which it would be impossible to raise objections.

" If it were desired, Mr. Chamberlain could ask the Czechoslovak Government whether it would be possible to consider, as a practical solution, the transfer to the Sudeten Germans of responsibility for the maintenance of order in those territories about which no doubt was entertained. The Sudeten Germans would create their own organisations in those territories, to replace the German troops, or would make use of organisations which were already in existence, under the control of German observers. Mr. Chamberlain would ask the opinion of the Czechoslovak Government and if Prague accepted this proposal, he would ask the Czechoslovak Government to withdraw their troops and police from the districts in which the Sudeten Germans would maintain order. In his reply to Mr. Chamberlain's letter, Herr Hitler insisted upon his conditions of yesterday. He admitted only one exception, namely, that he would not occupy militarily the territories subject to plebiscite.

" Herr Hitler's claims may be summed up as follows:

" 1. He demands the immediate recall of military and other authorities and of the police from those Sudeten territories which he claims as German.

" 2. He demands the military occupation of these territories.

" Mr. Chamberlain, for his part, demands that Herr Hitler should define his claims in a memorandum, and says that when he has received this memoradnum, he will send it to-morrow, by air, to Mr. Newton, the British Minister in Prague. Mr. Chamberlain states to Hitler also, that at the present moment he does not see what more can be done than to send this memorandum and return to London.

" Mr. Chamberlain demands at the same time from Herr Hitler a promise that he will not start any military action against Czechoslovak territory until such time as he has received an answer from Prague, as such an action would compromise future negotiations, if such negotiations should take place.

" Mr. Newton received first the message about mobilisation (saying that there was no objection to the Czechoslovak mobilisation), and afterwards he received the above information from Godesberg. He is supposed to draw the attention of the Czechoslovak Government to the fact that the announcement of mobilisation might provoke the issue of an immediate order to the German troops to invade Czechoslovakia.

" (*Signed*) SMUTNÝ."

All this information was, of course, of extraordinary importance, and it was evident that something was likely to happen immediately. In the evening of September 23 the members of the Syrový Government met at the residence of the President of the Republic, together with the political Cabinet of Dr. Hodža and the Presidents of the Coalition parties. Those present at this meeting were *unanimously* of the opinion that it was necessary to order the mobilisation of several classes. This step was indeed, quite natural, because until then Czechoslovakia, under the pressure from the Western Powers, had taken no great military precautions, although Germany had already called up 2,000,000 men and Poland also, since September 20, had

concentrated several divisions on the Czechoslovak frontier and
even Hungary had already increased the numbers of her men
under arms. When even the two West European Governments
drew our attention to the necessity for greater measures of
defence, because they felt that the efforts to arrive at an agreement with Germany were failing, it was obviously the duty of
those responsible for the safety of Czechoslovakia to order
mobilisation.

At 10 p.m. on September 23 the announcer of the broadcasting
service asked listeners to stand by their receivers, and half an
hour later he announced that the President of the Republic had
ordered the mobilisation of all classes of men up to the age of
forty. After reading the mobilisation order, the announcer made
an appeal to all citizens ending with the following words: " Our
cause is a just one."

It is not easy for a Czechoslovak who lived through those
moments to describe what was happening at that time in his
country; the memory of it remains too painfully vivid. . . . The
whole atmosphere was changed immediately throughout the
country. Whereas, since September 21, when the Government
had yielded to the Franco-British pressure, the Czechoslovak
people had been living in an atmosphere of depression and grief,
they now raised their heads cheerfully as they were called to
arms for the defence of their country. It is difficult to explain how
it was possible, but it is a fact that the first reservists reported
at their stations in Prague only a quarter of an hour after the
mobilisation was declared. Everyone hurried and everyone was
helpful, in order that the mobilisation should be carried out as
quickly as possible, with the result that on September 24 and 25
many more reservists came into the barracks than could possibly
have been expected, and the officers found considerable difficulty
in dealing with them all. The behaviour of the Czechoslovak
women also was admirable: they did not conceal their natural
anxiety and their eyes were filled with tears, but mothers were
helping their sons and wives their husbands, so that they should
be able to carry out their duty as quickly as possible. It was clear
to each and everyone that here was a just cause to be defended.
There was no one who did not gladly and of his own free will
come forward to help in the defence of the country and of

freedom. It will, moreover, remain for ever the pride of our people that not for a single moment did they succumb to war hysteria, and not a single voice was raised in hatred against the enemy. The people proved that it was prepared for any sacrifice, however terrible—and the sacrifice which it was prepared to make would have served not only our national self-defence, but also the interests of Europe as a whole. Such a people was worthy of a better fate than that which was inflicted upon it a few days later and that which it suffers to-day.

The sentiment and behaviour of the Czechoslovak people during those magnificent days were described in an unforgettable manner by Karel Čapek when he wrote on September 25 in the *Lidové Noviny*:

" Only too often of late have we listened to appeal after appeal to keep calm, but to-day, at last, that calmness to which we have been adjured has become a splendid reality. Throughout our Czechoslovakia there prevails an absolute calmness which is born of our certainty, of our decision, and of our realisation that there is no way of avoiding what is inevitable. Calmly and soberly, our menfolk have come forward in answer to the summons to perform their supreme duty. You should see them in the villages, in the small towns and in the cities—everywhere you will witness the same spectacle as they hasten to join the colours as quickly as possible in response to the call of duty. The youths, with their suitcases on their shoulders; the married men, accompanied by their wives and children; the women and children cheering those who are leaving their homes; the people who must go on with their work, whether in the fields or in the factory—all of them are behaving quite normally, however moved they may feel, for they have not been taken by surprise. They look as though they were simply going to their normal work, for it seems as natural to our men to defend their country as to earn their daily bread. It is a historic effort which is being made without any pomp and ceremony. Ours is indeed a great nation."

The mobilisation was carried out with exemplary efficiency and all went absolutely according to plan. Within a few days we had placed on a war footing an army of over 1,500,000

well-trained men from every branch of the services, adequately
staffed with excellent officers and non-commissioned officers.
This did not represent by any means the whole of the military
forces of which we could dispose, for only twenty classes, i.e.
those consisting of men up to the age of forty, had been called
up. In September we mobilised somewhere about thirty-five
divisions, but we could easily have mobilised a further ten
divisions.[1] The actual number of those mobilised, though very
considerable, was of less importance, however, than the fact that
the Czechoslovak Army, which had been created with great
care and effort during the previous twenty years, was composed
of really well-trained soldiers and was staffed with highly
qualified officers and non-commissioned officers. It is of importance, also, that the majority of its units were mechanised, and
that our metallurgical and engineering industries, which far
surpassed in productive capacity those of Italy, could keep these
amply supplied with material of first-class quality. So far as
both military training and technical equipment are concerned,
the Czechoslovak Army was at least on a par with the German
Army, and there was no other army in Central Europe, Poland
not excepted, which could face comparison with it.[2] Moreover,
the morale of the Czechoslovak Army was exceptionally high.
Indeed, in this respect, it would have been difficult to find its
equal, for it represented the concentrated essence of a united
Czechoslovak nation, grimly determined to defend itself to the
last breath.

On September 24 the Government declared the Republic to
be in a state of readiness for war and the Chief of the General
Staff, General Ludvík Krejčí, was appointed Commander-in-
chief of the armed forces. The Government and the entire administration, as well as all private enterprises, were subordinated

[1] I emphasise this because the Press of Western Europe mentioned as a rule a
force of only thirty-five divisions, as though Czechoslovakia had only that number
of divisions at her disposal. In actual fact, as I have stated, the total military
strength of the Republic was forty-five divisions, of which only thirty-five were
mobilised at the end of September, 1938.

[2] This was only fully realised by the British the following March, when the
whole military equipment of the Czechoslovak Army fell into German hands.
" The motorised equipment of the Czechoslovak Army," wrote *The Times* correspondent on March 24, 1939, " is greatly superior to that possessed by the Germans
—knowledgeable Czechs expressed the deepest contempt for the German material
which rolled into Prague last week. . . . The disarmament of the Czechoslovak
Army has at least doubled the number of heavy guns possessed by Germany."

to the military authorities. The necessary administrative, economic and financial measures were taken in connection with the mobilisation and the state of readiness for war. Everything went off without a hitch. This was possible, of course, only because every citizen without exception had volunteered of his own free will. This was most apparent in the rapid organisation of the whole system of communication and transport,[1] and in the organisation of air raid precautions. The maintenance of supplies for the Army as well as for the civil population in the larger towns was no less successfully organised. The careful and far-sighted financial policy adopted by Dr. Kalfus, Minister of Finance, and Dr. Engliš, Governor of the National Bank, who were jointly responsible for preventing chaos in the State and public finances and for creating a considerable reserve, enabled the heavy requirements of the Army over a considerable period of time and the vast expense of the mobilisation to be met without any serious dislocation of the finances and economic life of the Republic. Women of all classes, moreover, showed great ability in playing an effective role during these difficult days when the whole of the Czechoslovak nation gave proof of its maturity, not only by its readiness to make the greatest sacrifices which patriotism might call for, but also by its initiative and by its ability to adapt itself quickly to the successful performance of many difficult tasks. The Czechoslovaks are no less capable than the French of rising to an emergency. President Masaryk taught his people that they must make up for their comparatively small numbers by working more energetically and more intelligently. This is attempted with a flourish of genuine humour such as is characteristic of both the English and the French. The Czech people as a whole are self-sacrificing, courageous and even heroic but they seldom boast about it. Their greatness is rooted in the human simplicity of a peasant.

The efficiency of the Czechoslovak mobilisation was, of course, somewhat disagreeable for Germany, whose propaganda therefore immediately disseminated " news " of disorders and of the opposition of the Czechoslovak people to their military obligations. The German official news agency, the D.N.B. (Deutsches

---

[1] Private people—even those who were not obliged to do so—willingly placed their motor cars at the disposal of the Army.

Nachrichten Büro) stated that railway wagons carrying Czechoslovak reservists were covered with inscriptions such as " Away with Beneš and Syrový," " We want work and bread," " We do not want to be cannon-fodder." The same propaganda agency announced that the majority of Sudeten Germans did not obey their mobilisation orders. In actual fact, however, although Herr Henlein announced by radio from Germany that those Sudeten Germans who obeyed their mobilisation orders would be committing an act of high treason against the German nation, even this threatening announcement had little effect on the Sudeten-German people. Apart from a few isolated exceptions, the Sudeten Germans obeyed unhesitatingly their mobilisation orders. The anti-Nazi Germans did so with the same enthusiasm as the Czechoslovaks themselves. Every day, however, the German propaganda tried to provoke the Sudeten-German people by stories of " massacres " of the Sudeten Germans, and the Henleinist *Freikorps* continued their brutal attacks on the frontiers; but all this was not sufficient to stir the Sudeten Germans into rebellion. On the contrary, proofs of Sudeten loyalty occurred, like that on September 25, when the training centre at Špičák in Šumava (Böhmerwald) was attacked, a local unit composed of eighteen Sudeten-German soldiers, whose relatives were among those who had gone over into Germany, was responsible for repulsing the attack and driving the invaders back beyond the frontier.

The falseness of the German propaganda at this time was very thoroughly exposed in the following official Czechoslovak communiqué, dated September 25:

" We have already on many occasions drawn attention to the lies which are broadcast from German radio stations. These lies are often proved to be lies by those who broadcast them. Thus we were informed at first by the German broadcasting stations that the Czechoslovak mobilisation had been a failure because half the reservists had not joined up. Later on, however, when anyone could see for himself that this was untrue, the German stations announced that the reservists had joined up, but that large numbers of them had deserted into Germany, which is also a lie.

" On another occasion the German broadcasting stations stated that the frontier was in the hands of German troops; but a little while later we heard the very same stations announcing that the frontier was thickly manned with Czechoslovak troops and that they were shooting anyone who tried to desert to Germany. Both statements were false, as was also another statement entirely without foundation which was broadcast from Germany to the effect that on Saturday night Sudeten-German deserters captured eleven soldiers of the Czechoslovak Army and took them into Germany.

" Still further evidence of the lying of the German propaganda is provided by the following incident: Not long ago, when private persons were being compelled to hand over any arms which they might possess, the German broadcasting stations protested that the Sudeten Germans possessed at most only old hunting rifles. Only last Saturday, however, there were found in the possession of Sudeten Germans at Ráj, near Frýstát, 200 hand-grenades and 220 lb. of explosives. These were, moreover, of German origin."

One could continue almost indefinitely with proofs of this sort, for in most cases the shameless lies which were a regular weapon of German propaganda could be very easily exposed. It is unfortunate, however, that this campaign of lying, accompanied by much threatening bluff, made an impression on the countries of Western Europe. I would nevertheless emphasise that, though this was its main objective, it made no real impression at the time on the Sudeten Germans, the vast majority of whom remained loyal to their duty as Czechoslovak citizens. In particular, the democratic anti-Nazi Sudeten Germans worked in faithful and loyal co-operation with the Czechoslovaks. I might perhaps mention, in confirmation of this statement, two further declarations which were made.

On September 27, the Executive of the German Democratic Youth Movement (which comprised numerous Socialist, Catholic, democratic, athletic and students' organisations) addressed the following manifesto to President Beneš:

" In this hour of fate, the German Democratic Youth of Czechoslovakia feels it necessary to assure you that it is ready to fight beside the other nationalities of this state in defence of the present frontier of our Republic. The mobilisation has incorporated thousands of young enthusiastic Germans into our Army, and thousands more are waiting for a sign from you to take up arms also if need should arise. We welcome the military measures which have been taken as a guarantee that the Republic has no intention of surrendering thousands of Germans who for twenty years, at the cost of very great economic and social sacrifices, have defended the ideas of our Republic.

" Considering Czechoslovakia as an indivisible unit, bequeathed to us by history, we wish to emphasise that only a democratic Czechoslovakia which offers equality to all its nationalities is able to assure national and social well-being to Sudeten Germans. As young Sudeten Germans, we want to prevent our life in the future from having to be spent in mental and social slavery such as German Fascism tries to impose upon our nation. We desire to continue to live and to work as free people in the Fatherland in which we were born and in which we have grown up. We are opposed to the transfer of the frontier districts, not only because it would deprive us of our freedom, but also because it would place Czechoslovakia in a terrible situation. The evacuation of the frontiers, which to-day are militarily occupied, would represent a serious danger to the future life of the Republic. In the past we have not been afraid to defend the democratic ideals of Czechoslovakia, and to-day we are not afraid to fight, arms in hand, for the integrity of our state.

" The German youth of all parties and all opinions is well aware of its obligations, and is united in firm determination to defend Czechoslovakia against external enemies as well as against their agents within our state.

" Upon us, dear President, you can unconditionally rely ! "

On the same day also (September 27) eight German Deputies and Senators belonging to the Communist Party issued a declaration in which they said : " We are expressing the desire of more than a million Sudeten-German democrats, Catholics, Socialists and Communists, as well as several hundreds of thousands of the former followers of Henlein, when we solemnly declare that the majority of Sudeten-German people refuses to be annexed to the Third Reich. We are absolutely at one with Czechoslovak democracy in our desire to defend the Republic, its democratic constitution and its territory against all armed aggression and against all blackmail. Henlein has no right to proclaim, in the name of the Sudeten Germans, his plan for the partition of Czechoslovakia. The Sudeten Germans who voted for the Henlein party did not vote for this plan, but for national equality within the framework of the Czechoslovak Republic."

These Germans were as good and as convinced German nationalists as were the followers of Henlein, but their will to stand side by side with Czechoslovak democracy in defence of the territorial frontiers of Czechoslovakia was not taken into consideration during the decisive international conversations. While the Czechoslovak mobilisation was going on, it became quite evident and convincing that a great part of the Sudeten-German people were sincerely devoted to the democratic Czechoslovak Republic, and that it was not only by verbal expressions of loyalty, but by acts of self-sacrifice and by their readiness to risk their lives that the German democrats proved their loyalty to the democratic Czechoslovak flag. What better proof could there be that there were other means of reaching a satisfactory solution of the Sudeten-German problem than the forcible disruption of the common life of Czechs and Germans which had lasted for hundreds of years. Furthermore, Czechoslovak democracy enjoyed at that time the fullest sympathy of German democrats other than Sudeten Germans. Their feelings were expressed in moving terms by the great German writer, Thomas Mann, who had become a Czechoslovak citizen only when he was deprived of his citizenship in the Third Reich, in his declaration published on September 28 in the *Die Volksillustrierte Zeitung*:

"I take the occasion of the twentieth anniversary of your Republic in order to express from the bottom of my heart to your brave State and people my sincere congratulations. Never before was I more proud and more thankful than I am now that I can call myself a citizen of the Czechoslovak Republic. It would suffice to explain my pride and pleasure in my association with the Czechoslovak nation to refer to its social and cultural achievements during the past twenty years. These feelings are enhanced, however, by this wonderful behaviour of our Republic during the hard test to which it is submitted to-day—behaviour which has justly earned the sympathy and respect of the whole world. It would be an unhappy Europe, a Europe ripe for slavery, that would leave in the lurch and abandon a State which is certainly prepared to make very great sacrifices in the cause of peace, but which, at the same time, stands up with touching determination against the will which aspires to bring about its destruction. The Czechoslovak nation is ready to undertake a fight for freedom, the importance of which greatly surpasses its own fate."

German authors living in exile in Paris sent on September 24 the following manifesto to Czechoslovak authors:

" Between you, the Czechoslovak authors, and us, German authors living in exile, is a fated association. Those dark forces which dominate our people and have driven us abroad threaten your people, your freedom and your culture. This association is no new one, but to-day the community of our ideals of freedom, peace, democracy and humanity is more evident than ever before.

" We have given proof, during several hard years of exile, that we are ready to fight for the irreplaceable basis of dignified human life, for we consider that life is valueless if lies, tyranny and slavery prevail. This gives us the right to say that we admire, and are thankful for, the preparedness, discipline and love of freedom which are evinced by the Czechoslovak people, united by the great humanitarian, Masaryk.

" In our thoughts and in our acts we are united with you, with the whole menaced Czechoslovak people, and especially with those German democratic citizens of the Czechoslovak Republic who to-day stand in the Sudeten-German territory as an advance-guard of freedom.

" In these moments which are, for you as well as for us, for your nation as well as for ours, equally terrible, we assure you of our entire solidarity. We greet you in the name of the fated association which unites us to-day in common anxiety and which, to-morrow, will unite us in common work for the future peace of our respective nations."

The mobilisation proved that we could rely on a great part of the Sudeten-German people and that the subversive Nazi Henleinist demagogy really only affected the unripe youth. At the same time, it provided an opportunity for a unique demonstration of the community of heart and mind between the Czechs and the Slovaks, a community which is not shattered by the semblance of things which occurred in March, 1939. It should be emphasised that the Slovak soldiers vied with the Czechs in the readiness with which they responded to the mobilisation order and in their willingness to make sacrifices. The leading Slovak politicians of all parties gave moving proof of their loyalty to a united state. Dr. J. Pauliny Toth, the President of the Slovak autonomist Protestants, proclaimed, even before mobilisation: " Slovakia and the Slovaks will not allow their Republic to be torn to pieces, whether by Hungarians, by Italians or by Poles. For us the Czechoslovak Republic is our only Fatherland and we shall fight for it to our last breath." *Slovák*, the official organ of Hlinka's party, wrote on September 25, in an article entitled, " All for the Defence of the Nation and the State ": " Let us be ready to defend our Fatherland, to defend the territory given to us by God, and to defend all those moral, material and national values which we have preserved many times by our own efforts, by our own knowledge and by our own blood. Our state is passing through a difficult time and we must help it; we must defend also our Slovak inheritance—our right to live as Slovaks, which was granted to us by our God and Creator."

The Association of Slovak Writers published a proclamation in which it was said:

" The Slovaks have awakened in the Republic to a new life. We feel the fated necessity of our present collaboration with the Czechs in the task of defending our state. We say to all Slovaks and Czechs: ' We would rather not exist than exist as slaves.' "

On September 22 and 23 the Deputy President of Hlinka's Slovak Catholic Party, Dr. Tiso, had important conversations

with the President of the Republic, at which the latter made
him a proposal regarding the realisation of Slovak autonomy
with a special Parliament and an autonomous administration.
This proposal was accepted on September 24 by the Executive
of the Slovak Catholic Party as a basis for negotiations. As early
as September 27 the most radical member of the Slovak autonomists, the Deputy Karol Sidor, announced in a radio broadcast
that Dr. Tiso, during his conversations with President Beneš,
had achieved everything that the Slovak nation needs, in
order that it may live in its own land and in Czechoslovakia,
and he went on to make the following appeal to the Slovaks:

" Be diligently obedient to the orders of your superiors
and of the national representatives. Only by such discipline
shall we assure the future of Slovakia and the integrity of the
Slovak land, our dear Country."

Between September 28 and 30 detailed conversations took
place between the Czechoslovak Government and the Slovak
representatives of all parties. In spite of all the understandable
difficulties with which they had necessarily to contend in
discussing such complicated questions, they arrived at an
agreement in principle—its implementation, however, was
spoilt by the catastrophic consequences of Munich. Successful
negotiations developed also with the representatives of Sub-
Carpathian Ruthenia regarding their representation in the
Government. It would be no exaggeration to say that the
mobilisation ranged side by side not only all the Czechoslovaks
and Ruthenes, but also, together with them all, the democratic
elements among the minority nationalities—in short, the whole
democracy of the Republic, whatever language it spoke, was
united in the defence of a just cause.

3. *The Attitude of the Little Entente and of Russia.*

The united will to resistance of the entire Czechoslovak nation
made a great impression on the other states of the Little Entente.
In Rumania, the number of declarations of sympathy and of
loyalty to the alliance steadily increased, and one of the
Rumanian divisional commanders, General Ion Anastasiu, even
went so far as to offer his services to the Czechoslovak Government.

Meanwhile the official policy of Rumania, directed by King Carol, was in all respects that of a loyal ally, who did not wish merely to confine herself to a narrow interpretation of the legal obligations of the treaty which bound her to Czechoslovakia. The time is not yet ripe for the publication of more intimate details with regard to Rumanian policy. It must suffice for the present to state what were its outward manifestations and to add that the Czechoslovak nation will never forget the faithfulness which was observed towards it during this difficult period by the Rumanians, under the leadership of King Carol.

We shall also remember with gratitude the unprecedented demonstrations organised by the Yugoslav people during this period. In all the larger towns—not only in Belgrade, Zagreb and Lyublyana, but also in the large towns in other districts—there were every day mass demonstrations in enthusiastic support of Czechoslovakia and in violent protest against the aggressive designs of Germany. These demonstrations were often pointed directly against the Government of Dr. Stojadinovitch, on account of its pro-German and pro-Italian policy. Consequently, an official ban was placed on all public demonstrations, but they continued all the same. Hundreds of Yugoslavs volunteered for service in the Czechoslovak Army. On September 27 the Association of Yugoslav *Sokols* came forward with a Resolution, which they forwarded to Dr. Stojadinovitch, declaring the loyalty of its members to their King and country and their readiness to make any sacrifice in that cause, and at the same time proclaiming their solidarity with their gallant cousins in the Czechoslovak *Sokols* and their faith in the triumph of truth and justice on the side of Czechoslovakia. Worthy of note among the numerous other public declarations of sympathy and solidarity with Czechoslovakia were those issued by the Yugoslav professors, authors and composers—signed by 150 well-known people, including over thirty university professors and some sixteen singers and actors of the National Theatre[1]—and by the Students' Peace Council

---

[1] " The Serbs, Croats and Slovenes regard the freedom and independence of Czechoslovakia as being of vital importance to the cause of truth and democracy, and as the surest guarantees of world peace and of the security of the Central European and Balkan states, as well as that of the national minorities within them "

in Belgrade, which called for the exertion of every effort by Yugoslavia in defence of the Czechoslovak Republic.[1] There can be no doubt, in fact, that the Serbs, Croats and Slovenes of every class were solidly in favour of the fullest co-operation with Czechoslovakia. If war had broken out, the pressure of public opinion in Yugoslavia would have forced the Government to range its forces immediately beside those of Czechoslovakia.

Similar demonstrations of public opinion in favour of Czechoslovakia took place also in Bulgaria.

The reaction of the smaller countries in Eastern Europe to the firmer attitude taken by Great Britain and France after Godesberg was striking. The moment that it seemed probable that the Western Powers would take definite action in opposition to Germany, the Central European countries began to give indications of their preparedness to stand up for themselves. It may be mentioned in this connection that Hungary was even at that time still very reluctant to associate herself with any action against Czechoslovakia. Her attitude was certainly affected by the increased firmness of the Western Powers after Godesberg, though more immediately, no doubt, by the action of the Rumanian and Yugoslav Governments. On September 25 the latter declared that, in the event of Hungarian aggression against Czechoslovakia, they would immediately fulfil their obligations towards the latter country. This declaration was made direct to the Hungarian Government, and the Czechoslovak Government was notified to that effect.

At that time also, Soviet Russia abandoned her attitude of reserve. It should in all fairness be pointed out that throughout the crisis Soviet Russia preserved an absolutely correct attitude towards Czechoslovakia, never for a moment leaving her in doubt that she would fulfil her obligations under the Pact of Mutual Assistance against Unprovoked Aggression which had been signed on May 16, 1935. These obligations were linked up with a certain procedure (stipulated in the text of the Pact) by the League of Nations, and, which was particularly important,

[1] " Czechoslovakia is in danger. We are irrevocably linked with our cousins in that country, because of our common struggle for freedom in the past and because of our present common danger. The threat to Czechoslovakia is a threat to peace, a threat to the independence of the smaller nations, and therefore a threat to us. Only by the united and determined resistance of every patriot and lover of peace in our two countries can Czechoslovakia be saved and our defence assured."

was conditional on the prior intervention of France. During the critical days before and after Berchtesgaden, the Czechoslovak Government put two questions to the Soviet Government:

1. Would the U.S.S.R. fulfil their obligations under the Pact of Mutual Assistance (i.e. would they come to the assistance of Czechoslovakia if France did so)? The answer was in the affirmative.

2. Would the U.S.S.R. fulfil their obligations arising out of their membership of the League of Nations? The answer was again unconditionally in the affirmative.[1]

The answers of the Soviet Government to both the questions put to it by the Czechoslovak Government were rightly considered to be so definite that, subject to the limitations mentioned in the footnote, Russian help for Czechoslovakia may be regarded as having been certainly assured. The Czechoslovak Government did not ask Soviet Russia to come to its assistance automatically, regardless of the terms of their mutual Pact, because it did not want to make it possible for Germany to declare a " crusade against Bolshevism." The Czechoslovak Government realised that, should this happen, the Western Powers, whose relations with Soviet Russia had been a trifle cold of late, might decide to adopt a passive attitude or perhaps even an attitude actively hostile to the Czechoslovak Republic. This attitude, we considered, might easily be adopted by Britain and France were Soviet Russia our only ally.

Certain Czechoslovak politicians (among them, be it noted, even some who were otherwise strongly opposed to Communism) considered the Government's anxiety in this respect somewhat exaggerated, especially since it was daily becoming more apparent that we could rely on no assistance from the Western Powers. Others, however, drew attention to the very reserved attitude adopted by Moscow with regard to the Central European crisis, and were doubtful whether Soviet Russia herself would be willing to intervene alone on behalf of Czechoslovakia against

[1] It should be added, in explanation of the foregoing, that a Protocol appended to the Soviet-Czechoslovak Pact of 1935 stipulated as follows: " It is also agreed that both signatories of this Pact will take steps in common to ensure that the Council of the League of Nations shall publish its recommendations as quickly as circumstances may demand, and that in the event of the Council failing, for any reason, to come to a decision, the obligation to assist would nevertheless be observed."

Germany. The Czechoslovak public was, on the whole, very grateful, of course, for Soviet Russia's loyalty towards their country, and for the fact that she, at any rate, far from trying to coerce their Government into making concessions to the Henleinists, was always warning them against making such concessions. The Russians, like Mr. Chamberlain himself in March, 1938, quite rightly maintained that the Czechoslovak Government should find a settlement of the minority problem within the framework of the democratic constitution. Any Henleinist demand which threatened to disrupt the Republic should not only have been disregarded but most strongly opposed.[1]

There were various stories in circulation during the Czechoslovak crisis regarding the intentions of Soviet Russia. In certain Paris and London circles it was stated (in such definite terms as to create an impression that the statement was based on official information) that Soviet Russia, conscious of her internal weaknesses and of the deficiencies of her armed forces, would refuse to fulfil her treaty obligations towards France and Czechoslovakia. It has subsequently been proved, of course, that these stories were not only untrue but were deliberately put about in order to confuse the public (and also the leading politicians) of Britain and France. As a matter of fact, the Soviet Commissar for Foreign Affairs, M. Litvinov, made a definite statement on September 21. He recalled that immediately after the annexation of Austria the Soviet Government had proposed to the Western Powers that they should discuss the consequences of this event, but that his proposal had been ignored.

" The Soviet Union," M. Litvinov continued, " bound to Czechoslovakia by a treaty of mutual assistance, has consistently refrained from any interference in the negotiations of the Czechoslovak Government with the Sudeten Germans, considering that these are a purely domestic affair of the Czechoslovak state. We have refrained from offering advice to the Czechoslovak Government, considering it inadmissible to advise it to make concessions to those whom it considers

[1] It must be recognised that the attitude advocated by Moscow, of refusing on principle any policy of concessions to Nazi expansionism, has been amply vindicated by the disastrous consequences to which the acceptance of such a policy has led.

guilty of prejudicing the interests of the nation, merely in order to absolve ourselves of the necessity of fulfilling our obligations resulting from that Treaty. Nor, on the other hand, have we given advice in the opposite sense.

" We have always appreciated the discretion of the Czechoslovak Government in not asking us whether we would fulfil our obligations in accordance with our Treaty. There is therefore no reason to imagine that our attitude in this matter was uncertain until, a few days before my departure for Geneva, the French Government addressed itself to us in order to discover what would be our attitude in event of aggression against Czechoslovakia.

" I gave, in the name of my Government, a perfectly clear-cut answer to the effect that we were determined to fulfil our obligations in accordance with our Treaty and to grant assistance to Czechoslovakia at the same time as France, by every means which is at our disposal. Our military authorities are ready to participate immediately in a Conference with the military representatives of France and Czechoslovakia, in order to determine what measures are required by the situation.

" Apart from that, we consider it advisable that the question should be brought before the League of Nations, if only under Article XI of the Covenant, in order

" (1) to mobilise public opinion and

" (2) to make quite clear the attitude of certain other states and their eventual active, or at least passive assistance.

" It is, nevertheless, necessary to make use of all possible means at our disposal for the prevention of armed conflict, and we consider that one of the measures suitable for this aim would be to call immediately a conference of the European Great Powers and other interested states in order, eventually, to prepare some collective action.

" About three days ago the Czechoslovak Government asked the Soviet Government whether it was prepared, in accordance with the Soviet-Czechoslovak Pact, to grant immediate assistance to Czechoslovakia, provided that France should honour her obligation by doing likewise. To this question the Soviet Government returned an immediate answer, in absolutely clear and positive terms. I think that it will be agreed that that was the answer of a loyal signatory of an international treaty and of a faithful defender of the League of Nations."

When, later on, reports began to circulate to the effect that Soviet Russia was making excuses to France, in order not to be obliged to fulfil her obligations, M. Litvinov explained, on September 23, before the Sixth Commission of the League of Nations that the operation of the Soviet-Czechoslovak Treaty was expressedly made conditional on France previously going to the assistance of Czechoslovakia:

" It was," said M. Litvinov, " the Czechoslovak Government which, at that time, insisted that mutual assistance between the U.S.S.R. and Czechoslovakia should be conditional on the assistance of France and that proviso was embodied in the Treaty. In other words, the Soviet Government has no obligation towards Czechoslovakia if, in the event of aggression against her, France adopts a negative attitude, and in that case would go to her assistance only as a result of a decision by the League of Nations in her favour. But nobody could say that such rendering of assistance is a duty, and actually the Czechoslovak Government has never raised the question of our assistance independently of that of France.

" After having accepted the Germano-Anglo-French ultimatum the Czechoslovak Government asked the Soviet Government what would be its attitude, or, in other words, whether it would consider itself bound by the terms of the Soviet-Czechoslovak Pact, if, Germany having presented further claims, and Anglo-German negotiations having proved unsuccessful, Czechoslovakia were to decide to defend her frontiers with arms.

" This second question was quite understandable, because, Czechoslovakia having accepted an ultimatum which envisaged the denunciation of the Soviet-Czechoslovak Pact, the Soviet Government undoubtedly had a moral right to denounce the Pact.

" Nevertheless, the Soviet Government for its part was not looking for a pretext for avoiding the implementation of its commitments, and replied that, even under the conditions referred to in the Czechoslovak enquiry, if France gave help to

Czechoslovakia, the Soviet-Czechoslovak Pact might be regarded as valid once more."

It must be admitted that Soviet Russia was quite right when she quoted the fact that she would be obliged to help Czechoslovakia only if France did so. It must be admitted also that Soviet Russia was never asked by Czechoslovakia for help outside the terms of the pact of mutual assistance. She cannot, therefore, be reproached with having failed to act in accordance with her treaty obligations. On the contrary, she showed in various effective ways that she understood the difficulty of the situation in which Czechoslovakia found herself and that she was ready to support her.

Soviet Russia's most important intervention during those critical days in September was the *démarche* which she undertook against Poland. On September 23 the Soviet Government informed the Polish Government that it would denounce the Soviet-Polish Pact of Non-aggression if the Polish Government persisted in sending troops to the Czechoslovak frontier. The Polish Government replied in a rather haughty manner to this Soviet Note, proclaiming that the Polish Government was not bound to offer anybody any explanation " of its defensive measures " and expressing surprise at the Soviet *démarche*, since no special military measures had been taken on the Soviet-Polish frontier. Nevertheless, the Russian *démarche* had an important influence on Warsaw. It may be taken as certain that if the two Western Powers had maintained that opposition, which was their first reaction to Hitler's ultimatum, Russia would have gone forward with them in a no less energetic manner, as was proved by the conversations between the British delegate at Geneva and M. Litvinov, the positive result of which was the issue by the Foreign Office of its definite communiqué in the evening of September 26.[1] The Soviet Government's intentions were very precisely defined in the Havas Agency's report from Moscow of September 27:

"A few days ago the Soviet Government announced, through the mouth of M. Litvinov, that, in view of the fact that Herr Hitler's unacceptable conditions had led France and

[1] See p. 183.

England to promise to help Czechoslovakia in the event of German aggression, it was likewise prepared to carry out its obligations. High authorities in Soviet Russia who had previously considered the situation as somewhat involved now consider that it has been cleared up. France and England have taken a stand on the side of Czechoslovakia, and there is no doubt whatsoever that President Roosevelt's declaration to Herr Hitler and Dr. Beneš has had a powerful effect in favour of world peace. It is considered that the world is only two inches removed from war and that only the close collaboration of the peace-loving Great Powers can prevent war. The diplomatic representatives of the Powers which are friendly towards Czechoslovakia, for their part, are quite convinced that the Soviet Government is perfectly sincere in its decisions to fulfil all its obligations towards Czechoslovakia with all its powers. It is considered to-day that the requisite conditions exist for the realisation of common agreement and for close military collaboration between England, France and Soviet Russia. The Soviet Government is willing to commence forthwith discussions to that end.

" On the other hand certain preparatory measures have been taken in Soviet Russia. Many tens of thousands of young workers, formed into regiments and divisions of all arms, have lately been carrying out real manœuvres in conjunction with the Regular Army in various parts of the Soviet Union. Thirty-five thousand young men are carrying out manœuvres in the Leningrad district, six thousand near Jaroslav, and many more thousands in Central Asia. Further manœuvres will take place in many other districts. New appeals are being sent to the Political Commissars and organisations of the Communist Party, urging them to intensify the campaign of recruiting men for service in the Army and Navy. One fact which is especially emphasised is that the recruiting of new naval units for service will entail an increase of the personnel of the Navy. Nothing can be seen yet to confirm the report that the mobilisation of reservists has commenced, but it seems that the Moscow barracks are more empty. A large number of lorries belonging to the Commissariat of Communications can be seen transporting groups of civilians who are accompanied always by a few men in the uniform of the Railway Militia."

I would mention finally, in this chapter dealing with the attitude of Soviet Russia—although, in doing so, I forestall what actually occurred—the Soviet Government's answer to President Roosevelt's proposal that an international conference should be held. The Note conveying this answer was delivered to Mr. Kirk, head of the American Embassy in Moscow, on September 28 and ran as follows:

" The foreign policy of the Soviet Union is inspired with a desire for world peace. The Soviet Union, renouncing the use of force in the settlement of international disputes, supported, at the time, the initiative of the Government of the United States in proposing, by the Kellogg Pact, that States should renounce war as an instrument of their national policy. In addition to this, at the suggestion of the Soviet Government, an agreement was signed on February 9, 1929, by the Soviet Government and numerous other States relating to the realisation of the Pact in its original spirit. In Central Europe events are occurring which threaten to lead to a world war.

" In this grave moment the Government of the Soviet Union cannot fail to appreciate the intervention of the President of the United States, who is appealing for a peaceful settlement of this conflict. The Soviet Government accepts gladly the proposal, addressed by the United States Government to the Government of the Soviet Union, to help in the prevention of war and in finding a peaceful solution of the present international crisis. The Government of the Soviet Union is investigating the obstacles which prevent Anglo-American mediation between Czechoslovakia and Germany, in spite of the willingness shown by Czechoslovakia to make sacrifices for the cause of peace. The Soviet Union considers the immediate calling of an International Conference as the most effective means of preventing eventual aggression and of averting a new world war. In March of this year, after the military occupation of Austria, an occupation which represented a threat to European peace, the Soviet Government proposed, in order to prevent very dangerous international conflicts later on, that a Conference should be summoned immediately, in order to devise practical ways of preventing aggression and of saving peace by collective effort. Faithful to its desire for peace, the Soviet Government is even now willing to support the proposal of the United States that an International Conference should be called, and is willing to participate actively in such a Conference."

All these facts go to prove the loyalty of Soviet Russia towards Czechoslovakia and the correctness of her attitude throughout the crisis. There was no reason to doubt that Soviet Russia would not fulfil her obligations if France did so. The Western Powers could have been certain that the immense might of Soviet Russia would be on their side, if they would take energetic steps against Germany. The question whether Soviet Russia could not, and if she could, why she did not react more actively during the September crisis does not arise. One of the most important reasons for this was certainly that she did not want to become involved alone in a war with Germany, which would have been almost bound, if Western Powers remained neutral, to lead to Japanese intervention against Russia in the Far East. There is no doubt, of course, that if the final fall of Czechoslovakia means a serious weakening of the Western Powers, and especially of France, a considerable loss was suffered also by Soviet Russia, whose position in Central Europe immediately became more difficult.

4. *Temporary Resistance by the Western Powers.*

The situation after Godesberg, as seen from Prague, showed one important improvement: The brutal attitude of Herr Hitler had opened the eyes of the Western Powers. They saw that no sooner did they make concession to Herr Hitler than he increased his demands, and that whenever he sensed their weakness, he adopted an aggressive attitude. They themselves had found by experience that it would be dangerous if they continued to give way to Hitler. This was why it was very important that France had partially mobilised, that the British Fleet had been called out and Czechoslovakia had been able to mobilise. The situation

of Germany had become less favourable: Britain and France had
begun to show signs of resistance to Hitler (they did not urge
Prague to accept the Godesberg ultimatum); Russia had made a
démarche in Warsaw; Rumania and Yugoslavia had warned
Hungary. The Czech newspaper, *Lidové Noviny*, very well
expressed the Prague view of the situation at that time:

" Our position has considerably improved, as a result of
our mobilisation and the events which accompanied it. . . .
We must not, of course, delude ourselves—we are still the first
to be attacked—but we now have the means of defending ourselves, and it would appear that this considerable change
has not been without influence in quarters where the decision
between peace and war will be made. We are not yet out of
the wood, but at any rate there seems no longer to be any
probability that a decision will be made about us, without our
being consulted. After the unfortunate experience we have
had, we cannot be certain that we shall not live to see further
pressure exerted on us from the West, but it seems improbable
that the negotiations for peace upon which we are engaged
can do other than end in a reasonable and proper agreement.
The lines of such an agreement have been suggested by Dr.
Beneš in his broadcast speech: ' It would be very much to the
advantage of our nation,' he said, ' that there should be a
reconciliation between France and England, on the one hand,
and Germany, on the other, and between us and Germany
and our other neighbours, and also that there should be
collaboration between us and the other States, more especially
those of Eastern Europe."

The achievement of this aim required, of course, a conference,
not a war, and a conference from which we were not excluded.
We were certain by this time that the policy of reaching a
" negotiated settlement " without any negotiation whatsoever
with the country chiefly concerned, was at an end.

" We all feel relieved," wrote the *České Slovo*, on the same
day, " at this definite abandonment of the shabby attempt to
decide about us—but without us."

There was good reason, indeed, to believe that the policy of the
Western Powers had reached a turning-point. This was proved,

not only by diplomatic reports regarding the attitude of the British and French Governments, but also by the articles which appeared in the Press of those countries. The Czechoslovak Press quoted at length an article entitled " Thus Far . . ." by Mr. Garvin[1] in the *Observer* on September 25, in which he wrote:

" The Nazi Power last week threw off the mask before the British Prime Minister and demanded in effect his total capitulation on their own soil. They counted that their armed advantage had made them already the masters of the earth. Not yet. If we are now forced to take up arms with no option left us but subjection, we shall never yield. Here we make the stand. Here we vow and dedicate ourselves utterly, if it should be required, to bear out that stand to the last breath. We shall undertake this and do it if we must so that the security of freedom shall be redeemed; and that bounds shall be set to open tyranny in such fashion as history shall for ever record and generations to come remember with thankfulness for as long as any freedom lives upon this earth."

In the Paris paper, *La République,* of the same date, Émile Roche, while pleading hard for an agreement with Germany and agreeing fully with the Anglo-French proposals, wrote:

" As we write, England and France are still trying to avoid conflict with Germany. . . . If Germany considers that she can take an advantage of this in order to enforce her demands by violence or by threats, it will not merely indicate that such a conflict exists, but would force on the attention of every Englishman and Frenchman the certainty of that conflict coming to a head. It may, perhaps, serve a useful purpose to make this statement now in this paper which indefatigably defends, and will continue to defend, peace—peace with honour and dignity."

These phrases were typical of those which appeared in the other organs of the London and Parisian Press, even those which were whole-heartedly in support of the official policy.

In proportion to our disappointment with the attitude adopted

[1] Garvin's attitude had been by no means friendly towards Czechoslovakia, especially during the months preceding the crisis.

by the Western Powers after the London Conference, were
our relief and gratitude as we received each report of the sympathy with the position of Czechoslovakia which was being
shown in those countries. The Czechoslovak papers were careful
to note every sign of this sympathy, and gave full publicity to the
impressive popular demonstrations in London and Paris. The
memorable declaration made by leading British authors, the
editorial remarks of newspapers, numerous articles and letters
written by various politicians and publicists in the Press, and,
indeed, every indication either of disapproval of, or of resistance
to, the fatal policy which had been embarked upon in London on
September 18 was received avidly and gladly in every corner of
the Czechoslovak Republic. The following three examples,
selected from among the many thousands of messages of encouragement which were received at that time, are indicative of
what was being felt in Britain and in France.

On September 23, the International Association of Authors in
Paris sent the following message to Czechoslovak writers:

" Jean Richard Bloch, André Chamson, Louis Aragon and
André Malraux (representing the French authors), H. G. Wells
(representing the British authors), and Bert Brecht (representing the refugee German writers in Paris) send herewith, as
a token of their absolute solidarity with the Czechoslovak
writers and with the Czechoslovak nation, the sum of 10,000
French francs which we have to-day collected from among
ourselves, and ask that this sum shall be considered as our
contribution to the Czechoslovak National Defence Fund.

" We hereby pledge ourselves to your country, which means
to us John Huss, T. G. Masaryk and Karel Čapek, and we
regard this action as a contribution to the cause of freedom,
without which culture cannot survive."

On September 21 a statement was issued by the British Labour
Party sharply condemning " the shameful surrender to Hitler's
threats and Britain's consent to the partition of the Czechoslovak
State." The statement added:

" It means the sacrifice, not only of a brave democratic
nation, but also of the interests of Britain, which are indissolubly linked with the sanctity of international law. Hitler's

ambitions will not stop short at Czechoslovakia, and no frontier, however remote, in Europe can henceforth be considered secured. Hitler's present triumph is only a prelude to further warlike adventures, which must eventually lead to a general war. Real peace is removed ever further from us by each surrender to force. If war is to be prevented and civilisation is to be saved, all the peace-loving nations must make a united effort to restore the rule of law."

The same day Mr. Winston Churchill published the following declaration:

" The partition of Czechoslovakia under pressure from England and France amounts to the complete surrender of the Western democracies to the Nazi threat of force.

" Such a collapse will bring peace or security neither to England nor to France. On the contrary, it will place these two nations in an ever weaker and ever more dangerous situation.

" The mere neutralisation of Czechoslovakia means the liberation of twenty-five German divisions, which will threaten the Western front; in addition to which, it will open up for the triumphant Nazis the road to the Black Sea.

" The acceptance of Herr Hitler's conditions constitutes the prostration of Europe before the force of the Nazis, who will gain very important advantages thereby. It is not Czechoslovakia alone which is menaced, but also the freedom and the democracy of all nations.

" The belief that security can be obtained by throwing a small state to the wolves is a fatal illusion. The war potential of Germany will increase in a short time more rapidly than it will be possible for France and Great Britain to complete the measures necessary for their defence.

" If peace is to be preserved in a lasting way, it can be done only by a combination of the forces of all those whose convictions and vital interests dictate resistance to Nazi domination. A month ago that was still possible to achieve, but the chance was lost."

Similar declarations became more numerous after Godesberg, and were regarded in Czechoslovakia as proof that resistance to the policy of force pursued by the Third Reich was stiffening rapidly in France and Britain. Thus the *České Slovo*, the central organ of the Czech National Socialist Party, wrote on September 25:

" Meanwhile, in the countries of Western Europe, there is a vigorous resurgence of the suppressed forces of resistance to the policy of sacrificing Czechoslovakia for the sake of a sickly chimera of peace. Such a peace is recognised as being in reality the humiliation of civilisation, and the spirit of freedom of thought throughout the world, before violence and the shameless plundering of the weak by the strong. The people of France and Britain are expressing their sympathy with us in a manner so overwhelming that the world cannot fail to be impressed. The future of our cause gleams bright before the eyes of a world which has suddenly become aware of the abyss of servitude, shame and desperation into which it will be plunged unless it checks itself on the brink. Surely everyone now realises that Czechoslovakia is only first in the line, and that if she falls, others too must sooner or later succumb. All over Europe resounds the slogan, ' Stand by Czechoslovakia !', as consciences awake and are translated into resistance, and we feel reassured again that we do not stand alone."

On September 24 it was generally known in Czechoslovakia that mobilisation on a large scale had been declared in France on the previous night and that important measures of mobilisation and defence were being taken in England also. Immense satisfaction was felt, moreover, when the news arrived in Prague that on the afternoon of September 23 M. Daladier had told a delegation of the Radical Socialist Party that in the event of Czechoslovakia being the victim of unprovoked aggression, France would, in accordance with her engagements, take the necessary steps to help her. This announcement meant, of course, that the bitter disappointment which had been felt by the Czechoslovak public on September 21 gave way to renewed confidence. There was a great sensation when it was learned that a general of the French Army (General Faucher) who had been in Czechoslovakia with the French Military Mission since 1919, and had been its chief since 1926, had asked the French Government to relieve him of his duties, and had placed himself at the disposal of the Czechoslovak Army. This gesture, by which a generous French officer protested against the attitude of his Government, made a great impression on the Czechoslovak public and rehabilitated in their eyes the honour of France. M. Bechyně was expressing the feelings of our whole people when he wrote in a letter to General Faucher:

" Your difficult and splendid gesture speaks to millions of Czechoslovaks. France, your Fatherland, will appreciate before long what a great service you have rendered her by your action. You are indeed a friend in need, and you have revived in the minds of us Czechoslovaks the picture of France eternal, great, generous and true. After the many hours of sorrow and humiliation through which we have passed because of some of your countrymen in Paris, you have now shown us the real France. During the last few days I have seen many men weeping in the streets, and have said to them, ' What are you crying about, you cowards ? We have still got our arms and our courage, so what is the use of weeping ? ' And they have answered me, ' We are crying because of the behaviour of the France which we loved.'

" In many a heart where that love has been dying, General, you have given it new life. We thank you."

Unquestionably one of the main sequels to Godesberg was a revival in the minds of Czechoslovaks of their affection for France, which had previously been dwindling, and of their deep sympathy for Britain. This was, of course, due to the fact that, both in France and in Britain, not only the public, but now the Governments also, were opposing Hitler's outrageous ultimatum, which had crudely exposed the expansionist designs of the Third Reich in Europe.

Mention has already been made of the fact that on the night of September 23–24 the French Government ordered a partial mobilisation,[1] and that on September 24 the British Government also took certain measures which amounted, in actual practice, to some sort of mobilisation of the British Army. These decisions clearly indicated that both Governments considered Hitler's

[1] The degree of mobilisation was extended on September 26.

demands to be inacceptable and were therefore preparing for resistance. This is proved also by the fact that the British Government, although it had forwarded the Godesberg Memorandum to the Czechoslovak Government, did not advise the latter to accept it. Similarly the French Government considered it impossible to advise Prague to accept it, and both in London and in Paris the representatives of the two Governments were in consultation with each other.

So far as the French Government was concerned, M. Daladier was now inclined to think that Germany should be resisted, an opinion in which he was confirmed by the knowledge that there was growing dissatisfaction with his policy of continual concession among the general public and even within the French Cabinet itself. Three of his Ministers (MM. Paul Reynaud, Mandel and Champetier de Ribes) had protested strongly against the ultimatum which forced Czechoslovakia to accept the London proposals of September 18 and had threatened their resignation. After Godesberg he inclined to agree with them that no further concessions should be made to Germany, a view which was shared by most of the important people in the French Army. The result was that, at the Cabinet meeting which took place on September 25, there was a sharp clash between M. Daladier and M. Bonnet, who was always in favour of further negotiations with Germany.

No less agitated discussions took place in the British Cabinet. In the evening of September 25 MM. Daladier and Bonnet flew to London for consultation with their British colleagues, which was resumed on the following morning. General Gamelin, Chief of the French General Staff, also attended these conversations. It is generally known that, though General Gamelin did not attempt to conceal the temporary shortcomings in the defensive preparations of France, he was nevertheless firmly convinced of the certainty and swiftness of a final victory by France, and that he made no secret of it.

On the Sunday evening (i.e. before the conversations with the French Ministers) the B.B.C. announced that on September 23 the British Government had informed the Czechoslovak Government that they considered the Czechoslovak mobilisation to be justified and that they could not recommend the acceptance of the Godesberg Memorandum, which they had delivered to them. It can be seen, therefore, that both official and unofficial opinion had stiffened very considerably against the acceptance of the German demands.

The Czechoslovak Government was informed about the contents of the Godesberg Memorandum on September 24, though the actual document was not handed to them officially until the night of September 24–25. It was at once submitted to careful examination in order that a detailed reply might be drawn up for the British Government. It was immediately obvious that the only possible answer would be a negative one, and it was in this sense that the Czechoslovak Minister in London, M. Jan Masaryk, drew up the Note which he handed to Mr. Chamberlain and Lord Halifax on Sunday, September 25.[1] This Note, which revealed clearly that it was the work of the son of our President-Liberator, T. G. Masaryk, ran as follows:

> " *September* 25, 1938.

" SIR,—My Government has instructed me just now, in view of the fact that the French statesmen are not arriving in London to-day, to bring to His Majesty's Government's notice the following message without any delay:

" The Czechoslovak people have shown a unique discipline and self-restraint in the last few weeks regardless of the unbelievably coarse and vulgar campaign of the controlled German press and radio against Czechoslovakia and its leaders, especially M. Beneš.

" His Majesty's and the French Governments are very well aware that we agreed under the most severe pressure to the so-called Anglo-French plan for ceding parts of Czechoslovakia. We accepted this plan under extreme duress. We had not even time to make any representations about its many unworkable features. Nevertheless, we accepted it because we understood that it was the end of the demands to be made upon us, and because it followed from the Anglo-French pressure that these two Powers would accept responsibility for our reduced frontiers and would guarantee us their support in the event of our being feloniously attacked.

[1] Note that this also took place before MM. Daladier and Bonnet reached London. This letter is published in Cmd. Paper 5847.

" The vulgar German campaign continued.

" While Mr. Chamberlain was at Godesberg the following message was received by my Government from His Majesty's and the French representatives at Prague:

" ' We have agreed with the French Government that the Czechoslovak Government be informed that the French and British Governments cannot continue to take the responsibility of advising them not to mobilise.'

" My new Government, headed by General Syrový, declared that they accept full responsibility for their predecessor's decision to accept the stern terms of the so-called Anglo-French plan.

" Yesterday, after the return of Mr. Chamberlain from Godesberg, a new proposition was handed by His Majesty's Minister in Prague to my Government with the additional information that His Majesty's Government is acting solely as an intermediary and is neither advising nor pressing my Government in any way. M. Krofta, in receiving the plan from the hands of His Majesty's Minister in Prague, assured him that the Czechoslovak Government will study it in the same spirit in which they have co-operated with Great Britain and France hitherto.

" My Government has now studied the document and the map. It is a *de facto* ultimatum of the sort usually presented to a vanquished nation and not a proposition to a sovereign State which has shown the greatest possible readiness to make sacrifices for the appeasement of Europe. Not the smallest trace of such readiness for sacrifices has as yet been manifested by Herr Hitler's Government. My Government is amazed at the contents of the memorandum. The proposals go far beyond what we agreed to in the so-called Anglo-French plan. They deprive us of every safeguard for our national existence. We are to yield up large proportions of our carefully prepared defences, and admit the German armies deep into our country before we have been able to organise it on the new basis or make any preparations for its defence. Our national and economic independence would automatically disappear with the acceptance of Herr Hitler's plan. The whole process of moving the population is to be reduced to panic flight on the part of those who will not accept the German Nazi régime. They have to leave their homes without even the right to take their personal belongings or even, in the case of peasants, their cow.

" My Government wish me to declare in all solemnity that Herr Hitler's demands in their present form are absolutely and unconditionally unacceptable to my Government. Against these new and cruel demands, my Government feel bound to make their utmost resistance, and we shall do so, God helping. The nation of St. Wenceslas, John Hus and Thomas Masaryk will not be a nation of slaves.

" We rely upon the two great Western democracies, whose wishes we have followed much against our own judgment, to stand by us in our hour of trial."

The Note delivered by M. Jan Masaryk informed the Western Powers, therefore, that Czechoslovakia considered Herr Hitler's Godesberg demands to be utterly and unconditionally unacceptable, and this view had, of course, to be taken into consideration during the Anglo-French negotiations. The far-reaching consequences of Herr Hitler's demands were described in detail by the Czech statesmen in a Memorandum which they completed in the evening of September 25. The Czechoslovak Government took steps also to inform the general public in their own country of the extent of Hitler's demands by publishing in the Press on September 26 the following communiqué:

" During the night of September 24–25 the British Legation in Prague, acting as an intermediary, transmitted to the Czechoslovak Government the Memorandum of the German Chancellor, Herr Hitler, which had been delivered to the British Prime Minister, Mr. Chamberlain, during his conversations at Godesberg. This Memorandum was received by the Czechoslovak Government on the understanding that it was based in principle on the Anglo-French proposals of September 19, which had been decided upon at Berchtesgaden and which they, acting on the advice of their British and French friends, had accepted, although they were aware of the heavy sacrifices which that acceptance would entail. They believed, however, that by these sacrifices they would assure the free development in the future of the Czechoslovak state and that they would obtain the international guarantees which were promised.

" A closer study of this Memorandum has shown clearly, however, that it is not a question of the Anglo-French Plan of September 19, but of quite new demands, which fundamentally go far beyond the framework of the Anglo-French proposals. This Memorandum represents, so far as one can understand it, entirely new demands made by Germany on Czechoslovakia in a manner which shows no desire to reach agreement, but merely a nakedly brutal design to destroy the viability and independence of the Czechoslovak state.

' The character of this Memorandum, which passes over in silence the question of possible guarantees of the Czechoslovak state, can best be seen from the fact that it abandons the basis of the Anglo-French proposals, which was the cession to Germany of Sudeten-German territory with a population more than 50 per cent. German and demands, in addition to those territories, further large areas which are predominantly Czech. The realisation of the German plan would mean the annexation by Germany of about 3,750,000 Czechoslovak citizens, of whom 2,800,000 are German and more than 800,000 Czechoslovak by race. Since the number of Czechs who live in the predominantly German parts of the Czech provinces is considered to be about 380,000, it is evident that the new proposal envisages the annexation of predominantly Czech territories containing nearly 450,000 Czechs.

" Moreover, the Memorandum does not stop short even with the satisfaction of this requirement, but demands that in yet other predominantly Czech territories a plebiscite should be held to decide whether they shall belong to Czechoslovakia or to Germany.

" The Memorandum concerns a territory with 1,300,000 inhabitants, of whom 1,100,000 are Czechs and 145,000 are Germans. It means that in all 820,000 Czechs would be annexed by Germany, while within the borders of the Czech provinces there would remain only 100,000 Germans. The figures are only approximate and are, of course, based on the Census of 1930.

" It is evident from this new Memorandum that the German Reich's Chancellor has put aside the pretext of self-determination and justice for the Germans in the Czech lands, and adopted a policy of demanding a territory which not only was never German, but also is not inhabited by racially German inhabitants. The Reich's Chancellor has not troubled even to mention the question of what guarantees of national existence would be given to the Czech minority in Germany, despite the fact that the present German nationality policy, as is practised to-day towards the Poles and Lusatian Serbs in the German Reich, is a policy of ruthless denationalisation.

" From the economic point of view, the territorial claims made in Herr Hitler's Memorandum also reveal a wish to destroy all possibility of independent life for the Czechoslovak Republic. They strike at the very foundations of the economic structure of Czechoslovakia by depriving her of vast industrial and agricultural resources. They disrupt her territorial integrity and break up her system of communications, not only in the Czech provinces, but indeed throughout the Republic. If these claims were conceded, the Republic would be deprived of all its industrial centres, with exception of Prague, Zlín and Plzeň, while the latter would, of course, be situated on the very frontier. Czechoslovakia would be deprived of her hop-production; she would be deprived of a large part of her forests, which are the basis for her paper and wood industry; she would lose the greater part of her iron, cotton, glass, ceramic, chemical and many other industries. All those industries, upon which depends the Czechoslovak export trade, would be destroyed or crippled. The natural result of this would be a lowering of the standard of living of the population and an increase of unemployment and of emigration.

" The Czechoslovak Republic would at the same time find herself faced with the new problem of looking after the masses of Czech and German people who would leave the territory annexed by Germany, for fear of the totalitarian and brutal Nazi régime.

" Closely connected with the economic losses with which Czechoslovakia is thus threatened are the catastrophic effects in the sphere of communications which the satisfaction of those claims would entail.

" The annexation of the territories demanded in Herr Hitler's Memorandum would cut the main rail and road communications of the Republic. Direct communication between Prague and North Slovakia would be impossible, as would also be communication between Prague and South-Eastern and Northern Moravia. The communications of the whole Republic would be disorganised and the state itself torn into three parts without any effective and direct communications between them. At the same time, Czechoslovakia would lose her docks on the Elbe and her access to Bratislava. In other words, she would be completely crippled.

" Compliance with Hitler's Memorandum would cripple the Republic also from a military point of view. The country, deprived of its natural mountain frontiers, narrowed by the tearing away of the vast German, as well as of the mixed and Czech, districts, and with its western portion joined with the eastern only by a narrow corridor, would be at the mercy of its powerful neighbours, and more particularly of Germany. This situation would be accentuated by the fact that the Republic would be deprived of its armament industries and of its principal defences, and would be unable, under the new territorial conditions, to construct new ones. In fact, compliance with Hitler's Memorandum would mean placing the whole of the western part of the Republic, i.e. Bohemia and Moravia, at the mercy of Germany.

" Since one cannot suppose that Hitler's Memorandum is based on ignorance of the nationality and economic situation of the Republic, one must regard it as deliberately designed to reduce the Czechoslovak state to a condition of absolute economic and political impotence and thus to prepare for the final domination of the Central European zone by the German Reich. The Czechoslovak Government has given ample proof of its sincere endeavour to solve the Sudeten-German problem by going to the utmost limits of concession, and even accepting the Anglo-French proposals as the basis for an agreement. This firm and definite desire remains unchanged by the formation of a new Government, under the Inspector-General of the Armed Forces, General Syrový, and this Government enjoys the confidence of all the Czechoslovak parties of the former Coalition Government.

" The Czechoslovak Government is persuaded that it is still possible to come to an agreement and to maintain peace, provided only that the Western Powers adhere to their proposals, which were agreed upon at Berchtesgaden and which were laid before the Czechoslovak Government on September 19 and were accepted."

This analysis should have sufficed to show that Hitler's Godesberg demands aimed at the complete destruction of Czechoslovak independence. But it should also be mentioned that the Anglo-French proposals, whose acceptance was forced on Czechoslovakia by the pressure of England and France on September 21, already dangerously threatened that independence. The Godesberg ultimatum went much further. Yet even so, when there were indications that the British and French Governments were preparing to put up serious resistance to Hitler's ultimatum, it was put about both in Britain and France by certain people who desired peace at any price (even at the price of the destruction of Czechoslovakia) that there were no fundamental differences between the Anglo-French proposals of September 18 and the demands made by Hitler on September 23. The only difference, it was argued, was one of procedure; it would therefore be a crime if war were permitted to break out merely on that account. Some of the newspapers even went so far as to publish maps purporting to show exactly what territory would be ceded to Germany under each of the two plans. The proposed new frontiers were, in both cases, so marked as to create an impression that Herr Hitler was not demanding much more than had already been proposed by the British and French Governments and accepted by the Czechoslovak Government. In order to maintain this tendentious impression, the territories in which (according to the terms of Herr Hitler's ultimatum) a plebiscite was to be held were not indicated. It needed no deep study, however, to see the great difference between the two proposals—

differences to which M. Daladier himself drew attention in a
speech delivered on October 4:

" When we left London we had the impression that our
plan would provoke indignant protest in Prague, but meet
with approval in Berlin.

" The Czechoslovak Government, in its heroic devotion to
the cause of peace, accepted that plan, but at Godesberg Herr
Hitler, in his interview with Mr. Chamberlain and in his
Memorandum, formulated new demands, regarding the
manner in which the plan should be carried into effect.

" That was why the progress of the negotiations, which had
been initiated as a result of Mr. Chamberlain's and my decision
to establish direct contact with the German Government and
seek a compromise, found itself arrested during the night of
September 23–24, and why, during the ensuing days, Europe
rushed towards a rupture of its peace.

" What, then, was the situation on September 24, at the
moment when Mr. Chamberlain arrived back in London from
Godesberg ? We had proposed the transfer to Germany of
those territories, inhabited by more than 50 per cent. of
Germans, in accordance with a certain procedure and up to the
limits which would be determined by an international commission. We had arranged for the exchange of population;
and we had offered the new Czechoslovakia an international
guarantee.

" What did Germany demand ? The immediate transfer of
certain territories and the creation of large plebiscite areas,
but without offering any real guarantees to the population
concerned, and without ensuring an international guarantee
for the new Czechoslovakia. It would appear that, so far as
Germany was concerned, she intended that the proposed
operation should assume the character of, and should have the
same effect as, a conquest, except that there would be no
recourse to arms.

" The divergence between the London plan and the Godesberg Memorandum was therefore obvious. It was one of
principle and of detail. Would it lead to a European war ?

" During those days of anguish two great tendencies became

evident in our country. We found them within every political party and within groups of all shades of opinion. One may say that these two tendencies vied with each other, under the influence of current events, in the conscience of every Frenchman. The first was to rely on negotiation; the second, to rely on firmness.

" So far as I was concerned, as head of the Government, I recognised, from the first moment, in both these tendencies the infallible instinct of the French people. I felt that the real solution lay in the synthesis of these two tendencies, and not in their rivalry.

" What the people of France wanted was to avert anything that would be irreparable—such as, for instance, German aggression. Such aggression, according to the terms of our Treaty, would have necessitated help and assistance by France. We should have asked you to honour your country's obligations.

" In view of the development of the German preparations, and to avoid the possibility of being surprised by a *coup de force*, we decided on September 24 on certain military measures which were intended, not as a provocation, but in order to put the country in a position to deal with any eventuality. Our military chiefs assembled our armed forces in order to be able to deal with anything which might occur. We did everything in order to defend ourselves effectively. Our military chiefs put our forces in a condition to fulfil their supreme duty to their fatherland.

" In London, we once more agreed with the British Government on concerted action. General Gamelin made a technical report on the effort we had already made and on those which circumstances might call upon us to make in the future.

" English and French alike, we were unanimous in our common desire for peace, as well as in our common will to oppose any aggression.

" In the evening of September 26, in an official communiqué issued to the Press in London, it was announced that if Germany attacked Czechoslovakia, France would go to her assistance and that ' Great Britain and Russia would certainly be on the side of France.' "

In the controversy which had arisen with those who maintained it was a matter only of " procedure," *Les Cahiers des Droits
de l'Homme* stated the real truth in its issue of October 1–15,
1938:

> " They consider, of course, as ' *procedure* ' the inclusion
> among those territories to be annexed and held by Germany,
> of regions where the German population does not attain 50 per
> cent.; the surrender to the Reich of all the material accumu-
> lated in the Czech fortifications; the provision of no guaran-
> tees for the lives and property of those German democrats and
> Czechs who would not wish to be exposed to the excesses of
> Nazism. Are these mere matters of procedure ? "

The differences between the London proposals and the Godesberg ultimatum can be summarised as follows:

1. The London proposals recommended the cession of terri-
tories in which more than half the population were German.
Hitler then demanded districts where less than 50 per cent. were
German, and even districts where the majority was Czech.

2. The London proposals refused a plebiscite. Hitler demanded
that a plebiscite should be held even in districts where there was
an unquestionable Czech majority.

3. The London proposals promised the " adjustment of
frontiers wherever necessary." This was taken to mean consideration for the vital necessities of geography, economics and
communications. Hitler simply claimed to dictate the frontiers
himself and would not tolerate any " adjustment." He even told
Mr. Chamberlain at Godesberg that his contribution towards
peace lay in the fact that he was now proposing a frontier which
was different from that which he would demand after a military
victory. A victory, it may be pointed out, which he would have
been unlikely to secure against the combined forces of Britain,
France, Czechoslovakia and Russia.

4. The London proposals assumed that the new frontier would
be delimited " under the supervision of an international body
which would include a Czechoslovak representative," and that,
until that delimitation was completed, the whole of the territory
concerned would remain under Czechoslovak administration.
Hitler, however, insisted on the immediate military occupation

(October 1) of the territories which he indicated. From this it was clear that what hè actually was aiming at was the occupation of strategically important positions and the surrender without compensation of all property in the occupied territories.

5. The London proposals envisaged the eventual exchange of population on a basis of the right of option, in order to be able to save the Czechs and anti-Nazi Germans from Nazi oppression. Hitler's ultimatum made no mention of this.

6. The London proposals promised Czechoslovakia " a general guarantee against any unprovoked aggression." In Hitler's ultimatum there was not a single word about this; Czechoslovakia was to be considered henceforth as a purely German sphere of interest.

It cannot be denied that the London proposals were very hard on Czechoslovakia and threatened the conditions essential for her independence. Yet, nevertheless, their realisation, especially if it had been discussed by an international commission in the presence of a Czechoslovak representative, and if, until its termination, Czechoslovakia had retained control of her military defences, still made it possible to ensure her the means of at least some economic and military defence, and thus the possibility of an independent existence. Whereas the Godesberg ultimatum demanded that Czechoslovakia should be delivered entirely into the hands of German domination. It was this ultimatum which was accepted in principle at Munich.

On September 25 and 26, however, London and Paris, fearing the consequences which have been described, and realising that Hitler wanted to achieve domination over the whole of Central Europe, still held out against the Godesberg ultimatum, and it was in this mood that the Anglo-French conversations terminated in the morning of September 26. Mr. Chamberlain described these events in his speech in the House of Commons on September 28:

" Conversations were resumed the next morning [September 26], when the French Ministers informed us that if Czechoslovakia were attacked France would fulfil her Treaty obligations, and in reply we told them that if, as a result of these obligations, French forces became actively engaged in hostilities against Germany, we should feel obliged to support them."

Having adopted this point of view and authorised the military experts to discuss the consequences which might result from this decision, the British and French Ministers agreed upon their " last effort " to save peace. Mr. Chamberlain himself has revealed the curious procedure which he adopted: " Meanwhile, as a last effort to preserve peace, I sent Sir Horace Wilson to Berlin on the 26th, with a personal message to Herr Hitler to be delivered before the speech that Herr Hitler was to make in Berlin at eight o'clock that night. The French Ministers entirely approved this initiative and issued a communiqué to that effect at midday." Mr. Chamberlain, in his letter sent to Herr Hitler by Sir Horace Wilson, proposed that immediate negotiations should take place between Czech and German representatives, in the presence of British representatives. His letter ran:

[Cmd. Paper 5847]   " LONDON,
                                  " *September* 26, 1938.

" MY DEAR REICHSKANZLER,—In my capacity as inter-mediary I have transmitted to the Czechoslovakian Government the memorandum which your Excellency gave me on the occasion of our last conversation.

" The Czechoslovakian Government now inform me that, while they adhere to their acceptance of the proposals for the transfer of the Sudeten-German areas on the lines discussed by my Government and the French Government and explained by me to you on Thursday last, they regard as wholly un-acceptable the proposal in your memorandum for the imme-diate evacuation of the areas and their immediate occupation by German troops, these processes to take place before the terms of cession have been negotiated or even discussed.

" Your Excellency will remember that in my letter to you of Friday last I said that an attempt to occupy forthwith by German troops areas which will become part of the Reich at once in principle and very shortly afterwards by formal delimitation, would be condemned as an unnecessary display of force, and that, in my opinion, if German troops moved into the areas that you had proposed, I felt sure that the Czecho-slovakian Government would resist and that this would mean the destruction of the basis upon which you and I a week ago agreed to work together—namely, an orderly settlement of this question rather than a settlement by the use of force. I referred also to the effect likely to be produced upon public opinion in my country, in France and, indeed, in the world generally.

" The development of opinion since my return confirms me in the views I expressed to you in my letter and in our subsequent conversation.

" In communicating with me about your proposals, the Government of Czechoslovakia point out that they go far beyond what was agreed to in the so-called Anglo-French plan. Czechoslovakia would be deprived of every safeguard for her national existence. She would have to yield up large proportions of her carefully prepared defences and admit the German armies deep into her country before it had been organised on the new basis or any preparations had been made for its defence. Her national and economic independence would automatically disappear with the acceptance of the German plan. The whole process of moving the population is to be reduced to panic flight.

" I learn that the German Ambassador in Paris has issued a communiqué which begins by stating that as a result of our conversations at Godesberg your Excellency and I are in complete agreement as to the imperative necessity to maintain the peace of Europe. In this spirit I address my present communication to you.

" In the first place, I would remind your Excellency that as the Czechoslovakian Government adhere to their acceptance of the proposals for the transfer of the Sudeten-German areas there can be no question of Germany ' finding it impossible to have the clear rights of Germans in Czechoslovakia accepted by way of negotiation.' I am quoting the words at the end of your Excellency's letter to me of Friday last.

" On the contrary, a settlement by negotiation remains possible and, with a clear recollection of the conversations which you and I have had and with an equally clear appreciation of the consequences which must follow the abandonment of negotiation and the substitution of force, I ask your Excellency to agree that representatives of Germany shall meet representatives of the Czechoslovakian Government to discuss immediately the situation by which we are confronted, with a view to settling by agreement the way in which the territory is to be handed over. I am convinced that these discussions can be completed in a very short time, and if you and the Czechoslovakian Government desire it, I am willing to arrange for the representation of the British Government at the discussions.

" In our conversation, as in the official communiqué issued in Germany, you said that the only differences between us lay in the method of carrying out an agreed principle. If this is so, then surely the tragic consequences of a conflict ought not to be incurred over a difference in method.

" A conference such as I suggest would give confidence that the cession of territory would be carried into effect, but that it would be done in an orderly manner with suitable safeguards.

" Convinced that your passionate wish to see the Sudeten-German question promptly and satisfactorily settled can be fulfilled without incurring the human misery and suffering that would inevitably follow on a conflict I most earnestly urge you to accept my proposal.

" I am,

" Yours faithfully,

" NEVILLE CHAMBERLAIN."

The initiative for this " last attempt " to save peace came from the side of Britain: Mr. Chamberlain suggested it to MM. Daladier and Bonnet. Mr. Chamberlain made up his mind to do something of this sort even before the arrival of the French Ministers in London. This was already apparent that Sunday afternoon, when, in the presence of Lord Halifax, he received the Czechoslovak Minister in London, M. Jan Masaryk, who handed them the Note, categorically rejecting the Godesberg ultimatum. Mr. Chamberlain realised that that ultimatum could not be accepted, but hoped to be able to find a way out by calling an international conference or a German-Czechoslovak Conference at which a British representative would participate. This Conference would decide how to bring into operation the Anglo-French proposals of September 18, and might at the same time

even grant some satisfaction of the Godesberg demands. It must
be realised that Mr. Chamberlain, even after Hitler's ultimatum,
never ceased to believe in the goodwill and pacific intentions of
the Chancellor of the German Reich, and was therefore convinced
that, if Hitler were satisfied with regard to the Sudeten-German
question, peace in Europe would be assured for a very long time.
He believed, moreover, the assurances given him by Herr
Hitler at Godesberg, that there would be no war on account of
colonies. This fatal miscalculation perhaps proves why he was
always so anxious to devise some means of satisfying Herr Hitler
with regard to his Sudeten-German demands. What he had in
his mind on September 25, when he spoke with M. Jan Masaryk,
is evident from the letter sent by the latter to Lord Halifax:

[Cmd. Paper 5847]   " LONDON.
                               "*September* 26, 1938.
  " SIR,—I have communicated to my Government the Prime
Minister's question which he put to me yesterday afternoon
and for which he wished an answer. This question of the Prime
Minister's, as I understood it, I transmitted to Prague as
follows:

  " ' Although Herr Hitler did say that the memorandum
handed to the Czechoslovak Government by His Majesty's
Government was his last word, and although Mr. Chamberlain doubts very much that he could induce Herr Hitler to
change his mind at this late hour, the Prime Minister may,
under circumstances, make a last effort to persuade Herr
Hitler to consider another method of settling peacefully the
Sudeten-German question, namely, by means of an international conference attended by Germany, Czechoslovakia
and other Powers which would consider the Anglo-French
plan and the best method of bringing it into operation. He
asked whether the Czechoslovak Government would be prepared to take part in this new effort of saving the peace.'

  " To this question I have now received the following answer
of my Government:

  " ' The Czechoslovak Government would be ready to take
part in an international conference where Germany and

Czechoslovakia, among other nations, would be represented, to find a different method of settling the Sudeten-German question from that expounded in Herr Hitler's proposals, keeping in mind the possible reverting to the so-called Anglo-French plan. In the note which M. Masaryk delivered to Mr. Chamberlain yesterday afternoon, mention was made of the fact that the Czechoslovak Government, having accepted the Anglo-French Note under the most severe pressure and extreme duress, had no time to make any representations about its many unworkable features. The Czechoslovak Government presumes that, if a conference were to take place, this fact would not be overlooked by those taking part in it.'

" My Government, after the experiences of the last few weeks, would consider it more than fully justifiable to ask for definite and binding guarantees to the effect that no unexpected action of an aggressive nature would take place during the negotiations, and that the Czechoslovak defence system would remain intact during that period.

" I have, &c.

" JAN MASARYK."

No further or more detailed information has hitherto been made public regarding the conversations between the British and French Governments, or the discussions which took place between their representatives from September 24 to 26. The outcome of these is, of course, known, and was the Munich Conference. It is obvious, however, that behind the scenes there took place a great struggle between those who favoured a firm stand and those who were for peace at any price, even if it meant the acceptance of the Godesberg demands. This lack of decision, which led fatally to Munich, was evident even during the period when Hitler was himself, by his exaggerated demands, forcing the Western statesmen to resist him. The general atmosphere of the conversations in London can be gauged from the following message from the Havas Agency in London, dated September 26:

" The presence of General Gamelin, Chief of the French General Staff, at the Conference of the British and French

Ministers which took place this morning [September 26] is enough to indicate the significance of those conversations.

" It is not unreasonable to assume that yesterday Mr. Neville Chamberlain and M. Edouard Daladier examined in the first place the diplomatic aspect of the problem arising out of the German claims in Czechoslovakia.

" The drastic character of the German demands could not but be unreservedly disapproved by the representatives of London and Paris, as well as being unanimously considered unacceptable by the public, both in England and in France.

" It is evident, therefore, that the British Government will maintain the attitude, which it has already adopted, of transmitting to Prague the terms proposed by the Reich, while taking the greatest care not to show any sort of solidarity with them.

" It is certain that the British Government intends to resist Germany if the latter insists on robbing the Czech people of their freedom, or on annexing part of their territory by force, but, nevertheless, it is expected that Mr. Chamberlain, in a last effort to maintain peace, will propose to the French Ministers that one last *démarche* be made in Berlin—' the very last concession to dictatorial methods.'

" Since Germany has had her radical demands satisfied in principle by the Anglo-French proposals, the French and British Governments might, in order to give further proof of their good faith, propose some means whereby the execution of their plan would be expedited.

" The evacuation of the Sudeten territories and the transfer of population might well be accelerated, though not necessarily to such an extent that it could be completed by October 1, which is the date fixed by Germany. After all, it is to the advantage of the Czech authorities that the existing state of tension should be relieved as speedily as possible on the basis of the settlement to which they have already given their consent.

" Germany would, in that case, have to declare herself for or against a peaceful settlement.

" It is to be hoped that the appeal made by Great Britain and France, which has received such timely support from the President of the United States, will be listened to in Berlin."

As the crisis came to a head, President Roosevelt had intervened by addressing an urgent appeal to Herr Hitler and Dr.
Beneš on September 26, in which he begged them " not to break
off the negotiations " but to find " a peaceful, fair and constructive settlement " of their dispute. In this appeal, which was
transmitted at the same time to Mr. Chamberlain and M.
Daladier, he said:

" It is imperative for peoples everywhere to recall that
every civilised nation in the world voluntarily assumed solemn
obligations in the Kellogg-Briand Pact of 1928 to solve controversies only by pacific methods. In addition most nations
are parties to other binding treaties placing them under an
obligation to preserve peace.

" Furthermore, all countries have to-day available for such
a peaceful solution of difficulties which may arise, treaties of
arbitration and conciliation to which they are parties. Whatever may be the differences in the controversies at issue, and
however difficult of pacific settlement they may be, I am
persuaded that there is no problem so difficult or so pressing
for a solution that it cannot justly be solved by a resort to
reason rather than by a resort to force.

" During the present crisis, the people of the United States
and their Government earnestly hoped that negotiations for
an adjustment of the controversy which has now arisen in
Europe might reach a successful conclusion. So long as these
negotiations continue, so long will there remain hope that
reason and the spirit of equity may prevail, and that the
world may thereby escape the madness of a new resort to
war.

" On behalf of the 130,000,000 people of the United States
of America and for the sake of humanity everywhere, I most
earnestly appeal to you not to break off negotiations, looking
to a peaceful, fair and constructive settlement of the questions
at issue. I earnestly repeat that so long as negotiations
continue, differences may be reconciled. Once they are broken
off, reason is banished and force produces no solution for the
future good of humanity."

President Roosevelt's appeal was thankfully received in Czechoslovakia, and it was in a similar tone that Dr. Beneš answered it immediately:

" Although it is Czechoslovakia who has already made the greatest sacrifices in the negotiations up to the present time, sacrifices which touch the country's vital interests, we are not breaking off negotiations, being desirous of seeing the conflict solved by peaceful means of agreement.

" Czechoslovakia also signed a treaty of arbitration with Germany and has already proposed to settle the present dispute under its terms and is ready to renew this offer.

" I believe that even to-day the dispute could be settled in a spirit of equity, without resort to force, and the whole Czechoslovak nation still hopes this will be the case.

" The Czechoslovak nation would defend itself if attacked, but it is profoundly convinced, with you, that in the end war solves no problem and that this is a case in which reason, a sense of humanity and the principle of justice should triumph."

Herr Hitler's reply maintained the Nazi leader's reputation for oratory. He did not forget to recall that the right of self-determination, proclaimed by President Wilson, was refused to the Sudeten Germans, nor omit the already familiar lies about Czech persecution of the Sudeten Germans. He ended as follows:

" I am convinced, Mr. President, that when you visualise the whole development of the Sudeten-German problem, from its inception to the present day, you will realise that the German Government has really not lacked either patience or the sincere desire for a peaceful understanding.

" It is not Germany's fault that there exists a Sudeten-German problem and that from it has grown the present impossible situation. The frightful fate of those human beings concerned in this problem allows of no delay in its solution. The possibilities of reaching a just settlement by union are thus exhausted by the proposals contained in the German memorandum.

" It now lies, not in the hands of the German Government,

but in the hands of the Czechoslovak Government to decide
whether they desire peace or war."

5. *The Counter-offensive of Germany, Italy and the Defeatists.*

During the days which followed Godesberg, however, there
was some misgiving in Germany lest Herr Hitler had overcalled
his hand. It was evident that he had not expected such a strong
reaction on the part of the Western Powers. Herr Hitler had
dared to deliver his ultimatum because he had been persuaded
by Herr von Ribbentrop in particular that England and France
would permit and would accept anything; but it now seemed
that Herr von Ribbentrop had either overestimated the influence
of those upon whom he relied in London and in Paris or he had
underestimated the strength of their opponents. It had clearly
become essential, therefore, that the rising tide of resistance in
France and in England should be checked, and the Nazis set
about doing this in the same manner which they had previously
found to be effective. They maintained a menacing attitude,
going on with their military preparations and even threatening,
in Herr Hitler's speech at the Sports Palace, a general mobilisation. This both intimidated the faint-hearted and provided
those who sympathised with the Nazi case with an additional
pretext for urging capitulation, owing to the necessity for the
" Führer " to save his threatened prestige. They strove, at the
same time, to prove that Germany had no desire for war, but
merely wished to win " justice " for the Sudeten Germans by
peaceful means, and that therefore Czechoslovakia's opposition
to the Godesberg proposals was an act of provocation. German
propaganda continued to insist that there was no difference
between the terms of the Anglo-French proposals of September
18 and those of the Godesberg ultimatum, and that, since
Czechoslovakia had accepted the former, France need no longer
consider herself bound by her treaty obligations to help her in
opposing the latter.

The Czechoslovak mobilisation was described as an act of
provocation, and, although it was known that Britain and
France had approved it, the Germans put it about that it had
been proclaimed at the instigation of Soviet Russia, who was
urging Prague on to war. Bands of Henleinist *Freikorps* were

sent to provoke riots and fighting on the Czechoslovak frontiers, which were very much exaggerated in the German reports, while Dr. Goebbels' workshop turned out tales of the persecution and killing of Sudeten Germans. Czechoslovakia was presented to the world as a peace-breaker and a country who was deliberately provoking war—her pacts guaranteed her only against " unprovoked aggression."

Meanwhile, with a tireless flow of partisan rhetoric, the Duce supported the Führer. In a speech delivered at Padua on September 24, he spoke of General Syrový, the head of the new Czechoslovak Government, as " a general whom everyone considered as being very well-disposed—indeed, too well-disposed—towards Moscow." and demanded that " the problem which now presented itself before the conscience of the nations should be thoroughly and finally solved." In Bellona, on the same date (September 24), he said of the French: " They do not know us and they are too stupid to be dangerous." When he began to realise that Britain and France were stiffening in their opposition, and felt that he should therefore double the force of his threats and menaces, while leaving the door open for retreat, his tone became more and more bellicose and pro-German, and his suggestion of " localised war " more practical. At Verona on September 26 he declared:

" The German Memorandum does not depart far from the terms of the proposal approved at the London Conference. It is evident that if the Czechs were left to their own resources, they would be the first to recognise that it was not worth while to become involved in a conflict, as to the result of which there could be no doubt. Now that the problem has presented itself in its three aspects (German, Hungarian and Polish) owing to historical forces which cannot be resisted, it should be solved thoroughly, and there is at this moment one man above all in Europe who must answer for what is happening, the President of the Czechoslovak Republic. He was the most obstinate, if not the greatest among those who disrupted the Austro-Hungarian monarchy. At that time he was already speaking about a Czech nation and writing about it in *The Czechoslovak Nation*, and was travelling everywhere, going even to Geneva. . . .

" If this conflict breaks out, it can be localised at the beginning. I myself still believe that Europe will not want murder and arson and that it has no desire to burn itself in order to ' cook the rotten egg of Prague.'

" One must, however, envisage a third possibility, i.e. one in which the character of the conflict will be such as to draw us in directly: if that occurs, we shall not hesitate at all, nor will we allow any hesitation. . . .

" It is useless for the diplomats to tire themselves in trying to save Versailles and the Europe which was constructed there, often with a colossal ignorance of geography and of history. The Versailles settlement is in its agony; its fate will be decided this week; and it will be during this week that a new Europe will be able to come into being, a Europe of justice for all and of reconciliation between the nations."

On the same day, speaking in Vicenza, he said suggestively:

" Hitherto Italy has taken no steps of a military character. But if the others continue to call up their reservists and to mass them on the frontiers, and if there are further naval concentrations, no one must be surprised if Italy also takes its measures."

By these speeches Mussolini rendered excellent service to Hitler. However, the latter deemed it politic to resume the initiative by concentrating interest on himself, and it was to this end that he delivered his warlike speech at the Sports Palace in Berlin. Not a letter of his Godesberg ultimatum was retracted. First, he threatened: " We have created such armaments as the world has never seen before. Now, German people, wear those arms ! " Then he tried to reassure his potential opponents: " Alsace-Lorraine does not exist for us. . . . All the territorial disputes between Germany and France are now suppressed." " I have held my hand out to England." He spoke of the agreement with Poland. Then he came to the Axis: The German and Italian nations " from the doctrinal and political point of view, linked themselves in a narrow and indissoluble friendship." The Austrian problem " was solved for the happiness of the entire great German nation. And here we are to-day," he continued, " face to face with the last problem which should, and will, be solved. This is the last territorial claim which I have to make in Europe, it is a claim which I will not abandon." He then passed on to the historic attack by the head of one state on the head of another, an attack which, though all three countries were nominally at peace, was echoed in the speeches of Mussolini: " The Czech State was founded on an unprecedented lie, and the father of that lie was called Beneš" [shouts: "Pfui!" " Hang him ! "].

Herr Hitler's speech was a very clever one. Relying on the insufficient knowledge of the problem in question which was prevalent in the West, he perverted the facts, and appealed to the peace-loving tendency which is deeply rooted in the Western democracies by promising peace to England and France. He argued that he was trying to obtain only what had already been accepted by the Czechoslovak Government and put on President Beneš all the blame for the threatened catastrophe of war.

We had experienced these tactics before and, in Czechoslovakia no one was particularly impressed. All our newspapers were unanimous in refuting Hitler's grossly offensive attacks, so full of inventions and lies, while our radio drew attention to the fact that during the Reich's Chancellor's speech the crowded audience could be heard shouting in rhythm: " We want war ! " The general opinion prevailed that Hitler's attempt to deceive Western European opinion by his peaceful assurances would not succeed. Faith in the Western democracies, and more especially in the United States of America, where Germany's aggressive attitude was provoking ever-growing resentment, had revived after Godesberg. This faith became more firmly established and was greatly strengthened when on the evening of September 26, while Hitler was actually delivering his speech, the British Foreign Office issued its notable communiqué, saying:

" It was authoritatively stated last night that during the last week Mr. Chamberlain has tried with the German Chancellor to find a way of settling peacefully the Czechoslovak question. It is still possible to do so by negotiations.

" The German claim to the transfer of the Sudeten area has already been conceded by the French, British and Czechoslovak

Governments, but if in spite of all efforts made by the British Prime Minister a German attack is made upon Czechoslovakia, the immediate result must be that France will be bound to come to her assistance, and that Great Britain and Russia will certainly stand by France.

"It is still not too late to stop this great tragedy, and for the peoples of all nations to insist on settlement by free negotiation."

Prague opinion at this time was very well described by the *Lidové Noviny* of September 27:

" Let us recognise the fact that Western Europe regards the demands made in Herr Hitler's memorandum as incompatible with the essential requirements of our state, and that therefore it does not consider them as identical with those of the London proposals.

" Let us recognise also the cardinal fact that Western Europe and, of course, also Soviet Russia approve of our preparations for the defence of our Country, and that France, England and Soviet Russia, for their part, have made such preparations as their interests demand and as are dictated by their international position and obligations.

" At the moment when Hitler, in his Berlin speech, was striving to force acceptance of his most extreme demand, Mr. Roosevelt's message of peace and conciliation, of reason and agreement, passed along the cables all over the world. To this message the President of the Czechoslovak Republic was able immediately to reply with his unconditional and whole-hearted agreement.

" Will this voice from another world, the voice of a real democracy, be heard ? Whether it is or is not, our armies stand by at the frontiers."

The actual course of events destroyed the hopes which were entertained in Prague, where, following on the mobilisation, all preparations had been made for putting the whole nation in a state of complete readiness for the defence of the State. Since September 26 the activities of the Western pacifists, whose attitude was one of complete defeatism, had become intensified.

Herr Hitler's speech at the Sports Palace was seized upon in certain interested quarters, and quoted as evidence that he had no aggressive designs upon either France or Great Britain. The speech was used as an argument to persuade the British and French public, exactly as it was intended by Hitler and Mussolini, that it would be ridiculous if war should break out merely over a question of procedure and over a matter which did not concern them. The vital strategic and military importance of Czechoslovakia as the ally of a Britain and France in acute danger from an aggressive Germany was steadily concealed. This type of defeatism, amounting to the cynical betrayal of national interests, was particularly prevalent in France, where *Le Temps*, on the afternoon of September 26 (in an issue dated September 27), published a letter from M. Pierre Étienne Flandin, in which he said:

" If the Government proposes that in due course France should afford military assistance to the Czechoslovak state, it is clear that this assistance cannot be afforded except in proportion as, and on condition that, similar military assistance may be agreed upon, in application of Article XVI of the Covenant of the League of Nations, by the other contractual parties which still recognise the validity of that Covenant, and especially by Great Britain.

" It is evident therefore that the French Government could not order a general mobilisation unless the same measure is taken in the British Empire; it being understood, of course, that mobilisation would entail the introduction of conscription in the British Empire, where it does not at present exist.

" Our British friends should, in all loyalty, be informed— and I have no doubt that MM. Daladier and Bonnet have done this—that the French Army would be unable alone, or even with the help of a small British contingent, to bear the strain of land operations on three fronts. Everybody knows that our classes of 1914–19, which are precisely those which would be the first engaged, are commonly known as the *classes creusés*, because they correspond with the deficient birth-rate of the war years. The French people would have difficulty in getting on its feet again, even if it were victorious, after the heavy loss of human life which infantry warfare involves. The French Government, though it need not exaggerate its insistence on the principle of equal sacrifices, since that principle is in keeping with the noble and generous character of the British nation, would have to agree with the British Government upon a plan for the earliest possible intervention of units of the British Army, equal in numbers, at least, to those which were engaged in the War of 1914–18. Such intervention must take place with far less delay than in 1914, since we may anticipate having to face an appreciably greater number of enemy divisions than during the last war, while, at the same time, we ourselves would be without the assistance which we then enjoyed."

On the following day, M. Flandin posted up in the streets a proclamation, which actually incited people to refuse to comply with any military measures. The proclamation was immediately confiscated. Undaunted, the French defeatists even went so far as to expose the military shortcomings of their fatherland to the admiration of the world. Afraid lest the British might be too active, they exaggerated their own military weakness, while at the same time trying to frighten Britain by their demand that she should immediately introduce general conscription and undertake beforehand the responsibility of financing the war. The suggestion, included in the letter from M. Flandin, quoted above, were made use of also in confidential diplomatic conversations. Attention was drawn to it also in the article in *L'Europe Nouvelle* which is quoted in Chapter II, 4. Absolute panic was created in French parliamentary circles; French deputies of different parties united to send resolutions or delegations to the Prime Minister and Foreign Minister, or even to the President of the Republic, asking urgently that negotiations with Germany should be continued. At the same time, they asked that Parliament should be summoned, in order that it might express its opinion on the matter of general mobilisation, and on the question of war or peace. Nearly all the Parties repeated some modification of the declaration which had been made on September 27 by the Members of the Opposition of the Right and of the Centre, namely that they considered it impossible that

" a matter which had been settled in principle should lead to hostilities on account of its method of execution." Much propaganda was devoted to the idea that the Communists were deliberately urging the world into a war, from which Bolshevism alone could profit. The fearsome imaginings which others merely hinted at, Charles Maurras fully described in *L'Action Française* of September 26:

" Will the slaughter go on for so long as in 1914–18 ? The chances are that it will be more bloody. And for whom ? And why ?

" The only one who will benefit will not even be some miserable politician like Cot or Mandel, but the decadent revolutionary, the great Slavo-Germanic anarchist, who will burst upon us in the West, as in the era of the great invasions.

" Nevertheless it would be better to follow the English proverb: ' Wait and see '; to wait, but to go on arming, rearranging all our alliances and reconstructing our own State.

" There is no doubt that Hitler may attack us.

" All right. If he does, we will react by simply defending ourselves and that will give our morale some of the advantages which we held in 1914. But to attack as in 1914, shouting ' To Berlin ! To Berlin ! ' and to allow ourselves to be brought back lamentably to Pantin and to Aubervilliers would serve but one cause, that of a new Commune under the colours of Moscow."

Anyone who opposed the ruthless demands of Germany, anyone who drew attention to the fact that the sacrifice of Czechoslovakia would bring about a dangerous weakening of France or dishonour the name of Britain, was declared a " war-monger," or a " Bolshevik." The defeatists in Britain and France made out that either Germany must be satisfied or war would break out. They thereby concealed the possibility, if the Anglo-Franco-Russian *bloc* were to stand firm, that Germany would become afraid of a war against a European coalition. In Paris, people could even be found who declared that the British Foreign Office communiqué of September 26 was " a suspicious falsification," though that communiqué was actually written by Lord

Halifax himself. This was perfectly well known in well-informed quarters in Paris, even during the period September 26–28, yet nevertheless publicity was deliberately given to the assertion that it was not authentic ! For the same reason, when the German official agency, during the night of September 27–28, denied the report regarding the announcement of general mobilisation in Germany for the afternoon of September 28, the French defeatists immediately gave publicity to the denial and accused those responsible for the report of being deliberate panic-mongers. Yet the report in question had been sent from Berlin by both Reuters and the Havas Agency, and its accuracy was admitted later by both Mr. Chamberlain and M. Daladier. Mr. Chamberlain, in his speech of September 28, said that Herr Hitler announced to Sir Horace Wilson his intention of proclaiming a general mobilisation at 2 p.m. on September 28. The same thing was said by M. Daladier in his parliamentary speech of October 4. In addition to that it has been officially stated that on September 27, at 5.40 p.m., Mr. Chamberlain sent a telegram to President Beneš informing him that, " according to the information which His Majesty's Government has received from Berlin," the German Army would probably invade Czechoslovakia the next day,[1] if by 2 p.m. (September 28) the Czechoslovak Government had not accepted Germany's conditions. While messages of this sort were passing between the Allied Governments, the French public was being informed that the report of German mobilisation was the invention of the " war-mongers " !

At the head of this campaign of defeatism in France was one of the leading French politicians, M. Flandin, who had, it must be admitted, the courage to act openly, whereas the majority of the other politicians who shared his views kept well in the background. This defeatism was most clearly evident in the parties of the Right and Right Centre, but it infected also the parties of the Left, as was shown by the resolution adopted by the Socialist teachers and postal officials, to whom pacifism, it must be remembered, is already a tradition. Their delegation was received, ironically enough in the circumstances, by the Minister of

---

[1] This message from Mr. Chamberlain to President Beneš is given in full on p. 194, below.

Foreign Affairs, M. Bonnet, to whom they handed the following appeal:

" We have no desire for war.

" At this grave hour, confident that we are expressing the sentiment of the vast majority of the French people, we declare our desire for a peaceful settlement of the present international crisis.

" Inasmuch as, only a few days ago, it was believed that agreement was possible and that the question of principle had been settled, how can it now be permitted that, on account of a matter of procedure, of self-respect, or of prestige, the statesmen should suddenly break off negotiations which have been going on for several weeks and should plunge the whole of Europe into the most terrible of wars ?

" We beg the French Government to persist in its negotiations, without letting itself be discouraged by the difficulties which it experiences.

" We beg that, during these negotiations, the French Government will bear in mind the intense desire for peace of its people, which has left so many victims on the battle-fields of Europe.

" We beg that due heed may be paid to the common-sense statement of President Roosevelt: ' It is necessary to make peace before, rather than after, a war. Force brings no solution for the future, nor for the good of humanity.' "

These views were shared also by a great part of the Radical Socialist and Socialist parties, who thereby, if not always actively, at least by their tacit consent, furthered the policy of defeatism.

There were, of course, many politicians and journalists who were in opposition to it, prominent among the former being the Ministers, MM. Mandel, Paul Reynaud and Champetier de Ribes, while the latter included the Deputy M. de Kérillis (*L'Époque*), M. Émile Buré (*L'Ordre*), " Pertinax " (*L'Europe Nouvelle*), M. Bidault (*L'Aube*), M. Jean Pupier (*La Journée Industrielle*), and MM. Leroux, Lévy and Rosenfeld (*Le Populaire*); as well as nearly all the British and French correspondents in Prague. There were also other newspapers which opposed the policy, such as *Le Petit Bleu, Les Cahiers des Droits de l'Homme* (in which MM. Dominois, Ancel, Mazon and Enfiére wrote with great vigour) and *La Bataille Socialiste* (M. Zyromski's paper). The opponents of the French Government were nevertheless in the minority and, having access to fewer public platforms and other means of publicity than their rivals, were forced to remain on the defensive. People like Blum and Herriot remained passive, much to their own embarrassment, as was candidly and succinctly confessed by the former when, at the time of the acceptance by Czechoslovakia of the London proposals, he said: " My feelings are a mixture of cowardly relief and of shame." The only Party which was consistently opposed to capitulation to Germany was the Communist Party; all the other Parties were divided on the issue into sections favouring " peace " and " resistance " respectively. In fact, France passed through a serious and profound political and moral crisis. The divided state of opinion had a paralytic effect on the Government, and was a source of considerable embarrassment to the Prime Minister and some of the other Ministers. M. Georges Bonnet, however, never wavered from his consistent advocacy of " peace," rather than " resistance," and thereby enjoyed a certain advantage over his colleagues. The attitude maintained by M. Bonnet and his followers found sympathetic expression in an editorial article in *Le Temps* of September 28 as follows:

" In yesterday's speech, Herr Hitler referred to the possibility of withdrawing his troops from the Sudeten-German districts which they had occupied, while a plebiscite was held. Order would be maintained in these districts by the British Legion, which seems to have volunteered for that duty.

" If that is really all that is meant by that passage in the Führer's speech, it might be accepted as a basis for negotiations.

" If one goes into the matter thoroughly, one cannot help coming to the conclusion that the situation can be summed up briefly as follows:

" 1. The Prague Government, acting on the advice of Great Britain and France, agreed to transfer to Germany those regions in which there is a German majority.

" 2. The German Government interprets this agreement as applying to a much larger area than Prague will recognise, but is apparently prepared to accept the proposal that a plebiscite shall be held under conditions which will be defined in due course, but which seem to be strict ones.

" 3. Having no faith in the sincerity of the Prague Government, Hitler is demanding the evacuation of the Czech forces from the greater part of the region concerned and its occupation by German troops by October 1. He is insisting also that no material shall be destroyed before this transfer.

" Regarded in this manner, the problem should not be insoluble. Questions regarding the size of the areas in which a plebiscite should be held and the method in which it shall be conducted can be, and indeed should be, settled by negotiation or arbitration.

" Then there is still the matter of the date of October 1. This it is which gives an unpleasant character to the Godesberg Memorandum, but, in his speech yesterday, Herr Hitler emphasised that this character was due only to fear that Czechoslovakia would not carry out the obligation which she had accepted.

" But, in a statement issued last night, i.e. after Herr Hitler's speech, Mr. Chamberlain said Great Britain and France would give some sort of guarantee to Czechoslovakia in return for the promise made by the Prague Government. He added that the British Government was ' prepared to ' give an undertaking ' that this promise of assistance would be honoured within a reasonably brief period, on condition that the German Government, for its part, would consent to the settlement of questions relating to the conditions of the transfer of territory by discussion and not by force.' Sir Horace Wilson, who saw Herr Hitler at noon to-day, must have informed him of this attitude. . . . That is indeed the crux of the matter. It is not insoluble, like a Gordian knot, and there is no need of a sword to cut it."

Such articles hardly do honour to the intelligence or integrity of French politicians.

More depended on France than on England, not only because

French interests were more immediately involved in Czecho-slovakia, but primarily because France possessed the best Army in the world. Alas, it was precisely during the period when the international crisis reached its summit and when there was need of the greatest firmness and decision which Herr Hitler, together with Signor Mussolini, would have had to respect, that political anarchy reached its maximum in France. Consequently, the defeatist forces gained ground and finally overwhelmed the straightforward party of " resistance." Under such circumstances, Mr. Chamberlain's " conciliation attempts " were made easy. Though the British Prime Minister and his followers met, even in Mr. Chamberlain's own party and especially in British public opinion, far greater resistance than M. Bonnet himself had to overcome, these two, in close alliance, carried the field in their respective countries. Thus the road to Munich was opened.

1. *The Last Attempts at Conciliation by Mr. Chamberlain.*

I HAVE mentioned that on the morning of September 26 the
British and French statesmen decided to make one " last
attempt " to save peace. This attempt took the form of Mr.
Chamberlain sending his adviser, Sir Horace Wilson, to Herr
Hitler with a letter, in which he suggested that further negotiations should take place at a German-Czechoslovak conference,
in the presence of a British representative. Sir Horace Wilson
went to Berlin by air and was received there by Herr Hitler at
5.30 p.m. on September 26. Herr Hitler told him (according to
Mr. Chamberlain's statement in the House of Commons) " that
he could not depart from the procedure of the Memorandum, as
he felt conferences would lead to further intolerable procrastina-
tions." This argument was used publicly that same night by Herr
Hitler in his bellicose speech at the Sports Palace. Mr. Chamberlain was persuaded that Herr Hitler had, as he expressed it, a
deep-rooted " lack of confidence " in the Czechoslovak Government and that it was necessary, therefore, to dissipate this
unfortunate impression. This was the reason why Mr. Chamberlain published, at 12.30 a.m. that night (September 26–27), the
following statement:

" I have read the speech of the German Chancellor and I
appreciate his reference to the efforts I have made to save the
peace.

" I cannot abandon those efforts, since it seems to me
incredible that the peoples of Europe, who do not want war
with one another, should be plunged into a bloody struggle
over a question on which agreement has already been largely
obtained.

" It is evident that the Chancellor has no faith that the
promises made will be carried out. These promises were made,
not to the German Government direct, but to the British
and French Governments in the first instance. Speaking for
the British Government, we regard ourselves as morally

responsible for seeing that the promises are carried out fairly
and fully and we are prepared to undertake that they shall be so
carried out with all reasonable promptitude, provided that
the German Government will agree to the settlement of terms
and conditions of transfer by discussion and not by force.

" I trust that the Chancellor will not reject this proposal,
which is made in the same spirit of friendliness as that in
which I was received in Germany and which, if it is accepted,
will satisfy the German desire for the union of the Sudeten
Germans with the Reich without the shedding of blood in any
part of Europe."

At the same time, Mr. Chamberlain tried to persuade Prague,
not only to accept his proposal of further negotiations with Germany, but to consent in advance to the rapid transfer of the
Sudeten-German territory. I have mentioned above that on
Sunday, September 25, Mr. Chamberlain had intimated to M.
Jan Masaryk that Prague should consent to negotiate " through
an international conference in which Germany, Czechoslovakia
and other Powers would participate." To this proposal the
Czechoslovak Government gave, in principle, an affirmative
reply, on condition, however, that at such a conference the
Czechoslovak Government would be permitted to make repre-
sentations about " many unworkable features " of the Anglo-
French proposals of September 18, and that during the negotiations " the Czechoslovak defence system would remain intact."
In spite of this compliance, fresh pressure was exerted on Prague
on the following day (September 27).

News reached London that Sir Horace Wilson's mission had
proved unsuccessful, and that Herr Hitler, in a conversation
which he had with him on September 27, had suggested to Sir
Horace that if he did not receive a satisfactory answer from the
Czechoslovak Government by 2 p.m. on September 28 he would
resort to military action and proclaim a general mobilisation.
Whereupon Mr. Chamberlain sent the following message, telegraphed from London, to President Beneš:

" I feel it my duty to inform you and the Czechoslovak
Government that His Majesty's Government have received

from Berlin, information which makes it clear that the German Army will receive orders to cross the Czechoslovak frontier immediately if, by to-morrow [September 28] at 2 p.m., the Czechoslovak Government has not accepted the German conditions. This means that Bohemia would be overrun by the German Army and nothing which another Power or Powers could do would be able to save your country and your people from such a fate. This remains true whatever the ultimate result of a world war might be. His Majesty's Government cannot assume the responsibility of advising you what you should do, but it believes that this information should be brought to your notice without delay." [1]

Mr. Newton, the British Minister in Prague, delivered this message to President Beneš, and shortly afterwards, at about 9.30 p.m. (on September 27) called on Dr. Krofta, the Czechoslovak Foreign Minister, taking him a further telegram from London. On this occasion, Mr. Newton communicated a new proposition to M. Krofta—which had also been presented to the German Government—concerning the way in which the "transfer " of the territory should be carried out in conformity with the Anglo-French proposals. On receiving this fresh proposition, Mr. Newton (according to what he said to M. Krofta) asked London " *ob es nicht überholt ist* " (whether it was not already out of date); to which he received the reply that he must present the proposition to the Czechoslovak Government. Mr. Newton therefore read out to the Czechoslovak Foreign Minister the official British telegram instructing the British Ambassador in Berlin to tell the German Government that, since Herr Hitler demanded the cession of Sudeten territory by October 1, the British Government would urge the Czechs to act as quickly as possible. This, Mr. Newton said, was the reason for presenting this new proposition, which was done in collaboration with the French Government. If Hitler had no confidence in President Beneš, he must trust the British Government to see that the plan for the cession of the Sudeten territory was punctually fulfilled.

The new British proposition, presented at the same time ran:

[1] Czechoslovak State Document.

" Since the Czechoslovak Government agreed in principle
to the cession of territory in the Sudeten regions, we are now
faced with the difficulty of reaching an agreement on the
actual procedure of the transfer. The Czechoslovak Government have rejected the proposals of Herr Hitler for a military
occupation of the whole territory by October 1, and His
Majesty's Government agree that these proposals are unreasonable.

" The enclosed proposal affords, in the view of His
Majesty's Government, a possibility of elaborating the guarantees concerning the essential conditions of the transfer, and
the British Government earnestly ask that the Czechoslovak
Government should give their full co-operation in putting the
time-table into effect. The British Government fully realise
the difficulties which the Czechoslovak Government will have
in accepting these proposals and also the material difficulties
which might occur in carrying them out. The Government
have, however, come to the conclusion that they must accept
these proposals, submit them and take full responsibility for
their realisation. The Czechoslovak Government should
clearly realise that the only alternative to this plan would be
an invasion and a dismemberment of the country by force and
that Czechoslovakia, though a conflict might arise which
would lead to incalculable loss of life, could not be recon-
stituted in her frontiers, whatever the result of the conflict
may be.

" The British Government propose the following time-table,
for which the British authorities would take a certain part of
responsibility for carrying it out.

" 1. German troops would occupy the territory round Cheb
and Aš outside the Czechoslovak fortifications on October 1.

" 2. Czechoslovak and German delegates, together with a
British representative, would meet in some Sudeten town on
October 3.

" The British representative would have the same voting
power as his German and Czech colleagues.

" At the same time the International Delimitation Commission, with a German, Czech and British member, would
meet.

" As far as possible the observers would arrive simultaneously, and, if possible, the British Legion. Later four British battalions could arrive. The Legion, the observers and the troops would be under the command of the Delimitation Commission. The duties of the delegates would be the following:

" (a) To take steps for the immediate withdrawal of the Czechoslovak troops and State police.

" (b) To fix the broad outlines for the protection of the minorities in the ceded areas and for the right of option and the removal of property. A similar agreement could be reached for the German minority in Czechoslovakia.

" (c) To give instructions, on the basis of the Anglo-French plan, which would be submitted to the International Delimitation Commission, for the determination of the new frontiers with the greatest expedition.

3. " From October 3 to October 10 the German troops would enter territory on which the delegates would declare that settlement was complete. This might be the whole territory, but it is also possible that this will be impracticable, as the Czech troops will not have yet been withdrawn completely, so that there would be a danger of clashes with the entering German troops. The International Delimitation Commission would, however, have to determine the final frontiers by October 31, and the Czech troops and police would have to be withdrawn behind this line while German troops would occupy up to this line.

4. " Further meetings of the delegates would consider whether it would be necessary to take further steps to improve the frontiers determined by the International Commission in October in order to take account of the geographical and economic requirements in different communities. It could be also considered whether local plebiscites might not be necessary or useful for this purpose.

" 5. Later negotiations would follow between Germany, Great Britain, France and Czechoslovakia in order—

" (a) To fix common measures for the demobilisation and withdrawal of troops.

" (b) For the revision of the present system of alliances of

Czechoslovakia and the introduction of a system which would jointly guarantee the new Czechoslovakia." [1]

It should be observed under what circumstances the British proposal to the Czechoslovak Government was made. It was announced at first that Herr Hitler would very probably cross the Czechoslovak frontier on the afternoon of September 28 if by that time he had not received full satisfaction from the Czechoslovak Government. The British Government was unwilling to bear the responsibility for giving any advice, but expressed the opinion that " Bohemia would be militarily crushed " and that " that remained a fact, whatever might be the final result of a possible world war." In the second Note, this British threat was pronounced more precisely: " whatever might be the result of the world war, the present Czechoslovak frontier would never be restored." This threat had already been used on many previous occasions in order to influence Prague to give in to Hitler's demands, and some British statesmen were somewhat disturbed when they saw that this argument (which in their opinion contained so much of human interest for the Czechoslovak nation) did not impress Prague. Only after these threats had been made sufficiently clear, was the proposal put forward concerning the stages in which the territory would be transferred—several points of this proposal appeared later in the Munich Agreement. Mr. Newton himself had doubts whether the proposal, at the moment at which it was made to the Prague Government, had not already been overtaken by events, nevertheless his Government insisted that he should deliver it. Actually, it was delivered to the Czechoslovak Government, together with a statement that it had already been delivered to the German Government, with a comment to the effect that the French Government agreed with it. Thus the reaction of Britain and France to Herr Hitler's threats that he would proclaim general mobilisation and attack Czechoslovakia was not to face this aggressiveness firmly, but to insist upon Czechoslovakia choosing the way designated by Herr Hitler at Godesberg. This action on the part of their Governments was never revealed either to the British or the French public. While treating aggressive Germany with all respect, they

[1] Czechoslovak State Document.

continually urged Czechoslovakia to give way to and satisfy
Germany. To justify their behaviour on the ground that it was
due to their anxiety to prevent Czechoslovakia from being
crushed was regarded as cowardly hypocrisy and an insult to the
Czechoslovak nation.

On September 28 the Czechoslovak Government accepted the
British plan together with its " time-table," but made important
conditions, pointing out in particular that on several points it
differed from the Anglo-French proposals of September 18. The
Czechoslovak Government insisted that it could not evacuate
its territory, demobilise its troops or abandon its fortifications
before the future frontiers had been exactly delimited and the
new system assured by international guarantee. In order that
it might not be susceptible to the charge that it wanted to
prolong the negotiations indefinitely, the Czechoslovak Government proposed December 15 as the final date of the evacuation.
The Note which was delivered to the British Minister that day
ran as follows:

" On September 27, His Majesty's Minister in Prague
submitted the proposals of the British Government concerning
a cession by stages to Germany of parts of the territory of the
Czechoslovak Republic.

" The Czechoslovak Government fully appreciates the effort
made by the British Government to reach a peaceful solution of
this problem, and the Czechoslovak Government has therefore, as always before, examined the proposals submitted to it
with the greatest care. At the instance of the French and
British Governments of September 18, the Czechoslovak
Government has accepted their proposals and they assure
them that they themselves ask for their full and loyal realisation. In order to avoid any doubts on this point, the Czechoslovak Government consents to the British and French
Governments guaranteeing their realisation.

" The Czechoslovak Government points out, however, that
the memorandum submitted at Godesberg, on September 23,
to Mr. Chamberlain, differs in so many essential points from
the proposals of the British and French Governments that
the Czechoslovak Government felt compelled to reject this

memorandum, and Mr. Chamberlain in his speech of September 27, declared that he ' well understands the reasons why the Czech Government has felt unable to accept these terms.'

" In the same speech, Mr. Chamberlain declared that the proposals made after the visit to Berchtesgaden—known as Franco-British proposals—' gave the substance of what Herr Hitler wanted.'

" The Czechoslovak Government accepts in principle the plan and the time-table submitted by the British Government. They must, however, point out that this time-table does not agree, in several points, with the Franco-British proposals.

" The Government accepts the whole of point 2, except the disposition about the composition of the Commission and delegates and the Delimitation Commission and point (a) which refers to the withdrawal of the Czechoslovak Army and police. As far as the composition of the Commission is concerned, the Czechoslovak Government proposes the inclusion of a French member and further that in case the delegates could not come to an agreement, the doubtful questions should be submitted for arbitration to a representative of the United States.

" The Government accepts also points 4 and 5.

" The Government has the following objections to points 1 and 3:

" There were no specific dates for evacuation fixed in the Franco-British proposals and the Czechoslovak Government interpreted it as meaning that evacuation would begin only after the International Commission would have finished its work.

" Further, in our opinion, the proposal of the British Government of September 27 differs in two fundamental points from the Franco-British proposals which the Czechoslovak Government have accepted at the instance of both Governments in the interest of peace, i.e.—

" 1. They demand the immediate evacuation of Cheb and Aš.

" 2. They demand an evacuation by stages beginning on October 10. In both cases this was to take place before there would be an agreement about the conditions of transfer concluded under the direction of an international organ, in which Czechoslovakia would be represented, as required in the proposals of September 19.

" Czechoslovakia cannot evacuate her territory or demobilise or leave her fortifications before the future frontiers have been determined precisely and before there would be determined and assured a new system of international guarantees, which was promised to Czechoslovakia in the Franco-British proposals. The procedure, suggested in them, could be speeded up, as the Czechoslovak Government has no wish, under any circumstances, to defer a final solution.

" The Czechoslovak Government would accept any date for a final evacuation, if all the conditions were fulfilled, i.e. when the work of the committee of delegates of the Delimitation Commission and the agreement about guarantees would be finished, whether this date be October 30 or any later date. At the same time, the Czechoslovak Government would agree to the fixing of a date which would determine the furthest limit. In this respect they would suggest December 15. If the work were concluded before, it could be an earlier date, between October 31 and December 15.

" The Czechoslovak Government further asks most urgently that it should be determined by diplomatic negotiations on the basis of what principles and what facts the new frontiers would be drawn, before the work of the delegates and the Delimitation Commission would begin. The Franco-British proposals adopt the principle that districts which have more than 50 per cent. of German population should be ceded. At the same time, these proposals admit the possibility of adjusting the frontiers in favour of Czechoslovakia, wherever this would be necessary: this British plan also stresses economic and geographical considerations.

" All frontiers, hitherto suggested from the German side, were fixed exclusively from the German point of view, without Czechoslovakia being able to say a word. This last German memorandum fixes a frontier which differs very considerably from that suggested in the Franco-British proposals. Czechoslovakia repeats emphatically that she cannot accept a plebiscite, as formulated in the demands contained in the memorandum of the German Government.

" Finally, the Czechoslovak Government stresses that it would gladly agree that any difference should be submitted for arbitration to Mr. Franklin D. Roosevelt, if in the advanced stage of negotiations, when an agreement had been reached on so many points of procedure, new difficulties and insuperable obstacles should arise, or that, as proposed by the President of the United States, an international conference should be called in the sense of the Note addressed on September 27 to Lord Halifax by the Czechoslovak Minister in London."[1]

By the time this Note was delivered, it had already been overtaken by the development of the situation since the evening of September 27. Sir Horace Wilson arrived back in London after 5 p.m. on that day and informed Mr. Chamberlain. His report was pessimistic: it contained a statement of Hitler's intention to proclaim a general mobilisation at 2 p.m. if Prague did not accept his demands by that time. It seemed that any hope of reaching agreement with Hitler was vain, and therefore Mr. Chamberlain broadcast that same evening, after 8 p.m., a speech of gloomy pessimism, pronounced in a low, disappointed voice. He declared how terrible it would be if war should break out " because of a dispute which occurs in a far-off country between people of whom we know nothing," especially when that dispute had already been settled in principle. He did not want to abandon the hope that it would nevertheless still be possible to save peace. "I would not hesitate to pay even a third visit to Herr Hitler if I considered that it would be of any use. But, actually, I cannot see what more I could usefully do in the way of mediation." For that reason he took certain military measures, but asked the public not to be alarmed, and he ended his speech as follows:

" However much we may sympathise with a small nation confronted by a big powerful neighbour, we cannot in all circumstances undertake to involve the whole British Empire

[1] Czechoslovak State Document.

in war simply on her account. If we have to fight, it must be on larger issues than that. I am myself a man of peace to the depths of my soul. Armed conflict between nations is a nightmare to me; but if I were convinced that any nation had made up its mind to dominate the world by fear of its force, I should feel that it must be resisted. Under such a domination, life for people who believe in liberty would not be worth living; but war is a fearful thing, and we must be very clear, before we embark on it, that it is really the great issues that are at stake, and that the call to risk everything in their defence is irresistible.

" For the present I ask you to await as calmly as you can the events of the next few days. As long as war has not begun, there is always hope that it can be prevented, and, as you know, I am going to work for peace to the last moment."

Owing to the circumstances in which it was delivered, this speech was differently interpreted in different quarters. Some people thought that Mr. Chamberlain was preparing public opinion for war, and indeed there can be no doubt that the British Prime Minister was at that moment not in a position to regard war as an impossibility. News came through from Berlin that German troops, armoured cars and tanks in large numbers were filing through the German capital and Reuter's and Havas Agency reports, sent after 11 p.m. on September 27, stated that Germany intended to mobilise on the following day. Mr. Chamberlain's " defensive measures " can, therefore, not be regarded as having been altogether unnecessary. At midnight the mobilisation of the British Fleet was ordered.

Feverish efforts were nevertheless continued to " save peace."

During that same evening the British Minister for the Co-ordination of Defence had informed the group of Tories most determined to resist capitulation to Germany that the military and, above all, the defence position of Britain and France was far from satisfactory. M. Bonnet's version of General Gamelin's report was used to prove that the French Army would remain incarcerated in the Maginot Line while the full force of the War was felt by the civil population behind the lines. Therefore immediately after Mr. Chamberlain's broadcast, London

advised Paris, where, as has already been stated, the defeatists'
campaign to " save peace " had just reached its climax, that it
was desirable that negotiations with Germany should still go on.
In this way, the ground was well prepared for a policy of total
capitulation to Germany and for the final sacrifice of Czechoslovakia. Herr Hitler's reply to Mr. Chamberlain's letter of
September 26 reached London at 10 p.m. on September 27 and
was as follows:

> " BERLIN.
> " *September* 27, 1938.

" DEAR MR. CHAMBERLAIN,—I have in the course of the
conversations once more informed Sir Horace Wilson, who
brought me your letter of the 26th September, of my final
attitude. I should like, however, to make the following written
reply to certain details in your letter:

" The Government in Prague feels justified in maintaining
that the proposals in my memorandum of the 23rd September
went far beyond the concession which it made to the British
and French Governments and that the acceptance of the
memorandum would rob Czechoslovakia of every guarantee
for its national existence. This statement is based on the argument that Czechoslovakia is to give up a great part of her
prepared defensive system before she can take steps elsewhere
for her military protection. Thereby the political and economic
independence of the country is automatically abolished.
Moreover, the exchange of population proposed by me would
turn out in practice to be a panic-stricken flight.

" I must openly declare that I cannot bring myself to understand these arguments or even admit that they can be regarded
as seriously put forward. The Government in Prague simply
passes over the fact that the actual arrangement for the final
settlement of the Sudeten-German problem, in accordance
with my proposals, will be made dependent not on a unilateral
German petition[1] or on German measures of force, but rather,
on the one hand, on a free vote under no outside influence,
and, on the other hand, to a very wide degree on German-
Czech agreement on matters of detail to be reached subsequently. Not only the exact definition of the territories in

[1] Decision?

which the plebiscite is to take place, but the execution of the
plebiscite and the delimitation of the frontier to be made on
the basis of its result, are in accordance with my proposals to
be met independently of any unilateral decision by Germany.
Moreover, all other details are to be reserved for agreement
on the part of a German-Czech commission.

" In the light of this interpretation of my proposals and in
the light of the cession of the Sudeten population areas, in fact
agreed to by Czechoslovakia, the immediate occupation by
German contingents demanded by me represents no more
than a security measure which is intended to guarantee a
quick and smooth achievement of the final settlement. This
security measure is indispensable. If the German Government
renounced it and left the whole further treatment of the
problem simply to normal negotiations with Czechoslovakia,
the present unbearable circumstances in the Sudeten-German
territories which I described in my speech yesterday would
continue to exist for a period, the length of which cannot be
foreseen. The Czechoslovak Government would be completely
in a position to drag out the negotiations on any point they
liked, and thus to delay the final settlement. You will understand after everything that has passed that I cannot place
such confidence in the assurances received from the Prague
Government. The British Government also would surely not
be in a position to dispose of this danger by any use of
diplomatic pressure.

" That Czechoslovakia should lose a part of her fortifications
is naturally an unavoidable consequence of the cession of the
Sudeten-German territory agreed to by the Prague Government itself. If one were to wait for the entry into force of the
final settlement in which Czechoslovakia had completed new
fortifications in the territory which remained to her, it would
doubtless last months and years. But this is the only object
of all the Czech objections. Above all, it is completely incorrect
to maintain that Czechoslovakia in this manner would be
crippled in her national existence or in her political and
economic independence. It is clear from my memorandum
that the German occupation would only extend to the given
line, and that the final delimitation of the frontier would take

place in accordance with the procedure which I have already described. The Prague Government has no right to doubt that the German military measures would stop within these limits. If, nevertheless, it desires such a doubt to be taken into account, the British and, if necessary, also the French Government can guarantee the quick fulfilment of my proposal. I can, moreover, only refer to my speech yesterday in which I clearly declared that I regret the idea of any attack on Czechoslovak territory, and that under the condition which I laid down I am even ready to give a formal guarantee for the remainder of Czechoslovakia. There can, therefore, be not the slightest question whatsoever of a check to the independence of Czechoslovakia. It is equally erroneous to talk of an economic rift. It is, on the contrary, a well-known fact that Czechoslovakia, after the cession of the Sudeten-German territory, would constitute a healthier and more unified economic organism than before.

" If the Government in Prague finally evinces anxiety also in regard to the state of the Czech population in the territories to be occupied, I can only regard this with surprise. It can be sure that, on the German side, nothing whatever will occur which will preserve for those Czechs a similar fate to that which has befallen the Sudeten Germans consequent on the Czech measures.

" In these circumstances, I must assume that the Government in Prague is only using a proposal for the occupation by German troops in order, by distorting the meaning and object of my proposal, to mobilise those forces in other countries, in particular in England and France, from which they hope to receive unreserved support for their aim and thus to achieve the possibility of a general warlike conflagration. I must leave it to your judgment whether, in view of these facts, you consider that you should continue your effort, for which I should like to take this opportunity of once more sincerely thanking you, to spoil such manœuvres and bring the Government in Prague to reason at the very last hour.

" (*Signed*) ADOLF HITLER."[1]

[1] *Correspondence respecting Czechoslovakia*, Cmd. 5847.

What followed afterwards was described by Mr. Chamberlain himself on the afternoon of September 28 in the House of Commons:

" About 10.30 I received from Herr Hitler a reply to my letter sent by Sir Horace Wilson. It is printed in the White Paper. A careful perusal of this letter indicates certain limitations on Herr Hitler's intentions which were not included in the Memorandum, and also gives certain additional assurances. There is, for example, a definite statement that troops are not to move beyond the red line, that they are only to preserve order, that the plebiscite will be carried out by a free vote under no outside influence, and that Herr Hitler will abide by the result, and, finally, that he will join the international guarantee of the remainder of Czechoslovakia once the minorities questions are settled. Those are all reassuring statements as far as they go, and I have no hesitation in saying, after the personal contact I had established with Herr Hitler, that I believe he means what he says when he states that. But the reflection which was uppermost in my mind when I read his letter to me was that once more the differences and the obscurities had been narrowed down still further to a point where really it was inconceivable that they could not be settled by negotiations. So strongly did I feel this, that I felt impelled to send one more last letter—the last last—to the Chancellor. I sent him the following personal message:

" ' After reading your letter I feel certain that you can get all essentials without war and without delay. I am ready to come to Berlin myself at once to discuss arrangements for transfer with you and representatives of the Czech Government, together with representatives of France and Italy if you desire. I feel convinced that we could reach agreement in a week. However much you distrust the Prague Government's intentions, you cannot doubt the power of the British and French Governments to see that the promises are carried out fairly and fully and forthwith. As you know, I have stated publicly that we are prepared to undertake that they shall be so carried out. I cannot believe that you will take the responsibility of starting a world war which may end civilisation, for the sake of a few days' delay in settling this long-standing problem.'

" At the same time I sent the following personal message to Signor Mussolini:

" ' I have to-day addressed a last appeal to Herr Hitler to abstain from force to settle the Sudeten problem, which, I feel sure, can be settled by a short discussion and will give him the essential territory, population and protection for both Sudetens and Czechs during transfer. I have offered myself to go at once to Berlin to discuss arrangements with German and Czech representatives, and if the Chancellor desires, representatives also of Italy and France.

" ' I trust your Excellency will inform the German Chancellor that you are willing to be represented and urge him to agree to my proposal which will keep all our peoples out of war. I have already guaranteed that Czech promises shall be carried out and feel confident full agreement could be reached in a week.'

" In reply to my message to Signor Mussolini, I was informed that instructions had been sent by the Duce to the Italian Ambassador in Berlin to see Herr von Ribbentrop at once and to say that while Italy would fulfil completely her pledges to stand by Germany, yet, in view of the great importance of the request made by His Majesty's Government to Signor Mussolini, the latter hoped Herr Hitler would see his way to postpone action which the Chancellor had told Sir Horace Wilson was to be taken at 2 p.m. to-day for at least twenty-four hours so as to allow Signor Mussolini time to re-examine the situation and endeavour to find a peaceful settlement. In response, Herr Hitler has agreed to postpone mobilisation for twenty-four hours.

" Whatever views hon. Members may have had about Signor Mussolini in the past, I believe that everyone will welcome his gesture of being willing to work with us for peace in Europe. That is not all. I have something further to say to the House yet. I have now been informed by Herr Hitler that he invites me to meet him at Munich to-morrow morning. He

has also invited Signor Mussolini and M. Daladier. Signor
Mussolini has accepted and I have no doubt M. Daladier will
also accept. I need not say what my answer will be."

Mr. Chamberlain's statement was supplemented by M.
Daladier in his parliamentary speech of October 4, as follows:

" Mr. Chamberlain's broadcast speech sounded a note of
warning that the situation was serious. We decided, therefore,
to make one final and supreme effort to save the situation.
During the night of September 27–28 we sent instructions
to our Ambassador in Berlin that he should seek a personal
audience with Herr Hitler, and to our Ambassador in London
that he should ask Lord Halifax to give instructions to his
Ambassador in Rome to beg Signor Mussolini to support the
idea of calling a conference. That was our response to the
spirit of the second message from President Roosevelt, who
has made such a generous contribution towards rendering
possible a peaceful solution.

"At 11.15 on September 27, M. François Poncet was received
by Herr Hitler and presented him, in the name of his Government, with definite proposals which could be carried into
effect immediately. Herr Hitler did not reject these proposals,
but said that he would give his reply in writing.

" Mr. Chamberlain, for his part, initiated a supreme effort
to bring together in Germany the heads of the Governments
of the four Great Western Powers. Signor Mussolini strongly
and successfully supported this initiative, with the important
result that a postponement of the German mobilisation for
twenty-four hours was secured.

" Herr Hitler immediately issued invitations for a conference in Munich."

At the time of writing nothing more is known of what took
place between the various Governments concerned during that
fatal night of September 27–28. Mr. Chamberlain explained the
course of events as though he had even then been acting quite
independently and on his own initiative, while M. Daladier spoke
as though the initiative for the conference came from Paris.

It may be recalled that on the evening of September 27 he said to the journalists: " On the international plane, the struggle for peace is not yet finished; the negotiations are still going on. Do not imagine that our diplomacy is inactive. It has made itself felt again to-day in several capitals." Events have proved, moreover, that there really can be no doubt that French diplomacy was very active at that time. Nor, for that matter, can anyone pretend that it was at all necessary for London to persuade Paris to send representatives to Munich—the French diplomats went there willingly and with at least as much spontaneity and relief as did the British.

M. Daladier claimed, in his speech, that the action decided on during the night of September 27–28 was in compliance with " the spirit of President Roosevelt's second message," but it is open to doubt whether the calling of the Munich Conference really satisfied the requirements of President Roosevelt's second appeal. The President of the United States, not satisfied by Herr Hitler's answer sent to him at 3 a.m. on September 28 (that is to say, at a time when the calling of a Four-Power Conference was already being discussed) sent a new, and this time very urgent, message, that negotiations for the solution of the conflict should continue. To that end, he proposed a conference " of all the nations directly involved in the conflict," which conference he said " could meet immediately in a neutral European region." Instead of that, however, a conference only of the four European Great Powers was called, and that in Germany itself ! Czechoslovakia was not even invited to participate in it—the Czechoslovak diplomats were allowed to come to Munich only in order to provide information should it be helpful to the British and French delegation. Unfortunately, it cannot be denied that President Roosevelt's efforts met with little goodwill in Paris. Proof of this was given by the French Press, which gave full publicity to the remarks made against the American intervention by M. Frossard, who, during those days, collaborated closely with the Governmental clique. The procedure proposed by President Roosevelt was, according to its author, accompanied by great risks, that it would meet many difficulties. On the other hand, the representatives of Germany, Italy, France and England could meet immediately, if necessary

to-morrow (i.e. September 29), and thus arrive quickly at a
solution of the conflict by the process of mediation regarding the
Sudeten-German territory. This criticism of the American initiative was naturally accompanied by a complete disregard of the
fact that Moscow had associated itself unreservedly with Mr.
Roosevelt's proposals and that it was in accordance with those
proposals that an international conference had in fact been
convened. Besides which, of course, no attention whatsoever
was paid to the fact that the Czechoslovak Government also had
agreed to the convocation of an international conference (this
was done in a Note delivered on September 26 by the Czechoslovak Minister in London, M. Jan Masaryk, to Lord Halifax),
but could hardly be expected to support a Four-Power meeting
at which it was not represented.

As early as September 25, Mr. Chamberlain had had in mind
an international conference, at which Germany, Czechoslovakia
and other Powers would participate. In the letter which he sent
to Herr Hitler on September 26, he suggested direct negotiations
between the German and the Czechoslovak delegates presided
over by English representatives, who would act as mediators.
The negative attitude of Herr Hitler and his threats of mobilisation were sufficient to make Mr. Chamberlain abandon that
plan. Thus the Western Powers, disregarding the United States
of America and paying not the slightest attention to the Soviet
Union, rushed into the Four-Power Conference alone. Hitler
was only too glad to " postpone " his mobilisation. It is certain
that the mobilisation of the British Navy acted as a considerable
deterrent, for, as soon as the news was published, the *Deutsches
Nachrichtenbüro* hastily contradicted the report that Germany
was mobilising and when, on September 28, it was already quite
sure that London and Paris had definitely decided to stand
firm this *démenti* was repeated in a more emphatic manner. Herr
Hitler was aware of the opposition of the leading people in the
German Army to a European war. Despite all the warlike
flourishes of Signor Mussolini, it was by no means certain that
Italy would dare to enter into a war against an Anglo-French-
Russian coalition. Signs were apparent of the popular resistance
in Italy to war, and Italian efforts at mobilisation met with
considerable difficulty. After Mr. Roosevelt's second appeal, in

which the inference was perfectly clear that Germany alone would be responsible for the outbreak of war, it was certain that the United States would come in on the side of Britain and France. Herr Hitler was, therefore, entirely isolated in the international as in the domestic field. With these immense odds against Nazi Germany and in particular against the person of Hitler himself, it will be even less easy to understand in the future, than it is to-day, how it was possible that the Western Powers capitulated before German threats.

The opposition in the German Army to Hitler's dangerous policy has already been mentioned in Chapter II, Part 1. The details of this opposition have been published by Professor Bernard Lavergne, a writer who is very careful to verify his material, in an article " *La crise européenne ou la grande défaite des démocraties,*" which he contributed to *L'Année Politique Française et Étrangère* of November, 1938. He expresses his belief in the information which was published by Geoffrey Fraser in *Le droit de vivre* of the previous month. It is for this reason, and because that information corresponds very largely with that already in my possession (from other sources) as early as September, that I think it worth while quoting it:

" REPRESENTATIONS BY THE GERMAN GENERAL STAFF AGAINST ANY DECLARATION OF WAR

" On Monday, September 26, the German General Staff, realising the gravity of the situation, decided to approach the Führer once more. A deputation consisting of Generals von Hanneken, Ritter von Leeb and Colonel Bodenschatz called at the Chancery of the Reich and requested to be received by Herr Hitler. They were sent away.

" At noon on the following day the principal generals held a meeting at the Bendlerstrasse. Hitler refused to receive them, but, in anticipation of this refusal, they had drawn up a Memorandum, which they handed in at his Chancery.

" The following is a brief summary, which I am in a position to give, of this historic document, which was divided into five chapters and three appendices, covering in all eighteen pages:

" Chapter 1 stresses the divergencies between the political

and military leadership of the Third Reich; it points out the
low morale of the German population, which renders it
incapable of sustaining the strain of a European war; and
finally it demands, ' in view of the low morale of the people,'
that, in the event of war breaking out, exceptional powers
shall be given to the military authorities.

" Chapter 2 describes the bad condition of the Reichswehr,
quoting numerous cases of insubordination and adding that,
in view of the political situation, the military authorities have
felt obliged ' to shut their eyes, in many serious cases, to the
absence of discipline.'

" Chapter 3 is devoted to an enumeration of various
deficiencies in armaments. Attention is drawn especially to
the unsatisfactory condition of some parts of the Siegfried
line, which was constructed in a hurry, and the absence of
fortifications in the Aix-la-Chapelle and Saarbrücken sections
is noted. In connection with the latter, anxiety is expressed
(quite unjustifiably, by the way) on account of the danger
which this would represent in the event of violation of the
neutrality of Belgium by French troops, concentrated in the
region of Givet. Emphasis is laid also on the grave shortage of
officers and N.C.Os.: no fewer than 48,000 officers and 100,000
N.C.Os. are necessary to bring the army up to complement,
and in the event of a general mobilisation eighteen divisions
would find themselves devoid of any leaders.

" Chapter 4 examines, from the military and from the
political points of view, the possible effects—very difficult to
calculate—on the Reich of a military defeat.

" Chapter 5 sums up the reasons why defeat must be
expected in any but a strictly local war. In the opinion of the
General Staff, the eastern front could not be held if the Russian
Army advanced through Poland; if the Russian Army
advanced through Rumania, the situation would be less unfavourable to Germany, but would depend very much upon
the attitude of Hungary—if Hungary remained neutral it
would be possible for Russia within seven or eight weeks to
deploy on the Czechoslovak front enough troops to paralyse
any German offensive. Of especial interest in this chapter is
the statement that less than 20 per cent. of the officers of the

Reichswehr believe in the possibility of victory for Germany.

" Appendix 1 deals with the air forces and Appendix 2 with passive defence (A.R.P.). The contents of these two appendices has, however, not been ascertained.

" Appendix 3, a military appreciation of the situation with regard to Czechoslovakia, arrives at the conclusion that the Czechoslovak Army, even if fighting without allies, could hold out for three months. It would be possible to send against Czechoslovakia only a part of the German forces, as it would be necessary to retain covering forces on the Polish and French frontiers as well as on the Baltic and North Sea coasts, and as it would be necessary also to keep a force of at least 250,000 troops in Austria to prevent any popular uprising and to guard against a possible Czechoslovak offensive. It states, in conclusion, that it is considered highly improbable that hostilities would remain localised during this three-month period."

"We are, of course, quite unable to know what were the Führer's reactions when he read this reasoned and well-documented memorandum emanating from so authoritative a source. It cannot have left him unmoved, but it would seem that the ' fifth sense ' (of divination) which he possesses inspired him to stick to his bluff. Therefore, when Sir Horace Wilson, Mr. Chamberlain's personal representative, called on him, he declared that if he did not receive satisfaction, he would order a general mobilisation at 2 p.m. on the following day.

" What actually happened ? At 10 p.m. on September 27, Admiral Raeder, chief of the German Admiralty, was received by the Führer. This visit was the climax of those efforts which the Chiefs of the German armed forces made to influence Herr Hitler. The position of Admiral Raeder was strongly reinforced by the report that the British Fleet was being mobilised. Hitler began to retreat. As a result of the interview with Admiral Raeder, he issued, through his official information bureau (*D.N.B.*), a retraction of the statement which he had just sent to Mr. Chamberlain. His bluff failed. Forced to the brink of war, and faced now with an unfavourable public opinion and with the solemn warning of the chiefs of

his Army, Navy and Air Force, he would have had to climb
down. Only a miracle could save him. That miracle took place!

" Who was responsible for that miracle ? Who was responsible for the new offer to Herr Hitler which led, within twenty-
four hours, to the Anglo-French capitulation at Munich, and
to the sacrifices of Czechoslovakia ? The Czechoslovak
Government, it should be remembered had, on four occasions
during the previous eight months, been dissuaded by France
from coming to terms with Germany.

" The Western Powers, in their anxiety to preserve peace,
which they could have preserved simply by standing firm,
rendered war in the near future and under conditions unfavourable to them well-nigh inevitable."

It was, however, with the immediate danger alone that the
statesmen of Western Europe seemed to be concerned. It is
not out of the question that the idea of solving the conflict
by means of a directory of the four European Great Powers
originated neither in London nor in Paris, but was suggested to
the Western statesmen from Berlin or from Rome, where it had,
for several years, been proclaimed as the way of salvation for
Europe. When, during the evening of September 27, Mr. Chamberlain declared in his broadcast speech that, if necessary, he would
consider the possibility even of a third visit to Herr Hitler, he
added that he himself did not know what useful purpose he
could serve so far as mediation was concerned. From this it would
appear that during those evening hours neither London nor
Paris knew very well what to do. Suddenly the idea was conceived of asking Signor Mussolini to mediate—until that moment
Rome had, on the whole, been ignored. This decision formed an
entirely new departure and the simplest explanation for it is
that it was suggested in London and in Paris that this road
would be viable.

2. The Munich Dictate.

The Czechoslovak Government was no less taken by surprise
by the decisions of the Western Powers on the night of September 27-28 than the general public: the Governments of London
and Paris carried on their negotiations without even informing

the Czechs, who were duly presented with a *fait accompli*. If hope had been expressed after Godesberg that the " devilish game about us and without us " would stop, on September 28 it was clear that in reality the devilish game was being continued. On the evening of September 28 the Czechoslovak Government was simply informed that on the following day a Conference of the representatives of the four European Powers would take place at Munich. The Government of our French allies did not even insist that at that Conference, where questions relating to Czechoslovak territory were to be discussed, Czechoslovakia should be represented on equal terms with the others and should be allowed to substantiate her attitude. Permission was granted that Czechoslovak diplomats[1] should attend the Conference, but only to give information to the British and French delegations. President Beneš made a last-minute appeal to Mr. Chamberlain and M. Daladier to have consideration for Czechoslovak interests. No answer was received from M. Daladier, but Mr. Chamberlain answered asking the Czechoslovak Government not to insist upon its conditions. This answer was given only on the evening of September 29, when the Conference had already begun, and it took the form of a message from the British Minister in Prague which ran :

" The remarks of the Czechoslovak Government to the proposed time-table were communicated to the Prime Minister, who will, of course, bear in mind the points for which the Czechoslovak Government have shown concern.

" Mr. Chamberlain has already assured his Excellency the President of the Czechoslovak Republic that he will respect in Munich the interests of Czechoslovakia and that he goes there with the intention of trying to find an accommodation between the points of view of the German and Czechoslovak Governments, so that steps could be taken for an orderly and just application of the principle of cession to which the Czechoslovak Government has consented.

" His Majesty's Government wishes to express their firm hope that the Czechoslovak Government will not obstruct the

---

[1] The Czechoslovak Minister in Berlin, Dr. Mastný, accompanied by two Councillors, Lisický and Masařík.

already difficult task of the Prime Minister by the formulation
of objections against the so-called time-table and by insistence
on them. The Czechoslovak Government should bear in mind,
as well as all the others concerned, the grave alternative if an
agreement for a new settlement should not be found.

" It is absolutely necessary that the conversations at
Munich should reach speedy and definite results, which would
lead to direct negotiations between Germany and Czechoslovakia. This can be reached only if the Czechoslovak Government is resolved, at the present stage of negotiations, to
give a wide discretion to Mr. Chamberlain and not to hinder
his decision by making absolute conditions.

" *September 29, 1938.*"[1]

There was no response in France to the warnings which came
from Prague, and very little in Great Britain. Although the
French Ministry of Foreign Affairs (Quai d'Orsay) had recently
been making a special endeavour to convince the French Government of the terrible results which would follow concession to
Hitler's demand their efforts were without result. It would be
relevant, at this stage, to quote the following notes, which have
already been published, made by Dr. Hubert Masařík of his
conversation with M. Lamarle, Counsellor of the French Legation
in Prague:

" Czernin Palace.
" I handed Lamarle a statement showing clearly how unjust
and ridiculous were the claims which Hitler was making. This
statement was based on an army map of nationalities. Lamarle
immediately outlined for me the principal points of a telegram
which he proposed to send to Paris, and in which he put
forward our views, which he shared with regard to the ' corridor ' in Moravia. His opinion was generally favourable
towards us. Speaking in confidence, he described to me a conversation which he had had a few days earlier with Herr
Kundt, who had shown him what his Party were demanding.
According to their demands, the new frontier would pass
through Česká Lípa (Böhmisch Leipa), Ustí (Aussig), Lubenec

[1] Czechoslovak State Document.

and Žlutice. Lamarle explained France's hesitancy—we have known each other intimately for the past four years—as being due to the deficiency of her Air Force and to her dread of an aerial bombardment of Paris. Veuillemin had, it appeared, returned from Germany very much upset. During the last few days, however, the situation had improved and we could rely on France. . . .

" On September 27, at the express wish of Lamarle, I was asked to point out again in detail at the French Legation all the differences between Hitler's claims and the Anglo-French proposals. Lamarle said that it was a matter of the utmost importance for us that London and Paris should immediately be convinced that Hitler was lying when he pretended that his proposals meant merely the carrying into practice of the Anglo-French plan.

" I went to the Legation with Dr. Boháč and for two and a half hours, in the presence of three members of the Legation and of the Minister, I analysed the border territories along the whole length of our frontier, pointing out the differences which existed between the two plans. I brought with me a map known as the Runciman map, on which the Czech territory is marked in red, the German territory in white, according to the density of population, and during the discussion this map proved to be the best and most effective argument in any negotiations on this subject. It was necessary, however, to complete it by marking on it the railways and the roads, a task which I had carried out that afternoon by the Institute of Geography in order that a copy might be sent to the French Government in the diplomatic bag. It was agreed between Lamarle and myself that another concise telegram should be sent to-day, and to-morrow we should send by aeroplane a detailed report, containing all relevant statistics and accompanied by a map.

" We analysed, district by district, first the territory claimed by Hitler and then, separately, the territory in which it was proposed to hold a plebiscite. I emphasised, and the French admitted, that Hitler's most dangerous trick consisted in counting the percentages of the inhabitants in the whole of the territory which it was proposed to cede to him, whereas the only fair procedure was to count them in each district separately, since the districts were time-hallowed entities, dating back to the days of Austria-Hungary, and had been recognised as such by the Henleinists themselves. Thus the French report is in fact based on the principle of regarding the districts as economic and administrative units. Lamarle and his colleagues recognised the necessity of maintaining the unity of the territory crossed by the railway line from Česká Třebová (Böhmisch Trübau) to Olomouc (Olmütz) and Moravská Ostrava (Mährisch Ostrau), of our retaining the territory round Opava (Troppau) and of smoothing away the dangerous salient below Brno (Brünn). They recognised also the injustice of enclosing in the territory to be transferred the towns of Břeclav (Lundenburg), Znojmo (Znaim), Jemnice (Jamnitz) and Jindřichův Hradec (Neuhaus) and the district round Domažlice; and the necessity of providing for communication between Plzeň (Pilsen) and Domažlice (Taus) railway communication with České Velenice (Gmünd). They were definitely in favour of the proposal to retain half of the district of Duchcov (Dux,) where there was, as we were able to prove, a Czech minority of about 50 per cent., which had been settled there for sixty years. Similarly they recognised the necessity of moving the ethnic boundary in the North from Roudnice (Raudnitz) in the district Litoměřice—Lovosice (Leitmeritz—Lovositz), and of making certain radical alterations in Hitler's map with regard to Eastern Bohemia.

" The report will be drafted in such a way that, as regards each district, the object of Hitler's exaggerated demands will be indicated, e.g. railway junction, industry, raw materials, strategical considerations, etc.

" After my explanation, the French realised that, so far as the plebiscite territories were concerned, it was a question whether Hitler was indulging in some cruel joking or was providing himself beforehand with something to give up, i.e. was arranging matters in such a way that he would be able, during the negotiations, to give up some obviously ridiculous claims in order to appear justified in insisting more strenuously than ever on the delimitation of the frontiers of the territories which he wished to have ceded to him at once. Lamarle accepted the following list of points which are most important for us:

" 1. The widening of the ' corridor ' in Northern Moravia, together with guarantees regarding the railway-line Třebová –Olomouc–Ostrava (Trübau–Olmütz–Ostrau).

" 2. The widening of the ' corridor ' in Southern Moravia, together with guarantees regarding railway communications, and regarding the withdrawal of the Germans to the natural frontiers of their majorities.

" 3. The division of the coal basin in Northern Bohemia.

" 4. A guarantee of the communications in the Šumava (Böhmerwald) and the maintenance of the existing frontier at Domažlice (Taus).

" 5. A guarantee of the communications with České Velenice (Gmünd) and Jindřichův Hradec (Neuhaus);

" 6. Essential compromises wherever there is a Czech minority of 30–50 per cent.

" The contradictions between the maps presented by Hitler and Henlein respectively also had a salutary effect on the French. All these were noted in our favour in the report.

" I have emphasised the fact that I have deliberately ignored strategic considerations which are of importance to France, because I am not qualified to deal with such matter.

(*Signed*) Dr. Masařík.[1]

It is unfortunately a fact, however, that these arguments, warnings, and appeals from her Czechoslovak allies, who were faced with mortal danger, had not the slightest influence on France. When M. Daladier described in the Chamber of Deputies on October 4 how he had accepted the invitation to go to Munich, he added: " I regret nothing." Brave words, but I would express my doubt whether history will justify them.

On September 29, sooner than had been anticipated, Herr Hitler, Signor Mussolini, Mr. Chamberlain and M. Daladier came to an agreement at Munich. After two conversations lasting through two afternoons and one evening, the agreement was completed and at 2 a.m. on September 30 it was published:

[1] Czechoslovak State Document.

" Germany, the United Kingdom, France and Italy, taking into consideration the agreement, which has been already reached in principle for the cession to Germany of the Sudeten-German territory, have agreed on the following conditions governing the said cession and the measures consequent thereon, and by this agreement they each hold themselves responsible for the steps necessary to secure its fulfilment.

" 1. The evacuation will begin on the 1st October.

" 2. The United Kingdom, France and Italy agree that the evacuation of the territory shall be completed by the 10th October, without any existing installations having been destroyed and that the Czechoslovak Government will be held responsible for carrying out the evacuation without damage to the said installations.

" 3. The conditions governing the evacuation will be laid down in detail by an international commission composed of representatives of Germany, the United Kingdom, France, Italy and Czechoslovakia.

" 4. The occupation by stages of the predominantly German territory by German troops will begin on the 1st October. The four territories marked on the attached map[1] will be occupied by the German troops in the following order: The territory marked No. I on the 1st and 2nd of October, the territory marked No. II on the 2nd and 3rd of October, the territory marked No. III on the 3rd, 4th and 5th of October, the territory marked No. IV on the 6th and 7th of October. The remaining territory of preponderantly German character will be ascertained by the aforesaid international commission forthwith and be occupied by German troops by the 10th of October.

" 5. The international commission referred to in paragraph 3 will determine the territories in which a plebiscite is to be held. These territories will be occupied by international bodies until the plebiscite has been completed. The same commission will fix the conditions in which the plebiscite is to be held, taking as a basis the conditions of the Saar plebiscite. The commission

[1] See sketch map based on the original. The sketch map illustrating the Godesberg memorandum of September 23 (see Cmd. 5847) is also reproduced.

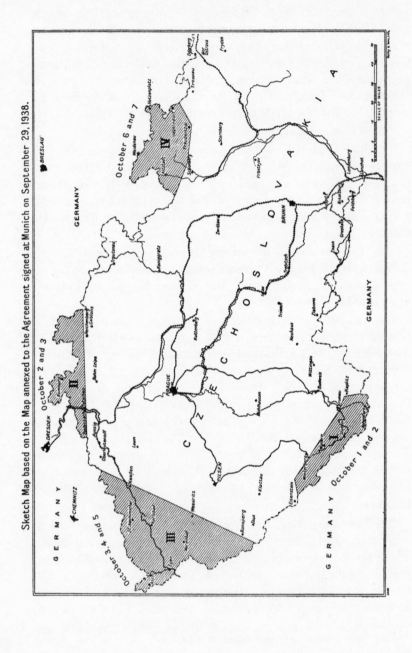

Sketch Map based on the Map annexed to the Agreement signed at Munich on September 29, 1938.

will also fix a date, not later than the end of November, on which the plebiscite will be held.

" 6. The final determination of the frontiers will be carried out by the international commission. This commission will also be entitled to recommend to the four Powers, Germany, the United Kingdom, France and Italy, in certain exceptional cases minor modifications in the strictly ethnographical determination of the zones which are to be transferred without plebiscite.

" 7. There will be a right of option into and out of the transferred territories, the option to be exercised within six months from the date of this agreement. A German-Czechoslovak commission shall determine the details of the option, consider ways of facilitating the transfer of population and settle questions of principle arising out of the said transfer.

" 8. The Czechoslovak Government will, within a period of four weeks from the date of this agreement, release from their military and police forces any Sudeten Germans who may wish to be released, and the Czechoslovak Government will within the same period release Sudeten-German prisoners who are serving terms of imprisonment for political offences.

" ADOLF HITLER.
" NEVILLE CHAMBERLAIN.
" EDOUARD DALADIER.
" BENITO MUSSOLINI."

" ANNEX TO THE AGREEMENT.

" 1. His Majesty's Government in the United Kingdom and the French Government have entered into the above agreement on the basis that they stand by the offer, contained in paragraph 6 of the Anglo-French proposals of the 19th September, relating to an international guarantee of the new boundaries of the Czechoslovak State against unprovoked aggression.

" 2. When the question of the Polish and Hungarian minorities in Czechoslovakia has been settled, Germany and Italy for their part will give a guarantee to Czechoslovakia.

" 3. The Heads of the Governments of the Four Powers declare that the problems of the Polish and Hungarian minorities in Czechoslovakia, if not settled within three months by agreement between the respective Governments, shall form the subject of another meeting of the Heads of the Governments of the Four Powers here present.

" All questions which may arise out of the transfer of the territory shall be considered as coming within the terms of reference to the international commission.

" 4. The four Heads of Government here present agree that the international commission provided for in the agreement signed by them to-day shall consist of the Secretary of State in the German Foreign Office, the British, French and Italian Ambassadors accredited in Berlin, and a representative to be nominated by the Government of Czechoslovakia."[1]

As soon as the Conference was concluded, this death sentence was conveyed by the British and French delegation to the Czechoslovak delegates who were present at Munich. How this happened is described in the following report by Dr. Hubert Masařík:

" At 3 p.m. on September 29, 1938, our aeroplane took off from Ruzyn. After eighty minutes' flight, we landed at Munich. The reception we met with at the aerodrome was roughly that accorded to police suspects. We were taken in a police car, accompanied by members of the Gestapo, to the Hotel Regina, where the British Delegation was also staying. The Conference was already in progress and it was difficult to establish any contact with leading members either of the British or French delegations. Nevertheless I called out by telephone first M. Rochat and then Mr. Ashton-Gwatkin. The latter told me he wished to speak to me immediately in the Hotel.

" At 7 p.m. I had my first conversation with Mr. Ashton-Gwatkin. He was nervous and very reserved. From certain cautious remarks, I gathered that a plan, the details of which Mr. Gwatkin could not then give me, was already completed in its main outlines and that it was much harsher than the Anglo-French proposals. On our red map, I explained to him

[1] *Further Documents respecting Czechoslovakia*, Cmd. 5848.

all our really vital interests. Mr. Gwatkin showed a certain understanding in the question of the Moravian corridor, though he completely ignored all the other elements of the problem.

" According to him, the conference should end at latest to-morrow, Saturday. Up to now, only Czechoslovakia had been discussed. I drew Mr. Gwatkin's attention to the consequences of such a plan from the internal political, economic and financial aspect. He answered that I did not seem to realise how difficult the situation was for the Western Powers or how awkward it was to negotiate with Hitler. On which, Mr. Gwatkin returned to the Conference, promising that we should be called at the first interval.

" At 10 p.m. Mr. Gwatkin took Dr. Mastny and myself to Sir Horace Wilson. There, in the presence of Mr. Gwatkin and at the express wish of Mr. Chamberlain, Sir Horace told us the main lines of the new plan and handed us a map on which were marked the areas which were to be occupied at once. To my objections, he replied twice with absolute formality that he had nothing to add to his statements. He paid no attention whatever to what we said concerning places and areas of the greatest importance to us. Finally, he returned to the Conference and we remained alone with Mr. Gwatkin. We did what we could to convince him of the necessity of revising the plan. His most important reply was that made to M. Mastny, to the effect that the British Delegation favoured the new German plan.

" When he again began to speak of the difficulties of negotiating with Hitler, I said that, in fact, everything depended on the firmness of the two Western Great Powers. To which Mr. Gwatkin answered, in a very serious tone: " If you do not accept, you will have to settle your affairs all alone with the Germans. Perhaps the French will put it more amiably, but I assure you that they share our views. They will disinterest themselves. . . .'

" At 1.30 a.m. we were taken into the hall where the Conference had been held. There were present Mr. Neville Chamberlain, M. Daladier, Sir Horace Wilson, M. Léger, Mr. Ashton-Gwatkin, Dr. Mastny and myself. The atmosphere was oppressive; sentence was about to be passed. The French, obviously embarrassed, appeared to be aware of the consequences for French prestige. Mr. Chamberlain, in a short introduction, referred to the agreement which had just been concluded and gave the text to Dr. Mastny to read out. During the reading of the text, we asked the precise meaning of certain passages. Thus, for example, I asked MM. Léger and Wilson to be so kind as to explain the words ' preponderantly German character ' in Article 4. M. Léger, without mentioning a percentage, merely remarked that it was a question of majorities calculated according to the proposals we had already accepted. Mr. Chamberlain also confirmed that there was no question except of applying a plan which we had already accepted. When we came to Article 6, I asked M. Léger whether we were to consider it as a clause assuring the protection of our vital interests as had been promised in the original proposals. M. Léger said, ' Yes,' but that it was only possible to a very moderate degree, and that the question would come under the International Commission. Dr. Mastny asked Mr. Chamberlain whether the Czechoslovak member of the Commission would have the same right to vote as the other members, to which Mr. Chamberlain agreed. In answer to the question whether international troops or British forces would be sent to the plebiscite areas, we were told that that was under consideration, but that Italian and Belgian troops might also participate.

" While M. Mastny was speaking with Mr. Chamberlain about matters of perhaps secondary importance (Mr. Chamberlain yawned without ceasing and with no show of embarrassment), I asked MM. Daladier and Léger whether they expected a declaration or answer to the agreement for our Government. M. Daladier, obviously embarrassed, did not reply. M. Léger replied that the four statesmen had not much time. He added positively that they no longer expected an answer from us; they regarded the plan as accepted and that our Government had that very day, at latest by 5 p.m. to send its representative to Berlin to the meeting of the International Commission and finally that the Czechoslovak official whom we sent would have to be in Berlin on Saturday, in order to fix the details of the evacuation of the first zone. The atmosphere was becoming oppressive for everyone present.

" It had been explained to us in a sufficiently brutal manner, and that by a Frenchman, that this was a sentence without right of appeal and without possibility of modification.

" Mr. Chamberlain did not conceal his fatigue. After the text had been read, we were given a second slightly corrected map. We said ' Good-bye ' and left. The Czechoslovak Republic as fixed by the frontiers of 1918 had ceased to exist. In the hall I met Rochat, who asked me what the reactions would be at home. I replied curtly that I did not exclude the worst and that it was necessary to be prepared for the gravest eventualities."

This Report needs no comment.[1]

For twenty years the Germans and their friends in other countries have denounced the Versailles peace terms, which they did not hesitate to describe as cruel " dictation." Yet the final negotiations at Versailles were participated in by a German delegation, and the peace terms were not presented to them until they had been thoroughly, and not hurriedly, worked out by a large body of specialists of every kind. At Munich, on the other hand, a totally different method was adopted: in a few hours a directory of four Great Powers determined the fate of a smaller state without even having the decency to listen to its views. No defeated nation has ever been treated in a worse manner. Nothing can justify that brutally cruel injustice. A small country was sacrificed to satisfy the ambitions of one, and the fear of war of two countries. Yet, even at this price, Europe did not secure any certainty of peace and calm, but was only brought nearer to catastrophe and plunged into a period of acute tension.

It was possible to come to an " agreement " within a few hours, because the Western Powers simply accepted Hitler's demands—there is no fundamental difference between the Godesberg Ultimatum and the Munich Decree. Mr. Chamberlain and M. Daladier pretended, of course, that the terms agreed upon at Munich represented a considerable improvement upon those demanded at Godesberg, and both statesmen justified the Munich Agreement entirely and exclusively on this basis. But let us just examine this claim. They point out that, whereas at

[1] Czechoslovak State Document.

Godesberg Herr Hitler demanded to occupy the Sudeten-German territory by October 1, at Munich it was agreed that this occupation should be carried out in stages by October 10—a date which appeared, it may be recalled, in the British time-table. What generosity on the part of Hitler to consent to wait ten days before he obtained all, and in some respect more than all, that he wanted ! Another improvement which was claimed was that, whereas at Godesberg Herr Hitler had himself dictated the new frontier, it was laid down at Munich that this frontier should be delimited by an international commission, which would include also a Czechoslovak delegate. In actual fact, the German simply dictated to the International Commission, and it was in vain that the Czechoslovak delegates asked Britain and France for their aid. And at the end of it all, the final frontier proved, as will be shown, to be even worse than that demanded at Godesberg. This came about quite simply; with no further fear of Czech military resistance once the fortifications and their " installations " had been handed over—by the treaty signed between Germany, Italy, Britain and France—the Germans simply insisted on the frontier they wanted. This frontier was naturally one which put Czechoslovakia completely at their mercy. They then dropped the idea of a plebiscite, upon which they had insisted at Godesberg.

One final and significant " improvement " was included in the Munich agreement. M. Daladier, when explaining these alleged " improvements " to his Chamber of Deputies on October 4, emphasised in particular the International guarantee which had been promised to Czechoslovakia, whereby " France and Great Britain undertook to associate themselves immediately and unreservedly with an international guarantee of the new frontiers of the Czechoslovak state against any unprovoked aggression, Germany and Italy, for their part, undertaking to give a similar guarantee as soon as the question of Polish and Hungarian minorities in Czechoslovakia had been settled." " I am convinced," said M. Daladier, " that, by means of these direct conversations, a just and honourable settlement will soon be agreed upon." The occupation of Czechoslovakia in March, 1939, adequately proved how " just and honourable " a settlement had been found ! M. Daladier's total ignorance of the train of events which he himself had helped to put in movement was shown by his declaration in the same speech: " It is true that the Munich Agreement has diminished the territory of Czechoslovakia, but the Republic can still live a free life, and we shall help her."

In March, 1939, the Czechoslovak people saw little of this " help " solemnly promised by the Prime Minister of France six months earlier.

3. *Czechoslovakia gives in.*

Shortly after 5 a.m. in the morning of September 30, Herr Hencke, the German *Chargé d'Affaires* in Prague, telephoned to the Ministry of Foreign Affairs, asking to be received by Dr. Krofta at six o'clock. It was indicative of how completely the situation had changed that Germany herself was now assuming an active role. Herr Hencke was received by Dr. Krofta at 6.16 a.m. and handed him the following Note:

" YOUR EXCELLENCY,—On the orders of my Government, I have the honour of submitting to you enclosed the text of the agreement and the supplementary protocol which were concluded at Munich on September 29 between the Chancellor of the Reich, the British Prime Minister, the head of the Italian Government and the French Prime Minister.

" At the same time, I wish to notify your Excellency that the German Reich Government invite the Czechoslovak Government to send one representative and one military expert to the sittings of the International Commission mentioned in Article 3 of the enclosed agreement, which will be held in the Foreign Office at Berlin on September 30, 1938, at 5 p.m., under the chairmanship of the Secretary of the Foreign Office, von Weiszäcker.

" I use this opportunity to assure your Excellency of my most profound respects.

" PRAGUE.

" *September* 30, 1938.

" (*Signed*) HENCKE,
" *German Chargé d'Affaires.*"[1]

[1] Czechoslovak State Document.

At this conversation, the German *Chargé d'Affaires* said that he had received no instructions other than to deliver the Note, but Hencke expressed his personal opinion that there was no difference between the Berchtesgaden and the Godesberg terms.

Three hours later, at 9.30 a.m. on September 30, a meeting of the leaders of the political parties was held at the President's Chancellery at the Hradčany, and a meeting of the Cabinet at the Kolovra Palace. Shortly afterwards there was a combined meeting of the Cabinet, the leaders of the political parties, the late Cabinet of Dr. Hodža's Government and Generals Krejčí and Husárek, as representatives of the Army. This meeting went on until noon, when it was decided unanimously to accept the Munich Decree.

While these meetings were in progress the Ministers of Britain, France and Italy had called officially on Dr. Krofta and had insisted that they must receive his Government's decision by noon. At 12.30 p.m., Dr. Krofta received all of them together and told them:

" In the name of the President of the Republic and in the name of my Government, I announce that we accept the decisions taken at Munich without us and against us. Our view upon them will be expressed later in writing. For the moment I have nothing to add. I want only to draw your attention to the necessity of persuading the German Government that the Press and radio campaign which has been conducted against us should now cease, for otherwise it will be impossible to carry out peacefully the programme laid down at Munich."

The French Minister, M. de Lacroix, agreed with what Dr. Krofta had said regarding the decisions, i.e. that they were " against us," and told him that M. Daladier wished him to express " his keen regret " about them. The British Minister, Mr. Newton, assured Dr. Krofta that Mr. Chamberlain had done everything he could for Czechoslovakia. The Italian Minister, Signor Fransoni, remained silent. Dr. Krofta concluded this obviously embarrassing conversation with these memorable words:

" I do not intend to criticise, but this is for us a disaster which we have not merited. We surrender, and shall endeavour to secure for our nation a peaceful existence. I do not know whether your countries will benefit by these decisions which have been made at Munich, but we are certainly not the last; after us, there are others who will be affected—and who will suffer from those decisions."

That afternoon the Committee of the Coalition majority, consisting of fifty members, met in the House of Parliament, and was informed by Dr. Hodža of what had taken place. The Committee discussed the matter until 7 p.m., but decided that they could do nothing to reverse the surrender, which had been accepted.

The Government announced its decision in the following communiqué, published in the afternoon of September 30:

" The Government of the Republic met at the Hradčany this morning under the Chairmanship of the President of the Republic. At this meeting the international situation as it has developed since the Four-Power Agreement resulting from the Conference at Munich on September 29 was seriously discussed. The decisions of the Munich Conference were announced to the Czech Government this morning.

" The Government has closely studied the details of those decisions and the circumstances which must be taken into account in connection with them. After careful consideration and study of the urgent recommendations made by the British and French Governments, and fully conscious of its responsibility before history, the Czechoslovak Government decided, with the unanimous consent of the responsible factors of the political parties, that the Four-Power Agreement of Munich should be accepted. They have made this decision, because they realise that it is necessary to preserve the nation, and that any other decision is to-day impossible.

" The Government of the Czechoslovak Republic, in announcing this acceptance, declares also before the whole world its protest against the decisions which were taken unilaterally and without our participation."

The difficult task of announcing this capitulation to the public fell upon the Prime Minister, General Syrový, who had become

famous during the heroic struggles of the Czechoslovak Legionaries, who fought during the World War on the side of the
Western democracies. He made the announcement by radio
at 5 p.m.:

" I am experiencing the gravest hour of my life. I would
have been prepared to die rather than to go through this, but,
just because I have already won spurs in the War, I, as chief
of the Army, must tell you frankly that before one goes into
battle one must size up and clearly recognise the overpowering
might of the enemy, and that one must then act upon one's
knowledge.

" We have had to chose between making a desperate and
hopeless defence, which would have meant the sacrifice of an
entire generation of our adult men, as well as of our women
and children, and accepting, without a struggle and under
pressure, terms which are without parallel in history for their
ruthlessness. We have been anxious to make our contribution
towards peace and we have been willing to make it—but not
in the way which we are now constrained to do.

" We were deserted. We stood alone.

" All the states of Europe, including our neighbours to the
north and to the south are standing to arms. We are in a
certain sense a bastion surrounded by forces which are far
more powerful than ours.

" Deeply moved by the situation, all your leaders, together
with the Army and the President of the Republic, have considered every possibility which lies before us. We have come to
the conclusion that, if we must chose between the diminution
of our territories and the death of our whole nation, it is our
sacred duty to preserve the lives of our people, in order that
it may not emerge weakened from this age of terror, and in
order that we may not be obliged to abandon our belief that
our nation will rise again, as it has done so often in the past.

" In this hour of fate we must all express our gratitude to
our Army, whose preparedness has preserved us in the presence
of a disaster which threatened the very existence of our
nation. It is no dishonour to yield to the decree of four Great
Powers who have such an overwhelming military supremacy.

" We shall accomplish the conditions imposed on us. We call upon our nation and our people to swallow their bitterness, their disappointment and their pain, and to help us to assure our future within our new frontiers. We all share the same fate and everybody must help to bring our country, though damaged, into the haven of peace. The most important thing is that unity and concord should reign amongst us, and that there should be no conflict within our ranks. . . .

" Our state will not be one of the smallest in the world. There are other states much smaller than ours will be but which are nevertheless healthy and resistant. The territories which will remain to us will give us the possibility of further cultural and economic progress. It is true we shall have less spacious boundaries, but then we shall be among ourselves, and many hindrances to the good and peaceful administration of our state will be removed. Our Army will continue to do its duty to defend our new frontiers.

" Let us, all of us, now see to it that our state shall return to health within its new frontiers and that its citizens are assured a new life of peace and fruitful labour. With your help we shall succeed."

Immediately afterwards there was read over the wireless an Army Order issued by the General Krejčí, Chief of the General Staff, saying:

" Soldiers ! the Czechoslovak Government, under pressure of world events, was obliged to accept the transfer of various territories of our state. We soldiers, who were the pride of the nation until now, must remain so in the future. Western Europe has asked this sacrifice from us categorically in order to prevent world war.

" In our oath we have promised the President of the Republic unconditional obedience. Destiny obliges us to fulfil this promise in the most painful circumstances. . . .

" A good soldier must endure failure, for even in it there is a manifestation of true heroism.

" Our Army was not defeated. It has preserved unblemished its good repute. It must preserve it always in the future. The Republic will have need of us. . . .

" We are confident that our nation will emerge successfully from its present difficulties. We soldiers will prove ourselves worthy of its trust. Our Government and our nation will find us ready for all sacrifices."

These messages were, of course, intended to prevent despair from seizing upon the public and to prevent the people from becoming panic-stricken. An even deeper impression was probably created, however, by the appeal made by the Czech poet, Josef Hora, which will remain for ever the expression of suffering of the Czech people:

" In the days of our sorrow when others, more powerful, have decided to beggar our ancient Country, lift up your heads, all of you, in pride and calmness. It is not we who should be ashamed. We wanted only peace and justice, and we have suffered a disappointment which will stand out in history for centuries to come, like the torture of our Saviour. It is all the more necessary, therefore, that the nation should summon up all its courage, faith and common sense. Do not stop thinking of a better future just because the present is bitter. At the will of the Great Powers our State is shrinking before our startled eyes, but our nation will remain a solid bastion for millions of citizens of the world who are hourly drawing closer to each other. Behold, in this most difficult hour the very foundations of the nation are being made stouter and more firm by the growing force of love. That is our dowry; that is our capital. Let our mutual love and our will for justice give us the strength not to despair or to lose our hope, our reason and our outward composure. Calmness and discipline are the necessary words which will open before us a vista of happier days to come. Not one of us is responsible for what has happened. Let that give us the pride with which we may face what is to come.

" Even if our hands tremble with rage, let us not lose faith in ourselves, in our leaders and in our future. May our sadness, our horror and our danger even increase our self-confidence. Hundreds of thousands of our children are growing up; may the sight of them fortify us to preserve a calm and creative attitude ! They will sing our national anthem with a new tone in their voices—for they will know more than we did and will have experienced more, and will therefore be stronger to resist than we have been. We are the bridge across which our young generations will enter life. Let us be a solid bridge !

"We can waste no more time, but must start to-day thinking out how to rebuild our Country, diminished in size, but with heart and mind still intact. The other day I was talking to a man who confessed to me that he had hitherto just lived for the day, seeking his own comfort and tolerant of weakness in himself and in others. ' From now onwards,' he told me, ' I want to live strenuously and sincerely, and shall yield to no weakness of spirit.' Many—indeed, I think all—of us have felt as he did during these days of bitter adversity. Such a people, such a nation as ours, will not lose its head under any circumstances. The leaves of illusion have been torn from us by the chill blast of experience, but the solid trunk of our faith still stands erect and unshaken. Let us go on with our work, firm in our belief that nothing has been taken from us which can weaken our national spirit. Through the winter of our present misfortune, let us look forward to the spring, for we must not imagine that spring will never come—it is we alone, however, who, by our calmness and dignity in these days of sorrow, can make it come. We must think, we must work, we must struggle towards that end. We must set our teeth and prepare to make any sacrifice in order that the injustices of to-day may be righted for our children, for our nation of to-morrow, for no one else can do that for us ! "

I shall not attempt to describe what the Czechoslovak people suffered during these days, though it is impossible for any foreigner to understand the depth of its sorrow and the bitterness of its disappointment. We feel no shame that people should have been seen weeping publicly in Prague and indeed throughout the Republic, or that some of our soldiers should have killed themselves. Immediately after the announcement of the capitulation, attempts were made to organise public demonstrations in Prague, but the public were too ready to respond to the appeal

made by the authorities for calmness and discipline. Everyone
wanted to be alone with his grief and with the burning torture
of his frustrated hopes. The bitterest disappointment was the
attitude adopted by the Western democracies with whom the
Czechoslovak nation had kept faith. " We believed," said Dr.
Zenkl, Lord Mayor of Prague, on September 30, " in the treaties
and in the solemn obligations which they imposed on the great
nations and powerful states, but they have considered the rights
of a small nation as of less importance than the brutal might of
one which is great and powerful. We have found ourselves again
at a crisis in history when might has taken precedence over
right." The horror which the Czechoslovak people felt was intensified by the announcement of the enthusiasm with which
Mr. Chamberlain and M. Daladier were greeted in London and
in Paris after their return from Munich.

The *Lidové Noviny* wrote: " The country is shrouded in deep
mourning, in which the words of the poet Viktor Dyk are heard
encouraging us to be brave:

" *The defeated cause is not lost,*
The nation remains, only the map is changed."

*   *   *   *   *

The very basis of the international and internal situation of
Czechoslovakia was to be transformed, and it was necessary to
act accordingly. In the first place, it was necessary to reconstruct
the Government. It is true that at the head of the new Government there remained General Syrový, and that some other
Ministers were taken over from the previous Government, but
several new elements had to be introduced: Dr. Párkányi came
in as the Minister for Carpathian Ruthenia and a Minister for
Slovakia would have been appointed if agreement could have
been reached with Hlinka's Catholic Party. A most significant
change was made, however, in the Ministry of Foreign Affairs,
where Dr. Kamil Krofta, a keen admirer of Masaryk and an
enthusiastic protagonist of his political and moral legacy, and a
devoted collaborator of President Beneš, was replaced by Dr.
Chvalkovský, who used to collaborate with Dr. Švehla, leader
of the Agrarians, and who was for several years Czechoslovak

Minister in Berlin and later in Rome.[1] In the manifesto in which
the President of the Republic said " Good-bye " to the retiring
Government, he said: " Recent events have forced us to change
our Government and make certain changes in the direction of
our internal as well as of our external policy, more especially in
relation to what is happening locally." The character of these
changes was indicated by General Syrový in a speech which he
delivered on October 5, announcing the programme to which
the new Government intended to work, as follows:

" The Government is anxious to carry out loyally the decisions
taken by the four Great Powers at Munich, while doing its
utmost to preserve and safeguard the vital interests of our new
state. The principles in accordance with which the Government
will direct its foreign policy may be expressed very simply:
friendly relations towards all, and especially towards our neighbours. The establishment of such relations is clearly dictated as
a result of our realisation that if we want to live safely and content we must collaborate with our neighbours."

General Syrový announced at the same time that the reasonable demands of Slovakia and Sub-Carpathian Ruthenia would
be satisfied.

On October 5, as soon as these changes of Government and of
policy had been effected in accordance with the changing situation, President Beneš, acting on his own initiative, not under
pressure of any kind, announced his resignation. In a farewell
speech which was broadcast at 9 p.m. he said:

" With composure and with calm, we confront our fate. In
these difficult times I have tried to safeguard the interests of
our State and I have tried to do what is right for Europe in
order to preserve the peace. We have now to reach an understanding with our neighbours. Their overpowering might has
been too great for us. In order not to jeopardise the life of our
State in the new circumstances, I think that as President I
should no longer stand in the way. As a convinced democrat,
I think it better to go. We remain democrats and we shall try
to continue to work with our friends, but my resignation is

[1] Where he was actually serving when he was summoned home to assume control
of the Ministry of Foreign Affairs.

imperative in order to accommodate our State to the new circumstances. It is still necessary for us to be loyal to all our friends. Our new State will now receive a more homogeneous structure. There will be no more grounds for dispute between us and our neighbours.

" The men who did not appreciate the many attempts of the Government to reach an agreement with the neighbours of Czechoslovakia were mistaken. As I was elected in another situation, I fear that the personal representative so elected might be regarded as an obstacle to an agreement and to its necessary development. I shall remain a convinced democrat. We shall develop quietly and adapt ourselves to the circumstances. We shall not renounce our old friends and we must try to win new friends. Our State had a special nationalistic situation. Now it becomes a national State, corresponding to the development of the national principle. This new condition will awaken the activity of the nation and give it a larger moral foundation. The culture of our nation will become stronger. The top of the tree is cut off, but the trunk remains. Let us descend to the roots. Some time the tree will put forth new leaves.

" We are still numerous enough to look to the future with confidence. We have avoided a catastrophe and we must not lose our heads even in this hour of utter misery. We have not shown a lesser heroism in doing what we did than if we had gone into battle. After all these sacrifices, we are happy to see that we have retained as a nucleus for our State a nation which will understand how to safeguard its own interests.

" Your country was in danger, but the danger will be greater now if you forsake your unity. All of you—manual and mental workers, peasants and soldiers—work for the interests of our State, so that you may go forward to a happy future. I address my particular thanks to our courageous Army. I remain with it in spirit and I wish it further success. I express my conviction that this people will preserve its confidence with energy and endurance, that it will continue to fight for national freedom, and that it will be as victorious in the future as it has been in the past.

" I do not leave the ship because the sea is stormy, but

because it is a political necessity. I remain conscious of my duties as a citizen. For all our citizens I wish better times in the future, both for them and for our beautiful country. Good-bye to you. Remain united, brave, and faithful."

Dr. Beneš' departure was very significant, for he left—indeed he had to leave—when the independent, free and democratic Czechoslovak Republic, of which he, in succession to T. G. Masaryk, was the personal symbol, met with disaster. His departure and the disaster which necessitated it, represented, moreover, a severe defeat for the Western democracies. The consequences of Munich, which it was even then not difficult to foresee, are now daily becoming ever more evident.

CHAPTER VI

The Munich Intermezzo

1. *The Dismemberment of Czechoslovakia.*

ALTHOUGH the decisions of Munich and Berlin were wiped out completely six months later by the occupation of the whole of Czechoslovakia in March, 1939, it would be a grave mistake to believe that the Munich frontier was itself just or proper. The Germans themselves by their action proved its untenability even after all consideration for Czech interests had been swept aside.

It was untenable strategically, economically and politically. Czechoslovakia was completely disarmed; its natural defences and prepared fortifications were one and all handed over to Germany. The result was seen in March when the German army overran the whole of Bohemia and Moravia within a few hours. Economically, not only Czechoslovakia, but Germany was adversely affected and above all the Sudeten-German districts were completely crippled. Even before March, 1939, the old Czechoslovak-German frontier was restored for all economic purposes. Politically the principle of self-determination was invoked only to be violated. Not only was the unwarranted assumption made that all Germans wished to join the Third Reich, but 719,127 Czechs were simply annexed by Germany. Many of these were Czechs living in purely Czech districts and they were annexed for reasons of purely power-politics. This annexation of non-German peoples was undersigned by the British and French representatives on the International Commission. Since German undertakings to the contrary preceded this annexation the Nazis had reason to suppose that Britain and France would continue to be indifferent to further annexation, such as that which took place in March. This was fortunately not the case. Yet the declarations of leading statesmen in Britain and France, after the German annexation of Czecho-Slovakia on March 15, 1939, proved how little the two Western Governments seemed to be aware of the harm which they had permitted six months earlier. It is for this reason that the mistakes and injustices of the Munich frontier have been exposed at some length in the Appendix. If Europe is ever to be reconstructed on a sound basis, there can be no return to Munich.

2. Czechoslovakia Internally Divided.

The Munich Agreement represented in all respects a terrible catastrophe for Czechoslovakia. Her state structure was shattered, her independence undermined. Such a shock was naturally bound to introduce profound changes in her entire policy. The exterior symbol of such future changes was the resignation of President Beneš. President Beneš' resignation indicated the interruption of the process of development of Masaryk's First Republic, externally independent and internally free, and marked the dawn of a " Second Republic," externally dependent upon the Third Reich, and internally changing from a unified state into a Czecho-Slovako-Ukrainian Federation based on authoritarian principles.

(a) *The Federalisation of Czechoslovakia.* The problem which first called for solution was the transformation of the Republic into a federal state. In the new situation created by the ruthless reduction in size and strength of Bohemia and Moravia, the two provinces which had always represented the nucleus of the state, the centrifugal forces quickly gained ground over the centripetal. In Slovakia Hlinka's Autonomists[1] came immediately to the fore. Although they represented only one-third of the Slovak people, they declared that they could no longer be satisfied with a decentralised administration and local self-government, and proceeded to make every effort to obtain such complete autonomy as would convert Czechoslovakia into a form of federal state. At the conference held by the Slovak parties in Žilina on October 5 and 6, the Ludáci forced the acceptance of their proposal of autonomy for Slovakia, which had been made in the Czechoslovak Parliament on August 17, 1938. A resolution adopted at Žilina, on October 6, demanded that " government and executive power in Slovakia should

---

[1] Slovenská Ludová Strana, popularly known in Czech as Ludáci. This Slovak Populist (Catholic) Party was led by the priest, Andreas Hlinka, till his death in the summer of 1938. It is referred to here alternatively as the Slovak Autonomists, the Hlinka Party and the Ludáci.

repose in a Slovak Government, composed of five Ministers, the
following matters only being considered as the concern of the
whole state: the activities of the Ministries of Foreign Affairs
and National Defence, the administration of the National Debt
and the issue of loans for purposes interesting the whole state;
the five Slovak Ministers should at the same time be members of
the Central Government in Prague. Dr. Tiso, Deputy Chairman
of the Slovak Catholic Party, was appointed Minister for the
Administration of Slovakia, and on October 7, at his proposal,
four other Slovak Ministers were appointed (two Catholics and
two Agrarians). Thus, under the Presidency of Dr. Tiso, the first
Government of an autonomous Slovakia came into being.

It was quite natural, of course, that a similar arrangement
should be made for Sub-Carpathian Ruthenia, which had been
promised autonomy definitely by the Treaty of St. Germain and
by the Czechoslovak Constitution. A Government of Ruthenia
was appointed on October 11, composed of four Ministers and
two Under-Secretaries of State, under the Presidency of Andrej
Bródy, a Parliamentary Deputy; the so-called Russophil interests being represented in it by MM. Bródy and Fencík, and the
Ukrainian interests by M. Revay and Dr. Bačinský. On October
26, however, M. Bródy was dismissed from his post, and three
days later he was imprisoned on a charge of high treason for
having, together with Dr. Fencík (who had in the meantime
fled to Hungary), favoured the Hungarian proposal of uniting Ruthenia with Hungary. Bródy was accused of having,
during a considerable period, worked on behalf of the Hungarian
Government. He was replaced as Prime Minister of Ruthenia
by Mgr. Vološín, representative of the Ukrainian movement,
and since that time Sub-Carpathian Ruthenia has changed its
name and status first into " the Carpathian Ukraine " and now
again into Ruthenia, province of Hungary. Since the capital of
the province, Užhorod, had been handed over to Hungary by the
Vienna decisions, the Government was obliged to move to Chust,
which thus, for the short space of a few months, became the
capital of the autonomous Carpathian Ukraine.

After long and difficult negotiations, the Czechoslovak
Parliament accepted, by a great majority, the law regarding
Slovak autonomy, as required by the Slovak Catholic Party.

Slovakia was granted an independent legislature and executive, while the Slovak Provincial Administration was to be appointed by the President of the Republic, advised by the Chairman of the Slovak Parliament. The official language, which was to be taught in the schools, was to be Slovak, but Czechs, as well as all Bohemian or Moravian administrative or business offices, would retain the right to use the Czech language, while the provisions stipulated in the Treaty of St. Germain of September 10, 1919, for the other nationalities would still hold good. The Central Parliament was to deal with everything regarding foreign relations and national defence (but Slovak soldiers would, in peace time, serve only in Slovakia in the services responsible to the local command), the Department of Civil Registration, Customs and Excise, Postal Office, State railways and other communication services, and Inland Revenue.

Changes of the Constitution and the passage of laws regarding the Constitution were to have had the support of specified majority of the Slovak deputies, the Central Government was to be such as would enjoy the confidence of a majority of the Slovak deputies, and the President of the Republic had to be elected by a majority of the Slovak deputies. All other matters were to come within the competence of the independent Slovak Parliament and Government, and the members of the Slovak Government were to participate in the decisions of the Central Government only with regard to subjects concerning Slovakia also. The Czechoslovak Parliament at the same time (November 19) passed in principle a similar law with regard to Sub-Carpathian Ruthenia, whose name was officially changed on December 31 to Carpatho-Ukraine. A change was adopted also in the official title of the whole Republic, for when, in accordance with the wish of Slovak Catholics, the Slovak nation was recognised as sovereign and separate, the name, Czechoslovakia, which expressed the idea of national unity between the Czechs and Slovaks, was changed into Czecho-Slovakia.

The constitutional laws on the autonomy of Slovakia and Sub-Carpathian Russia were published on November 22, 1938 (*see* Nos. 299 and 328 of the *Collection of Laws and Decrees*). It was, of course, incomparably easier to extort by political pressure the legal recognition of autonomy for Slovakia and the

Carpathian Ukraine than it was to create an autonomous life in these small and backward provinces. The Slovaks and the Ukrainians were not politically mature enough for such a far-reaching autonomy as they achieved in November, 1938. The political, economic and cultural conditions which would have made it possible simply did not exist. Both these provinces awoke to independent life only in 1918, when the majority of the people were illiterate and completely backward in national and political consciousness. Through the systematic work of the Czechs, who furnished the men for the administration and financed the cultural and economic advance of Slovakia and Sub-Carpathian Russia, together with the ardent patriotism of a handful of Slovaks and Carpathian Russians, the two countries had advanced astonishingly quickly during the last twenty years. But twenty years were not, of course, enough for the creation of conditions necessary for an autonomous, still less for a completely independent life. The best Slovaks and Ruthenians realised this clearly and they therefore did not ask for autonomy, but only for progressive decentralisation. Even inside the Hlinka party there were politicians who were conscious of the danger of establishing the radical autonomy which was demanded by the party. Furthermore, the Slovak Autonomists had never succeeded in any election in polling more than a third of the votes in Slovakia. The laws on autonomy of November, 1938, were passed only because the Czechoslovak Republic had been so weakened and broken at Munich that the road was open to every type of demagogic radicalism. Furthermore, the Slovak extremists knew that their aspirations were looked on favourably by the Germans, who wanted to weaken Czechoslovakia as far as possible—the Henlein movement had served that purpose, the Slovak autonomist party were to serve it later.

The following economic figures may illustrate the fact that the basis for Slovak autonomy was altogether illusory. Even after Munich, the crippled Czech countries raised 75 per cent. of the grain production. The remainder was in Slovakia and Sub-Carpathian Russia. Some 80 per cent. of all industrial enterprises were in the Czech countries, 17 per cent. in Slovakia and 3 per cent. in Sub-Carpathian Russia. About seven-eighths of the production capacity were in the Czech districts, while only one-eighth was in Slovakia and Sub-Carpathian Russia. The share of Slovakia in the national income was about a tenth of the whole. The taxation and consumption capacity of the Slovaks and Ruthenes was incomparably lower than that of the Czechs. Out of all capital savings, which were estimated at about 58 milliard crowns in the old Czechoslovakia and about 38 milliards in the post-Munich republic, about 90 per cent. was in the Czech districts and 10 per cent. in Slovakia. The Czech countries thus represented about 85 to 90 per cent. of the whole economic power of the state even after the Munich Agreement.

Just as before, it was therefore necessary that even after the federalisation of the state the Czech countries should support Slovakia and Sub-Carpathian Russia financially and economically. It was also necessary to help these two autonomous countries in administrative and military matters in order to build up their autonomous life. The anti-Czech agitation organised by Slovak and Ukrainian extremists thus merely speeded up the final break-up of the state, and the loss of independence not only of the Czechs, but also of the Slovaks and Carpathian Ukrainians.

(b) *The New President of the Republic and the New Government.*— It was only after the foregoing changes in the constitutional and political structure of the state had been effected that it was possible to proceed with the election of a new President of the Republic. On November 30, 1938, Dr. Emil Hácha, Chief Justice of the Supreme Administrative Court, was elected to that office by the votes of 272 out of a total number of 312 Deputies and Senators who were present. The election placed at the head of the state an old and highly-respected judge, who was a democratic Conservative, but who had previously not taken part in any political activities. He was elected by the votes of all the Czechs and Slovaks except the Communists, who handed in blank cards; the German Parliamentarians, repeating their post-war tactics, did not attend the election.

General Syrový's Government, upon which had fallen the particularly difficult and most ungrateful task of maintaining the authority of the state during a wild period shaken by revolutionary events, resigned, and on December 1 a new

Government was formed. This new Government was headed by M. Rudolf Beran, President of the strongest political party, the Agrarian Party, and President also of the Party of National Union, which had recently been formed. M. Beran was well-known for his efforts to reach a friendly understanding with the Third Reich and with Henlein's party. As Minister of Foreign Affairs, there remained Dr. František Chvalkovský, a sympathiser with the policy of the Berlin-Rome Axis; as Minister of National Defence, General Syrový; as Minister of Finance, Dr. Kalfus. The Deputy, M. Karol Sidor, the most passionate advocate of Slovak autonomy, was appointed delegate for Slovakia; Dr. Jiří Havelka was appointed Minister without portfolio, Dr. Havelka was a specialist in administrative questions and was later appointed to the direction of the Office of the President of the Republic. For the various other departments, some of which were merged into one another, experienced specialists were appointed as Ministers.

The only new Ministers who were actually already in Parliament and who had previously been politically active were the Prime Minister, Rudolf Beran, and the Slovak representative, Karol Sidor. This represented, of course, a great departure from the principle of party government upon which Czechoslovak democracy had hitherto been based.

The President of the Republic at the same time appointed a Government of Slovakia, composed of five members, and headed by Mgr. Jozef Tiso, and a Government of Carpatho-Ukraine, composed of two members, and with Mgr. Augustin Vološín as Prime Minister.

On December 16 the Slovak delegates were appointed to the common Czech-Slovak Ministries of Foreign Affairs, National Defence and Finance.

(c) *Authoritative Democracy in Bohemia.*—Meanwhile great changes took place in the internal political system of Czecho-Slovakia. Prior to the September crisis, the political system of Czechoslovakia was based on numerous political parties, each of which was run in a disciplined manner by its own bureaucracy. These parties represented various social classes or economic groups, but they were somewhat of a mixture between political parties and professional corporations or groups. After the catastrophe, however, it was considered necessary to simplify this complicated system; the party leaders therefore decided to reorganise all political groups in Bohemia and Moravia into two parties. The first of these parties, the Governmental party of " National Union " was a merger of the former Agrarian, Small Traders, Czech Catholic, National Union and Czech Fascist Parties, together with a part of the Czech National Socialist Party; the other, in opposition to the Government, was the " Party of Labour," composed mainly of the former Czech Social-Democrat Party, but containing also the rest of the Czech National Socialist Party.

As early as October, the Czech Social-Democrat Party announced its secession from the Socialist International; this action was one of several which expressed the disillusion felt generally by all our people—disillusion with all international movements and organisations. The complete absence of support from abroad in September had made them look for the salvation of what remained possible to save in relying on their own strength and resources, however small they might be, rather than to faith in international obligations. At the end of 1938 the Communist Party was dissolved, and by a decree dated December 23, 1938, it was stipulated that new political parties might be founded only by permission of the Government.

In Bohemia and Moravia an attempt was made to reorganise political life on the basis of two parties, and it was intended in this way to continue, though to a very limited degree, in the democratic tradition of the nation. It is easy to understand, however, that during a period of a great upheaval, when, in fact, it is necessary to build up a new state, there must inevitably be an increase of the authority and concentration of power in the hands of the executive. For this reason, the Czecho-Slovak Parliament, in December, 1938, passed a new and very sweeping Enabling Act, valid for a period of two years, which granted the President of the Republic the right to change even the Constitution and constitutional laws by his personal decree. Thus a system of authoritarian democracy was introduced in Bohemia and Moravia. In practice, all power was concentrated in the hands of the Government and executive—the parliament became only a decorative ornament. It was also clear that the granting of autonomy to Slovakia and Sub-Carpathian Russia necessitated new Parliamentary elections; also in Bohemia and in Moravia. But in the meantime this necessity was not particularly pressing—there were many more important tasks to face. Thus the existing Parliament remained in operation— though only on paper. The organisation of the two new parties, the Government Party of National Union and the opposition National Labour Party went ahead. Progress was slow, however, and little enthusiasm was shown by the people who were too distressed by the Munich catastrophe to take much interest in party alignments which must have seemed rather artificial. Also the fact that the two parties did not differ very clearly from each other in the most important principles of their programme prevented the real success of either. Their political orientation and activities were more or less in agreement. The whole artificiality of political life organised on this basis was apparent in the fact that the National Labour Party, which was supposed to represent a loyal opposition, had to be prevented at all costs from achieving a majority over the Government Party of National Union. The Opposition leaders themselves were aware of this. For if it had happened, there was danger that Berlin would immediately have intervened, since the Nazis were from the outset determined not to allow a party to assume power in Prague which was recruited largely of former Socialists. In practice, it so happened therefore that behind the new façade of two artificially created parties the former more or less successful collaboration of the representatives of the old parties continued unabated. The situation was best characterised by the fact that the Prime Minister, Beran, did not, even under the new conditions, sever his relations or abandon his collaboration with the Chairman of the National Labour Party, the Deputy, Hampl, who had been the Chairman of the Social Democratic Party. The names of these two politicians suggest that the political re-grouping was carried out in such a way that the majority rallied round the Agrarians, whose leader was Beran, and the minority round the Social-Democrats, who were led by Hampl.

This, of course, did not exhaust all political activity in the Czech provinces after Munich. The different Fascist groups became very vociferous—the less support they had among the people the more vociferous they became. Before Munich these groups were quite unimportant. The Fascist Party of the former General Gajda and the " League " of the Deputy, Stříbrný, were declining and the group called " Vlajka " was almost unknown to the wider public. Even after Munich the majority of people continued to ignore the Fascists. The latter thought that they would gain popularity by a violent Press campaign against ex-President Beneš, who had left Czechoslovakia for England on October 22, 1938, because he did not want to cause difficulties to the Government by his continued presence in the country. After such a devastating catastrophe, it was only natural that people should ask who was responsible for it. They wanted to find an answer which was simple and easy to explain, so the Fascists found it easy to put about that " President Beneš was to blame for everything, and in particular for his policy of co-operation with the Western democracies." In the middle of October a Parliamentary Commission was appointed for the purpose of deciding who was responsible for the national disaster. This Commission very soon found that among those who were to blame were not only President Beneš, Dr. Krofta, his Foreign Minister, and their faithful collaborators, but all those who accepted and adopted their policy—and this policy had been accepted by all but a very few of the leading politicians and political parties. It soon became obvious, moreover, that the campaign of defamation against President Beneš met with strong popular opposition and that, instead of antipathy being created against him, sympathy increased for the man who accepted the consequences, political as well as personal, of a national disaster for which he was not to blame. The Czechoslovak people were not so ready as were certain volatile sections of the intelligentsia of Prague to reach a mistaken verdict.

The demagogic campaign which tried to throw all responsibility only on the former President, Beneš, was openly condemned by Deputy Ladislav Rašín, a political opponent of Beneš, when he declared in Parliament in the middle of December, 1938: " I consider it necessary in the higher interests of the State that the Government should try to ascertain the responsibility for the national catastrophe. But this responsibility cannot be ascertained by newspaper campaigns. I therefore propose that the Government should take the necessary measures to investigate the question by an objective and independent body. It should be investigated in its whole breadth and length from the policeman who fired a shot, though he should have waited to be killed, up to the former President of the Republic. Do not let us forget that between this policeman who did not obey the order to commit suicide and thus created an " incident " and the President who was mistaken in believing in the honour and loyalty of our allies are a number of persons, also among us Deputies, among Ministers and Prime Ministers, who also have their share of responsibility and their share of the guilt."

In the same speech, Deputy Rašín, who had belonged to those politicians who refused to capitulate before the Franco-British ultimatum of September 21, 1938, and would have preferred even an isolated war, criticised the whole policy of concessions to the Nazis and declared: " I know very well that the time is not propitious for the solemn announcement of a revisionist programme, but I cannot say, as one of the speakers before me did, that what has happened is settled for good and all. As long as I shall live, it will not be settled for me. In the soul of the nation there must still burn a flame of national faith. A nation is great only in the strength of its courage, in the ardour of its belief and the greatness of its resolution to suffer and make sacrifices for the future. The Czech nation waited three hundred years for the restoration of its independence. The Poles waited for decades for their resurrection, the Hungarians waited twenty years for revision. We also must wait again, must keep alive the flame of faith. It must not be extinguished; we must not become the victims of resignation; the nation of Hussite warriors must not become a nation of mean slaves."

On the same occasion the Nationalist Deputy Schwarz pronounced a very courageous speech. He openly objected to Czecho-Slovakia joining the Rome-Berlin Axis: " Is what has happened to us, not enough " he said, " that some people would want us to lose again in the next great struggle with the German-Italian alliance ? " Though an opponent of Communism, he thanked expressly the Russian ally, " who

alone, not only kept the Treaty, but was ready to help even
far beyond the obligations of these treaties." Both these
speeches were, of course, suppressed by the Censor, but they
quickly spread among the public. There is no doubt that they
expressed the sentiment of the people, on whom the propaganda
of the Fascist groups could have no deeper influence if only for
the reason that the Fascists tried, by all possible means, to curry
favour with the German Nazis.

The Fascist elements also began to excite anti-Semitic
passions. Unfortunately, a certain number of Czech lawyers and
physicians all too eagerly trimmed their sails to the wind and
extorted from their organisations various measures directed
against the Jews. It is all to the honour of the Czech people that
it was not carried away by the anti-Semitic flood. On the
contrary in several country towns a sort of voluntary " referen-
dum " was organised, which always resulted in favour of the
Jews. This spontaneous reaction of the people against the anti-
Semitic agitation was all the more remarkable because the
Government and the Press, out of fear of Berlin, did not dare to
counter anti-Semitism in public. Nevertheless, the Government
tried discreetly to prevent these ugly excesses. People in economic
life pointed to the dangerous consequences which anti-Semitism
would have on Czecho-Slovak trade, especially in the Anglo-
Saxon countries. One of the Ministers declared, " You will either
export goods or Jews," and this saying quickly spread among
the public, though it could not be published in the Press. The
Government yielded only slowly and with obvious reluctance to
the pressure of the Nazis, who demanded the " liquidation of the
Jews." Only at the end of February, 1939, internal circulars, or,
rather, decrees, were issued which advised the removal of Jews
from leading or conspicuous positions in the administration and
in public life, but even then the procedure was to be considerate.
One must concede that the post-Munich Beran Government
acted moderately in the Jewish question as in other matters. It
put the brake on excesses and tried to preserve at least some of
the main principles of democratic policy. Nevertheless, it was
not popular. The people, accustomed to freedom and hating
Nazi barbarity, suspected the Government of too much subservience to Berlin without apparently sufficiently realising that

after Munich it had become impossible effectively to resist the wishes of Berlin.

The position of the Government was really very difficult: it inspired no confidence among the people, who were filled with the hope of reparation for the wrong committed at Munich; at the same time, it was exposed to continuous pressure from Berlin, which suspected it of being not consistently and sincerely loyal to the Third Reich. The Germans in Bohemia and Moravia accused it of refusing their demands and of returning to the " Anti-German" tendency of the Beneš régime. The Czech Fascists were dissatisfied because it still hesitated to introduce the methods prevalent in the Third Reich. Finally, it was exposed to the continuous blackmail of the Slovaks and Ruthenes. But at least Beran had enough opportunities to convince himself how superhumanly difficult it was to live " in friendship " with the Nazis, a theory which he had continuously advocated in former times.

In addition to these immensely difficult political conditions, the Government had to face grave economic, social and financial tasks. The care for the refugees from the occupied territories was an especially painful problem. At the end of January, 1939, there were about 170,000 of whom about 12,000 were anti-Nazi Germans and about 7,000 Jews. It was impossible to solve this problem without help from abroad. After fairly protracted negotiations in London and Paris, a British and French loan to the amount of £16 million was granted at the beginning of February. It may be interesting to quote the Prague weekly, *Přitomnost* of February 15, 1939, on the actual effects of this loan:

" Let us first discuss the contribution made by France. France does not give us any cash at all. France lent us, during the depression of 1932, 700 millions of gold francs in several instalments. That amounts to about £4 million. These are now taken over by France and France will pay the interest and redemption of the debt. But the interest and redemption thus saved will not remain in Czecho-Slovakia. The 35 million francs which represent the interest and redemption service must be paid into a special account, out of which foreign currency will be given to refugees who want to emigrate from the country. This means that the Government must first secure this foreign currency and then will have to allow its export. This settles the French contribution. Let us glance at the British share in the loan. First of all, out of £12 million, £4 million are a gift to the Republic. But the Republic is obliged to distribute these £4 million under British-French supervision to the refugees from the Sudeten territory who want to emigrate. One family gets £200 each as a gift. Those who have the means must pay for themselves; the poor ones get it for nothing. A higher exchange rate is calculated for those who can afford it and the money gained is used for the fund, which thus increases its means for the emigration of further refugees. About a fifth of these £4 million has been distributed already: only about 3,000 refugees have so far profited from it. On the whole, only about 10,000 people will be able to emigrate on this money, because certain families will be given more than £200. If only £200 was given to each family, between 15,000 and 20,000 refugees would be able to leave the country. The arrangement so far is a good one since nobody, for instance, can be admitted to Australia who has not £200 free abroad. Without this gift, these people could not emigrate at all.

" Out of the whole loan there remains then only £8 million, which we have not yet accounted for. This forms the real loan. About a third of this sum will be used for the necessary redemption of bank-notes. A further £2,000,000 will have to be assigned to the Emigration Fund and will have to be paid in pounds, as they will not be paid out to us any more. As may be remembered in the first days after Munich Great Britain advanced £10 million on a bigger loan which was then proposed. As we are now promised only £8 million, £2 million were paid actually in excess of the final sum and these £2 million will have to be paid into that £4 million Emigration Fund into which Great Britain will pay a correspondingly lower sum. Thus only £6 million are left for an actual loan, or less than 1 milliard crowns. It will be remembered that originally a loan of about £30 million was discussed.

" Thus the whole ' economic assistance ' which was promised

by Great Britain and France, when they forced us to accept the Munich Agreement, finally comes to a reduction of our export quotas to France by half and to the £6 million British loan."

This was the position after Munich. After the annexation of Czecho-Slovakia by Germany in March, 1939, the whole loan has lost its original basis. We can only express the hope that the money which it was designed to procure for Czechoslovakia will be used for the support of the new unfortunate refugees from the country.

The Prague Government tried to alleviate the social difficulties and unemployment by the construction of a motor road from the west to the east of the republic, by the erection of labour camps, by the introduction of compulsory labour, by the pensioning of older state employees, by the dismissal from public service of all married women, etc. Many of these measures were, of course, harsh and even inhuman. But the extraordinarily difficult situation in which the state was placed was a valid excuse. One must take into account the fact that the resources of income for the state had been reduced by 40 per cent. in consequence of the cession of the rich frontier districts and that the production capacity of the country had been lowered by about 35 per cent. Nevertheless, the Government tried, by all means, to preserve order in the state finances. After difficult negotiations with the Slovak Government, which made very large claims on Prague and was very reluctant to make any sacrifices for common expenditure, the common state Budget was announced on February 18, 1939, in which expenditure was estimated at 3,191,367,000 crowns and income at 3,191,616,000 crowns. About 44 per cent. of the expenditure was assigned to the defence of the state and 33 per cent. to the state debt. Military expenditure was lowered in comparison with last year by 700 millions. The Budget of Bohemia and Moravia (these provinces, though in area they represented only half of the republic, represented in population three-quarters, in economic resources seven-eighths and in taxation resources almost nine-tenths of the state Budget), showed the inevitable deficit: compared with 5,902 million expenditure the income was estimated only at 4,638 millions.

Public instruction required 1,172 millions; public works, 863 millions; social services and health, 705 millions; 450 millions were earmarked for the motor-road, 580 millions for the reconstruction of the railways and postal services. The Slovak Budget estimated expenditure for administration at 1,193 millions and income at 886 millions, for state enterprises expenditure at 1,178 millions and income at 974 millions, besides 645 millions of investments. The large deficit was to be reduced by a " voluntary " loan which the Slovak Government proposed to float.

These figures give an approximately correct picture of the financial and economic situation of Czecho-Slovakia as she was being rebuilt in reduced circumstances after Munich. Though the Czechoslovak people were considerably impoverished by the Munich " agreement," the financial burdens of the state did not diminish in proportion. All the more important is it therefore to stress that even after the terrible shock of the September crisis of 1938 the Czech people continued to be punctual in the fulfilment of their duties as tax-payers. The Minister of Finance, Dr. Kalfus, could declare with justified pride on February 18, 1939, that the " working of our economic and financial machine had not been substantially impaired. The people even in the districts near the frontiers where the cession of territory was taking place, continued to work, to reap, to plough, to go to the factories and offices and to pay the taxes regularly. They simply believed in their nation and government. Not many nations, even with centuries' old traditions, could have carried on better under such tragic circumstances. This fact inspires us with a fervent hope for the future. We have suffered immense economic losses, but we have not lost belief in ourselves and this faith will lead us again to a better future." When he spoke thus in the middle of February, Dr. Kalfus could not foresee that within less than a month the Czecho-Slovak nation would again be overwhelmed by a new catastrophe.

(d) *The Totalitarian Régime in Slovakia.* In Slovakia the situation developed differently from that in the Czech territories. In the conditions existing in Slovakia, which were politically and socially far more primitive and culturally much more backward than in the Czech districts proper, the political " primitives," represented by Hlinka's Autonomist Party, came to the top. That party seized power in Slovakia and forced all others to give up the struggle. This was possible, not through its own resources, but only because the Czechs had been crippled by the German occupation, and because Germany gave every possible assistance to the Catholic politicians, many of whom as subsequent events proved, were working in close collaboration with the Nazis. The Nazis intended, and in fact secured, that Slovakia should become a tool of the Third Reich. The geographical and strategic situation of Slovakia placed it in an admirable position to act as an instrument for German manœuvres, not only against the Czechs, but also against the Hungarians and Poles.

In the six months which followed Munich, the Slovak autonomists (Ludáci) with effective help from the Nazis, organised in autonomous Slovakia a totalitarian, single-party régime. Under the leadership of Karol Sidor, they organised Hlinka Guards—complete with uniforms, decorations and brutal habits, copied from the Nazi S.A. and S.S.—and set up concentration camps, even before they had started arresting " awkward " people ! The Slovaks adopted as their slogan the variant, " One God, one Nation, one Leader ! "

The Communist Party was dissolved as early as October 9,[1] and all the other parties were either dissolved or forced to dissolve themselves, the only one which was allowed being the Catholic Party of " National Unity," founded on October 8.

A large number of various cultural, professional and sporting organisations were also dissolved, among them being the Czechoslovak *Sokol* Movement, whose property was simply confiscated by the dominant Ludáci. The Press was entirely " *gleichgeschaltet* " and many of the Slovak newspapers were stopped, though German papers were treated more leniently.[2] Anti-Semitism was not merely tolerated, but was directly supported. At the same time the slogan: " *Von s Čechami!* " (" Out with the Czechs ! ") was introduced. Czech professors,

[1] The Communist Party was dissolved also in Carpatho-Ukraine at the same time. In the Czech provinces its activities were stopped on October 20, but the Party was not dissolved until the end of December.

[2] In Bohemia several German papers were stopped because they had lost their readers, who had been annexed by Germany, but, on the other hand, the import of papers from Germany was recommenced.

teachers, officials and judges were mercilessly dismissed, and more than 9,000 Czechs employed in the Government and other public services were discharged; the Fascists of the reactionary Catholic Party could not tolerate the presence of the more progressive Czech elements. This hasty dismissal of Czech officials caused, of course, serious deficiencies in the administration.

Autonomy, which the Slovaks did not win by hard work, but rather extorted for themselves by taking advantage of the tragic conditions into which Czechoslovakia was thrown, proved an " Eldorado " for many adventurers; while any Slovak who remained faithful to the idea of Czechoslovak national unity was treated with contempt if not with violence. The fate of the ex-Minister, Dr. Ivan Dérer, one of the truest of Slovak patriots, who had done for the Slovak nation infinitely more than all the Ludáci and their followers combined, is typical: after Munich, Dérer became a sort of refugee, living in Prague, because in Slovakia he would certainly be harassed and persecuted by Sidor's Hlinka Guards for his loyalty to the idea of the national unity of Czechoslovakia. Equally typical of what went on in this Munich era was the case of Professor Vojtěch Tuka, who was condemned in 1929 to several years of imprisonment for high treason in conspiring with Hungarian revisionists; in 1939, he was reinstated with honour, played a prominent part in putting Slovakia under the protectorate of Germany and is now Minister of the Interior in that German-ruled province.

Hatred of the Czechs, which was deliberately fostered for years by the Slovak autonomists, had many causes. Much harm was undoubtedly done by the short-sighted bureaucratic policy of centralisation pursued in Prague, and also by the somewhat tactless behaviour of some of the Czechs employed in Slovakia, who did not appreciate sufficiently the susceptibilities of the Slovaks, a primitive people whose national consciousness was only just coming to life again. But a deeper cause of this unfriendliness was the new-found nationalism of the Slovaks, which, having been consistently trampled underfoot by the Hungarians was first able to develop in the Czechoslovak Republic. Hence it considered itself in opposition to the Czechs, who were both numerically, politically and culturally far stronger than themselves. Nationalism needs for its development a certain amount of antagonism against some other nation; the Hungarians were beyond the frontier and were very weak after the World War; whereas the Czechs who were coming into Slovakia appeared as rivals to the rising Slovak element. Especially among the younger Slovaks it was forgotten that without Czech help it would have been impossible to organise the administration and public life of Slovakia. It was indeed the Czechs and a handful of Slovak patriots who made possible the cultural, economic and social progress of the Slovak people. For not only were these provinces culturally backward and their people illiterate, but they were also without sufficient capital of their own, hence it was necessarily the Czechs who provided roughly-speaking 30 milliards of Czech crowns for capital expenditure, in Slovakia and Sub-Carpathian Ruthenia. The work that was done and the capital which was invested benefited, of course, not only the provinces to which they were devoted, but the whole of the Czechoslovak Republic, for it was a matter of vital interest to all that the cultural and economic level of the Slovak and Ruthene people should be raised. But the younger generation of the Slovaks and the Slovak nationalist demagogues underestimated the constructive work carried out by the Czechs for their country. The Autonomists' dèmand was, in fact, to be exclusive master in a house which was built mainly by the efforts of the Czechs. If the loyalty of the Czechs towards the Western democracies was poorly rewarded, they were no more fortunate as regards the loyalty of the Slovaks.

Though the new masters of Slovakia soon realised that the united advance of Poland and Hungary was directed primarily against Slovakia, and that, in the territories occupied by the Hungarians, Slovaks were persecuted and even shot, the authorities in Bratislava no longer had the possibility of drawing the logical conclusion—that Czech help was not without value and that considerable advantages lay in co-operation with the Czechs.

Although a certain amount of appeasement ensued after the election (on December 18, 1938), of the first Slovak Parliament, this movement was rapidly cut short in March, 1939. The election was, of course, organised on Nazi lines; only one list of candidates was presented to the electorate, only official propaganda was allowed, and the voting was, in practice, not secret, but public. Under such circumstances, it was not surprising that, according to the official announcement, 97·5 per cent. of electors voted in favour of the Government. The highest percentages of votes declared not valid occurred in districts with a Protestant majority[1] and in the districts of Eastern Slovakia. A certain number of candidates belonging to the former Agrarian Party and to the other non-Marxist parties were allowed to appear on the governmental list, but not a single Czech candidate was allowed. Although the Czechs were much more numerous in Slovakia than the Germans, representatives of the Germans, as well as of the Hungarians, were entered òn the list of candidates and eventually elected. In this way sixty-three Deputies were " elected," and, since 1,263,687 votes in all were recorded, each candidate represented about 20,000 voters.

The Slovak Parliament was solemnly inaugurated on January 18, 1939, in the presence of the Prime Minister of the Central Government, M. Beran, and the Minister of National Defence, General Syrový, as well as other representatives of the Central Parliament. Speeches were made on this occasion urging the importance of friendly relations between Czechs and Slovaks. The improvement of these relations had been much advanced already by the visit of President Hácha to the High Tatra Mountains during the last days of December, 1938, but the factor which had most influence in inclining the new rulers of autonomous Slovakia towards a *rapprochement* with the Czechs was undoubtedly their painful experiences with the Poles and the Hungarians.[2]

Dr. Sokol was elected President of the Slovak Parliament and on his advice (in accordance with the principle of the new law regarding Slovak autonomy) the President of the Republic appointed a new Slovak Government, again headed by Dr. Tiso, and increased in number from five to six Ministers. The reconstruction of the Tiso Government was not without political significance. It was of considerable importance that the radical

---

[1] The Protestants in Slovakia are as a rule nationally and culturally much more advanced than the majority of the Catholic population.

[2] Slovakia was at this time being flooded with Slovak refugees from the territories occupied by Hungary, in which the pre-War policy of persecution and Magyarisation was adopted.

autonomist, Matúš Černák resigned and that he was replaced in the Ministry of Education by the more moderate Jozef Sivák. The young, thirty-five-year-old, secondary school-teacher, Černák, had been appointed Minister in the Prague Government the day after the mobilisation of September 24, at the suggestion of the Hlinka party. When, however, the Munich catastrophe happened, he immediately exploited the situation and on October 3, presented demands which amounted to an ultimatum, asking for the surrender of all power in Slovakia into the hands of the Hlinka party. At the same time he resigned as a demonstration. At the conference at Žilina, held on October 6, 1938, which resulted in the proclamation of Slovak autonomy, he adopted the extreme radical point of view. In the Tiso Goverment, Černák represented the sharply anti-Czech tendency and he more and more identified himself with those who, following Tuka's example, demanded the complete independence of Slovakia. His resignation from the Government on January 20, 1939, was generally considered as a symptom of some willingness on the part of the Slovak Government to check the extreme separatist elements. At that time the general political situation and the difficulties with administration and finances, severely shaken by the events, had really brought home some of the advantages which the Slovaks derived from their association in a common state with the Czechs to many leading Slovak politicians, among them even Minister Sidor. But the very change of mind which became apparent among some of the more soberminded Slovak autonomists was the signal to the Slovak extremists and the German Nazis collaborating with them to make real consolidation of the relations between Czechs and Slovaks impossible. Thus, after a short respite which lasted approximately from the end of December, 1938, to the end of January, 1939, the Slovak extremists, led by Tuka and Mach, began in obvious concert with their German protectors, to intensify their agitation for an independent Slovak state.

(e) *Chaos in the Carpathian Ukraine.* In Sub-Carpathian Russia, which at the end of December, 1938, was renamed " Carpathian Ukraine," the post-Munich situation was extremely confused. Since October, 1938, German influence had become dominant even in the internal affairs of the province. Germany at first opposed the cession of Sub-Carpathian Russia to Hungary and her point of view prevailed at the Vienna Conference of November 21. The country was, however, deprived of its most fertile southern regions and lost its two most important towns, Užhorod (Ungvár) and Mukačevo (Munkácz). The railway connection with Slovakia was interrupted. Hungarian and Polish terrorists continued to attack the frontier regions: skirmishes and even small battles were the order of the day. At the same time, the country was flooded with specious agitators for the foundation of a " Great Ukraine." The Ukrainian agitators came from Galicia, Vienna and Germany and had every support from the Nazis. M. Revay, Minister of the Interior, granted them citizen rights with extraordinary alacrity, so that they could freely pursue their activities in all parts of the country. People whose only qualification was their zeal for a Greater Ukraine were called to fill leading political and administrative positions. There had always existed in Ruthenia a considerable rivalry between those with Ukrainian and those with Great Russian sympathies. The régime was now completely controlled by representatives of the Ukrainian movement, and, naturally, opposed by people of Great-Russian sympathies. The difference between the two groups was also partly religious: the Ukrainians were Greek Orthodox, the Russophiles were Russian Orthodox; and partly linguistic: the former spoke Ukrainian, the latter Russian.

Mgr. Vološín, the Premier of the autonomous Government, an ailing old man, a Ruthenian patriot of undoubted merits and good intentions with a sincere regard for the Czechs, but weak and purely parochial in his outlook, floundered helplessly in this political and administrative confusion. This simple priest, who had worked hard for the extermination of illiteracy among his people, had never dreamt of becoming Premier. The task which he had to face would have defeated even a man of the greatest experience and firmest resolution. At the beginning, Mgr. Vološín wanted to lean on the Czech officials and soldiers, who alone were capable of preserving order in the administration. But the ambitious young Ukrainian nationalists wanted as soon as possible to get hold of all positions held by Czechs. At the instigation of German Nazi agents, therefore, they turned against the Czechs just as the radical Slovaks had done. Nevertheless, the behaviour of the Ukrainians towards the Czechs was, at least in the first months after Munich, better than that of the Slovak autonomists. It began to deteriorate only after January, 1939, especially under the influence of the Germans.

After the establishment of the autonomous Carpathian Ukraine, the Germans behaved as masters of the country. They made it clear to everybody that the country could preserve its autonomy only with German help. The Carpathian Ukrainians thus saw in Hitler their main protector against the Hungarians and Poles and thought it necessary to fulfil all his actual or supposed wishes. In the second half of November, 1938, the Secretary of the German Legation in Prague, Dr. Hoffmann, arrived at Chust, which had after the loss of Užhorod become the new capital of the country, and was everywhere welcomed with great ostentation. Germany despatched agents and officers to Sub-Carpathian Russia as early as October and November, 1938. In spite of the snow on all the mountains, many of these were said to be carrying on geological research ! The Germans resident in the Carpathian Ukraine organised a National Socialist party and its representative became a Secretary of State in the Chust Government. The Ukrainian youth was organised according to their instructions into a uniformed " troop " called *Sič* which was headed by Fedor Revay, the brother of the Minister of the Interior. *Sič* was an imitation of the Hlinka Guard in Slovakia. In political life totalitarian tendencies got the upper hand and, of course, anti-Semitism flourished in a country with a Jewish population of 15 per cent. There was at first some hesitation as to what should be done with the political parties. In October it was only the Communist Party which was actually forbidden and dissolved. The other parties were to be " concentrated." The Minister of the Interior, Revay, was in an embarrassing situation: hitherto he had been a Social-Democrat, but he quickly became a Ukrainian nationalist with totalitarian predilections. On January 19, 1939, the Chust Government suddenly announced that elections for the autonomous diet would be held on February 12. The lists of candidates were to be submitted on January 22, i.e. in three days. This alone sufficed to secure the Government against all possible opposition. At first a list of candidates representing the Great-Russian tendency was submitted as well as the Government list, but then the Government made a secret arrangement with certain members of this opposition, that their list of candidates should not be presented after all. By such tricks, the Government achieved its aim: the people were confronted with only one list of candidates, on which Germans and Czechs were also represented (but no Hungarians and no Jews). But the Ukrainians were not yet out of the wood! On January 26 a disagreeable accident happened to the Chust Government: they decided that day to dissolve all political parties and to recognise only one legal party called the " Ukrainian National Union." This decision was taken without attention being paid to the fact that the dissolution of the parties would have resulted in the loss of their mandates in the Central Prague Parliament for all the Carpathian representatives—thus also for Minister Revay. According to the Constitution, it even had the consequence that none could have become a candidate for any legislative assembly inside a period of six months. The Chust Government, which was not exactly strong in legal matters, realised its mistake only after its decision had been published and was thus forced to revoke its original decision to dissolve all parties. On February 7, however, the Supreme Administrative Court in Prague decided that the original decision was in fact binding and that the Sub-Carpathian members of the National Assembly had one and all lost their mandates in consequence. This meant that the Carpathian Ukraine could no longer be represented in the Prague National Assembly by its Deputies and Senators. In the " elections " to the autonomous Diet held on February 12, 1939, the single list of Government candidates swept, rather naturally, the poll and was returned with about 90 per cent. of the votes. Nevertheless, in Chust, the only place where the elections were secret, a great number of people absented themselves and a third of the voters rejected the Government list. In the circumstances, however, no set-back counted. The Ukrainian Diet was to meet in March and it would certainly have manifested in favour of Great-Ukrainian nationalism.

Ukrainian propaganda in Sub-Carpathian Russia had been considerably intensified since October, 1938. It was, of course, instigated and supported from Germany by all possible means. The German Nazis called the Carpathian Ukraine the " Piedmont " of the aspirations for a unified Greater Ukraine. This little country was to be the centre of free Ukrainian propaganda and activity. As mentioned before, Ukrainian agents began to assemble from all sides and were most effectively supported by the two brothers Revay—Julian, the Minister of Interior, and the other, Fedor, who was first the leader of the *Sič* organisation and since January the Chairman of the totalitarian party of " Ukrainian National Union." In their public pronouncements, the Carpathian Ukrainians were more cautious: thus the Premier Vološín told a correspondent of the *Matin* (in an interview published on January 3, 1939): " It is certain that the Ukraine in Poland and Soviet Russia is formed by one and the same people and that we have many sympathies for our brethren. But I repeat: this is a problem which concerns the Big Powers and we are too small to interfere with it actively— it is our first duty to keep pace in everything that concerns foreign policy with the Czecho-Slovak federation." This is a moderate pronouncement, though it would certainly appear to indicate approval of Great-Ukrainian aspirations.

The agitation spreading from Sub-Carpathian Ruthenia was followed with growing concern in Poland. The Ukrainians in Eastern Galicia were encouraged in their aspirations when they saw how, on the other side of the Carpathians, a free life of their co-nationals was developing. Contacts were inevitably established between the Ukrainians on both sides of the Carpathians. The Polish Government could not remain indifferent to this unrest among the Ukrainians, which was being quite openly supported by representatives of the Chust Government. The Poles protested against this agitation to the Central Government in Prague. The Prague Government was, it is true, formally responsible towards any foreign state, but at the same time it did not have sufficient executive power to influence the autonomous governments of Slovakia or the Carpathian Ukraine. On January 6, 1939, there was a sharp armed clash with many casualties between Hungarian detachments and Ukrainians and

Czechs. Two days later a new clash occurred near Užhorod. These frontier clashes continued. It was not always easy to ascertain which side bore the responsibility for them. It was obvious that the German Nazis welcomed and indeed stirred up continual tension between the Danubian states. These incidents were, nevertheless, " settled " by diplomatic negotiations between Prague and Budapest, and an agreement was reached according to which armed persons were not to enter a certain frontier zone; frontier incidents continued.

The Prague Government was in an extremely awkward position: though it bore full responsibility, it had no effective power in the autonomous regions of Slovakia and Carpathian Ukraine. In the latter province disorder was even more rampant than in Slovakia. The serious deterioration in public law and order between October, 1938, and January, 1939, showed that a more energetic interference was necessary if even the elements of public order were to be restored. For this reason, the Prague Government decided that the Czech General Lev Prchala should be appointed as third Minister of the Government of Carpathian Ukraine (up till then the Government had only two Ministers, Vološín and Revay). General Prchala, who was appointed on January 16, 1939, had been prominent before in the Carpathian Ukraine and knew the country intimately. Prague did not omit to inform Berlin of the appointment and received the impression that German official circles had no objections. In spite of this, however, General Prchala's arrival in the province was immediately seized upon by German Nazis on the spot, who incited the Chust Government against the appointment of a " Czech general " to the Government of the " autonomous " Ukraine. Minister Revay protested against it by a special telegram sent to the German Ministry of Foreign Affairs. Demonstrations against General Prchala were prepared at Chust with the full support and active participation of the German Nazis. The Germans, once again, were playing a double game. They took one line in Prague and a wholly different one in Chust. Apparently the German Government did not yet consider the moment propitious for a definite step: in the meantime it was content to increase irritation and tension between the Czechs and Ruthenians, as between the Czechs and the Slovaks. The Nazi tactics of gradually disrupting their opponent internally continued. But for the time being the conflict was provisionally settled. General Prchala assumed his post and worked hard for the pacification of the agitated and confused country which had become the victim of divergent foreign propaganda and intrigue. It was due to the Czech Army that the provisioning of the people was assured and that the main administrative and economic needs of the country were fulfilled. Nevertheless, the discontented elements led by the brothers Revay and incited by the German Nazis still continued to fret against the consolidation which General Prchala tried to bring about. March, 1939, saw their complete abandonment by the Germans.

(*f*) *The Liberated Sudetenland.* We have tried to sketch the internal development of the mutilated and disrupted Czechoslovak Republic in the first four months after Munich. We shall now briefly touch on the events in the Sudeten-German regions which had been detached from Czechoslovakia on the pretext of the principle of self-determination.

In the first weeks after Munich, the Henlein adherents were, of course, overjoyed by their liberation. Konrad Henlein was appointed Reich Commissioner for the Sudeten area, although it was a former Reich Commissioner for Prussia, Head of a Department in the Reich Ministry of Interior, Dr. Bracht, who became second in command and not another prominent member of the party. All actual administrative power was concentrated into the hands of this very experienced administrative official. The former Henlein Deputy, Karl Hermann Frank, known for his extreme radicalism, became the second representative of Henlein, largely for tasks involving " representation." These appointments and division of functions were most symptomatic: the former prominent members of the Henlein party were given minor representative functions, while the key positions in the administration of the Sudeten districts were filled with reliable experts from the Reich. The National Socialist emigrants, who had fled to Germany in former years (as, for instance, the former Deputies, Jung and Krebs), who had not always seen eye to eye with the Henlein leaders, also clamoured for their share. But the hopes and demands of many ambitious Henleinists were not fulfilled to the extent they had expected. The Reich Nazis treated them as they had treated the Austrian Nazis after the annexation of Austria. They satisfied them only so far as it suited their interest and reserved the real leadership and decision for themselves. This was one of the first reasons for the disillusionment of many Henlein adherents. Besides this, there soon began discrimination among them: they were divided according to the time they had joined the party and their behaviour before Munich.

Within a few weeks, many of Henlein's adherents had been sobered and were already discontented with their fate. They had imagined their " liberation " quite differently: they wanted to become the masters, who would dominate the Czechs, the " Marxists " and Jews, while now they were subordinated to new masters of truly Prussian efficiency. The Sudeten Germans, who never in history had belonged to Germany, were not accustomed to the barrack-room discipline introduced by the Prussians.

The Sudeten people were given ample opportunity of seeing with their own eyes the glories of Hitler civilisation. In the first days of October a triumphal welcome of the liberator Hitler, who, with other famous leaders of the party, visited the towns of the " liberated " Sudeten areas, was staged with considerable pomp. In the first days of November (between the 9th and 11th of that month) another impressive show was arranged: these were the Jewish pogroms which, accompanied by disgusting atrocities, shocked the entire civilised world. In towns which had lately formed part of the Republic of Masaryk, scenes of indescribable horror occurred. Jewish women, stripped of their upper garments by the representatives of Hitler culture, were chased with their children through the streets: some Jewish children were beaten to death. These savage scenes excited surprise and disgust among many of Henlein's supporters. Before they were " liberated " most of them had thought that the descriptions of anti-Semitic atrocities committed by the Nazis in the Reich were merely *Greuelpropaganda* invented by the Czechs and Marxists: now they saw with horror that reality exceeds everything they had been told.

Soon also discontent began to spread among them for economic and social reasons. The Nazis began to introduce all the various

" voluntary " taxes and subscriptions, and began to carry out
their well-known " Socialist " demagogy which forced the employers to provide extensive social services irrespective of the
economic strength of the works in question. The middle class was
the first to be hit by the Nazi economic system. Thus, ironically
enough, just those strata of society who had been the main
voting reserve of the Henlein party paid the heaviest price for
Henlein's policy. Minor employers of labour, business men and
tradesmen soon learnt to their cost that they had served their
use as voting ciphers, but that the " freedom " which they had
got was merely freedom to be exploited and finally bought out
by the Nazi system of giant monopolies. Even the peasants soon
found that it was the big landowners who gained most from the
new situation. The land which had come under the Czechoslovak
Land Reform of 1919 was, in several places, confiscated from its
present owners and handed back to the big proprietors.

In the short space of two months the price of food rose considerably in the Sudeten districts; this was the unavoidable
result of the forced detachment of the largely industrial Sudeten
area from the Czech agrarian hinterland. The difference of price
levels in Reichenberg between October and December, 1938,
was as follows: bread rose from 3·10 kč. to 3·60 kč., butter
(1 kilogram) from 22–24 to 30–34 kč., sugar from 6·30 to 6·90, one
egg from 0·65–0·70 to 0·90–1·10, pork (1 kilogram) from 16–
20 kč. The price level went up also, because the economic and
currency conditions had to be adapted to conditions in the Reich.
Thus, for instance, in December, 1938, it was possible to buy
with 1 mark 3 lb. of rye-bread and 1 lb. of sugar. But before
in Czechoslovakia 8·30 kč. (the value corresponding to 1 mark)
bought 3 lb. of wheat bread of much better quality, 1 lb. of sugar
and 1 lb. of the best white flour of a quality now unobtainable in
Germany. The Nazis certainly tried to win the labouring masses
by extorting all sorts of financial advantages for them from the
employers, but not with much success. The failure was due
mainly to political reasons: too many labour officials, whether
in the party or the trades unions, were subjected to persecution
for their " Red " opinions. The Nazis dealt too severely with the
Sudeten-German workmen, who were accustomed to the well-
developed Czechoslovak social services and to complete political

freedom. Compulsory labour was introduced and even the most skilled workmen (such as glass-blowers) were commandeered for the building of roads regardless of their abilities, which might have been used more economically elsewhere. After January 1, 1939, the eight-hour working day was abolished in practice, and a ten-hour minimum became the rule in the greater part of the country, even though wages remained the same. In these conditions, the Sudeten workers began to demonstrate as early as December by partial or larger strikes in many factories. The " ringleaders " were immediately punished and several sent to concentration camps.

The " liberation " of the Sudeten-German people was accompanied by a merciless persecution of all anti-Nazi Germans, whether they were Socialists, Communists, Catholics or Liberals. Many thousands were arrested and sent to concentration camps. Thousands tried to save themselves by flight to the Czech territories; we have already quoted the numbers of these luckless refugees. As in Vienna, the suicide rate showed a sharp upgrade. These suicides were not only among Jews, but also among anti-Nazi " Aryans " and several hundreds were recorded.

Even at Munich 720,000 Czechs were annexed by Germany and thus surrendered to Hitlerite oppression. About 380,000 Germans remained in Czechoslovakia. The German Czecho-slovak Governments came to a special agreement about these minorities on November 20, 1938. According to this agreement the two governments expressed their willingness to come to terms on questions concerning the " preservation and free development " of both minorities and to establish a permanent Committee composed of official delegates appointed by the two Governments, which was to debate all these questions. Thus reciprocity and parity was preserved on paper, though in reality Germany could and did do anything she liked. While the 380,000 Germans in Czechoslovakia claimed a highly privileged position for themselves and were supported by the whole weight of the Empire, the 720,000 Czechs who had been annexed to Germany by force, were completely at the mercy of their new rulers and did not even dare to appeal for help from Prague. They were verbally reassured that their " national " rights would not be curtailed and no attempt made to denationalise them. It fact the Nazi pressure was as immediate as it was thorough. Their societies and different cultural or sporting organisations and institutions were dissolved; 80 per cent. of the Czech schools were closed down; often this happened because teaching in the Third Reich was intolerable and frequently dangerous for Czech teachers. By all means, fair and foul, Czech business and tradespeople were forced to sell their establishments to Germans at low prices and frequently at very short notice. Henlein's followers stuck on shops signs " Czech Shop " next to signs " Jewish Shop " and organised a systematic boycott of the Czech element. In order to create a good impression, a single Czech periodical was " permitted " at Opava (Troppau) and this paper translated into Czech news and sentiments dictated by the Nazis. Thus every conceivable means was employed to deprive the Czech minority of the cultural and economic conditions for the " preservation and free development " of their nationality which had been promised to them in the Agreement of November 20.

As in Austria, so in the Sudeten-German areas, Hitler, after the military occupation, staged the comedy of popular consent to the annexation by organising a plebiscite. On December 4, 1938, supplementary elections to the Reichstag were held in the occupied territories. They were preceded by an enormous election campaign—Hitler, Hess, Frick, Goebbels, Ley, Henlein and other leaders of the Nazi movement made declamatory speeches. In order to make complete victory certain, all the known methods of terrorism were used, and the elections were practically public. Thus, according to official statistics 2,491,920 voted " Yes " and only 32,922 voted " No " or were invalidated. These results were laughable and once again the Nazis discredited their work by over-zealousness and expected the world to believe that overnight the Sudeten-German-Democrats, who had represented nearly a third of the total votes, had seen the error of their ways, and, together with 720,000 Czechs, had almost all changed into adherents of the Hitler régime. It would be irresponsible to quote the reliable information I have received from individual towns on the falsification of election results: there is no use in handing over defenceless people in these places to the ruthless persecution of the Gestapo. I will only mention what is obvious also from the official German statistics that the Chodove (Czechs round about Domažlice) kept up their tradition of courage also in these elections and registered a great majority of votes against the Hitler régime. Furthermore, soon after the elections, open demonstrations against the Nazi domination began to increase also in the Sudeten-German regions: there appeared inscriptions on walls like " Long live Czechoslovakia ! " " *Hitler nieder, Beneš wieder !* " etc.

After a few months of Nazi rule, disillusion and discontent crept over the former adherents of the Henlein party. It became more and more apparent what criminal folly had been committed by the brutal disruption of the centuries' old common life of the Czechs and Germans in these lands.

The " Sudetenland " was only a concept on paper, and not a geographical or ethnographical reality. Since this territory was composed of 4 or 5 fragments which had no connection with each other it was impossible to create a single administrative unit out of them. Thus the individual Sudeten districts were incorporated in the neighbouring German districts from the administrative point of view and only in Northern Bohemia was a special " *Gau* " created with the capital in Reichenberg. It was much more difficult to reorganise the economic structure of the Sudeten-German districts, for it was chiefly in the economic sphere that the pernicious consequences of the brutal disruption of the Czech-German unity in Bohemia and Moravia had become most apparent. Thus the Sudeten-German economists invented ingenious plans for the preservation of the old economic unity. The total effect of such plans was to keep the old customs frontier as it was before Munich. In March, 1939, it was the political frontier which was swept away; the economic frontier had to all intents and purposes already been removed. Prague was forced to consent to the continuance of commercial relations with the Sudeten area unfettered by Customs barriers. Others pressed Czecho-Slovakia to conclude a full Customs and currency union with the Reich so that the centuries-old contact with the Czech and Moravian hinterland should be officially recognised by the Germans. This is in fact what has happened. Many projects of new roads, railways and roadways could have been realised only if these communications could have traversed

Czech territory. All these and similar difficulties were removed by one stroke, when in March, 1939, Hitler simply annexed the whole of Bohemia and Moravia. Thus it was indirectly confirmed that the disruption of these countries on the principle of nationality had been a practical absurdity and that their inseparable connection must be restored one way or the other.

(g) *Czechoslovakia as Vassal of the Reich.* After Munich no alternative was left open to the mutilated and disrupted Czechoslovak state but to become the vassal of the German Reich. Completely deprived of all means of effective defence, she could not avoid the necessity of seeking favour with Berlin. A change in foreign policy was thus inevitable. This change was announced as early as the beginning of October by the Government of General Syrový. After his election, the new President of the Republic, Emil Hácha, told a representative of the German News Agency: " Our first endeavour will be to create permanently good relations with the German Reich. We want these relations to be loyal and sincere." Similar views were expressed by the new Premier, Rudolf Beran, in the Government declaration which he read in Parliament on December 13, 1938.

In the parliamentary debate which followed this declaration, the chief speaker of the new Government Party of National Union, the former Agrarian Deputy, Josef Černý, declared emphatically that the foreign policy of the preceding Governments had been mistaken and said: " We accept the historical decision (the Munich Agreement) conscious of the fact that we have preserved peace by heavy sacrifices and that we have found the way, we hope, to friendship with our greatest neighbour, Germany. . . . We had been unable to judge correctly of the strength and greatness of our neighbour and its importance for us, and we have sometimes overrated the international agreements, which every day became more problematic for us. . . . We thus change the orientation of our internal and foreign policy and change it on principle and consistently." The Czecho-Slovak Government tried to conduct its policy on these lines and it met with no opposition even from the opposition Labour Party. Among the people, however, resentment against Germany inevitably persisted, and it was difficult for the politicians to persuade them of the necessity for this new orientation which had been forced on the state by the Munich " agreement."

The drastic deterioration in the position of Czechoslovakia became obvious when Germany succeeded in extorting a corridor which would connect Silesia with Austria through Moravia. Simultaneously with the final determination of the frontiers on November 19, 1939, an agreement was signed in Berlin between Germany and Czecho-Slovakia, which gave Germany the right to construct a motor-road between Breslau and Vienna and a canal connecting the Danube and the Oder. The motor road was to be built by a German firm, was to be the property of the Reich, was to enjoy an extra territorial régime; the Customs and passport control would have been only German as well as the road-police; the Czech road-system was to be linked up with it. Thus a strip of Czecho-Slovak territory, 65 kilometres in length, was simply to be cut out of the body of the country because it suited the military requirements of Germany. A corridor between Silesia and Austria, by shortening the interior lines, would have had considerable strategic importance for Germany. The construction of the road continues. In December, 1938, work was started on the construction of a horizontal motor-way to lead from Western Bohemia via Jihlava (Iglau), Brno (Brünn), Zlín, Žilina, Prešov to Tačevo on the Rumanian frontier. This motor-road was to be purely Czecho-Slovak, but it was obvious that it would be used by Germany for her economic and especially military needs. In January, 1939, Germany extorted the right of transport in sealed carriages on all Czecho-Slovak railway lines— a right destined in the first place for the transport of German troops. Thus Germany exacted that all Czecho-Slovak communications should be at her complete disposal, to be used in peace and war as it suited her purposes.

The main wish of the Prague Government was to preserve the possibility of neutrality, while establishing friendly relations with Germany. The only desire of the people was that the nation which had been deserted by almost everybody at the decisive moment should be able to stand aside in any possible European conflict.

The Prague Government asked the Great Powers to fulfil their promise, given at Munich, to guarantee the frontiers of the new Czecho-Slovakia. This obligation was expressed quite clearly in the Munich Agreement, and both M. Daladier and Mr. Chamberlain had repeated it in their Parliamentary pronouncements. When the final frontiers had been agreed upon with Germany on November 20, 1938, the Czecho-Slovak Government reminded the Great Powers of their solemn under-taking to guarantee the new frontiers. But the diplomatic conversations which were held with the individual governments met with no success. Germany herself, of course, had no interest in fulfilling this promise, and the Western Powers likewise shirked the question. Czechoslovakia had fulfilled every one of the cruel conditions which had been imposed on her by the Munich Agreement of the Four Powers: yet not one of these Four Powers kept their only obligation, though they had under-taken it most solemnly at Munich. Czecho-Slovakia was aband-oned. In March, Germany simply drew the consequences.

After Munich Germany was no longer content with the Czecho-Slovak desire for friendship, or with the complete subservience of Czech foreign policy. She was resolved to draw the maximum profit from the fact that the Czechoslovak nation was now at her mercy. Germany saw no reason to allow this weakened nation to preserve even the modicum of independence which Munich had left to it. It was a principle of the Pan-German Nazism that Czecho-Slovakia was within the German " living space." In practice, this meant her complete subordina-tion to Nazi despotism.

Germany used for this purpose the same preparatory methods which she had used before Munich. Her first objective was to disrupt Czechoslovakia from inside. It was a great success for Nazi policy that Czechoslovakia had been transformed into a federal state soon after Munich. This, as we have shown, allowed the Nazis to incite the Slovaks and Ruthenes against the Czechs and to create constant friction between them. The reactionary semi-Fascist elements among the Slovak clericals were a docile instrument. While Prague tried to preserve a policy of neutrality, Bratislava proclaimed the necessity of Czecho-Slovakia joining the Anti-Comintern Pact and thus of supporting the Rome-Berlin Axis. The Slovak Minister, Karol Sidor, who was a member of the Prague Central Government, made several violent pronouncements on this point. He was supported by the Slovak Minister of Propaganda, Šaňo Mach. In Bohemia, they found support among the Fascist groups, under the leadership of corrupt and discredited people like the former Minister, Stříbrný, who years previously had been condemned by Parliament for bribery, and the former General Gajda, who had been discharged from the Army for espionage. Besides them, there was a pro-Nazi group, *Vlajka*, which was, however, unknown to the wider public. But, as has already been said (*see* Chapter VI, p. 249), none of these little groups had any influence on the Czech people or on the official policy of the Prague Government. For this reason they had to be more and more effectively supported by the German Nazis.

Nazi policy also exploited, for its own uses, just as before Munich, the German minority which had remained in Czecho-Slovakia. It did not amount to more than 380,000 people, or approximately a little over 3 per cent. of the whole population (before Munich there were over 20 per cent. Germans in the country). But the Nazis claimed for this *Volksgruppe* quite extraordinary privileges. In the debate in Parliament on December 14, 1938, the Deputy, Kundt, who had since Munich become the Nazi leader in Bohemia and Moravia, expressed the hope that all departments of state and all members of the Czech nation would recognise the fact that the Germans who had remained in Czecho-Slovakia were " members and representatives of the German National-Socialist community under the leadership of Adolf Hitler." It was on this assumption that Kundt based his activities.

In Bratislava and Chust the German pretensions were met with alacrity. In Slovakia the leader of the Slovak Germans, Herr Karmasin, became a Secretary of State and practically supervised the Tiso Government. When at the end of 1938 the Slovak Government suddenly decided to take a census, Karmasin protested, lest the census should reveal a decline in the number of Slovak Germans. The Premier, Tiso, immediately accepted his objections and complaints and the census was called off. Nothing could be done in Slovakia against the will of Herr Karmasin. This representative of Nazism did everything to Nazify Slovak political life as completely as possible. Under his leadership the Germans were organised exactly as they are in Germany: besides the uniformed political party, semi-military formations were founded for the Slovak Germans under the title *Freiwillige Schutzgruppe*. Nazi flags and badges were everywhere allowed and brutal anti-Semitism consistently applied in all walks of life. The Karmasin storm troops co-operated with the Sidor Guards, who had been organised with the direct assistance of the Nazis. The Slovak extremists who worked for a complete dissociation of Slovakia from the Republic were intimately allied with them. On January 31, 1939, the anniversary of the instalment of Nazism in Germany, a Slovak-German society was founded in Bratislava. It was symptomatic that Professor Vojtěch Tuka, fanatical enemy of the Czechs, who had been condemned to fifteen years' imprisonment for high treason in 1929, was elected President. Tuka declared at the first meeting of the new society that the Slovak nation thanked Germany and its leader for the attainment of her right of self-determination. " There is no doubt," he said, " that the Slovaks will later attain their aim, a Slovak state. . . . If Germany," he added, " must have recourse to arms in order to preserve European peace (!) we would want to fight shoulder by shoulder with our German comrades. . . ."

In Carpathian Russia the Nazis gained a similar influence. Herr Oldofredi became the " leader " of the Carpathian Germans, who do not number more than about 14,000. Like Karmasin, he became a Secretary of State in the Chust Government. On January 21, 1939, he declared officially that the political programme of the Germans in the Carpathian Ukraine was nothing more than a desire to collaborate in the reconstruction of the country and act as mediators between the German Reich and the Carpathian Ukraine. Therefore Herr Oldo Frodi worked together with Nazi agents and German officers who had been sent to the Carpathian Ukraine and tried to make the Chust Government serve the interests of Nazism. He naturally found ready support from the two brothers Revay. Fedor Revay became the President of a Ukrainian-German society.

The Nazis, of course, supported the Ukrainians against the Poles, and even tried also to exploit the anti-Polish mood of the

Czechs, which, after the invasion of Těšín, was considerable. In December, 1938, Nazi propaganda distributed anti-Polish pamphlets among the Czechs which showed a map on which Polish territory as far as Cracow was entered as Czech. This incitement of one nation against the other—Slovaks and Ruthenes against the Czechs, Czechs and Ruthenes against the Poles, Poles against the Czechs and Ruthenes, Slovaks against the Czechs and Hungarians—was the slogan of the Nazis, who, by inflaming conflicts between these small nations, hoped to establish Pan-German domination.

While the Nazis were able in Slovakia and the Carpathian Ukraine to develop freely their destructive activities with the connivance and even support of Government quarters, in Bohemia and Moravia they met with considerably greater resistance. The Czechs, even after Munich, were not ready to submit without demur to Nazi despotism. Immediately after the Munich catastrophe, many Czechs had found some consolation in the prospect that, after the loss of its extensive frontier territory, the state would at least be a completely national state and practically homogeneous as far as nationality was concerned. With considerable relief, it was realised that at least the German minority which remained in the country was numerically insignificant. It soon became apparent, however, that these 380,000 Germans intended to extort even larger privileges than those which had originally been demanded for a minority which numbered more than 3 millions. Kundt, who, like Henlein in his time, had once counted as a " moderate," ordered the Prague Government to recognise the privileged position of the German *Volksgruppe*, of which he was the leader. In defiance of the laws of the democratic Czech Republic of which they were the citizens, the Germans began to behave as if they obeyed the laws and customs of the Third Reich. All German institutions and organisations, whether political, cultural, social or economic, were Nazified. In all the German institutions, including the schools, which after all were still subject to the authority of the State, the anti-Semitism of the Nürnberg laws was introduced. Jewish professors, teachers, lawyers, and doctors were expelled, and Jewish children in the schools were forced to sit on special benches. These measures were in direct contradiction to the

Czecho-Slovak legal and constitutional order; this was a matter of complete indifference to the Nazis, whom Munich had put in the position to dictate far beyond their own frontiers. They therefore criticised the Czechs more and more sharply for being " unable to get rid of the pernicious Jewish influence," and when the Prague Government still hesitated to introduce anti-Jewish legislation, it was charged by the Nazis with intentions inimical to Germany. In the first weeks after Munich the opinion was general that the German University in Prague and the polytechnics in Prague and Brno would be moved to Germany—if only because the number of students would now be insufficient. But in January, 1939, Berlin decided that these institutions should stay where they were, so that they might remain " focal points of German culture." The Sudeten Germans from the districts handed to Germany by the Munich Agreement were compelled to continue in their studies in Prague and Brno, and were allowed to study elsewhere in Germany only with special permission. At the opening of the new term at the German University in Prague in January, 1938, a provocative National-Socialist demonstration was staged at which it was openly proclaimed that all German institutions of university rank were to be centres of Nazi culture and propaganda in Czecho-Slovakia.

National-Socialism, it should be remembered, was declared illegal in Czechoslovakia in 1934. It was only after the German campaign had begun in the spring of 1938, and Anglo-French pressure was being put on Prague to " come to terms with Henlein," that it was again permitted.

Prague was considerably surprised at the line the Nazis took on the question of option. It was to be expected that the majority of Germans who had remained in Czechoslovakia would opt for Germany. It soon became clear, however, that the Nazis were not interested in diminishing the numbers of Germans in Czechoslovakia. They therefore exerted considerable pressure on all Germans to give up their intention to opt for Germany and to remain within the Czechoslovak Republic. Those who insisted on opting for Germany were forced to sign a declaration saying: " *Ich optiere gegen den Willen des Führers.*" Kundt, however, explained the situation to the Germans at

Brno: " For us Germans the Czecho-Slovak passport is only a formality. In reality you remain members of the German Reich with a special mission." Only those Germans who had special permission from the Nazis were allowed to opt for Germany, either for economic or military reasons.

After January, 1939, the representatives of the Nazis in Czecho-Slovakia became even bolder. The former Henlein Sudeten-German Party had been as early as October, 1938, transformed into a National-Socialist party under the leadership of Kundt and had treated German Socialists, Communists, Catholics and Democrats with the same brutality as the German Jews. Kundt declared at the conference of the *Deutsches Arbeitsamt* held on January 3 and 4, 1939: " *Das Deutschtum in der Tschecho-Slovakei betrachtet sich trotz seiner gegenüber früher weitaus geringeren Stärke politisch als Faktor, welcher sowohl ein Recht auf Eigenleben, wie auch Anspruch auf die weitere Mitgestaltung eines Raumes besitzt, der von deutschen kulturellen und wirtschaftlichen Leistungen seit Jahrhunderten wesentlich bestimmt wurde.*" This sentence contained a whole programme whose actual meaning was understood only two months later when German troops occupied the whole of Czecho-Slovakia. It was the task of Kundt's Germans to serve as pioneers of this operation.

Herr Kundt announced at the beginning of January that the Germans in Czecho-Slovakia demanded absolute autonomy; that they did not regard themselves as a minority, but as the apostles of a great and special mission, which had been revitalised by the Munich Agreement; and that they must have complete liberty to profess openly their National-Socialist doctrine. These requirements were re-stated in greater detail by Herr Kundt in the *Prager Zeitungsdienst* of January 17 as follows:

1. Absolute liberty and the right to carry on undisturbed their political activities as National-Socialists for all Germans in Czecho-Slovakia: this provision to cover not only their programme, but also their organisation and their publicity.

2. The maintenance of Germans in their existing posts and employment. " It has become a recognised custom to dismiss Germans from their employment, even in private enterprises. Such a practice we consider as contrary to the new

spirit of collaboration," states the correspondence which is quoted.

3. The maintenance of autonomy and the right to determine the character of German education and cultural life. German culture and German teaching, must be able to find a home in Czecho-Slovakia wherever any Germans live.

4. The exclusion of Jews from all connection with the relations between Germans and Czechs. " We know sufficiently well what role the Jews have played in the relations between our nations, because they desire to fish in troubled waters and ' roast their chicken on the Czech stove.' "

5. The establishment of good relations by the Czechs towards the German Reich and the German people, not only in economics and culture, but also in politics. " That is a matter which must be arranged between Prague and Berlin, but we Germans living in Czecho-Slovakia are intimately concerned with it and are therefore greatly interested in it."

6. The development of a good relationship between the Germans in Czecho-Slovakia and the Czecho-Slovak Government. " The present era demands of us something better than playing a game of hide-and-seek. We do not want to carry on a polemical discussion with the Czech people, but to co-operate with them. If there are still among the Czech editors some who regard it as an essential part of Czech policy to indulge in polemics with the Germans, then it is up to the Czech nation to get rid of these *provocateurs*.

" The German national group," he adds in conclusion, " wants merely to lead its own life in its own way—but in the fullest possible sense. It would like, as far as possible, to share a *common ideology* with the Czech people, but no German, either in Germany or in Czecho-Slovakia, has any intention of *forcing his ideology on the Czechs*. The new form of Czech political life must spring spontaneously from its Czech background, and must adapt itself in its development to its environment. In so far as there exist among the Germans any desire to meddle in the national affairs of the Czechs, it is limited to *the expression of a wish* that this development may take place smoothly. The fulfilment of this wish would be to the interest not so much of the Germans as of the Czechs."

The Reich German Press hurried to give weight to Kundt's demands; and, of course, threats addressed to Prague were not missing from their recommendations. The Czech political world was indignant at these demands and several Czech papers gave vent to their bitter feelings. Thus the *Národní Politika* wrote on January 15, 1939: "If a small German minority voluntarily remains on our [Czech] side of the frontier, it is not exactly tactful to draw attention to its existence and needs by these warlike tones; such tones should belong to the past, especially since this small minority has, without any alteration, the same rights which hitherto had been enjoyed by the large German minority. The Czech minority in the Reich would be happy if it could only speak about its tragic position." The Czechs drew attention to the fact that the Germans in Bohemia and Moravia had more schools than they could possibly need: 234,000 Germans living in these two provinces had 1 university and 2 polytechnics, 124 elementary schools, 38 higher elementary schools, and 14 secondary schools, besides some 13 training colleges and 31 schools for apprentices. If the principle of parity would have been carried out, the Czech minority in Germany, numbering 720,000 people, should have had no less than 300 elementary schools, 80 upper elementary schools, 32 secondary schools, some 100 training colleges and 6 institutions of university rank. Actually, as we have shown above, Czech schools in the territories occupied by Germany after Munich had been closed down summarily.

The Germans, of course, considered such demands when they came from Czechs to be wholly unacceptable; blinded by Pan-German pretensions, the Nazis assumed that the Czechs should simply submit and recognise by the light of nature their privileged position.

But however justified the indignation of the Czech public, the Prague Government had no alternative but to accept German dictation. In February, 1939, an agreement was concluded between the Premier, Beran, and the Nazi leader, Kundt, that Herr Kundt should, as the leader of the German national group, discuss with two members of the Prague Cabinet the question of the legal position of the German national group which (according to Herr Kundt's definition) " is a member of the German national

community under the leadership of Adolf Hitler." In a lecture
which Herr Kundt delivered in Prague on February 17, 1939,
he reminded his audience that during the Middle Ages the
Czech rulers " not only called the Germans into the country,
but also gave them privileges, so that they could act as Germans,"
and continued: " I demand for the German national group in
Czecho-Slovakia, at least the same rights which these old
privileges granted to those Germans. It was they who helped
this country and the Czech nation to attain all that is most valuable in their present high standard of culture. I demand therefore
that the Germans should be free people, who shall live, work and
expand according to National-Socialist laws, according to
National-Socialist customs and according to National-Socialist
justice in private and public life. With a voice in the affairs of
the country, I demand that they live autonomously under their
own leadership, so that a new life for the two nations in these two
countries of mature civilisation may grow out of the present
ruins. In this spirit and with this firm resolution, I extend my
hand and wait for those Czechs who will have the courage and
the ability, sincerely and as spokesmen of their nation, to accept
this hand in the interests of a new life."

Let us ignore the historical absurdity of deducting Nazi racial
claims from Mediæval law, which was founded on the privileges
of individual estates such as the German burghers. It is sufficient
to notice that the leader of the Nazis in Bohemia was demanding
privileges. The Nazis claimed, not only equal, but special and
higher rights for the Germans than for the Czechs whose Republic it was. The spirit of brutal Pan-Germanism eager to establish
German domination, breathed from every word of Kundt's
pompous declaration. Again, the Nazi spokesman did not omit the
dark threats which invariably accompany every one of their
pronouncements: " It is high time, for history does not wait."
Kundt had had instructions to show discontent.

And Berlin proceeded to use this discontent to increase its
pressure on Prague. The Reich Press gave full support to Kundt's
demands and abused the Czechs for ignoring German " rights "
and " returning to the mistakes and errors of the Beneš régime."
It was with some irritation that Berlin perceived that even the
Government headed by Beran (who had always been praised by

the Germans for his views favourable to an agreement with Henlein and Hitler) was unwilling slavishly to submit to every German wish.

It was in this somewhat unfavourable atmosphere that the Minister of Foreign Affairs, Dr. F. Chvalkovský, paid a visit to Berlin on January 21, 1939. Chvalkovský's visit coincided with a German Press campaign, which was inciting the Carpathian Ukrainians against the appointment of General Prchala to the Chust Government and condemning the " dangerous obstinacy " displayed by Prague. Since several Czech papers, including even the Agrarian *Venkov*, voiced objections to the exaggerated demands of the Germans, the *Berliner Tageblatt* of January 20, 1939, warned Prague not to " revert to the blind and aggressive mentality of former times." At the same time, the *Deutsche Diplomatisch-politische Korrespondenz* insisted that Czecho-Slovakia should adapt its relations with the remaining minorities " to the new situation." The German official responsible for this article distinguished in this respect between the Slovaks and the Czechs: " In Slovakia the relations between the Slovak nation and German national group were never, even after the war, at all disagreeable. The concrete promises of the Slovak Premier, Tiso, show the natural way in which Germans can collaborate as active and respected members of the state community in the reconstruction of the country. . . . The Czechs must realise that their country is closely bound up with the German living space, and that therefore the Germans in this area do not constitute a foreign body, but represent a living member of their mechanism —as is proved also by the historical development up to the present day. It is no longer possible to shut one's eyes to these realities, but account must be taken of them in a completely realist spirit."

With all this frank talking, Minister Chvalkovský must have been prepared to hear some sharp words on his arrival in Berlin. He was not disappointed. On January 21 he had consultations with Ribbentrop, and was received by Hitler the same afternoon. With brutal frankness Hitler told Chvalkovský that the Czechs must draw the consequences from their defeat. M. Chvalkovský was ordered to listen to the main charges against his country:

Prague still hesitated, as if hoping that the situation could change.

It was incomprehensible that the Prague Government should still treat the Jews and the adherents of the Beneš régime with consideration.

It was astonishing that it should still keep its old alliances and not repudiate even the treaty with Soviet Russia.

There were symptoms that the Czechs were conducting a policy of camouflage and sabotage.

It was intolerable that the Prague Government should ignore the rights and demands of the German " national group " in Czecho-Slovakia.

Ribbentrop and Hitler then formulated their precise demands: (1) the demands of the German minority in Czecho-Slovakia should be satisfied according to the proposals submitted by Kundt; (2) the Beneš régime should be thoroughly " liquidated " throughout public life, especially in the Administration, the Army and the Press; (3) radical measures against the Jews must immediately be taken; and (4) the Army must be reduced, both as to numbers and to equipment. It was further demanded that Prague, on its own initiative, should give expression to its positive attitude to Germany. From the words and hints of Ribbentrop and Hitler, it became clear that Germany wanted Prague to sever all its existing ties with other Powers, to join the Anti-Comitern Pact and officially to announce its adherence to the Berlin-Rome Axis. In economic questions, Berlin did not ask directly for a Customs union, but only for closer collaboration on the basis of preferential duties. Germany wanted, by trading with and through Czecho-Slovakia, to assure herself of a supply of foreign currency which she could not have gained if Czecho-Slovakia had then joined a Customs union with the Reich. It was, however, insisted emphatically that the Czechs should not build new industries which could compete with the Sudeten-German industry and that they should in general respect the economic needs of the ceded Sudeten territory. Germany then demanded a part of the gold and exchange reserves of the Czecho-Slovak National Bank which would correspond to the economic resources of the annexed territory while categorically

refusing, on principle, to take over the corresponding part of the
Czecho-Slovak National Debt. In short, the political dependence
of Czecho-Slovakia on Germany was now being used for its
economic exploitation. It was made clear that the Czecho-Slovak
communications were to be at the disposal of Germany and that
railways and roads should be built on Czecho-Slovak territory to
meet German requirements.

After Chvalkovský's return from Berlin, it was said in Prague
that the Minister had tried to explain the Czech point of view
and had opposed the more extravagant German demands. As
far as there was any such opposition, it can only have been
of the most timid kind, since, not only is M. Chvalkovský a
more than flexible opportunist, but, after Munich, the Prague
Government had no effective means of resistance. The German
Press took it for granted that Prague would submit to everything. Thus, the Essen *National Zeitung* wrote on January 23:
" We expect that the Czecho-Slovak nation will not be prevented
from distinguishing her true friends from her enemies. We hope
that the last remains of the Beneš adherents still in office will
soon cease to influence the policy of present-day Czecho-
Slovakia." There was no mention, of course, of reciprocal
obligations incurred by Germany towards Czecho-Slovakia:
Pan-Germans have rights and demands on others, but no
obligations. When Chvalkovský reminded Ribbentrop of the
German promise made at Munich to guarantee the new frontiers,
he was refused with the cynical " explanation " that, for the
moment, this question was not urgent and that it would be
considered only later, when Prague had given proofs of its goodwill towards Germany. Prague would first do well to free itself
completely from the influence of international Jewry and from
any foolish hopes which the anti-German views of President
Roosevelt may have excited among the Czechs.

The Czecho-Slovak public was never informed about the
concrete demands made to Minister Chvalkovský during his
Berlin conversations. It was only warned of their serious
implications in a communiqué published on January 24, which
said: "There is no doubt that Germany, in pursuit of her programme of a reorganisation of Central and Eastern Europe, has
the intention of incorporating Czecho-Slovakia into this whole

as a factor which will enjoy equal rights with the other states of
the Danube Basin, of the Vistula and the Balkans. Our situation
towards Germany is somewhat special, as the Czech lands are
geographically and historically in a much closer relation to the
German lands than any other state. . . . [After the tension of
1938] it is natural that the mutual relations of the new Czecho-
Slovakia and the German Reich are passing through an experi-
mental stage, and are still in a very delicate atmosphere, and
that there exists an almost unlimited number of complex
questions which present the most varied difficulties. It will be
necessary to overcome these difficulties patiently, step by step."

The Government prepared the public by this tortuous explanation for the disagreeable measures with which it was
intended to satisfy Berlin. The sharper course was heralded by
the suppression, on January 25, 1939, of the *Národní Osvobození*,
the paper of the Czechoslovak legionaries, who were devoted to
the policy of Masaryk and Beneš. Even after Munich, this paper
had had the courage to defend this policy and to plead for Beneš
against unjust attacks. Soon afterwards several other periodicals
were suppressed, among them the Nationalist weekly, *Národní
Myšlenka*, edited by the Deputies Rašín and Klíma, and a
Beneš weekly edited by the Deputy Moudrý, and the historians
Slavík and Werstadt. Not only in the pro-Fascist, but also in the
Agrarian Press new and more savage attacks on the Beneš régime
began to appear. In this respect, the chief editor of the *Venkov*,
Rudolf Halík, particularly distinguished himself. On February 5
he wrote in his paper: " Humanitarian democracy [this is his
term for the régime of Masaryk and Beneš] became a perverse
cult of everything Left and is responsible for the national
catastrophe, by its suppression of the truth and its disregard of
reality. It fraternised with Bolshevism and considered an
African colony and the Communist-anarchist atrocities in
Spain as nearer to its heart than the life of its own nation and
its relations to its closest neighbour." The Agrarian and pro-
Fascist journalists quickly imitated the Nazi vocabulary and
customs in order to please Berlin. Halík, though not the only,
was at least one of the most thorough of the converts. He
proclaimed war on all Liberal literature, which he dubbed
" refuse " literature on the model of *Asfaltliteratur*.

The Premier, Beran, asked the public in several speeches which he pronounced from the end of January onwards to understand the necessity of friendship with Germany, and he criticised publicly the Beneš régime which was so hated by Germany. On January 27 he said: " All dangers are not yet past, and it would be really fatal if wide circles would believe that there is no danger any more and if we would mislead the public into thinking that some miracle might happen. We must draw all the consequences from our political and economic situation in the Central-European area." He therefore promised the German minority the " greatest understanding " for their needs and Germany " a sincere settlement of our political and economic relations to the German Reich." On February 22 he declared: " We are liquidating unreservedly all remains of the old régime which still create mistrust against us abroad. Our policy towards our neighbours, especially towards Germany, and also towards our minorities, will be frank and completely loyal. The minorities will have as many rights as we have ourselves." Even before (in a speech of January 29) he had said that the " belief in a return of the former political régime can hurt us immensely, more so than many people seem to think." He was warmly supported by his Foreign Minister, Chvalkovský, in a similar pronouncement on February 20: " Good neighbourly relations to Germany are not only the basic tendency of the foreign policy of the Government, but a necessity of internal politics. We must not toy with Fate, if Munich is not to become the prelude to a new catastrophe. We must combat any propaganda which tends to keep alive among the people vain hopes for a return of the old times. Those who criticise us to-day should be answered that they conducted and propounded for twenty years a foreign policy which suited them, and that we, to-day, carry out a policy which through their fault we are compelled to adopt. To proclaim pacifism and support disarmament, to drive the nation to war, to care for Geneva and the security of the Abyssinian frontiers and to forget about the frontiers of one's own country—such a policy we will leave to the judgment of history. Let us leave alone questions of Right and Left, ideology, Geneva, collective security and similar empty slogans. All that we have to do is to look after our own interests: let us keep our own counsel and leave the direction of the world to the Great Powers."

It is perhaps not known in Western Europe that M. Chvalkovský, as diplomatic representative of the Republic and one of its most important Ministers, had an active share in the foreign policy which he was now condemning and that he even declared to President Beneš in the summer of 1938, only a few weeks before Munich, that no other foreign policy could be adopted than that which had been pursued since the foundation of the Republic.

The Prague Government was trying hard to satisfy Berlin according to the wishes expressed by Herr von Ribbentrop to M. Chvalkovský on January 21. It tried hard, not only in all its pronouncements, but also in its actions. On January 27 Chvalkovský had a long conference with the Nazi leader, Kundt. Since the beginning of February, a special commission of all Ministries, with the Minister of Justice, Krejčí, in the chair, settled one after the other all the individual claims and complaints of the German minority. It was, of course, no longer alluded to as a " minority," but as a " national group." It was, however, obvious from the pronouncements made by Kundt (which are quoted above) that the Germans were not satisfied, but, on the contrary, rather encouraged by the mere existence of this Commission to ask for more. In the beginning of February certain anti-Jewish measures began to be introduced; this was done through confidential and unpublished Government decrees, in order not to excite too much opposition, at home and among the English-speaking public. Jews were removed successively from the administration, from banking, economic, social and cultural institutions. The Agrarian *Venkov* justified these steps on March 2 rather lamely by saying:

" We do not persecute anybody for being a Jew. But the non-Aryan element will not and must not have more rights and influence with us than we can permit for national, economic and social reasons."

At the same time an attempt was made to be considerate to those Jewish families and enterprises which had become completely assimilated to their Czech environment—but even in these slight concessions the German Nazis saw a proof of the " insincerity " of the Prague Government. On February 1 the Government issued decrees which ordered a revision of Czecho-Slovak citizenship for certain categories of people, and which changed the rules about the residence of aliens in such a way that it practically amounted to an expulsion of foreign emigrants, especially German. Writing after March 15, one can but regret that not all of these had been expelled in time so that after the occupation of Czecho-Slovakia numbers fell into the hands of the Gestapo. At the end of February a German-Czech " Anti-Comintern League " was being prepared. Kundt's *Press Correspondence* gave the following explanation: " *Die klare und deutliche Trennung von allen bolschevistischen und halbbolschevistischen Tendenzen ist das erste und wichtigste Lebensgesetz der neuen Tschecho-Slovakei . . . Aussen—und innenpolitisch gesehen, ist der tschecho-slovakische Staat nur denkbar auf der Basis des konsequenten und kompromisslosen Antibolschevismus, denn das Münchner Abkommen hat für die Tschecho-Slovakei nicht nur eine grenzpolitische Veränderung, sondern eine zwingende Entscheidung im Ideenkampf Europas mit sich gebracht. . . . Die Einstellung gegen den Bolschevismus und damit zusammenhängend, gegen das Judentum, wird in Berlin als Masstab des Vertrauens des national-sozialistischen Deutschlands zu der neuen Tschecho-Slovakei betrachtet.*" The Nazis demanded the domination of Czecho-Slovakia, not only politically, strategically and economically, but also the subjugation of the Czecho-Slovak people to the Nazi ideology. For the Nazis, it is of vital political importance that other nations should not support ideas inimical to the continued sway of the somewhat peculiar doctrines of the German Nazis. Hence their own vital necessity to interfere in the domestic affairs of others—and above all, of their intended victims.

The political demoralisation of the Czechs was to be accompanied by their military disarmament. Prague tried to meet Berlin also on the demand of reducing the Army. At the beginning of March, an official announcement was made that preparations for the reorganisation of the Army were shortly to be concluded. The number of units was to be reduced considerably in proportion to the reduced territory and population of the

state. A part of the officers and N.C.Os. were to find new employment either as secretaries of local authorities or as commanders
of the proposed labour camps. But even then a considerable
number would have remained without work. It was, of course,
necessary to reduce the Army in the reduced state even if
Germany had not pressed for it. But Germany was in some haste
for this measure, being afraid that in a certain emergency the
cadres of the Czechoslovak defensive forces might once more
become dangerous to her. She asked only for a reduction of the
Czecho-Slovak Army, but in fact tried to accomplish its disruption
as soon as possible. She therefore insisted that all higher officers,
who did not please her, should be removed. The first of these
steps was the resignation of General Ludvík Krejčí, the Chief of
the General Staff, who resigned at the instance of the Prague
Government on February 18, ostensibly for " reasons of health."
At the end of January the last members of the French Military
Mission left Prague; its chief, General Faucher, had left Prague
in November, 1938.

All these measures and actions of the Prague Government,
which still did not satisfy the German Nazis, were received by
the Czech public with unconcealed resentment. Even before
this time, the cleavage between the Government and the people
had become apparent. Munich had not contributed to any
decrease in the anti-Nazi opinions of the Czech public, but had
rather intensified them. Therefore, as we have already said, the
public often made the Beran Government responsible for actions
to which it was forced against its own will by Berlin. Beran tried
frequently to find a compromise between the demands of the
Nazis and the feelings of the Czech people. But he did not inspire
confidence; he was compromised by his advocacy—long before
the September crisis—of a policy of collaboration with Germany
and the Sudeten-German Party. Therefore the people saw in
him, as they saw in Chvalkovský, the Minister of Foreign Affairs,
and in other leading Agrarian politicians, all too willing and
ready servants of Berlin. These politicians found themselves in a
position which became increasingly difficult: they themselves
realised more and more clearly that an agreement with Nazi
Germany was an illusion, since Berlin did not want friendly
collaboration, but the complete subjugation of Czecho-Slovakia.

In the measure in which they were forced to make larger and larger concessions to the Nazis, they lost support among their own nation. The attacks on the Beneš régime in the Press had an effect exactly contrary to that which was intended: a people who had considerable political education compared the former freedom during the time of Masaryk and Beneš with the humiliating state of affairs after Munich, when the dependence of the nation on the Third Reich was steadily increasing. It was therefore impossible to eradicate from its mind the memories of a former régime and the belief in its resurrection. The more Government quarters combated the popular hope of a return to the free past, the more passionately did the people cling to their hopes. The conviction spread that President Beneš would set to work in his exile, just as he had during the World War, for the restitution of the freedom and independence of the nation. Various opportunities were used by the public to demonstrate openly for the former President, who had become the symbol of national resurrection. All efforts to struggle against this deep-seated mood of a nation which passionately clings to its freedom and national rights were in vain.

While Government quarters seemed to the broad masses of the Czech people far too amenable towards the Nazis, Slovak radicals and pro-Fascist Czech groups accused them of indecision. These groups had no support among the Czech people, which are genuinely democratic, but they began to assume importance only when they were directly supported by the German Nazis. Not unnaturally, therefore, the Czech Fascists sought out their Nazi patrons. General Gajda, whose abnormal and unscrupulous ambition had already led him once to betray Czech military secrets, now assiduously sought Nazi favour. The Nazis, whose disruption plans it admirably suited, did not hesitate to use his services; his former hyper-nationalist days were forgotten and the fact that he had at one time accused the Masaryk régime of " Germanophile treason " was forgiven him. General Gajda adapted himself to the changed circumstances with his usual alacrity and determined to climb to a leading position, even with the help of the Nazis and at the expense of the Beran Government. The adherents of the radically pro-Nazi group *Vlajka* had nothing to learn from his example. These pro-Fascist groups tried first to dominate the Government Party of " National Union," and at their political meetings tried to demonstrate their extreme radicalism, which was frequently directed against the Beran Government itself. The Government therefore began to take steps against them and to warn the public against their disruptive activities. In the beginning of March a meeting of the group *Vlajka* was dissolved—this step was ascribed by the German Nazis to the Minister of the Interior, O. Fišer, who was, as we shall tell later, to be removed from his post at their instance. The Government wanted, at the same time, to mollify some of Gajda's exorbitant ambitions by reinstalling him to the rank of a General (on the retired list). By a decree of the President of the Republic at the beginning of March, all the consequences of his actions, for which he had been punished, were annulled and Gajda thus could again become a general of the Czecho-Slovak Army. Gajda was thus, more than ever, encouraged in his ambitions, and he appeared immediately on the stage as soon as the German Army had occupied Prague. The public reproach which President Hacha administered to General Gajda at this time was the only remonstrance during the entire crisis which President Hacha permitted himself. It cost little for one servant of the Nazis to reproach another.

The pressure of the Nazis and Czech Fascists was apparent, also, when, at the end of February, some Government spokesmen began to question the need for a second party besides the Government Party of " National Union." Suddenly the Government Press started to point to the " danger that the second party would become a rallying point of those who do not want to break with the past." The Labour Party, for its part, behaved more than loyally towards the Government, and advocated, in complete agreement with it, the necessity for friendly relations with Germany. But it did not earn either thanks or recognition for this attitude, and its whole position in the public life of Czecho-Slovakia was as anomalous as it was unenviable; it could not develop in free competition with the Government Party, since its success in any elections would have thrown the state, dependent as it was on the Third Reich, into a serious crisis. It was, therefore, suggested that the two parties, Government and

Opposition, should agree on a single list of candidates for the elections to Parliament which were to be held in Bohemia and Moravia. In spite of this, the radicals still insisted that the Labour Party should simply dissolve, and they were able to point out that in Slovakia and the Carpathian Ukraine there were régimes of only one party. The Press of the German Nazis also naturally held up the conditions in Slovakia as a model for Prague. Thus, against the will of many leading politicians, who knew well the feelings and predilections of the Czech people and wished to save at least some of the main features and institutions of democracy, totalitarian tendencies prevailed more and more in the second Czecho-Slovak Republic. This also was a consequence of Munich, and one which was not only foreseen, but advocated by Lord Runciman in his famous Report: " if necessary, legal measures should be taken to bring such agitations to an end "—the " agitations " referred to was opposition by Czech democrats to the neighbouring aggressive dictatorships. The Czechoslovak nation was forced to become a vassal of the Third Reich, not only in politics and economics, but also in its ideology.

3. On the Way to Pan-German Hegemony

The consequences of Munich were disastrous, not only for Czechoslovakia, but for the whole of Europe. Yet many people in France and England sincerely believed that peace—by which they meant their own security—would be adequately assured, for some time to come, at least, if Germany were allowed to extend her domination over Czechoslovakia and Central Europe. Whatever may have been the causes which led the Western Powers to adopt the policy of Munich, the hopes which were attached to it were not fulfilled. Within a few months of September 30, 1938, it became evident that peace was by no means assured, but that, on the contrary, the danger of war had only been increased, by the serious weakening of Great Britain and France and the strengthening of Greater Germany.

The reason for this change in relative strength, which was becoming every day more and more apparent, was not difficult to find. The face of Europe was bound to change according to the fate of Czechoslovakia, which lay in the centre of Europe, at the crossroads between west and east and north and south.

Bismarck's well-known saying that " the master of Bohemia is the master of Europe " would seem to have been proved correct at Munich, as it had been at Versailles. When, in June, 1938, I spoke in London about the strategic situation of Czechoslovakia I said: " We do not go so far as to pretend that the destiny and prosperity of Europe depend exclusively upon the fate of Czechoslovakia, but it cannot be denied that an independent Czechoslovakia is the principal support for the independence of every other state in the Danube Basin and the Balkans, and may, therefore, be regarded as the basis of the existing situation in Central Europe." Munich has shown this argument to have been correct.

(a) *The Strategic Strengthening of Germany.* After Munich the Germans themselves admitted, since they no longer had any reason to conceal it, their real aims in the Czechoslovak dispute. These were most completely expressed by the editor of the *Frankfurter Zeitung*, Rudolf Kircher, on November 27, 1938, when he wrote:

" The most difficult and most important of our tasks—the breaching, on our eastern flank, of the Czecho-Franco-Russian barriers and the establishment of new friendly relations with Prague—is now definitely behind us. The crisis through which we have just passed has provided us with precise information about the value and importance of various states, both great and small, and especially about their determination. The power which resides in our united German people has revealed itself clearly to us, and to the rest of the world. It is easy to see that our own economic and political, and especially our strategic situation has been greatly—one may even say extraordinarily—strengthened by the solution of the ' Czecho-Slovak question.' The removal of the menace which was represented to us by the Czecho-Slovak salient, penetrating into our south-eastern flank, and the construction of an impenetrable wall of fortifications on our Rhineland front are regarded by experts throughout the world as completely reversing the strategic situation in Europe. Strategic considerations are not always the only ones, even for those who believe that armed conflict is inevitable, but they are the most important. It is evident to any well-informed person that no English or French, and, even more, no American rearmament can compensate for this reversal of the strategic situation.

" For Germany, and, we may add, for Italy, the sources of supply of foodstuffs and raw materials have considerably increased. The transformation of our relations with South-East Europe will certainly not damage our situation ! The fact that England and France can obtain from overseas an abundance of everything which they need, and the fact that the United States will construct a new Atlantic Fleet (to release eventually the British Fleet for service elsewhere) mean much less to Germany than is believed in the West. . . .

" There is at present time no insoluble conflict between the Western Powers and Germany. In that case, of course:

" (1) Germany, acting in full accord with Italy, will in future play the leading part in the countries of South-East Europe.

" (2) The increase of Germany's power on the Continent can entail no renunciation of her just colonial claims.

" (3) This double reality is not incompatible with the situation of England as a World Power, or with the prosperity of France as a Continental and colonial Power:

" (4) It should be recognised that the great partner of Germany, Fascist Italy, is predestined to be the directing Power in the Mediterranean and that England's claims in the Mediterranean, Red Sea and Indian Ocean are limited by the natural rights of a powerful Italy. And, finally, France, whose lines of communication with Northern Africa need not be protected unless they are jeopardised by her adoption of an unreasonable policy, should recognise that in the Mediterranean, as well as in Eastern Europe, the new relations between Powers can no longer be modified by alliances. Briefly, the status quo which has hitherto existed in Europe changed entirely, and this should be considered an irrevocable fact."

It is unquestionable, of course, that the strategic situation of Germany was remarkably strengthened by the " solution of the Czecho-Slovak question." In the first place, it disposed of a dangerous and serious enemy. In the opinion of German military experts, the Czechoslovak Army was, as regards its equipment, technique, training and morale, in every way superior to any other in Central Europe, not excepting the Polish. In certain respects—as was seen after the military occupation of Bohemia and Moravia—Czechoslovak equipment was superior even to the German. In Eastern Europe Czechoslovakia and Russia alone had built powerful walls of fortifications for the defence of their frontiers, and after the fall of the Czechoslovak fortifications, which were so constructed that their reduction would have taken a comparatively long time, the German Army meets with no further effective wall of fortifications until the Russian frontiers.

What the Czechoslovak armed forces were really like was stated frankly by General Faucher, head of the French Military Mission in Prague, in a conversation with M. de Kérillis, which was published in *L'Époque* on December 24, 1938:

" Excellent soldiers. Excellent officers' corps. Excellent equipment. And in addition to these, an intense patriotism and a will to defend to the last their national soil. It was a marvellous Army."

Questioned about the alleged inadequacy of the Czechoslovak fortifications on the southern (Austrian) frontier, General Faucher replied:

" That is incorrect. It is true that the fortifications of that frontier were less substantial than those on the other frontiers, but even before the annexation of Austria very serious work had been undertaken. After the *Anschluss*, i.e. since March, they have been materially strengthened by works in reinforced concrete, by anti-tank obstructions and by a comprehensive system of trenches. The line was a solid one."

As regards aerial assistance from Russia, General Faucher said:

" The support given during the early days would certainly have been weak, but the Czechoslovak aerodromes were so exceptionally well-situated from a strategic point of view that it would have been possible to achieve considerable results with very little material. Czechoslovakia was like a huge aerodrome projecting into the very heart of Germany. It needed only a few minutes for her aeroplanes to reach Berlin, Vienna, Dresden and Breslau, the principal industrial centres of Eastern Germany. Thanks to this fact, Czechoslovakia held an important trump card in her hand."

General Faucher gave, in conclusion, the following explanation:

" There were no Sudeten regiments. There were the Sudetens scattered throughout the Czechoslovak units. The Sudetens could not, therefore, have deserted *en masse,* and consequently there would have been no desertion on a large scale. Apart from a few who would have run away at the very beginning, the bulk of the contingents of German origin would certainly have conducted themselves very well. Do I need to tell you that even to-day I know Sudeten officers who refuse to leave the Czechoslovak Army ?

" The experiences of the World War, reinforced by the more recent lessons of the Spanish war, have shown the resisting power of a courageous Army which holds its ground. Even in the hypothetical event of Czechoslovakia standing alone against Germany, I am of opinion that it would have been possible to prolong the struggle for some months. You must bear in mind that the Czechoslovak Army had forty good divisions; in other words, as compared with the whole of the German forces, the differences would have been no greater than that which existed between the French and the German troops at Verdun."

Germany no longer has to fear forty Czechoslovak divisions,[1] most of which were motorised, and all without exception equipped with the most modern weapons, turned out by the two great armament works at Plzeň and Brno. To defeat the Czechoslovak Army, sixty to sixty-eight divisions would have been required; these will now be available for use by Germany wherever she may need them. A few divisions will be sufficient

[1] It is probable that this number would have been further increased during the war by at least five divisions.

to assure herself against the risk of a revolt of the Czech people. Germany need no longer be afraid of aerial attacks originating from Czechoslovakia, which would have endangered Vienna, Munich, Nürnberg, Dresden, Leipzig, Breslau, Cologne and Berlin.

That this analysis of the consequences of Munich is by no means exaggerated is proved by Captain Liddell Hart, Military Correspondent of *The Times*, among others, in an article which appeared in that paper on February 8, 1939, as follows:

" We have now to face the fact that the German re-occupation of the Rhineland, the *Anschluss*, and the satisfaction of German, Hungarian, and Polish territorial claims upon Czechoslovakia have brought far-reaching changes in the strategic balance. While these events have removed any justifiable excuse for war, they have inevitably had a one-sided effect upon security in the military sense. The Germans gained, not only by the release of forces, but by relief from the anxiety caused by Czechoslovakia's geographical position as an operational air base uncomfortably close to vital points. The drawbacks of fighting a two-front war were deeply impressed on them by their experience in 1914–18, and the risk of a repetition was no small restraining factor. The French, on the other hand, lost what was a powerful distraction to the German power to concentrate against them. In case of war, the forty divisions which the Czechs might have mobilised from their resources would, by subtracting a large part of the German strength, have been an indirect addition to that of the French. In these circumstances, there was no real need for the two Regular divisions which we might have made available. But now, instead of the prospect of a fairly even balance, the French see themselves facing heavily adverse odds. This has made them more anxious than ever for a promise of direct support on land from us, and on a scale much larger than was before contemplated.

The foregoing by no means exhausts, however, the catalogue of what Germany gained by her victory at Munich. Her economic gains were no less important. In order that we may realise the magnitude of the economic potential of Czechoslovakia as she was, let us recall at least the more important facts. Czechoslovakia, who inherited 80 per cent. of the industrial plant of Austria-Hungary, was one of the six most important industrial states in Europe (Germany, England, France, Italy, Belgium and Czechoslovakia). Her war industries had a greater production than those of Italy—in 1937 she produced 90 per cent. more raw iron and 15 per cent. more steel than Italy. In the Eastern European zone, which stretches from the Baltic to the Ægean, 3,000,000 tons of raw iron and about 4,700,000 tons of steel were produced in 1937, out of which Czechoslovakia produced 1,700,000 tons of raw iron and 2,300,000 tons of steel. Czechoslovak heavy industry produced more than that of the other eleven states in this zone put together—including Poland. By the domination of Czechoslovakia, Germany has neutralised to her own advantage more than half the economic war potential of the whole of the Eastern part of Central Europe. By the annexation, which was the inevitable consequence, this war potential is now added to the German. The other states in this zone are incapable of supplying themselves with war material from their own resources, and have therefore been rendered even more dependent than before on Germany. Czechoslovak industry was able alone to provide adequate supplies of war material to Rumania and Yugoslavia—to a certain extent she did this at a heavy financial sacrifice—and even to some other states in addition. Czechoslovakia possessed, moreover, a formidable chemical industry, whose capacity surpassed by far that of the other Central European states. The Germans rightly called Czechoslovakia the " armoury of the world." Now it is the armoury exclusively of Germany and the German allies. Germany's war potential was increased to an extraordinary degree first by the virtual destruction of Czechoslovak independence and later by the occupation of the country.

At the end of November the German Press published the following outline of the present strength of the German Army:

" The German Army, after the *Anschluss* of Austria and of Sudetenland, comprises eighteen army corps and forty-three divisions, plus three mountain divisions, five armoured divisions and a brigade of cavalry, and is divided into fifteen military commands.

" While the *Anschluss* of Austria, according to Captain Morawski, of the Ministry of War in Berlin, led to the establishment of two army corps, one of which consists only of mountain troops, the Sudeten territories have been divided up between the adjacent army corps (Nos. 4, 8, 17 and 18)."

The *Berliner Börsenzeitung* wrote with considerable satisfaction on January 1, 1939, about the increases in the German military forces which had been achieved during the year 1938:

" Over and above the general reorganisation of army corps which has been necessitated by the annexation of Austria and the Sudeten territories, there have been created, in the shape either of mechanised troops or of garrisons for the fortifications, the equivalent of more than six active-service divisions.

" Special efforts have been concentrated on motorisation and mechanisation: a present-day army contains five divisions of heavy tanks and four divisions of light tanks. A large number of units have been mechanised and at the time of the march into the Sudetenland, out of an effective total of thirty divisions, fifteen were motorised or mechanised."

Germany's strategical position was vastly improved, not only by the fact that she had got rid of the Czechoslovak Army, which represented a serious potential opponent to her own, but also by the fact that the danger of being at war on two fronts, i.e. in the west and in the east, was considerably diminished. Czechoslovakia, allied both to France and to Russia, made possible military co-operation between the west and the east against Germany. There is no object in puzzling over the question of which route Soviet Russia would have chosen in going to the assistance of Czechoslovakia, since those who understood the situation are well aware that a route would have been found. In any case, it does not really matter how soon the Russian Army would have intervened on the Central European Front, for, had there been concerted action between Britain, France and Russia, Czechoslovakia would certainly have held out for a much longer time than would have been necessary for the transport of Russian troops to her assistance. The important fact is that Russia was at that time willing to intervene and that Czechoslovakia wanted her help; the Czechoslovaks were not in the least afraid to allow the Russian Army to enter their territory, but, on the contrary, were anxious for its co-operation. At the present time it would be necessary, if Russian intervention were to be as effective as it would have been in September, 1938, for Poland to enter into the same relationship with Russia as existed formerly between Russia and Czechoslovakia. Polish-Russian relations are far more problematical, however, since Poland has many reasons[1] to be afraid of the entry of a Russian army into her territory. In any case, the destruction of Czechoslovakia, which formed a sure link between France and Russia, has made immediate, rapid and successful military co-operation between the west and the east extremely difficult. Poland alone would be an insufficiently powerful substitute for Russia as an ally of the Western Powers. Even with Russian aid, the Eastern Front, in the event of war, will be far further back from Germany's vulnerable points than it was in September, 1938. The risk for Germany of having to fight on two fronts is considerably reduced by this great push forward in the German offensive. It is no secret that the main reason for the opposition of many of the leaders of the German Army to Herr Hitler's military adventure was their fear of a war on two fronts. As a matter of fact, Hitler shared that fear—until after Munich, when his success in substantially diminishing that risk greatly strengthened his position and no less greatly weakened the Army's opposition to his daring policy. Ever since that time, Nazi influence in the Army has continually increased.

(b) *The Building of Mitteleuropa.* The fall of Czechoslovakia opened for Germany an unimpeded passage to the whole of the Danube Basin. Only after Munich was Germany in a position to undertake, with some hope of success, the realisation of her grandiose plans for the organisation of that *Mitteleuropa* which was to stretch from the North and Baltic Seas to Asia. No time was wasted before launching an intensive campaign to this end.

[1] These are in connection not only with her social conditions, but also with the nationality problems created by her Ukrainian and White Russian minorities.

In October, 1938, Dr. Funk, the German Minister of Economics, made a tour of visits to Belgrade, Sofia and Ankara, of which the *D.Z. am Mittag* of October 17, immediately after his return to Germany, wrote as follows:

" Yugoslavia, Bulgaria and Turkey represent a sort of Balkan axis which stretches from the German frontier to the Black Sea. This makes it possible to discuss large economic plans concerning all the three countries, e.g. building large roads and continuous telephone cables. Germany proposes to grant these countries long-term credits for goods supplied to them and to conclude with them trade contracts for a period of several years, so that their producers may be able to count on definite deliveries to Germany at definite prices. Furthermore, thanks to the great importance of the Danube, there will be built up for the south-east an economic area which will stretch from the North Sea to the Black Sea and will be naturally self-sufficient. South-Eastern Europe and Asia Minor have nearly everything that Germany needs and, besides that, Germany buys in those countries more than twice as much as England, France and U.S.A. combined."

German policy is very active towards this end and is achieving considerable results. There is no doubt that Germany brings certain benefits to the agrarian states of the Danube Basin, but they pay for it by having their economic system bound more and more closely to Germany, with consequences which naturally ensue. At any rate, Germany herself benefits from it, and is able to supplement from those countries what she lacks in cereals, foodstuffs and raw materials, and as early as the end of November, Dr. Schacht was already speaking of the improved condition of Germany's resources. The autarchic tendencies of German economy, inspired originally by military considerations, have been furthered considerably by the improvement of Germany's trade with the Danubian countries.

In Ankara, Dr. Schacht offered the Turkish Government a loan of £12½ million[1] to finance the reconstruction of the mines and industries of Anatolia, in which Germany was to collaborate by supplying materials, machinery and technicians.

[1] A few months previously England had granted Turkey a loan of £16 million.

Bulgaria depends for more than 80 per cent. of her commerce upon Germany. At the end of October it was announced that the German Government had proposed that, for a period of twelve years, Bulgaria should supply Germany with all her surplus products (tobacco, fruit, cereals, pigs), and receive in exchange armaments, machinery and manufactured goods. At the same time, German experts, engineers and mechanics would install the plant required for the improvement of Bulgarian communications and public works, irrigation, etc. The prices for the goods supplied by Germany and the wages of the German mechanics would be fixed in advance for the whole period. A German economic mission visited Sofia at the beginning of January, 1939, since when economic relations between Germany and Bulgaria have become more and more extensive.

While in Belgrade, Dr. Funk drew up a new Commerical Treaty with Yugoslavia, and on October 25 a new Clearing Agreement was concluded with Germany providing for stabilisation of the rate of exchange at between 14·30 and 14·70 dinars to the mark (the current rate). Another agreement was signed which regulated the quotas and contingents of Yugoslavia's exports to Germany, so that they should not exceed the value of her imports from that country.

In Rumania, Dr. Ley, chief of the Labour Front, had already inspected the oil-fields in the middle of October, and on December 15 a Trade Agreement was signed in Bucharest, whereby Germany undertook to take from Rumania goods to the value of 10,000 million lei (about £1,538,000), of which 25 per cent. would consist of oil or oil products.[1] The value of the mark was fixed for purchases by Rumania at 40·5 lei, and for purchases by Germany at 41·5 lei.

Meanwhile, in the same period, economic pressure on Hungary and Czechoslovakia was being increased. Germany forced Hungary to accept an arrangement whereby the entire Hungarian agricultural production, especially that of cereals, pigs and fats, was placed at her disposal, while, under the pretext that Hungarian industry is in Jewish hands, Germany discouraged that " artificial " industry and suggested that further industrialisation of Hungary should be stopped. As regards Czecho-Slovakia,

[1] The rest of the Rumanian oil production is reserved for England and France.

Germany's policy in the post-Munich era was to attempt to establish the greatest possible hold on her economic system, while maintaining the possibility open to an independent Czecho-Slovakia of obtaining foreign exchange. It was realised that the establishment of a customs union between Germany and Czecho-Slovakia would cripple the export trade of the latter with other countries, especially the Anglo-Saxon and American countries, and for this reason Germany at first preferred to maintain her commercial relations with Czecho-Slovakia on the basis of a system of mutual preference. The small economic disadvantages which resulted for the Germans by Czechoslovakia becoming, in the eyes of the trading world, a mere extension of Germany, were more than compensated by the German seizure of all her economic resources and capacities in March, 1939.

The foregoing shows how Germany made use in Central Europe of the opportunities opened by Munich. The *Deutsche Bergwerk-Zeitung*, of January 2, 1939, in a review of German trade relations with South-East Europe, said that much of Germany's exports had been diverted from overseas to the Balkan countries, while imports from those countries now amounted to 12 to 15 per cent. of total German imports, as against only 4 per cent. from the Danubian area in 1925–9. These proportions were further increased by the annexation of Czecho-slovakia and the consequent addition to Germany of Czech trade with South-Eastern Europe, which had been systematically fostered by the economic Little Entente.[1] The ultimate aim of Germany's economic policy is the creation of an economic *bloc* composed of Germany and the states of the Danubian Basin and of the Balkans. After the destruction of Czechoslovak independence, this aim was no longer unattainable.

(c) *Hungary.* The first country to feel the effect of the new situation created by Munich was Hungary. She had been seriously threatened by German pressure ever since the annexation of Austria, and now, after the fall of Czechoslovakia, which also served as a bastion between Hungary and Germany, she was no longer able to withstand that pressure. The tragedy was that, ever since the Treaty of Trianon was signed, Hungary and

[1] See *The Bulletin of International News*, Vol. XVI, No. 1, p. 35.

Czechoslovakia had been on terms of hostility, and every attempt, however, cautious, to bring about a reconciliation between them had failed. When the independence and unity of Czechoslovakia were destroyed, Hungary benefited by acquiring the southern districts of Slovakia and Carpathian Ruthenia. The Hungarians had to pay dearly, however, for this gain of territory; and after Munich they were threatened with passing completely under the domination of the Third Reich. Italy, upon whom Hungary had relied ever since 1927, even helped to contribute to the suppression of the feeble remnant of resistance within Hungary to becoming a vassal of Germany—that was the real significance of Count Ciano's visit to Budapest on December 19, 1938. M. Kanya, the former Foreign Minister of Hungary, whom Germany did not consider sufficiently reliable, was forced to resign at the end of November and on December 10, 1938, his place was filled by Count Csáky, who was more amenable to Berlin. In a public declaration, made immediately after his assumption of office, Count Csáky gave a public assurance that Hungarian foreign policy would be to maintain friendly relations with Germany and Italy. During Count Ciano's stay in Hungary from December 19–22, 1938, the gravitation of Hungary towards the Berlin-Rome Axis was accepted and assured. On December 30, 1938, the Prime Minister, M. Bela de Imrédy, said:

" Hungary is bound to Germany by an ancient fraternity of arms, to Italy by esteem for an ancient adversary. . . .

" The aims of the policy pursued by the two Great Powers of the Axis are to provide a more solid basis for peace in Europe and to create there a more just order, in which the Hungarians will play the role to which they are entitled. . . . We shall pursue a foreign policy of reliance on the Axis, but we shall pursue it as an independent nation, which is conscious of itself and is at the same time pursuing its own objectives."

M. Imrédy felt obliged to stress the fact that Hungary intended to maintain her " independence," since the domination of his country by the Berlin-Rome Axis, or rather by Germany, was causing considerable anxiety in Hungarian political circles. Some Hungarian politicians expressed certain fears quite openly.

For instance, Count Bethlen, a former Prime Minister, writing in the *Pesti Naplo* of January 1, 1939, warned his countrymen of the danger which the pursuit by Germany of her plans in the Ukraine would entail for them, since it might lead to a new invasion of Central Europe by the Slavs.[1]

This same January 1, one of the leaders of the Opposition, M. Tibor Eckhardt, wrote in the *Magyar Nemzet*:

" Hungary has never been and never will be a servant of Germany. There will be no unconditional surrender. We are not a high road, offering itself for use by other nations. We are opposed to the policy of ' Divide and Rule.' Hungary's historical role is to organise the Danubian Basin. Hungary will never renounce the Carpathians, which form her natural frontier. She should pursue a foreign policy of national independence, based, on the one hand, on the friendship and collaboration with Germany, Italy and Poland, but taking into consideration the great Western nations which have economic and financial power."

But these protesting voices, which expressed the indignation felt by Hungarians at the subjection of their country to German hegemony, were unable to arrest the inevitable course of events; Germany took good care to break down the opposition inside Hungary. M. Imrédy's Government found itself obliged, willy-nilly, to foster the tendency towards the introduction of a régime which, if not entirely totalitarian, was at least strongly authoritative. The Hungarian Nazis, supported, of course, by Germany, exercised an irresistible pressure in that direction upon the Government, using for this purpose in particular the demand for radical land reform and anti-Semitic agitation. The German Press wrote openly that it would be advisable for Hungary to " liquidate the artificial industries which are in

---

[1] " Whether the attempt succeeds or fails, it might cost us Hungarians our lives, while Germany would, at the very worst, come out of it poorer by one lost illusion, but the richer by an experience gained." He concluded his article as follows: " For twenty years past Hungary has done nothing to prevent the annexation of Austria and of the Sudeten territory. We have rejected any attempt at a restoration, whether alone, or in company with Austria. We have refused collaboration with Austria and Czechoslovakia. We have not accepted any of the projects for a Danubian Federation, because these projects were directed against Germany. To-day the mind of every thoughtful Hungarian is full of fear for the future."

the hands of Jews, and concentrate on agriculture." The Government began to introduce strong measures against Jews, some of whom committed suicide. Germany also made very good use of the German minority, which numbers between 500,000 and 650,000. On November 26, 1938, the Nazis defied the Hungarian law by founding the *Volksbund der Deutschen in Ungarn*, which is supposed to unite all National-Socialist Germans in Hungary, and in the *Völkischer Beobachter* of December 15, Dr. Basch, President of that organisation, formulated the following demands:

" 1. The recognition of the Germans in Hungary as a national community in the eyes of the law.

" 2. The solution of the question of German education merely by the issue of orders and without regard to the wishes of the parents. The establishment of a training college for German teachers, as well as of a German polytechnic and a German secondary school. The German language to be made the language of instruction in all nursery and elementary schools for German children.

" 3. The abolition of all obstacles to the founding of German daily and weekly papers.

" 4. The granting of facilities for the establishment of any kind of German organisation, and in particular of charitable and youth organisations.

" 5. The permitting of voluntary collections.

" 6. Religious instruction, and the conduct of religious services for Germans to be in the German language. Foundation of a seminary for German priests.

" 7. In case of necessity, the uniting of all Germans in their own political party."

Dr. Basch mentioned at the end that Herr Hitler had proclaimed that he would respect the existing frontiers of Hungary.

Dr. Basch's demands, so apparently innocent, were merely a copy of those made by Henlein, adapted to suit the situation in Hungary. Since the Germans in Hungary do not live in a compact unit alongside the German frontier the promise to respect the Hungarian frontiers was easy and cost little to make. It does not prevent Herr Hitler from proclaiming the right to interfere in Hungarian politics in such a way as to assimilate (*gleich-schalten*) Hungary completely into Germany. Although the leader of the Hungarian Nazis, Dr. Basch, had been imprisoned for three months during the Government of M. Gömbös for insulting the Hungarian nation, the Hungarian Government must now respect him. In an article published in the *Pester Loyd* of December 25, Dr. Imrédy announced that he would create a special Government department to deal with the minorities, and announced further concessions to the German minority:

" The Hungarian Government will create German nursery schools, a German teachers' college, German elementary superior schools and a German secondary school.

" Agricultural courses in German language will be organised.

" The Hungarian authorities will be obliged to make use of the German language in their dealings with members of the German minority.

" In the churches of the German minority the sermon will be delivered in German and the hymns will be sung in that language.

" The Germans will have the right to publish their newspapers, to organise their own associations and to take collections on behalf of their institutions."

That these concessions were, in fact, exceptional ones, made only under pressure from Germany, was shown by the fact that no such concessions were promised to the Slovak and Ruthenian minorities, which numbered, even then, after the first Hungarian occupation of territory in Czechoslovakia, between 500,000 and 600,000. These minorities are, on the contrary, being deprived of their schools and of their cultural and political institutions, which existed under the Czechoslovak administration. The Slovak minority in Hungary is once again, as has already been described, being cruelly persecuted.

The subjection of Hungary to the Third Reich became quite patent in the middle of January, 1939. On January 13 the German, Italian and Japanese Ministers called on the Hungarian Foreign Minister, Count Csáky, and he informed them that Hungary was willing to join the Anti-Comintern Pact. On January 16 Count Csáky visited Berlin, staying there until

January 18 and having a long conversation with Herr Hitler. In the official communiqué issued on January 18, it was stated that their views on foreign policy were exactly similar and that the old and well-tried friendship which existed between the countries would be still further developed. This euphemistic statement amounted to a public admission that Hungary had passed under the domination of the Nazis. The adherence of Hungary to the Anti-Comintern Pact is a matter of great importance. The German Press seized the occasion to blame M. Kanya, the former Hungarian Foreign Minister for not having believed in the might and greatness of the National-Socialist Germany and for having refused, lest he offended England and France, to join the Anti-Comintern Pact. Hungary now decided—or, more correctly, after the loss of Czechoslovak independence she was forced to decide unilaterally and unconditionally—in favour of the Berlin-Rome Axis. Her adherence to the Anti-Comintern Pact was misused by Germany, of course, for the purpose of exerting pressure on the other Danubian states, and above all on Rumania and Yugoslavia. Germany, having crippled Czechoslovakia, assured herself in January, 1939, of Hungary as a convenient jumping-off place, not only against Rumania, but also against Russia in pursuit of her Ukrainian plans. In return for her support, Hungary was promised help in her revisionist claims in Transylvania, which Germany will sooner or later support in the event of Rumania's refusing to pass under Nazi domination. At the same time, the domination of Hungary by Berlin made it easier for Germany to intensify her pressure upon Prague. The German threat to partition Slovakia between her neighbours played an important role in determining Slovak action in March, 1939.

Russia retaliated to Hungary's decision to adhere to the Anti-Comintern Pact with the breaking-off, on February 4, 1939, of diplomatic relations with Hungary, on the ground that that decision had been forced upon Hungary from outside and that therefore Hungarian policy had ceased to be independent. It was evident, of course, that Moscow intended by this demonstration to warn all the other Danubian and Baltic states not to follow the example of Hungary by adhering also to the Anti-Comintern Pact. It was thus intimated that they would certainly find themselves very awkwardly situated if Moscow adopted an unfriendly attitude towards them.

In the post-Munich situation, it was difficult, of course, for the smaller countries of South-Eastern Europe to find the courage to resist Germany, yet even then Germany met, and will continue to meet, and have to overcome, the opposition of large numbers of people in this part of the world, especially of those whose particular interests are in any way in conflict with the aims of German policy. This divergence of interest arises time after time even in the relations between Germany and Hungary. Though in September, 1938, Germany put a stern veto on Hungary's desire to acquire Carpatho-Ukraine, in March, 1939, this desire was realised, though Slovakia, or the greater part of it, still remained " independent."

That Hungary never renounced her desire for the return of Sub-Carpathian Ruthenia was proved by Colonel Beck, the Polish Foreign Minister, who, in a written answer to a question asked by a Member of Parliament on January 23, 1939, defined the attitude of the Polish Government with regard to the question of a common Hungaro-Polish frontier:

> " The Polish Government knows of Hungary's aspirations to recover Sub-Carpathian Ruthenia and to create a common frontier with Poland. As long as the Hungarian Government pursues a policy to that end, it can count on the goodwill and support of Poland and on her complete sympathy. She is content merely to watch the development of events and, should a dangerous situation arise, the Polish Government will take the measures necessary to meet it."

It was evident that the question of a common Hungaro-Polish frontier was kept open by Budapest and Warsaw. If Hungary desired it, in order to increase her territory and thus to achieve gradually the complete restoration to her pre-War frontiers, Poland was anxious that the Carpatho-Ukraine should disappear from the map. After Munich it appeared that the Germans regarded it as a " new Piedmont " from which might originate a movement for the liberation and unification of all the Ukrainians, including, of course, those who live under Polish oppression. There is no more reason to believe that Germany abandoned this intention in March, 1939, than there was to believe that Poland and Hungary had finally abandoned their desire for a common frontier in September, 1938. Over this question there is still a latent conflict between Germany, on the one hand, and Hungary and Poland (with Italy standing discretely behind them), on the other. On January 22, 1939, less than two months before the Hungarian occupation took place, the German *Diplomatic Correspondence*, expressing the views of the Foreign Minister, wrote sharply against those in Hungary who were opposed to the decisions made by the Vienna arbitrators on November 2:

" It is unfortunate that we should find once more, despite the efforts of the Hungarian Government, which could not fail to realise the incalculable consequences of any such development, that such an attitude has been adopted in the ranks of the Opposition, which, as Germany cannot but be surprised to note, is composed of partisans of the Popular Front, Jews, reactionaries and other discontented people. While Germany, together with Italy, has borne all the risks, the elements which have been mentioned, in their unseemly arrogance and ingratitude, act within the country as though they suspect the leader of the German state of wanting to eliminate Hungary just at the moment when she had completely acquired her ethnographical frontiers. It cannot be overstressed that at Munich Germany won a victory for the ethnographical principle. The Sudeten Germans returned to Germany and the Polish and Hungarian national groups were also returned as a result of the Munich Agreement to their mother countries. If now the discontented Hungarian elements, in defiance of all political realities, insist that Hungary cannot be satisfied with less than the whole territory which formerly belonged to the Crown of St. Stephen, they are dreamers who must be awakened to the realisation of the fact that the old crown of the Germans was no less proud than that of St. Stephen."

In other words, Hungary must not try to get more than what Germany will allow her, and Germany will allow Hungary to take what she—for the moment—does not directly want.

Realpolitik, however, means for the Germans that no decision is final except that which actively contributes to—and advances—German well-being and German ambitions.

(*d*) *Yugoslavia.*—So far as Yugoslavia was concerned, Berlin and Rome hoped that, even if she would not openly join the Axis she would take no action which would embarrass them. Yugoslavia, being directly adjacent to both Germany and Italy, was naturally obliged to step warily where the Axis was concerned, especially since these two Powers pursue their European policy as a united *bloc*, and Yugoslavia, after the fall of Czechoslovakia, had no force in Central Europe upon which she could rely. Under such circumstances, it was not difficult to predict that the hunting visit paid by Count Ciano to Dr. Stojadinovitch, Prime Minister of Yugoslavia, at Bělje, in Slovenia, on January 20–22, 1939, would not be without some positive results for the Berlin-Rome Axis. According to the official communiqué, the statesmen had " studied together certain European questions which were of common interest to Italy and Yugoslavia, and had both decided to continue their mutual collaboration for the reinforcement and further consolidation of peace and good order in their sphere of Europe, doing so with the consent of all the other states concerned and in connection with a recent statement by the countries neighbouring on Yugoslavia, which had found a favourable response in Belgrade." This was a direct hint at the efforts for a friendly understanding between Hungary and Yugoslavia for which Roman diplomacy was working—not always in absolute agreement with Berlin. Italian diplomacy was still trying, somewhat timorously, to balance the German predomination in Central and Balkan Europe by its influence, and after Munich played with the idea of supporting a friendly understanding, perhaps even of collaboration, between Poland, Yugoslavia and Rumania. At the same time, Italy was anxious to assure, at least in Yugoslavia, its economic position, which was being threatened more and more directly by the economic expansion of Germany. Publicly it was declared, as Count Ciano told the Press on leaving Yugoslavia, that " every diplomatic act in this sense [Danubian co-operation] is being done within the frame-work of the Rome-Berlin Axis."

The policy of Stojadinovitch became more and more favourable towards the Berlin-Rome Axis, but he was nevertheless afraid to join the Axis openly. He was prevented from doing more mainly by internal political considerations. In the elections for the Skupština, held on December 11, Stojadinovitch failed to achieve the success he expected. It is true—as it is true of all Balkan elections—that the Opposition failed to obtain a majority, but, in spite of all the obstacles with which it met, it considerably increased its representation as compared with the elections of 1935, and the Croat Opposition in particular, far from being weakened, gained in strength. It was well known that the Yugoslav Opposition was opposed to Dr. Stojadinovitch's foreign policy, which they criticised precisely because of its leaning towards the dictatorships of the Axis and away from the European democracies. Even the authoritative Government in Belgrade was obliged to pay a certain deference to Yugoslav public opinion and was, of course, at the same time anxious to avoid being directly involved on the side of Italy against France, and still less against Great Britain,[1] in a Mediterranean conflict, Finally, Belgrade was unable completely to ignore Rumania, and could not associate itself with a German policy of open hostility towards that country, especially if that policy were expressed in terms of Hungarian revisionist claims, since similar claims could very easily be extended at a later date against Yugoslavia, which contains some 500,000 Hungarians. In spite, therefore, of a certain leaning towards the Berlin-Rome Axis, the Belgrade Government, even under Stojadinovitch, tried to maintain an attitude of strict neutrality; it would have been delighted if, in fulfilment of Mr. Chamberlain's dream, with which Prince Paul is very much in sympathy, an agreement were to have been achieved between the Four Great Powers.

Condemned by force of circumstances and the character of its leaders to a passive policy of waiting, Dr. Stojadinovitch's Government, and even its successor, was forced, not always too unwillingly, to tolerate German economic and political penetration into Yugoslavia, merely attempting to balance it to some extent by collaboration with Italy. The policy which has been

---

[1] Prince Paul's visit to London from November 21 to December 6, 1938, was not without influence in this respect.

pursued was, however, full of dangerous contradictions. While it was of vital interest to Yugoslavia to maintain the situation created by the Paris Peace Treaties, the Belgrade Government nevertheless inclined towards the Berlin-Rome Axis, which was challenging the *status quo* by a somewhat disingenuous appeal to the " ethnical principle." This principle provides justification for the revisionist claims of both Hungary and Bulgaria, neither of which can be satisfied except at the expense of Yugoslavia— and, of course, also of Rumania. By the end of 1938 the Hungarian Press was already demanding quite openly that the Hungarians who live in Yugoslavia would be granted autonomy. In addition to this, the German minority, although it numbers merely some 40,000, was becoming more and more presumptuous in its claims.

The right of self-determination was also being claimed by the Croat Opposition, led by Dr. Matchek. The Deputies of the Croatian Agrarian Party, together with the Independent Democrats, decided in Zagreb on January 15 that they would appeal to " every element within their state " as well as to the other states, and especially the Great Powers, to see that the Croat question should be settled in accordance with the principle of self-determination, and that the existing intolerable and dangerous situation should be brought to an end. They went on to declare that the historical rights of the Croats were being ignored. The resolution in which these demands were being formulated recalled, it is true, the friendship of the Croats towards the Serbian nation, but at the same time it stressed the point that the Croatian nation could not indefinitely tolerate being denied its right of existence and freedom, as well as its right to determine its own future. An important point in this resolution was the declaration that treaties concluded and all obligations contracted by the Belgrade Government were damaging to the Croat nation and were therefore not considered as binding upon them. The example of Munich, at which a country was partitioned by the Four Great Powers in ostensible response to the demand of the Sudeten-Germans for self-determination, evidently influenced the Croats in such a way that their demands became more radical.

The deterioration of the position in Central Europe and of the relations between Serbs and Croats has been the irrevocable

consequence of the " realistic opportunism " practised by Prince
Paul and Dr. Stojadinovitch since 1936. Imitating the tactics of
Colonel Beck, the Polish Foreign Minister, they started to
" complement their old friendships by seeking new ones." In
practice, this meant that they turned their backs on France and
Czechoslovakia, limited the functions of the Little Entente to
defence of the Treaty of Trianon against Hungary and, in
drawing closer to Italy and Germany, they passed more and
more under their influence. Dr. Stojadinovitch is second only to
Colonel Beck in his responsibility for the overwhelming strengthening of German influence in Central Europe. It is these two
statesmen who are to blame for the fact that the road was
opened for the expansion of Nazi imperialism in Europe. To-day
it is seen that they are no less guilty of sacrificing the interests
of their respective countries than they are of having destroyed
the independence of others. Dr. Stojadinovitch failed even to
divert from Yugoslavia the effects of the demand, supported by
the dynamic Powers, for treaty revision in Central Europe and
in the Mediterranean zone, while his friendship with Berlin and
Rome did not even suffice to throttle the Croatian movement.
The results of his policy were wholly lamentable. He deprived
Yugoslavia of the confidence of her friends, and exposed her,
practically isolated, to the pressure of Germany and Italy,
which, after the occupation of Albania, was shown to present an
acute danger to Yugoslav integrity. In spite of his pact with
Bulgaria and his flirtation with Hungary, he never succeeded in
silencing their revisionist claims. So far as domestic affairs were
concerned, he so aggravated the tension between the Croats and
the Serbs that the former became intransigently radical in their
national claims, and, so far as the peasants are concerned, no
less radical in their social demands. These failures were by no
means compensated for by the temporary improvement of the
economic situation for which Stojadinovitch strove.

Dr. Stojadinovitch fell sooner than he expected. His attitude
during the elections, when he presented himself everywhere as a
Führer, displeased Prince Paul, and the result of the elections of
December 11 indicated to anyone who understood the situation
the complete failure of Dr. Stojadinovitch's policy (see above,
p. 313). In spite of an electoral system designed to favour the

Government, and in spite of terrorism at the polls, the Opposition succeeded in increasing its vote. The régime began to totter. Ten days after the elections there was a reconstruction of the Cabinet whereby Mgr. Koroshetz, the leader of the Slovene Catholics, who had been disturbed at the increasing Nazi pressure on Slovenia, left the Government and the Croat representation was increased. Mgr. Koroshetz's fears were shared by the leader of the Bosnian Moslems, M. Spaho, and, without the participation in the Government of these two non-Serb politicians, Dr. Stojadinovitch was unable to maintain even the fiction of the " national unity of the Yugoslavs." Not even were all the Serbian representatives in his Government in agreement with his policy. The radical resolution of the Croats of January 15, 1939 (see p. 314), created a considerable impression: and it was feared that the intransigent Croat Separatists might establish ascendancy over the more conciliatory Dr. Matchek.

In this way behind the scenes a change was prepared which could, of course, be carried out only with the consent of the Regent, Prince Paul. During the night of February 3, five Ministers handed in their resignations, a successor for Stojadinovitch having already been found, and on the following day Dr. Stojadinovitch, taken by surprise by what had happened, handed in his resignation. During the night of February 5–6, a new Government was appointed, with Dr. Dragiša Tsvetkovitch at its head. The new Prime Minister had already, prior to this, tried to reach an agreement with the Croats, and it was this fact which indicated him as the leader of a new Government, whose main tasks were to be the conclusion of an agreement with the Croats and a general reconciliation on domestic issues. In March official conversations were opened between Tsvetkovitch and Matchek and appeared to be progressing well, but the task of international reconciliation was hampered, not only because of Yugoslavia's serious external position after the occupation of Albania, but also by a tense domestic situation. The Croats will not be contented unless a federal Constitution of the State is adopted; it will be necessary, in order to placate the Serbian and Croatian Opposition, to relax the existing dictatorial régime and to admit a greater degree of political liberty. Such a policy would, however, certainly create a considerable diminution of confidence in Rome and Berlin, where the announcement of Dr. Stojadinovitch's fall was received with ill-concealed disapproval. The German Press tried to explain away the changes by pretending that the efforts to satisfy the Croats were of a similar character to those which led to the federalisation of Czechoslovakia, but the *Angriff* made no secret of its annoyance:

" Stojadinovitch represented a programme. He was one of those few leading people who represent the new Europe, towards the creation of which he contributed not a little in freeing Yugoslavia from the rigid system established at Versailles by concluding treaties with Italy and Bulgaria, as well as by his friendly attitude towards Germany, which enabled him to turn his country into an active and independent factor in the politics of Europe. For these reasons, he has been much attacked in France and also in London, where he was a great obstacle in the path of those who wanted to stop the German *Drang nach Südosten*, especially after the annexation of Austria and the Sudeten territory by Germany, by piling up British commercial warehouses in the Balkans. Dr. Stojadinovitch's foreign policy has many opponents in his own country also, especially in Slovenia."

In Rome also a very reserved attitude was adopted towards the new Tsvetkovitch Government for, in Dr. Stojadinovitch, Count Ciano had lost a colleague for whom he had a special liking and with whom only a few weeks earlier he had discussed the possibility of a very intimate collaboration. In these circumstances, the task which confronted Tsintsar Markovitch, the new Foreign Minister of Yugoslavia, on his accession to office was not easy, even though, so far as personalities were concerned, the fact that he had until then been the Yugoslav Minister in Berlin and was on friendly terms with the German authorities tended to make matters less difficult. The Tsvetkovitch Government inherited from Dr. Stojadinovitch the liability of " friendship " with the Berlin-Rome Axis, and it would be very dangerous for Yugoslavia to antagonise her neighbours by renewed friendships in the west. After the Italian occupation of Albania and the direct threat to Yugoslavia, it is less likely than ever that Yugoslavia will be allowed to diverge very much from the Axis. The new Government, so long as it is occupied with internal reorganisation, will be obliged to maintain friendly relations with Germany as well as with Italy, otherwise those " dynamic " Great Powers would not hesitate to intervene " dynamically " in Yugoslavia. Germany and Italy find intervention easy in proportion as the internal solidarity of the political and moral forces of the country have been disturbed by the implacable " realism " of Dr. Stojadinovitch's régime.

(e) *Rumania.*—Rumania was also threatened by the removal of the obstacles to German expansion into the Danube Basin. During the September crisis, Rumania behaved with exemplary loyalty towards her Czechoslovak ally and there is no doubt of what she would have done in the event of hostilities. This attitude on the part of Rumania was not, of course, viewed with favour by Germany. After Munich, Rumania was obliged to adapt herself to the changed situation. In the middle of November King Carol visited London and Paris. These visits merely served to impress on the Rumanians the desire of the two Western Powers to continue in the spirit of Munich, to disinterest themselves as far as possible in the affairs of Central Europe. It was clear that even their economic interests in this part of the world would remain on the whole very limited. In such circumstances it was natural that on his way back King Carol should have stopped in Germany and had there on November 27, in Leipzig, a conversation with Field-Marshal Göring. The German Press immediately took the opportunity of stressing the fact that Germany was Rumania's most important commercial partner, and they advised the Rumanian Government to make every possible effort to extend its economic relations with the Reich. In December a new commercial treaty between the two countries was signed, which foreshadowed the far-reaching treaty of March, 1939.

At the same time, however, political relations between Germany and Rumania became rather worse. This was due to the harsh measures taken in Rumania against the Iron Guard. The activities of this organisation had remarkably revived in November and several outrages had been committed by its members. On November 30 it was announced that their imprisoned leader, Codreanu, together with several Iron Guard leaders, had been killed while attempting to escape. The Rumanian authorities, profiting from the fatal experience of others, took merciless and vigorous steps against the Iron Guard. This action aroused great dissatisfaction in Germany, where the Iron Guard had always enjoyed, to say the least, considerable sympathy. The German Press immediately launched a campaign of vilification against King Carol, insolently referring, of course, to the Jewish origin of Madame Lupescu. The *Angriff* published Madame Lupescu's photograph and that of her father with an inscription, " Ugly Jews," and wrote: " Rumania is in flames. Jewish terror rages through the enslaved land. The dwarfs of corruption have their dirty hands full. Where Judah rules, blood flows and the prisons are full."

The *Börsen Zeitung* compared the shooting of Codreanu with the killing of Señor Sotelo in June, 1936, which had been the signal for General Franco's rebellion, and suggested that the consequences might be the same in Rumania as they had been in Spain.

German threats against Rumania were not empty, nor without purpose. It is absolutely necessary for Germany to have the Rumanian oil. Rumania seemed to be faced therefore with two alternatives; either she would have to submit to German hegemony, or she would have to share the fate of Czechoslovakia. Germany, by drawing Hungary into her political orbit, has reached the very frontiers of Rumania. Whenever they may wish to do so, the Germans can inspire Budapest to raise her claim to Transylvania, in which 1,500,000 Hungarians are living. German policy takes a careful interest in the 800,000 Germans who live in Rumania, among whom Nazi propaganda has been active for a considerable time, with unquestionable success. Finally, Germany does not forget to threaten Rumania by stimulating the Bulgarian claim for Dobrudja. On January 19, 1939, the [Bucharest correspondent of the *Frankfurter Zeitung* wrote to his paper:

" It is clear to the Rumanians themselves that a permanent agreement with Bulgaria would certainly be worth while, and that in this frontier dispute, which is unimportant for the Great Rumania to-day, Rumania should make a sacrifice."

The Sofia Correspondent of the Göring *National Zeitung* wrote in a similar tune in February, 1939:

" During the political debates in the Bulgarian Parliament several speakers demanded the revision of the ' dictated ' peace. Bulgarian official circles are speaking now for the first time of the necessity of satisfying their country's revisionist claims. What adds weight to the Bulgarian claims is that they were not drafted in general terms, but limit themselves to a mere rectification of the Bulgaro-Rumanian frontier. This rectification can be justified on racial grounds—that is to say, Bulgaria can appeal to the Munich principles and to the actual results of the Vienna arbitration."

Besides supporting the Hungarian, Bulgarian and German minorities in Rumania, Nazi propaganda disposed of yet another means of breaking down the resistance of Rumania: it would inspire new activity on the part of the Iron Guard, whose members cherish their semi-Nazi faith with greater fanaticism as the Rumanian Government's intolerance of their activities increases.

After Munich, Rumania found herself, in fact, in a very difficult situation. Her relations with Poland, with whom she has a treaty of alliance,[1] though not altogether bad, were uncomfortable. Poland was not a little displeased with Rumania when Colonel Beck failed to obtain her consent, in October, 1938, to the establishment of a common frontier between Poland and Hungary. It was also comprehensible that the Rumanians, although they desired close co-operation with the Poles, were nevertheless not anxious to share with them all the risks which ensued from their uncertain relations with Russia and with Germany. As far as Rumania was concerned, after Munich had severed close relations between Eastern and Western Europe and had allowed German influence to become so much more powerful, she was more afraid even than before to enter into closer relations with Russia, and must often have regretted having failed to seize the favourable occasion for doing this, which presented itself in 1935, after the signature of the

[1] Drawn up for application, not against Germany, but against Russia !

Franco-Soviet Pact.[1] This failure on the part of the Rumanians meant that the question of Bessarabia, whose annexation by Rumania has not yet been recognised by the Soviet Government, still remains unsettled.

The new Foreign Minister of Rumania, M. Gregory Gafencu,[2] was faced with the task of trying to solve these complications in the foreign policy of his country. He immediately tried to strengthen the alliance with Poland, of which he had always been a keen supporter, and attempted to secure the support of Italy in the hope that by coming under the defensive wing of the southern partner of the Axis (who cannot desire that his northern partner should completely dominate the Danube Basin and the Balkans) he would provide his country with the best defence against the pressure of Germany. It was along these lines that M. Gafencu carried on his negotiations with Dr. Stojadinovitch, during his visit to Belgrade on February 1–2, 1939. The most important matter which they discussed, however, was the settlement of their respective relations with Hungary. Dr. Stojadinovitch was supposed to be acting as mediator and to arrange that any reconciliation between Yugoslavia and Hungary should be accompanied by a similar one between Hungary and Rumania. The two statesmen hoped to conclude a pact of non-aggression between their states and Hungary, but Hungary insisted that the question of the Hungarian minorities, not only in Rumania, but also in Yugoslavia, should first be settled.

Further developments—above all after the occupation of Czechoslovakia—proved that all efforts for a *rapprochement* with Hungary had been in vain. Hungary, under the influence, scarcely concealed, of Germany, demanded with increasing insistence the fulfilment of her claims in Transylvania. At the same time Bulgaria was actively encouraged by the Nazis to raise her claim for the Dobrudja. Italian aid for Rumania against these two threats was not noticeable. M. Gafencu soon realised that there was little to be expected on the part of the Italians.

For Rumania, the meeting of the Permanent Council of the

---

[1] Rumania's policy with regard to Russia has nevertheless been more far-sighted than that of Dr. Stojadinovitch, who forgot, as soon as he became Prime Minister in 1935, that he had formerly been a keen advocate of the establishment of friendly relations with Russia.

[2] Appointed on December 21, 1938.

Balkan Entente at Bucharest was of far greater importance. On February 22, 1939, the four Balkan States (Rumania, Yugoslavia, Turkey and Greece) reaffirmed their determination to maintain "absolute respect for their frontiers." Pursuing further diplomatic activity in this direction, Gafencu strengthened Rumanian-Turkish collaboration by his visit to Ankara in April. For Rumania the free passage of British and French warships through the Dardanelles into the Black Sea was of vital importance.

Meanwhile the Polish-Rumanian Alliance was reaffirmed during the visit of M. Gafencu to Warsaw on March 4–6. Throughout this period, Rumanian-Russian relations, though correct, left much to be desired. It was not till the second half of April that they began to show an improvement.

After the death of the Patriarch, Miron Christea, M. Calinescu, a strong and determined man who enjoyed the full confidence of the King, became Prime Minister. M. Calinescu's energetic dealings with the Iron Guard had certainly done nothing to improve Rumanian relations with Germany, whose pressure on Rumania was increasing daily.

The situation of Rumania after the annexation of Czecho-Slovakia in March, 1939, became exceedingly difficult. To save herself from immediate danger, Rumania signed on March 23 a further trade agreement with Germany. This agreement was of capital importance: if it were to be executed, it would deliver practically the whole of the Rumanian economy into the hands of the Germans and Germany would be able to establish a form of economic protectorate over this country—with all the consequences which would inevitably ensue. From March onwards Rumania was directly menaced by the Pan-German aims of the Nazis. Once more, and in spite of Munich and the rebuff to King Carol in November, 1938, Rumania sought the support of Great Britain. In view of the serious deterioration in international relations, the important geopolitical position of Rumania on the Black Sea and her important sources of raw materials, the British Government decided on April 13 to give a formal guarantee to Rumania (as to Greece) against all aggression.

*   *   *   *   *

From the foregoing survey of the situation in the various Danubian states, it can be appreciated how completely, after the fall of the Czechoslovak bastion, the portals of the Danube Basin were opened to the Nazis. Germany was persuaded that the Great Powers of the west, and more particularly France, had renounced at Munich their claims to influence in the Danubian Basin and started openly to speak of it as part of her exclusive power-political sphere. Germany was obliged, of course, to have a certain consideration for her Italian ally, who was naturally not enthusiastic at the increasing predominance of German influence in the Danube Basin and the Balkans and tried furtively to diminish it to some extent.[1] Germany felt, however, that her supremacy over Italy in the Danube-Balkan zone was incontestable, and therefore encouraged Italy's plans of expansion in the Mediterranean, especially in so far as they weakened the position of both France and Great Britain. It was for this reason, in particular, that when Count Ciano visited Belgrade it was emphasised in German public statements that there was no rivalry between Germany and Italy on the Danube. In point of fact, Italy was by then so much in need of German support for the realisation of her expansionist aims in the Mediterranean that she could not afford to compete with her on the Danube. German arrogance in this part of the world speaks very clearly in the following lines, published in the *Deutsche Allgemeine Zeitung* of January 24, 1939:

" We are witnessing the resurrection of a natural tendency which was killed at Versailles; but to-day it is not due to the influence of dynastic ambition, such as that of the old Dual Monarchy, but to the influence of the great river which has its source in the Reich. The Berlin-Rome Axis has re-established natural conditions in the Danube Basin. No other agency could do that, especially since the Danube is no longer the focus of the Russian, Turkish and Habsburg aspirations."

To put it briefly, Munich intoxicated Germany with hope that there was no longer any force which would be able to frustrate the realisation of the Pan-German dream of *Mitteleuropa*.

---

[1] It is for this reason that Italy favoured the idea of a common frontier between Poland and Hungary, that she would welcome the realisation of Colonel Beck's scheme of " a neutral *bloc* " in Central Europe, that she cultivates a friendship with, and tries to increase her commerce with, Yugoslavia and that she would like to have a *rapprochement* with Rumania.

In the meanwhile, Italy, cut off from the Danube by Germany, seeks consolation by trying to satisfy her ambitions in the Mediterranean. Different versions were circulated, after Munich, in Italy of the idea which was expressed on January 1, 1939, in the *Popolo di Roma*, as follows:

" To-day more than ever the future of Europe depends on the action of the Axis and on the resistance which it encounters. That resistance must sooner or later either give place to an understanding, in which case there will be a peaceful reorganisation of Central Europe and the Mediterranean, whereby they will pass, as they should do, under the domination of Germany and Italy—or else there will be no yielding, in which case we must be prepared for a very serious situation in Europe."

Germany is, of course, only too pleased that Italy should direct her efforts in this direction, and naturally supports her in doing so. Thus the *Frankfurter Zeitung* wrote on January 1, 1939:

" Whatever the New Year may have in store, we shall certainly find there three things: the Berlin-Rome Axis will be stronger than ever; we Germans, by our energy and our sacrifices, will found the life of our Reich more firmly than ever before upon the magnificent territorial basis which we now possess; and in the Mediterranean a new question concerning the fate of Europe will be decided. England and Italy have already decided it, so far as they are concerned. Will France and Italy succeed in establishing a balance between themselves ? "

Italy does not quite realise, perhaps, that by involving herself in a conflict with France she would be playing into the hands of Germany. Even if (which is, of course, absurd) she should defeat France, she would be in no way strengthened against Germany, since she could win only with the help of Germany, who would demand of her a very heavy price for German assistance. Italy already depends to a terrifying extent on Greater Germany, who has now become her direct neighbour. Any further strengthening of the German position in Central and Eastern Europe would fatally weaken Italy, and no extension of her power in the Mediterranean could relieve her from the pressure of German expansion. No Italian action can annul the fact that since the destruction of the independence of Austria and Czechoslovakia the German Army has been able to take up a position of strategic advantage at the very gates of Trieste and very close to the Adriatic.

(*f*) *Poland.* It was in relation to Poland, however, more than to any other country, that Munich strengthened Germany. By ridding herself of Czechoslovakia, Germany removed the only obstacle which prevented her from reverting to her traditional policy, expressed with such brutal clarity in the Treaties of Brest-Litovsk and Bucarest in 1918. By these well-known peace treaties (which, of course, Germany never referred to as " *diktat* ") Germany tried to make herself master of the Ukraine and Rumania, to bring Poland under her control and establish firmly her domination of the Baltic. She was frustrated in her aims in 1918–19, first of all by the victory of the Western Powers, and later by the existence (at first passive and then active) of Soviet Russia.

The Peace Treaties which ended the War of 1914–18 were buried, however, at Munich, but it was not to the pre-War period of peace, but to the period of hostilities to which Europe returned, and Germany renewed once more her efforts towards the goal of Brest-Litovsk. This is the explanation of her zealous support after Munich for the maintenance of an autonomous Carpatho-Ukraine, and her firm insistence at Vienna on November 12 that the demands of Poland and Hungary should be refused, although they were supported by Italy. After six months of intensive Nazi activity Carpatho-Ukraine was nevertheless allowed to be acquired by Hungary. This meant in no way that this Ukrainian province had ceased to be regarded by Germany as a very convenient jumping-off place against Poland, Rumania and Russia.

By supporting this " Ukrainian Piedmont," Germany became involved on this score also in a latent conflict with Poland, where some 5,000,000 to 7,000,000 Ukrainians are living in direct contact with the Carpatho-Ukraine. The proclamation at Munich of the " ethnic principle " as the basis of the reorganisation of Europe naturally inspired Ukrainians in Poland to insist more urgently and hopefully on their right of self-determination. They immediately expressed quite openly their opposition to the efforts made by Poland to secure the occupation of Carpatho-Ukraine by Hungary. On October 11, 1938, in the Cathedral of St. George at Lwow the Ukrainians held a solemn Mass, at which they thanked God for the creation of the Carpatho-Ukraine as an autonomous country. Afterwards there was a procession of about 20,000 demonstrators, shouting: " Long live the Ukraine ! " " Away with the Magyars ! " Because the Polish police took drastic measures to stop it, this demonstration was repeated on a much larger scale the following day. Further demonstrations were held in favour of an autonomous Sub-Carpathian Ruthenia and against its union with Hungary; at all these demonstrations there was agitation for the union of all Ukrainians in one independent state. Counter-demonstrations were organised by the Polish nationalist students and led to violent skirmishes. Ever since then the Polish Ukrainians have rioted continually and much blood has been shed.

In the middle of October the Ukrainian National Democratic Party (U.N.D.O.) addressed a memorandum to the Polish Government, protesting against the idea of a common frontier between Poland and Hungary and proclaiming the national demands of the Ukrainians. The nature of these demands was revealed on December 8, when the Ukrainian Deputies proposed in the Polish Parliament the creation of an autonomous Halič and Volyň, inhabited by the Ukrainians. It was proposed that these districts should be united for administrative purposes and that they should have an independent Parliament and Government. Foreign affairs, defence and finance were to be run centrally, but all international treaties would require ratification by the Parliament of the autonomous Ukraine. The military forces stationed in Ukrainian territory should be composed of natives of that territory, except when some national emergency should require the departure from that principle. The Polish and the Ukrainian languages should both be regarded as official languages. The Prime Minister and the more important members of the Ukrainian Government should at the same time form part of the Central Government at Warsaw.

These proposals were roughly modelled on the terms of the

autonomy which had just been granted to the Slovaks and
Carpathian Ukrainians in Czecho-Slovakia and naturally aroused
a veritable storm of opposition on the part of the Poles. On
December 21 the President of the Polish Parliament (Sejm)
informed the Ukrainian deputies that it was impossible to accept
their proposals, because to do so would entail a change of the
Polish Constitution for which it would be necessary that the
proposals should be endorsed by one-fourth of all deputies (fifty-
two), whereas their proposals were endorsed only by fifteen
deputies. Subsequently, the Polish Prime Minister, M. Skla-
dkowski, declared himself against the claims of the Ukrainians.

Nevertheless, on January 4, the Ukrainian National Democratic Party published in Lwow a resolution proclaiming:

" The Ukrainian nation protests against the domestic and
foreign policy of Poland, which aims at the destruction of the
Ukrainian element and its vital interests. This policy can be
accepted neither by the U.N.D.O. nor by the Ukrainian nation.
*Only the granting of absolute independence to the Ukrainian nation
within the framework of the Polish state can solve our problem.*"

This resolution was delivered to the office of the Polish Parliament in answer to the rejection of the proposals for Ukrainian
autonomy. The Ukrainian nationalists in Poland are becoming
more and more radical every day, and are sharply critical of the
Polish foreign policy, complaining that, whereas formerly it was
based on friendship with Germany, it is now seeking to organise
an anti-German *bloc* together with the Bolsheviks. The Deputy,
Vasil Mudryj, during the Conference of the U.N.D.O. which
took place at the beginning of January, 1939, expressed a hope
that " the might of Germany would still force Poland to range
herself with Germany." While some members of the U.N.D.O.
proposed at this Conference that a programme after the model of
the Henlein's Karlsbad points should be drawn up, the representatives of the more radical section were of opinion that the
Polish Ukrainians should look for help from abroad. The latter,
who considered the granting of mere autonomy to be insufficient,
considered that assistance should be accepted from those who
were anxious to help them to obtain full independence. In the
middle of January there were heated discussions in the Budget
Committee of the Polish Sejm and Senate between the Poles and

the Ukrainians. The Ukrainians persist in demanding autonomy, and one of their deputies, Celevič, has reminded the Poles that the Ukrainians form to-day a nation with great dynamic force and with which it is impossible to experiment.

This " dynamic force " of the Ukrainians is, of course, inflated with enthusiasm by the dynamic force of the Nazis. The Ukrainian nationalist emigrants are concentrated in Berlin, where they consult the Nazi leaders. The autonomous Carpatho-Ukraine became for a while the Eldorado of these people, who worked in close collaboration with the local Germans and with their representative, who was a Secretary of the State in the Chust Government. Together with the Nazis from the Reich they visited the province regularly, in order to prepare the ground for any possible future action. In addition to that, Ukrainian-Nazi propaganda was active even before the German occupation of Prague, where the Ukrainian organisations in Czecho-Slovakia were concentrated. On January 21, 1939, they organised a demonstration in Prague to celebrate the twentieth anniversary of the proclamation of the foundation of an independent and united Ukraine, issued on January 22, 1919, in Kiev,[1] and pledged themselves to work in the spirit of that proclamation. At the beginning of January, General Popov, the Ataman of the Don Cossacks and leader of the Ukrainians who have fought for the liberation of the Ukraine and of the Cossacks, paid a short visit to Prague, where he had conversations with Czech politicians before going on to Berlin. As early as November and December, provocative leaflets and newspapers in the Ukrainian language were being published in Prague, while Ukrainian propaganda bureaux were set up in Vienna and in Rome. Ukrainian agitators were trying to win sympathy in Belgrade also. Colonel Melnyk, the successor of the famous leader of the Ukrainian emigrants, M. Konovalec, who was recently murdered, was also very active, working, of course, like his predecessor, in the closest collaboration with the German Nazis. Nor are the fairly numerous Ukrainians resident in America neglected, and the Executive Committee of the organisation adopted on December 25, 1938, a Resolution which stressed the " necessity of creating a Great Ukraine which would

---

[1] This action was strongly supported at the time by Germany.

unite all the territories belonging at present to Russia, Poland and Rumania." The Ukrainians of America declared their support for compatriots in their fight for self-determination and ended with a protest against Poland in the following terms:

" No agreement can be concluded with Poland. That is why the Ukrainians have to fight to tear their Fatherland from Polish hands."

Poland, of course, followed with anxiety and disapproval the Ukrainian propaganda which was carried on from Czecho-Slovakia and several times protested to the Prague Government, notably on December 18, when the Polish Government handed to the Czecho-Slovak Government a memorandum drawing attention to the activities of certain organisations in Czecho-Slovakia which appeared to aim at the formation of an independent Ukrainian state and reminding them that the existence of these organisations might have a harmful effect on relations between Poland and Czecho-Slovakia. The Czecho-Slovak Government replied that the Polish complaints would be carefully investigated and that it had no desire to tolerate any irredentist activity within its territory against foreign countries, since it was anxious to live on good terms with all its neighbours. It was stated in Prague that the Ukrainian movement was organised in the Carpatho-Ukraine, where it was inspired, not by Czecho-Slovakia, but by Germany. In the middle of December, 1938, M. Alexandrovski, the Soviet Minister in Prague, pointed out to the Czecho-Slovak Foreign Minister, Dr. Chvalkovský, that the Soviet Government would consider any campaign organised for the formation of a " Great Ukraine " as a hostile action.

It was well known, of course, in Warsaw that the centre of Ukrainian propaganda was not in Prague, but in Berlin, and for that reason relations between Poland and Germany became cooler after Munich. Apart from the Ukrainian question, the problem of the German minority did not help to promote friendship between the two countries. The Germans complained bitterly against the brutal behaviour of the Poles towards the German minority in the Těšín district, which the Poles had seized from Czechoslovakia. And the representatives of the Germans in

Poland made vigorous demands to the Polish Government for the recognition of their national rights.[1]

The possibility of giving support to the Ukrainian and the German minorities in Poland was a powerful weapon in the hands of Germany against Poland. In addition to this, however, the Reich extended and strengthened its position in Danzig, which is now administered by Nazis only and in accordance with instructions obtained from Berlin. The elections which took place in December in Memel and which were run entirely under the sign of the swastika, were made use of, not only to remind the Poles again of the German claims on this town, but also as a threat to Lithuania. After these elections, in which the Nazis were successful in gaining only one more mandate, Dr. Neumann, the " Henlein " of Memel, declared that the Memel Germans would remain united with Lithuania only on the following conditions: (1) that they obtained complete autonomy; (2) that Germany should be granted unrestricted rights in the Memel harbour. Otherwise, he said, the Memel Germans would ask Germany to intervene.

On December 12 the French and British Ambassadors in Berlin made a *démarche* before the Minister of Foreign Affairs, asking that the Memel Statute should be respected. It was easy for Germany to dispel the anxiety of the Western Powers, as for the moment she did not intend to embark on any very violent action, since she knew that, in the changed European situation, Lithuania would surrender immediately Memel was demanded. As early as December 17, the Foreign Minister of Lithuania had declared that his country was ready to satisfy the German demand for the autonomy of Memel, " within the terms of the Memel Statute," but that it would, of course,

[1] Immediately before Herr von Ribbentrop's visit to Warsaw in January, the German Senator, Hassbach, handed the Polish Government a long memorandum containing the complaints and demands of the German minority in Poland. It is interesting to note that in this memorandum Senator Hassbach protests against the attitude adopted by the Polish authorities when they say that they would treat the German minority in Poland with reciprocity, i.e. in the same way as the Polish minority is treated in Germany. This makes it clear that the Germans demand an exceptional position for their minorities in foreign countries, but do not admit the principle of reciprocity as regards minorities resident in Germany ! Having devoted so much space to the Germans in Poland, it would be unfair not to mention that the representatives of the Lithuanian minority, who live in the district round Vilna, announced their claims in very modest terms on January 4, 1939, and that the actions of the Ukrainians and other minorities in Poland are not without influence also on the White Russians, who are denied all rights, although there are more than 1,000,000 of them in Poland.

defend itself against any attempt by a Great Power to dominate it politically or economically. The German occupation of Memel in March, which was not resisted by the Lithuanian Government, proved this all to be a matter more or less of words. Lithuania was necessarily obliged to take into account the strengthened position of Germany, as also were the other two Baltic states, Latvia and Esthonia. It was questionable at that time to what extent these states could look for defence in a *rapprochement* with Poland, who, of course, after Munich even more than before, worked for this *rapprochement*, especially with Lithuania.

Immediately after Munich it was clear that Germany was trying to strengthen further her position in the Baltic; hence her intensive interest in Danzig and Memel, which indicated the probability that her eyes were on the Lithuanian and Esthonian coasts. One of the reasons for Germany's announcement at the end of December of her intention to increase the number of her submarines and cruisers was that she considered it necessary to strengthen her naval forces in the Baltic, where she was anxious to achieve supremacy. By the spring of 1939, it was clear that all this was directed not only against Russia, but against Poland. The German plan of joining Eastern Prussia with the rest of Germany by an " extra-territorial motor-road " running through the Polish Corridor into Pomerania was meant very seriously. The almost simultaneous occupation of Memel and Czecho-Slovakia in March, 1939, meant that Poland was in direct and immediate danger, which caused the British Government to take action. The smaller Baltic states however, as was seen during the Anglo-Russian talks in the summer of 1939, sought security in non-aggression pacts with Germany rather than in joining the Anglo-Russo-French security system.

Germany's pressure on Poland increased extraordinarily in every way after Munich, and the Polish Foreign Minister, Colonel Beck, tried to counteract it by three-fold action. In the first place he openly interested himself in the establishment of a common frontier between Poland and Hungary, as was evident from his proclamation of January 23, which has been mentioned above. Colonel Beck never abandoned the idea of forming a " neutral *bloc* " composed of Poland, Hungary, Yugoslavia and, if necessary, also of Rumania, under the patronage of Italy. It was Beck's optimistic opinion that this *bloc* could be directed, according to circumstances, either against Russia or against Germany, and it would be characterised by the fact that Poland would have a predominant position in it. Its policy, he considered, would be to stand aside, under cover of neutrality, from all conflicts between the Great Powers of Western Europe. It was not the events of the spring of 1939 alone which made nonsense of this plan. From a practical point of view, its neutrality could only have been maintained in the event of a conflict between the four Great Powers of the west, in which Russia was not entangled, for under any other circumstances its neutrality would have been illusory. It was precisely for this reason that Colonel Beck was trying to maintain friendly relations with Moscow, as well as with Berlin, in order to prevent co-operation between Germany and Russia, which would entail mortal peril for Poland. At the end of November Colonel Beck prepared a new surprise for Europe. On November 26 the following communiqué was published in Warsaw:

" The series of conversations which have recently taken place between the People's Commissar for the Foreign Affairs of the U.S.S.R., M. Maxim Litvinov, and the Polish Ambassador in Moscow, M. Waclaw Grzybowski, have enabled the following statement of the situation to be made:

" 1. All the existing agreements between Poland and the U.S.S.R., including the Non-Aggression Pact of July 23, 1932, remain in force completely as the basis of relations between Poland and the U.S.S.R. The Non-Aggression Pact, which was originally concluded for a period of five years and which was extended on May 5, 1934, for a further period extending to 1945, presents a sufficiently broad basis to guarantee the infrangibility of peaceful relations between the two States.

" 2. The two Governments regard with favour the extension of their commercial exchanges.

" The two Governments are in agreement about the necessity of a positive settlement of a series of current questions connected with their treaty obligations, and in particular of questions which remain undecided and the clearing up of recent frontier incidents."

This important communiqué was at first understood everywhere as meaning that Poland was turning towards Russia, in
order to obtain her support against Germany. There is no doubt
that Warsaw intended it as a protest against the Vienna arbitration of November 2, which, in accordance with the wishes of
Germany, had frustrated temporarily the plan of a common
frontier between Poland and Hungary. The official Polish
Agency (P.A.T.), in a commentary published on November 26,
at the same time as the communiqué, drew attention to the fact
that, for the sake of assuming good relations between Poland
and Russia, this declaration was sharply critical of the Vienna
arbitration, and announced in this connection:

" This declaration may also be regarded as a hint to
Germany and, in the second place, to those within and without the country who support certain minority nationalist
movements which tend to create an irredentism which
menaces the sovereignty of the Polish state."

This Polish-Soviet declaration was naturally not received with
enthusiasm in Nazi quarters, where it came in for some criticism.
Thus, for example, the *Danziger Vorposten* of November 29 wrote:

" Poland wanted to avenge herself for the Vienna arbitration.
One might have expected some such demonstration on her part.
It is worthy of note, however, that Warsaw has been unable to
find as a partner in her demonstration anyone but Moscow.
That is expressive of Poland's political position in Europe."

At the same time, however, a much more important paper,
the Essen *National Zeitung*, protested against the suggestion
that the Polish-Soviet declaration would prejudice the relations
between Poland and Germany and stated that the declaration
was not directed against Germany. In any case, it was evident
that Warsaw did not want to expose herself unilaterally against
Germany. She contented herself with improving her position in
Moscow and, having done that, she felt strengthened against
Germany. Various minor disputes between Poland and Russia,
and in particular some concerning their frontier and express
railway communication between Kiev Šepetovka and Zdol-
bunovo, were settled, and it was announced that important
commercial negotiations would begin in February, 1939.

At the beginning of January Colonel Beck prepared another surprise for Europe: He was spending his Christmas vacation on the French Riviera and it was expected that he would meet the French Foreign Minister, M. Bonnet, but he went instead on January 5 to see Herr Hitler at Berchtesgaden. Following this, on January 25–27, the German Minister of Foreign Affairs, Herr von Ribbentrop, made an ostentatious visit to Warsaw. The official communiqué stated that the results of this visit " show once again that collaboration between Poland and the Reich, which has stood the test of the last five years, has not only contributed towards a continual improvement of Polish-German relations, but has become in the new situation a valuable contribution towards present appeasement in Europe."

Beyond that no more definite news leaked out to the public. Warsaw announced semi-officially that during the conversations with Herr von Ribbentrop nothing took place that might cause anxiety to the Western Powers, or that would be directed in an unfriendly way against other states; at the same time it was announced that Poland's alliances with France and Rumania remained intact. An agreement was reached regarding the settlement of the problem of the Polish Jews who had suddenly been ordered last autumn to leave Germany. Although nothing definite is known about the conversations between Colonel Beck and Herr von Ribbentrop, it can be safely stated that they came to an agreement (only temporary and very fragile) on the following basis: Germany promised that her plans for creating the Great Ukraine were not " actual " and that therefore Poland need not consider herself as being threatened by it; in return for this assurance, Poland promised that she would maintain "neutrality " in any conflict between the Berlin-Rome Axis and the Western Powers. Within two months, Colonel Beck had his common frontier with Hungary and the destruction of Carpatho-Ukraine in his pocket, and was rapidly defining " neutrality " to mean " mutual assistance " with the Western Powers.

For her part, Germany had by no means diminished pressure on Poland and even in January, 1939, Herr von Ribbentrop must have felt quite satisfied, when he left Warsaw, that, even if he had not achieved all that he desired, he had means of ensuring that Warsaw should nevertheless continue to respect

Berlin. Colonel Beck still tried to manœuvre in every direction. Even on the very day when Herr von Ribbentrop was arriving in Warsaw, he defined his policy in an interview, which was published on January 25, 1939, by the North-American Press Alliance, as follows:

" The guiding principle of Polish policy is the maintenance of good relations with her neighbours. That is the reason why the Polish Government attaches so much importance to its relations both with Germany and with the U.S.S.R. The second principle is that of loyalty to Poland's alliances with France and Rumania. And the third is to oppose any decision taken with regard to questions which interest Poland about which Poland has not been consulted. Poland's interest in such questions being governed largely by their distance from her frontiers. . . . Our aim is to preserve peace, which is essential for any positive work. Poland's decisive position between Russia and Germany is quite natural, and is due to the general belief that we refuse to participate in any plan of aggression directed against the one or the other of our two neighbours. . . .

" Poland is interested in the colonial problem for two reasons: she is looking for places to which her population can emigrate and from which she can procure raw materials for her industries. At the present time, in accordance with her principles, Poland is looking for collaboration with those countries which have colonial territories."

This interview is very expressive of Colonel Beck's character. His policy was a very risky one and he could pursue it only for as long as Germany and Russia did not ask him to decide between them. For, fundamentally, Beck's policy consisted in the attempt not to commit Poland seriously in respect of any country, to have a free hand in respect of all, and to manœuvre ably between every country and especially between Germany and Russia. Though this policy may have succeeded for a time in diverting Pan-German aggressive expansion towards the Danube, it did not succeed in withdrawing Poland for ever from the danger of Nazi imperialism. The stronger Germany became in the Danube Basin, the greater became the German threat to Poland: for this, if not for its fatal consequence for Europe as a whole, a grave historical responsibility will always weigh heavily on the policy of Colonel Beck. It was, to a large extent, Poland, by her destructive opposition to a policy of collective security, who facilitated the development of the forces of Pan-Germanism in Europe. The Polish attempt to oppose it by the formation of a " neutral *bloc* " composed of Poland, Hungary, Rumania and Yugoslavia was, as we have already seen, completely futile. This *bloc* would inevitably have been an artificial construction, without any solid foundation, and would have collapsed the moment German aggression took place in Central Europe or the moment Russia intervened on the side of the Western Powers. It was just this policy of Poland which proved how fragile the theory of " neutrality " really was : when Count Ciano, during his visit to Warsaw on February 25 to March 1, pressed Poland to guarantee strict neutrality in the event of a conflict between the Axis and Britain and France, the Polish Government refused to give any such categorical promise. In the official communiqué published on March 1, it was stated that the two Foreign Ministers had " again established that a spirit of friendship, and perfect cordiality exists in the relations of the two countries, and is yielding positive results." It was not difficult to understand that these results were, in fact, very meagre. Moreover, M. Bonnet made a simultaneous declaration in which he said that Colonel Beck had left no doubt about the readiness of his country to honour her treaty obligations with France.

It was precisely during the visit of Count Ciano that violent demonstrations against Germany took place in Poland as an answer to the persecution of Poles in Danzig. The Government had considerable difficulty in calming public opinion, which was becoming more and more excited. On March 2, the Polish Government transmitted to the Danzig Senate a Note containing the Polish demands for a guarantee of the rights of Poles in the Free City. From this moment onwards, the tension between Germany and Poland became more and more strained and has been dangerously in evidence since the German occupation of Czecho-Slovakia and Memel. Nazi propaganda began to let loose the same threats against Poland which were formerly hurled against Czechoslovakia. At the same time, the behaviour of the Germans in Poland reached the state of over-excitement already so familiar. At the end of March, Germany demanded the return of Danzig to the Reich and the right to build a motor-road through the Polish Corridor, while the German Press made allusions to the rights of Germany in Upper Silesia and there was talk of a German occupation of Bohumin, which the Poles had seized from the Czechs in October, 1938. This town represents a very important junction of lines of communication. Confronted with this growing danger, Poland was obliged towards the end of March to proclaim partial mobilisation. Finally, international tension became so grave that Great Britain decided to give Poland a guarantee of independence. Mr. Chamberlain announced in the House of Commons on March 31:

> " I now have to inform the House that during that period [consultations with other Governments], in the event of any action which clearly threatened Polish independence and which the Polish Government accordingly considered it vital to resist with their national forces, His Majesty's Government would feel themselves bound at once to lend the Polish Government all the support in their power. They had given the Polish Government an assurance to this effect."

On April 4 Colonel Beck arrived in London and on April 7 the results of the talks which had taken place with the Polish Foreign Secretary were made public.

> " It was agreed that the two countries were prepared to enter into an agreement of a permanent and reciprocal character to replace the present temporary and unilateral assurance given by H.M. Government to the Polish Government.
> " Pending the completion of the permanent agreement, M. Beck gave his Majesty's Government an assurance that the Polish Government would consider themselves under an obligation to render assistance to his Majesty's Government under the same conditions as those contained in the temporary assurance already given by H.M. Government to Poland.
> " Like the temporary assurance, the permanent agreement would not be directed against any other country, but would be designed to assure Great Britain and Poland of mutual

assistance in the event of any threat, direct or indirect, to the independence of either.

" It was further recognised that certain matters, including a more precise definition of the various ways in which the necessity for such assistance might arise, would require further examination before the permanent agreement could be completed.

" It was understood that the arrangements above mentioned should not preclude either Government from making an agreement with other countries in the general interest of the consolidation of peace."

This declaration, like the one which followed on April 13 concerning the guarantee given by Britain and France to Rumania and Greece, stressed the decisive turn in British policy which had been brought about by the total occupation of Czecho-Slovakia. It also showed that Poland also could only secure her vital interests by adopting the principles of collective security. The continued presence at the helm of Polish and British affairs of those who had so long opposed this policy meant a certain amount of indecision in its application. It was with considerable unwillingness that it was recognised that the policy of collective security could be enforced only by an alliance which bound not only the two Great Powers of Western Europe, but also Soviet Russia. This necessity would become self-evident on the day in which either Poland or Rumania were the victims of German aggression.

(g) *Russia*. The policy of Russia has been characterised since Munich by a certain degree of abstention which has disturbed many of the Foreign Offices in Europe. In reality, however, there was no reason to be surprised at this. During the crisis of September, 1938, the Soviet Union adopted an attitude which showed a real sense of its responsibility, and it was ready to fulfil unconditionally its obligations under the terms of its treaties with Czechoslovakia and France. The necessary military preparations were immediately made, and in the conversations which M. Litvinov had at Geneva with M. Comnen, the Rumanian Foreign Minister, every arrangement was made for the passage of Soviet troops over Rumanian territory on their way to

Czechoslovakia. If there had been any uncertainty[1] regarding the attitude of Moscow, the British Foreign Office could not have published its famous communiqué of September 26, in which they spoke openly of Russian help. Britain and France, however, preferred Munich. They had, in fact, throughout the Czechoslovak crisis, acted independently of the Soviet Union, and they sought Soviet support only after Godesberg, when a conflict with Germany seemed certain. Otherwise, the two Western Powers—though France was in fact bound by the Franco-Soviet Pact—directed their action without any consultation with Russia, whom they kept severely at a certain distance. The Soviet Government stated in an official communiqué, published on October 4, 1938, that:

" In the course of the interviews of M. Bonnet with M. Souritz and of Lord Halifax with M. Maisky, which took place during the final period, the two Ambassadors of the Soviet Union were given no information other than what had appeared in the daily Press. There was no sort of a conference and still less an agreement between the Governments of U.S.S.R., France and England with regard to the fate of the Czechoslovak Republic or to the question of concessions to the aggressor. Neither France nor England consulted the U.S.S.R., but confined themselves merely to informing the Soviet Government of what had already happened."

Moscow can justly refuse any responsibility for Munich, and the Soviet Press sharply attacked France and England for having facilitated the tremendous victory of Germany. On October 25, 1938, the official Soviet newspaper, *Izvestija*, wrote:

" The general public both in France and in England, as well as in Germany and Italy, are becoming more and more bitterly aware of the fact that the Munich Agreement is not a treaty of peace, but a treaty of war—and above all of war which is carried on openly by underhand methods, and with every kind of cruelty and treachery, against the peoples of

---

[1] It is well known that the certainty that Russia would intervene was based on the conversations which took place at Geneva after September 25 (i.e. after Mr. Chamberlain's failure at Godesberg) between Lord de la Warr, first British delegate at the League of Nations, Mr. Butler, Under-Secretary of State for Foreign Affairs, and M. Litvinov.

Europe, against their liberties and against their independence.

" Hitler's speech at Saarbrücken, Germany's colonial demands, the German insistence on an air force almost three times greater than that of Britain, the renewal of Italian pressure with regard to Spain, the commencement by Japan of military activity in South China and the threat to Hong Kong —all these events show clearly that the Munich Agreement is not the end, but the beginning of a period of activity on the part of the aggressors which is directed straight against England and France.

" No well-informed politician can have any doubt of the power of the Soviet Union or of its ability to be a decisive force in a discussion with those who are organising war. And every government knows that the Soviet Union will fulfil it obligations in Europe.

" If those who are responsible for the policies of France and England have nevertheless capitulated, it is not because they have been mistaken, but because they have preferred capitulation to victory. Paris and London must therefore accept full responsibility for the fruits of their capitulation at Munich and for its consequences, for they have consented to that capitulation in full consciousness of what they were doing. There is no reason, moreover, to suppose that all the problems which the governments of Europe have tried to solve once and for all by consenting to a shameful plot with the Fascist aggressors will not rise up again before them."

The President of the Soviet Government, M. Molotov, expressed himself very sharply on this subject on November 7, 1938, on the occasion of the twenty-first anniversary of the Russian Revolution, in a speech delivered before Josef Stalin, members of the Government and leading politicians:

" The second imperialist war," he said, " has already begun over an immense area, stretching from Gibraltar to Shanghai. The democratic Powers are pretending to be powerless before the aggressors; but in reality they do not wish to intervene seriously against them, because they are afraid of the workers' movement. The Soviet Union, homeland of Socialism, alone has stood up to aggression. . . .

" German Fascism has incited the Japanese Army to test the strength of the Soviet Army. The infantry, the artillery and the air force of the Soviet Union have taught the Japanese a lesson and Germany has thus received her reply. . . . The Soviet Union alone has not allowed herself to be terrorised by the aggressors; she has proved to the whole world her loyalty to her obligations. The English and French Governments are trying to make people believe that the Munich Agreement is a victory for peace. Who is the victor ? Who is the vanquished ?

" We have seen, in the first place, a victory of England and Germany over France, whom they have persuaded to dishonour her obligations towards Czechoslovakia. We have then seen the victory of the four most powerful capitalist states, Germany, England, France and Italy, over Czechoslovakia. The Soviet Government alone remained to the very end firmly determined to face up to its engagements and to help Czechoslovakia."

The fatal consequences of Munich were reflected in the immediate policy of the Soviet Union in the fact that it stressed its reserve with regard to direct conflicts in which the Four Western Great Powers might become engaged. The Franco-Soviet Pact still remained formally in force, but that it was certainly no longer fundamental to the policy either of France or of the Soviet Union was proved in April during the Anglo-French efforts to reach once more an agreement of that sort with Russia. The relationship between the Western Great Powers and Soviet Russia had cooled very considerably. If it had become true that the Western Great Powers would adopt a passive attitude in case Russia were attacked by the anti-Comintern Powers, it was also very probable that Russia would not hurry to secure France and England, in the event of their becoming involved in a conflict with the Berlin-Rome Axis. Just as France tried to hide herself behind the Maginot Line, not caring any more about Central and Eastern Europe, so Russia, too, retired behind her western fortifications, and took refuge in the vastness of her territory. The passivity of France and Great Britain towards the dynamic Powers led to the passivity and reticence of Russia. These were the indisputable consequences of the breakdown of the system of collective security—consequences which the Western Powers were forced to reverse by intense and dangerous diplomatic activity in the spring of 1939. It is inevitable, if no reciprocity of obligations exists, each will try to defend himself as he can, without regard for the others, and in spite of the formal existence of treaty obligations.

For a while many Western European politicians were persuaded that Germany would leave the Western Powers alone, and that she would direct her expansion towards Central and Eastern Europe. This idea was reinforced after the Chamberlain-Hitler declaration at Munich concerning the solution of all questions between Germany and Great Britain by mutual consultation, and especially after the signature of a Franco-German Treaty of Friendship on December 6, 1938, in which Germany solemnly recognised the existing French frontier. Germany openly proclaimed Central and Eastern Europe as her sphere of influence and admitted only a certain measure of participation in that area for Italy. In London and in Paris these ideas did not meet with any serious resistance, and Mr. Chamberlain even went so far on November 1, 1938, in the House of Commons, as to say :

" What is the position of Germany in relation to the states of Central Europe ? Geographically, she must occupy a dominating position there. She does now. As a matter of fact, in so far as these states are agricultural in character, the nature of the trade between them and Germany is complementary. . . . So far as this country is concerned, we have no wish to block Germany out from those countries or to encircle her economically."

These words by the British Premier, which referred to the activities of Dr. Funk in South-Eastern Europe, were naturally understood by Germany to mean that the British Government recognised her claim to a predominant position in Central Europe. This was the inevitable construction put upon the policy of Britain and France at Munich. In these new circumstances, Germany, no longer fearing any intervention on the part of the Western Powers, continued to build up her *Mitteleuropa* and to make preparations for her audacious plan for a Great Ukrainian State. In both these cases she was bound to come up against Russian interests.

Russia could not regard with indifference the domination of the Danube Basin and the Balkans by Germany, while the plan of a Great Ukraine directly concerns her own territory. In the Soviet Union there are more than 31,000,000 Ukrainians (German propaganda quotes a much higher figure of more than 43,000,000). The Soviet Ukraine is one of the richer Soviet Republics, and its importance is very much increased by the fact that it extends to the Black Sea. For Germany, it would mean a most fertile supply of grain, and it has a highly developed dairy-farming industry. In addition to that, the territory of Soviet Ukraine produces 40 per cent. of the iron and fifty-five per cent. of the coal of the entire Soviet Union. The tearing away of the Soviet Ukraine would be possible only as a result of a war in which Russia was defeated. It is quite true that separatist movements have often started in the Soviet Ukraine,[1] but it is also certain that the Soviet régime is in absolute control of the administration, economic institutions and the Army. In all the main administrative posts there are Russians as well as Ukrainians. The Soviet Government could, moreover, make very effective use of the impression which would be created on the workers and peasants if they were told that " Fascists from abroad " wished to deprive them of their material advantages which the Revolution has given them—the anti-Bolshevik argument would not have the effect which is intended on the people, who for twenty years have been brought up in the Bolshevik creed with an exclusivity of which only a totalitarian régime is capable. Actually, the Soviet Ukraine enjoys a considerable degree of autonomy within the framework of the Soviet Union, and this fact could be made use of by the Soviet authorities, who would point out, as a contrast, that the Ukraine, " liberated " by the Germans, would become a colony, exploited by the Germans, and that its independence would not even be apparent. Nor would this be any exaggeration.

If the Ukrainian problem is developed to the full by Germany, the Soviet Government will naturally not hesitate to conduct a

---

[1] This was shown by several trials.

vast campaign of propaganda among the Ukrainian peasants in
Poland, and, if necessary, also in Rumania and in the Carpatho-
Ukraine. Since the peasants in these countries live for the greater
part under miserable conditions, enjoying low economic, social
and cultural standards, they would certainly be susceptible to
the lure of Communist agitation. German propaganda tempts the
Ukrainians with nationalist slogans; Soviet propaganda could
use Socialist slogans and would also be able to show what a
comparatively high degree of autonomy is being enjoyed by the
Soviet Ukraine. From this it is apparent that the Soviets have
ample means to enable them to face with equanimity the possible
effects of Nazi agitation among the Ukrainians. It is clear that
the agitation for liberating and uniting the Ukrainians might
very well lead to the foundation of a United Ukraine, not under
the domination of the Nazis, but under the protection of the
Soviet Union—in any case, it would seem probable that if
40,000,000 Ukrainians became united they would probably not
tolerate the protectorship of Germany, but would certainly very
soon turn against their " liberators."

It would be naïve, to say the least of it, to suppose that Moscow
would surrender the Ukraine without a fight. Such suppositions
are based upon the idea that the drastic purges carried out in the
Soviet institutions and especially in the Army have weakened
the Soviet Union to such an extent that she would be unable to
defend herself militarily against a foreign enemy. The Soviet
Union has certainly great internal difficulties and the purges
were no doubt a sign of a very serious internal crisis. But difficulties, sometimes very serious, although of another aspect, are
experienced also by Germany and Italy. If it is true that the
dictatorships in these countries would crumple up only under
the shock of a lost war, it is difficult to understand that causes
less serious would lead to the fall of the Soviet dictatorship.
The Soviet régime is at least no less stable than that of the Nazis
or the Fascists, and in any case it is capable of effective defence
against external attack. Attention was drawn to the huge
difficulties connected with the Nazi plans of the Great Ukraine
by General Sikorski, former Polish Prime Minister, in an article
aptly entitled " Unrealisable Plans." The article, which is a very
sober analysis of the military capacity of Soviet Russia, was

published on December 31, 1938, in the *Kurjer Warzsawski*. We quote the following extract from it:

"Though it is true that Germany's war potential has been enormously increased as a result of the annexation of Austria and the destruction of the Czechoslovak bastion, that is far from meaning that Germany is already in a position to dictate her will to the world. She has been able to abuse the confidence of her partners at Munich, she has been able to make political and racial arguments over-ride those of geography, economics and strategy, but I say once more that that is not enough to enable Herr Hitler to win fresh victories merely by threatening war and without striking a blow. The very fact that the newspapers of Germany and Italy publish new demands each day has certainly contributed towards a mass awakening against ' the Munich spirit.' . . .

" Neither the adversaries nor the partisans of Moscow have illusions any longer about the weakening of the Red Army after the recent purges. The decimation of the senior officers and the decapitation (in a literal sense) of the whole of the High Command, cannot but have profoundly shaken the morale of the troops. The execution of a military leader who was as popular as Marshal Tuchachevsky has certainly dumbfounded the rank and file, and done much harm to the national defences. If Stalin thinks—as did the monarchs of Tsarist Russia—that the Army is devoted to him alone and that there is no bond of comradeship between the men and those who lead them, he is very much mistaken. For, if that were so, the Red Army would consist merely of slaves, unfit for war or for the defence, not only of the state, but even of the very régime. One other enigma about the Red Army is the problem of the peasants; no one knows just how far agrarian reform has progressed under the Soviet régime and it is this which is bound to influence enormously the fighting value of the Army.

" One must not, however, let oneself be misled about the offensive value of the Red Army. Apart from its air force, it is unsuitable for warfare outside the borders of the Russian state or for use in large-scale operations. This situation might, however, become radically changed if Russia were threatened with invasion of its territories by a German Army. It might then be taken for granted that the Soviet Army, which is the largest in the world and perhaps also the best equipped, would respond in a disciplined manner to the appeals of the Government and of the military command. Helped by the unmeasurable area of Russia and by the absence of roads, it could put up an effective resistance to the invader, whose motorised divisions would not know how to move about in an area without roads or shelters. . . . On its national soil, the Red Army, even though it is Bolshevik, is a formidable foe. This is a truth which must not be misunderstood, especially as the Russian peasant is excellent when on the defensive. He has memories, moreover, of former occasions on which German troops have entered his country.

" All this is well known, of course, in Berlin. The difficulties of conducting a campaign into the heart of Russia have always frightened the German High Command. Schlieffen himself held a high opinion of the resisting capacity of the Russian private soldier, almost invincible on his native plains. These traditions, born in the time of Napoleon, have survived the whole of the nineteenth century; they were maintained during the Great War, and even to-day are still taken into account by the leaders of the Reichswehr in their strategic calculations.

" It is possible, however, that the Nazi politicians want to forget these difficulties, although they are inherent in any campaign on Russian soil; this alone would provide an explanation of their dream of a crusade in the Ukraine; psychologically this is quite possible, for nothing makes one so giddy as easily-won success. It may therefore not be out of place to recall that the strategic doctrine of the Third Reich— crushing assault, rapid and murderous warfare, dispatch of motorised divisions along the roads leading to certain definite places—is not applicable in the Russian plains; nor would it be possible to count on the rapid wearing-down of one's adversary: all such things simply do not apply in Russia.

" There remain, then, only the hopes of a rising of the civil population, of an armed rebellion or of separatist movements in certain regions. All observers of Russian affairs will tell you, however, that such hopes would prove without foundation in the event of an invasion of Russia by Hitler's Germany."

This evidence is the more important because it is given by an outstanding Polish soldier, and it is for that reason that it has been quoted. In any case, it is evident that Nazi action in the Ukraine would not be easy, but would, on the contrary, be very difficult and dangerous. In the Soviet Union they speak about these Nazi plans with a frankness which leaves one in no doubt. Suffice it to quote from merely one speech, by the Prime Minister of the Soviet Ukrainian Government, M. Petrovski, on December 12, in which he declared that " the Russians and Ukrainians together would defend their rights against any aggression, from wherever it might come," and then he quoted literally the words of Stalin:

" If these pigs will put their noses in the Soviet garden, they will be punished in such a way that they will lose their taste for it."

On the same occasion the chiefs of the Ukrainian Red Army stressed that:

" The Russian Army would not fight the war on Russian territory, as in 1914–18, but on foreign territory."

It seems that the Soviet Government has hitherto considered it unnecessary to alarm the public too much about the danger of German intrigues in the Ukraine. Russia continues, of course, to perfect and augment the defensive forces on her western frontiers, but in the meantime is waiting. Relations between Russia and Germany remain uncertain and strained, but, in spite of that, there were still, in January, negotiations in progress between them, regarding the maintenance and, if necessary, the extension of their mutual commercial exchanges: the possibility is not necessarily excluded of these exchanges including raw materials for their armament industries. Russian relations with Ankara remained friendly, in spite of the Nazi attempts to obtain greater influence in Turkey. The Turks, though not completely unresponsive to the German overtures, remained distrustful, especially of Italian aspirations to hegemony in the Mediterranean. On this point the Turks found themselves generally in agreement with Greece and Rumania, and, after May 12, with the British.

On the whole, the orientation of the Russian foreign policy was well described in the dispatch of a Press agency, sent on January 23, 1939, from Moscow, which stated:

" For the moment (according to political circles of Moscow), the aims of the Soviet foreign policy are as follows:

" 1. *Rapprochement* with Warsaw, Bucarest, Ankara.

" 2. Maintenance of existing pacts with the capitalist states.

" 3. Collaboration with the United States in the Far East.

" 4. Fight against Japanese expansion in the Far East.

" 5. Close collaboration with all the countries in the framework of the League of Nations.

" The rumours put about concerning conversations with Germany have been categorically denied by Moscow. On the other hand, it is stated that relations between Moscow and Prague will not undergo any change except in the event of Czechoslovak adhesion to the Anti-Comintern Pact. It is stressed in Moscow that Stalin is hostile to a policy of isolation."

Anger against Britain and France was by no means allayed by Anglo-French diplomatic passivity during the six months which succeeded the Munich Agreement. At the Eighteenth Congress of the All-Union Bolshevik Party, which was held at the beginning of March, 1939, the Soviet leaders criticised the policy of Great Britain and France very severely, accusing them of " deliberate failure to check the aggressors." Stalin, in a speech on March 10, explained the attitude of the British and French Governments as being actuated by fear of revolution, which they considered might happen if the non-aggressive states went to war, but this, he explained, was not the main reason. The main reason was that the majority of these states, notably Britain and France, had repudiated the policy of collective security, of giving a collective rebuff to aggressors and had, in fact taken up the position of non-intervention and adopted a policy of neutrality. This policy led to world war, and " behind it," he went on, " one perceives the desire not to hinder the aggressors in their dark plans. Let Japan, for instance, start war in China, or, better still, against the U.S.S.R., or let Germany get deeply involved in East

European affairs and in a war with the U.S.S.R. Let all those participating in the war get stuck deep in the mud of war; encourage them secretly; let them exhaust each other; and when they are sufficiently exhausted, then enter the stage with fresh forces—' in the interests of peace ' of course—and dictate your conditions. They had given Germany Austria and then the Sudetenland and then Czechoslovakia in violation of all their pledges; they had put about in their Press lies about the ' weakness of the Russian Army, the decay of the Air Force and disorder in the Soviet Union,' thus pushing the Germans further eastwards and promising them an easy prey. This policy," Stalin ended, " looks more like encouraging than discouraging an aggressor."

An even more violent criticism of British policy was expressed on March 12 by M. Manuilski:

" The plan of the British *bourgeoisie*," he said, " is to sacrifice the small East European states by pushing Germany eastwards against Russia. They hope by that counter-revolutionary war to divert Germany's colonial claims by letting her smash her teeth on the Soviet fist—and thus to secure for many years a British Imperial hegemony over Europe."

Manuilski even went further and accused certain British quarters of wanting to share Spain and the Mediterranean with Italy at the expense of France. They would, he maintained, be prepared to do the same in China once Japan was sufficiently weakened to accept a Far-Eastern " Munich," with Britain as arbiter.

" By their bandit plans," he went on, " they merely dig their own graves. They merely prepare the partition of their own Empire by the German Fascists and the break-up of the capitalist system, if Germany does attack the Soviet Union."

The occupation of Czechoslovakia and the change which it brought about in British foreign policy resulted in an improvement in the relations between the Soviet Union and Great Britain. Between March 23–28, a British Trade Mission visited Moscow and the official communiqué declared that " personal contacts established between representatives of the two Governments would doubtless assist the consolidation of Soviet-British relations and also international collaboration in the interests of a solution of the problem of peace."

Nevertheless, there appeared to be still a certain measure of hesitation and reserve in the attitude of the British Government in regard to Moscow.

When the Soviet Government proposed about March 20 an international conference to consider the question of German aggression, the British Government " declined the proposal on the ground that it was premature." But the steps which the British Government was forced to take to prevent immediate aggression in Eastern Europe necessitated co-operation between the two Western Powers and the Soviet Union.

* * * * *

To sum up: the post-Munich period between September 30 and the occupation of Prague, showed a steady deterioration of international relations. Permanent tension between Germany and England, accentuated by the tension between the former and the United States; chronic mistrust between Germany and France, towards whom the Nazis are behaving with ever-increasing haughtiness and even arrogance; sharp tension between France and Italy and, in connection with it, severe struggle for position in the Mediteranean between the Berlin-Rome Axis and the Western Powers (a struggle which has been dangerously aggravated by General Franco's victory); constant attempts by the Axis to isolate France entirely and to weaken or disrupt Franco-British co-operation; increased armaments of all the Great Powers and other states; the continued militarisation and Nazification of the entire German nation; the calling up of Italian reservists; increasing unrest of all smaller states bordering on Germany in the west and in the north—all these served to show the need for that Anglo-Russian *rapprochement* which the Nazis had always feared and to indicate that, by sacrificing Czechoslovakia and giving Germany a free hand in Central and Eastern Europe, Western Europe had neither bought, nor otherwise assured, a lasting peace.

Germany is firmly decided to pursue her plan for the Pan-German domination of Europe and of the world, along the route which was thrown open to her at Munich by the Western Powers. It is possible that M. Daladier did not realise the tragic meaning of the words which he used of the Munich Agreement: " It may one day be seen that at Munich, in the space of a few hours, the whole world changed in appearance."

Seven months have barely passed, yet anyone can see that on September 30, 1938, the world was changed to its very foundations. That great British statesman, Winston Churchill, in his speech in the House of Commons on October 5, 1938—a speech which will live in history—pointed out the consequences of Munich in the following terms:

" We have sustained a total and unmitigated defeat, and France has suffered even more than we have. . . . All is over. Silent, mournful, abandoned, broken, Czechoslovakia recedes into the darkness. . . . I venture to think that in future the Czechoslovak State cannot be maintained as an independent entity. I think you will find that in a period of time, which may be measured by years, but may be measured only by months, Czechoslovakia will be engulfed in the Nazi régime. . . .

" We are in the presence of a disaster of the first magnitude which has befallen Great Britain and France. Do not let us blind ourselves to that. It must now be accepted that all the countries of Central and Eastern Europe will make the best terms they can with the triumphant Nazi Power. The system of alliances in Central Europe upon which France has relied for her safety has been swept away. . . .

" We have passed an awful milestone in our history, when the whole equilibrium of Europe has been deranged, and the terrible words have for the time being been pronounced against the Western democracies: ' Thou art weighed in the balance and found wanting.' "

The months which elapsed after the fatal decisions of Munich sufficed to show that the road had been laid open for the establishment of Pan-German hegemony in Europe, and perhaps beyond the seas.

CHAPTER VII

The End of Munich

1. The German Plan for the Liquidation of Czecho-Slovakia.

EVERY month which elapsed from the fateful month of September, 1938, onwards, made it increasingly clear that European peace had not been ensured at Munich for any length of time. It became plain how accurate had been the foresight of the Czechoslovak Government when, rejecting the Anglo-French proposals on September 19, 1938, they had pointed out:

1. That, after accepting them, Czechoslovakia would, " sooner or later, fall completely under the influence of Germany."

2. " The balance of power in Central Europe and Europe as a whole would be destroyed," a state of affairs which " would have far-reaching consequences for all other countries and, in particular, for France."

In the preceding chapter we showed how conditions had developed in Czechoslovakia, and in Central Europe generally, from Munich to the month of Febrary, 1939. From this account it was obvious how greatly Germany had been strengthened when the ramparts of the Czechoslovak bastion fell. The Third Reich was now free to start upon a Pan-German advance, the purpose of which was to gain the control of Central Europe and, indeed, of the whole of Europe. The regions from the Baltic to the Black Sea and the Ægean were thrown into a state of confusion. Everywhere the Nazis sought to increase the divergencies from which they might derive an advantage. In these proceedings they were encouraged by the attitude of the Western Powers, from which they obtained the impression that these two Powers were leaving them a free hand in Central and Eastern Europe. The more aggressively and insolently, however, they acted, the greater was the vigilance, if not the resistance, which they aroused among all those who felt themselves menaced. Munich had not produced appeasement, but had increased the general uncertainty and the international tension. Great Britain was compelled to accelerate the speed of her armament, which had gradually attained huge proportions. France was threatened with an ever-increasing insolence by the demands of Italian Fascism. In the United States of America there was an increase of opposition to the brutal aggressiveness of the dictatorships, and this was accompanied by an increase in the defensive preparations of the great American democracy. Soviet Russia withdrew into a position of expectant reserve, which caused uneasiness on all sides; in February, 1939, the possibility of a German-Russian *rapprochement* again began to be mentioned. Although Japan achieved new conquests, she failed to break the Chinese resistance and was compelled to continue an expensive war. The struggle in Spain went on longer than the Berlin-Rome Axis had expected and Franco did not prove victorious until March, 1939. In various countries of Central Europe, after the first alarm caused by Munich, there were plain signs of efforts at resistance to the Nazi schemes for obtaining control of this area. In this respect, what perhaps tended most to encourage these nations was the resolute attitude of the American public and of President Roosevelt against the aggressive tendencies of the German National-Socialists and their savage methods. Such signs of opposition showed themselves even in crippled Czechoslovakia, the moral strength of whose people had not been broken by the effects of the Munich arrangement.

All these matters caused uneasiness to the rulers of the Third Reich. They saw that they must, by some decisive act, make sure of the enormous gain which they had derived from Munich. Their alarm at the development of international politics was increased by difficulties at home. The Munich victory had not met with that response from the German people which the Nazis had expected; among the bulk of the population, Hitler's course of action in September, 1938, had aroused some misgiving that, by the risks which they were incurring with such recklessness, the Nazis might easily plunge Germany at any moment into a fearful war. The annexation of the Sudeten Germans had not caused any particular enthusiasm among the German people. There was no decrease of the economic and financial difficulties. All sections of the population had to shoulder burdens which were becoming greater and greater. This merely caused social tension to become more acute. Industrial output was handicapped by many hitches and defects, both as regards manufacture and organisation. The spectre of impending war affected all public and private life.

There were many indications that the time factor would operate against Germany. Hitler accordingly decided to undertake some spectacular action in 1939. During the confidential discussions in January and February, 1939, between the leading German politicians and military authorities, Hitler explained the necessity for some decisive step in this year. While, on the whole, there was agreement as to the necessity of consolidating the Munich success and settling accounts with their opponents, there was a notorious difference of opinion as to whether action should be taken against the West or the East. The military leaders were inclined to take the view that action in Central Europe would involve less risk. The political leaders, including also Göring and Ribbentrop, judged that it was necessary first of all to break the opposition of the West; among the reasons which they urged in favour of this point of view was that they could rely unconditionally on Italian help only in a scheme of aggression directed against Great Britain and France. Hitler was disposed to associate himself with this opinion championed by the politicians. The question was not settled with complete finality, and Hitler postponed the final decision till it could be taken in accordance with the later development of the situation. On two matters, however, an immediate decision was reached at these discussions in January: (1) The German General Staff should rapidly complete the plan for the occupation of Holland and for an advance through Switzerland. (2) A scheme should be elaborated for the complete liquidation of Czecho-Slovakia. The occupation of Holland was conceived as a manœuvre for alarming Great Britain and France; as soon as this process had been accomplished, Hitler would offer the Western Powers " conciliatory negotiations," and would promise to evacuate Holland on condition that Great Britain and France satisfied the demands of the Axis. The manœuvre would be strengthened by a concentration of German troops on the Swiss frontiers and also by Italian mobilisation.

The liquidation of Czecho-Slovakia was regarded by the Nazis as a necessity in either case, but they attached the utmost importance to it precisely in its bearings upon the scheme of aggression against the West. In advancing against the East they could more easily leave Czecho-Slovakia in its Munich form, for in this eventuality their purposes would have been served if they occupied Plzeň, with the Skoda Works, Moravská Ostrava, with its important metal industry, and a number of other strategical centres. In all other respects, they were certain of having the Czecho-Slovak ways of communication completely at their disposal and of being able to make whatever arrangements they might please in Slovakia and the Carpathian Ukraine. Should they decide upon action against Rumania, Hungary appeared to be an even more convenient rallying point than Carpathian Ukraine alone. In this case, they could make an offer to Hungary by which, in return for joint action with Germany, she would receive Rumanian Transylvania. If Germany took action against Poland, it would be enough to occupy the Ostrava area and Bohumin rapidly; in view of the docile attitude of the Slovak and Ruthenian Governments, Germany would have a completely open road to the Carpathians. After the manner in which Poland behaved towards Czechoslovakia in September, 1938, the Nazis assumed that the Czechs and Slovaks would not assist the Poles if they were attacked by the Germans. For action against Russia, it might suffice for the Nazis, at least for the first stage of hostilities, to secure their position by setting up a Fascist and strongly anti-Bolshevist régime in Prague which would forcibly suppress the traditional sympathies of the Czechs for the Russians; the military occupation of Bohemia could, for the time being, be postponed.

But for any action against the West it was not possibly to rely on half-measures in Czechoslovakia. War with the Western Powers would certainly last for some time, and from the very beginning would disturb the whole world. Great Britain and France would seek support, not only in the United States and Soviet Russia, but also in the smaller nations of Central Europe. In Bohemia, from the very outset, efforts would be made to throw off the Munich yoke. The cadres of the Czechoslovak Army and large supplies of armaments were still available. While Munich had produced a detrimental defect upon the devotion of the Czech people to British and French policy, it had not destroyed their belief in world democracy, and the brutal methods adopted by Germany after Munich increased their repugnance to Pan-German Nazism. The idea of revenge seethed in the heart of every true Czechoslovak. In case of a war between Germany and the West (similarly, of course, too if Russia were involved) the first favourable opportunity would be seized in Bohemia to undertake armed resistance against the Third Reich.

The Nazis were well aware that these feelings prevailed in Czecho-Slovakia, and they realised that the Czech people submitted only from necessity to the official policy of the Prague Government. The Germans cherished no illusions that they would succeed in winning over this hard and stubborn nation, which in September, 1938, showed by its action that it was ready to fight for its liberty, and only refrained from fighting because it was not allowed to do so. It became increasingly clear to the Nazis that if they undertook any warlike operation on a large scale they must first take precautionary measures by stamping out any possibility of organised armed resistance on the part of the Czechoslovak people. Since they were being urged on by the general international situation and their internal difficulties to start some kind of determined action in Europe, they first of all had to liquidate Czecho-Slovakia, which continued to be dangerous to them even in its Munich form. The destruction of Czecho-Slovakia once and for all was the main condition of any expansive action by the Nazis in Europe.

This intention of Hitler's, which was decided upon already in January, 1939, and fixed finally at the beginning of February, remained, of course, unknown to the outside world. It was not until the end of February and the beginning of March that rumours of any definite character began to circulate. But even in the second half of January disturbing indications as to the hostile attitude of Berlin towards Prague were increasingly revealed. We have already given an account of how from January onwards the attitude of the Germans as regards Bohemia and Moravia became more and more exacting; the willingness of the Prague Government to meet successively all their demands did not produce any signs of satisfaction on their part, but, on the contrary, their attitude became more arrogant still. On February 17 Konrad Henlein declared at Litoměřice: " The area of contest comprised by Prague with its University must be preserved for the young generations of Sudeten Germans." After him, Kundt explained more clearly what the issue was; he expressed the hope that " before very long it would be possible to establish such relations between Germans and Czechs that this historic area of Bohemia and Moravia would become a link in the European chain against enemies in the East and in the West." In February the Reich's German Press adopted an even more threatening tone than in January when urging that the Germans in Bohemia should be granted the privileged position demanded for them. Thus, on February 18, the *Frankfurter Zeitung* said:

" The Czechs are located right in the centre of the large vital space [*Lebensraum*] and of the historic zone of influence exercised by the German people. Any reasonable right of the national groups should not be based upon the number of Germans remaining in Czecho-Slovakia, but upon the importance of their task and their natural connections with the bulk of the German people. For the task of the Germans in the Czech, Slovak and Carpatho-Ukrainian territories is to constitute a vital and solid centre between the neighbouring countries."

Kundt's newspaper Press rebuked the Prague Government for being half-hearted and for not making up its mind to cancel the pact with Moscow, to introduce the system of a single state political party, to take energetic action against the Jews, to adjust clearly the relations towards Slovakia and Carpathian Ukraine, to grant the rights of the German national group, to suppress the " whispering propaganda " which was maintaining false hopes among the people that there would be a return to the past, etc. It became more and more obvious that Kundt's Germans had been entrusted with the special task of bringing about the internal disruption of Czecho-Slovakia. As we shall soon see, a similar task was allotted also to the members of the Slovak Autonomist Party.

There were also other disturbing signs that a hostile course of action had been decided upon against Prague by the Nazis. In

January Germany suddenly stopped the work of the Commission which had been dealing with the delimitation of the Munich frontiers. Germany had not arranged for any Customs houses, etc., to be set up on these frontiers; the German Customs and Excise officials had been instructed that, for the time being, they were not to migrate with their families to the new frontier localities; and it was thus more and more evident that Germany regarded the new frontiers as a merely provisional arrangement. In January, too, the preparatory work for building an extra-territorial motor-road from Breslau to Vienna was stopped. At the same time there was a striking decrease of German interest in the construction of a Czech motor-road from west to east. While the tone of the German Press towards Prague became more violent, the Vienna wireless station in February began to broadcast in Slovak a campaign of incitement against the Czechs which, as time went on, emphasised more and more the demand for complete independence of the Slovaks in a state of their own, completely severed from all connection with Bohemia. When the Prague Government made diplomatic protests to Berlin, the reply of the German authorities was that they had no influence on the wireless station at Vienna. Matters became more serious when it was ascertained that from the middle of February onwards special police detachments began to be organised in Germany, similar to those which were formed as a prelude to the occupation of the Saar and of Austria; as, however, these detachments were organised at various localities in Germany, including the western regions, it was not possible to discover immediately for what purpose they were intended. But from the close of February onwards the transfer of German military units also began, while at the beginning of March it became clear that they were directed towards the Czecho-Slovak frontiers, not only in Silesia and Saxony, but also in Bavaria and Austria.

Between March 6 and 10 there was an accumulation of reports which clearly showed that Germany had finally decided to liquidate Czecho-Slovakia. The main features of the scheme were as follows: About March 15 some kind of violent action against Czecho-Slovakia would be started; Slovakia would proclaim its separation from Bohemia and complete independence; on March 12, the day of Nazi celebrations for the " German heroes," incidents would be provoked to show how brutally the Czechs behaved towards the Germans living in Bohemia and Moravia, and then these "persecuted" Germans, possibly also the Slovaks, would appeal to Hitler for help against the Czechs; this would provide adequate preparation and justification for the Germans to intervene in Bohemia; the Czech territories would be occupied and they would receive certain forms of autonomy within the German Empire; this process would involve the transformation of the internal régime into a totalitarian régime in co-operation with the Czech Fascists.

Action was then taken in accordance with this scheme, which was followed practically in every detail. The only divergence of any considerable character was that the plan was not started as late as March 15, but a few days before; this was caused by the initiative which Prague took against Bratislava in the night between March 9 and 10, an intervention which had not been foreseen by the Nazis. As a result of this, however, their plan for the liquidation of Czecho-Slovakia was not frustrated, but merely accelerated.

2. *The Separation of Slovakia.*

The course of action aiming at the separation of Slovakia from Bohemia was an important item in the Nazi scheme; its purpose was to produce the impression that the initiative had proceeded from Czecho-Slovakia itself. We have already explained how the Nazis had established themselves in Slovakia. They had secured from Tiso's Government everything they had demanded. They used every possible device to incite the Slovaks against the Czechs and, in particular, to encourage the radical separatist wing of the Hlinka People's Party. In February these radicals, the real leader of whom was Professor Tuka, although he remained in the background, renewed their activity, which in the preceding weeks they had slightly moderated. Tuka made no secret of what he had in mind. On December 6, 1938, when he was ceremoniously welcomed back to Bratislava from his domiciliary arrest in Plzeň, he declared: " It is only a nation living an independent national life to whom homage is rendered and the inviolability of whose frontiers are recognised. We must build up Slovak independence." Tuka insisted that the Žilina resolution of October 6, 1938, for an autonomous Slovakia within the Czechoslovak Republic had been passed only by means of backstairs intrigues against those who had wanted, there and then, to proclaim Slovak independence. In February, 1939, he told a correspondent of the Paris *Le Temps* (the interview was published on March 2):

" Czech imperialism does not disarm. It does not accept the radical changes which occurred in October and the autonomy of Slovakia. It is biding its time. In spite of the protests of the Government at Chust, the Czechs have sent one of their generals to Carpathian Ukraine. If the manœuvre succeeds in Ukraine, they will send another Czech general to us here for the purpose of making us submit to them. . . . The Czechs and the Slovaks are two different peoples; Bohemia and Slovakia are two separate worlds. Here the Slovak people are waiting, and if their expectations are disappointed, they will lose patience."

Tuka's henchman, Šano Mach, the head of Slovak propaganda, said quite candidly to the correspondent of the French newspaper: " Our ideal is complete independence and the sovereignty of the Slovak state."

It was on these lines that the radical group comprising the followers of Tuka continued to agitate with increasing boldness from February onwards. In fact, they began to put forward the demand that South-Eastern Moravia, which from time immemorial has been inhabited by what are known as " Moravian " Slovaks, should be added to Slovakia. In the *Slovak*, the Press organ of the Autonomist Party, Dr. Bednarik wrote on January 26, 1939: " The Slovak nation will have to secure the demand that its ethnical frontiers should also be the political frontiers of Slovakia." The Moravian Slovaks, who for centuries past have lived side by side with the Czechs of Moravia, had never felt any desire to abandon this life in common and to join Slovakia. They replied with scornful derision to the agitation of the radicals in the Autonomist's Party.

The only newspaper in Slovakia which took an open stand against these radicals was the *Nàrodnè Noviny*, representing the Protestant Autonomists, one of whom, M. Vančo, was a member of the Government; there were also many others who did not agree with the Autonomist Party, but did not venture to come forward in open opposition. On the whole, the Slovak Government tolerated their mischievous proceedings. Its President, Tiso, who had always been lukewarm in national matters (he was more of a pro-Magyar than a Slovak), did nothing to hamper the separatist tendencies. The Minister Durčanský was a tool of the German Nazis. Sidor, a member of the Central Government at Prague, was prompted mainly by personal ambitions tinged with an anti-Czech bias. Unlike the Prague Government, which contained a number of genuine patriots and distinguished experts, the power in Slovakia was mostly in the hands of persons whose moral qualities were questionable and whose administrative abilities were lacking, opportunism and greed, eagerness for a comfortable life without any exertion, were camouflaged behind the slogan of Slovak nationalism and Christianity.

The claims of Bratislava on Prague were continually on the increase. The Slovak Government kept extending its demands, even as regards military matters, the obvious tendency being to bring about the establishment of a separate Slovak Army. But Slovakia was too poor economically to be able, from her own resources, to defray the cost of her autonomy. Bratislava had the audacity to demand from Prague that the Czechs should make themselves responsible for Slovak deficits; Bratislava supposed that this request would be met if Prague were threatened with the danger of Slovak separation.

The Prague Government began to lose patience. Both for reasons of general policy and also on financial grounds, it was anxious, as Prime Minister Beran said, to " reach a clear agreement on all sides and for a long period." On March 1 and 2 the Prague Government conferred with the Slovak Ministers, Sidor and Teplanský. At these proceedings it was resolved that in the following week " the whole of the Slovak and the whole of the Czech Governments should meet at Prague for the purpose of consolidating the general line of its further course of action." The concrete demands of Prague were that the Slovak Government should solemnly associate itself with the constitutional state order and have nothing more to do with the Slovak radicals and separatists, or, in fact, with any movements incompatible with the constitutional order. As foreign affairs formed a joint matter for both Governments, Prague could not allow Slovak Ministers to negotiate with foreign states without the knowledge of the Ministry of Foreign Affairs, as had happened when, on February 28, Pružinský, the Slovak Minister of Commerce, and Durčanský, the Slovak Minister of Transport, had suddenly made their appearance in Berlin. In the same way, it was necessary to bring about a clear understanding on all matters connected with the Army and the joint finances; it will be readily understood that Prague was unwilling to agree that the Army should be split up into a Czech and a Slovak service.

The Slovak Ministerial Council met on March 4, and then again two days later, to discuss their reply to Prague. The proceedings were difficult, as there was a conflict between the tendency to maintain the existing state of affairs and the tendency to pursue a separatist policy. The Nazis did everything in their power to handicap the negotiations by introducing disturbances. On March 3 demonstrations were staged at the well-known health resort of Piestany; Karmasin, the German State Secretary, made them a pretext to launch an accusation against the Jews there. On March 4, Šano Mach, the chief of Slovak propaganda, declared at Bratislava that, " in view of the present international situation, it would be a national catastrophe not to construct a Slovak state." At the same time, there was a further strengthening of demagogic agitation against the Czechs and also against the Jews. It was under these circumstances and precisely at this juncture that the " Slovak loan for economic revival " was launched; the campaign of agitation against Czechs and Jews had already led to the flight of capital from Slovakia to the Czech territories, so that it was clear that these methods were the least suited for facilitating the success of the loan in question.

Finally, on March 6, late in the evening, an official Slovak communiqué was issued in which it was stated that " the Slovak Government regarded the political and constitutional status of the province of Slovakia as settled by the constitutional law concerning the autonomy of Slovakia." From this it could be inferred that the more prudent elements had gained the day over the radicals. This, however, was an error. It was a significant fact that this official communiqué was not published by a single Slovak newspaper except the *Nàrodnè Noviny,* which, from the outset, had opposed the efforts of the separatists. The other Slovak newspapers published curious comments on the resolutions of the Slovak discussions. Thus, on March 7, *Slovak* wrote:

" The Slovak line of action is straight and keeps uncompromisingly to the highest interests of the Slovak nation, building its new independent home in free Slovakia. At the last discussions it was decided that Slovakia is to maintain a free hand in the building of its better future, and will not allow itself to be bound by any considerations with regard to foreign interests, nor will it become the slave of foreign ideologies. Slovakia is aware that the fate of Central Europe cannot be determined without the great German nation and, for that very reason, not against the interests of Greater Germany. The new Slovakia . . . has sincerely taken its place by the side of those great nations which have begun and are continuing the struggle against Judæo-Marxism."

Similarly, *Slovenska Politika* wrote:

" In these grave times Slovakia must choose a path which is the most advantageous to the future of the Slovak nation and likewise nearest to its heart; that is the path to the definite political and economic assurance of Slovak independence."

This was a deliberately engineered confusion; on one side, the official communiqué concerning the Slovak discussions on March 6 declared that the Constitution was acknowledged to be valid, while, on the other, the Government Slovak Press ignored this communiqué and openly continued its campaign for the independence of Slovakia. It is particularly remarkable that the newspaper *Slovak* made an express reference to Germany. The wording of this reference was not sufficiently vague to be misunderstood; it was intended as a threat to Prague by Germany. This article in *Slovak* is a public document which confirms that the German Nazis had already reached an agreement with the Slovak Radicals as to a joint course of action against Bohemia.

The clear declaration demanded by Prague had not been made. On the contrary, the confusion had become worse. The German Nazis had taken good care that this should be so. Precisely at this moment the wireless station in Vienna intensified its campaign in the Slovak language against the Czechs and explained that the purpose of the discussions carried on by the Slovak Government was to satisfy the wishes of the Slovaks for complete independence.

While these events were taking place in Slovakia, Prague intervened in Carpathian Ukraine. On March 6 the President of the Republic dismissed from his office Julian Revay, Minister of the Interior, and distributed the functions in the Ukrainian Government in such a way that its President, Mgr. Augustin Vološin, was entrusted both with education and justice, General Prchala became Minister of the Interior, of Finance and Transport, and the newly appointed member of the Government, Stefan Kločurak, a personal friend of Vološin's, was placed in charge of economic and social matters. From a political point of view, this reconstruction was remarkable because of the departure of Minister Revay from the Ukrainian Government. Even in the Press the reasons for this change were adequately made clear: Minister Revay and his brother were the most zealous supporters of the Greater Ukraine agitation and also the advocates of a national Ukrainian totalitarianism within the country: they took measures of all kinds quite independently, without any regard to the common state, and, like the Slovak radicals, they took into account only the wishes of the German Nazis. As a result of this action on their part, the Central Government at Prague was confronted with ever greater difficulties; as regards foreign politics, it became difficult to maintain friendly relations with Poland and Hungary, while in home affairs it was an increasingly hopeless prospect to try to restore order in the small Carpathian region which was kept in a continual state of disturbance by all kinds of agitation and terrorism. It was for these reasons that Revay was removed and the position of General Prchala strengthened. The energetic intervention of the Prague Government took Revay by surprise. He was in Prague on

March 6 and was there handed his order of dismissal. He thereupon proceeded to Germany. At Chust the Ukrainian nationalistic organisations made a protest and called upon Vološin to hand in his resignation. Vološin, however, refused to do so. Revay's adherents looked for support from the German Nazis and they obtained it when the German propaganda started attacking Prague, which, it alleged, was trying " to renew the old system of Czech domination in the Carpathian Ukraine," and also incited the Ukrainian nationalists against the Czechs. Before very long, these radicals had ample proof that the Nazis had used them only as puppets which had been thrown away when they no longer served any useful purpose.

The intervention of Prague in the affairs of Carpathian Ukraine showed that the Prague Government was determined to put a stop to the mischievous activity of the Ukrainian and Slovak radicals. *Venkov*, the leading Government paper, wrote on March 8: " If the influence were allowed to remain in the hands of those who are rallying round Professor Tuka, the whole Slovak nation would pay dearly for such a policy. . . . In many cases there are foreign elements misleading a part of the Slovak people to adopt an anti-Czech course of action. These people in foreign service must be detected and removed by the Slovak people. It is high time that we knew exactly how we stand."

In accordance with the previous week's agreement, after the Bratislava deliberations a joint meeting of the Czech and Slovak Government was to be held. But the only Slovak Ministers who came to Prague were Sidor and Teplanský (the latter had previously been an Agrarian). Tiso, the President of the Government, remained in Bratislava. This circumstance also showed that the Slovak Government was still under the thumb of the radicals.

After lengthy conversation on March 9, the Prague Government decided on a radical step: it was resolved to dismiss the Tiso Government and suppress the separatist agitation. On the evening of the same day, the Czecho-Slovak Army received instructions to occupy all buildings of any importance in the Slovak towns during the night of March 9–10, and to take action against the subversive elements wherever they might attempt resistance. These military measures were entrusted to the charge of General Eliáš, Minister of Transport. During the night of March 9–10 the Army did actually secure all points of any importance; in the early hours of the morning all necessary measures were also taken at Bratislava. Tiso was then handed the decree of the President of the Republic which deprived him of his office, together with the Ministers Durčanský, Pružinský and Vančo. Tiso took the decree, but protested against it. He was then placed in custody in a monastery where he resided. Moreover, various radicals, including Tuka and Mach, were either interned or warrants were issued against them. These measures were essential if conflicts and disturbances on a considerable scale were to be prevented.

The public, which was without definite news, had merely an inkling that in some way or other a settlement of the strained relations between Prague and Bratislava was being prepared, but on the morning of March 10 it heard from the Czecho-Slovak wireless bulletin the news of the dramatic change which had been effected in Slovakia. This wireless bulletin emphasised the fact that not the slightest change had been made as regards the autonomous position of Slovakia and that the new Government would do everything that had been neglected by the previous Government, which, by finding continual pretexts for serious disputes, had caused unrest in Slovakia. The bulletin also promised that the new Government would secure considerable financial assistance from the Czech regions.

The bulletin, too, contained one particularly interesting passage: " Anyone who tells you that the German Empire wishes to separate Slovakia from the Czecho-Slovak state is a lying adventurer." These words were not chosen only for a propagandist purpose, but accorded with the opinion of the Prague Government. It can be readily understood that before deciding upon its intervention in Slovakia, Prague had endeavoured to ascertain the attitude of Berlin. From the replies made by the German *Chargé d'Affaires* in Prague, the Czech Government assumed that Berlin regarded the whole dispute with the Slovak Government as " an internal matter " of Czecho-Slovakia and that it had no objections to the measures which Prague proposed to adopt against the Slovak separatists. It is still uncertain to what extent the Wilhelmstrasse deliberately deceived Prague; there are some indications which suggest that Hitler's resolution to liquidate Czecho-Slovakia once and for all was known only to a very small circle of his closest collaborators —Ribbentrop, of course, was among them, but possibly he did not think it advisable to tell everything to the leading officials in the Foreign Office. It may even be probable that Hitler was not averse to the Prague intervention against Bratislava; since it was immediately utilised for speeding up the execution of a scheme which had already been drawn up. At the outset, however, it may have been considered best to let the Czechs cherish the illusion that Germany did not object to this action in Slovakia. According to Hitler's doctrine, a lie is one of the admissible implements of Germany diplomacy.

Simultaneously with the dismissal of Tiso's Government, the President of the Republic appointed Josef Sivák as President of the new Government. Teplanský continued to be a member of the Government and that same night was sent from Prague to Bratislava to take charge of the Government there, since Sivák, at that particular moment, was on his way to Rome, where he was to act as delegate at the Coronation of the Pope. This in itself caused a certain amount of difficulty, which was increased when Sivák, replying from Rome, declined to accept the post of Prime Minister. In Bratislava, too, events were not developing as Prague had expected. With the help of Karmasin, the political leader of the Germans in Slovakia, and the German Consul in Bratislava, the dismissed Minister Durčanský and Murgaš, commander of the Hlinka Guards, succeeded in escaping to Vienna. With the help of the Germans in Bratislava, the Hlinka Guards began to demonstrate, and as the Czecho-Slovak Army had received the order to have recourse to arms only in case of extreme necessity, the demonstrators became increasingly reckless. On the evening of March 10 Durčanský broadcast a message from Vienna in which he emphatically repudiated the intervention of the Prague Government as " unconstitutional " and urged the Hlinka Guards and the Slovak people to offer resistance. The Vienna wireless station continued almost uninterruptedly to broadcast anti-Czech messages in Slovak and called upon the Slovaks to persevere in their struggle for the complete liberation of Slovakia.

In Prague it had been arranged with Sidor, who was still in the capital, that Sokol, Chairman of the Slovak Diet, should be summoned to the President of the Republic. He arrived in the forenoon of March 10 and, after consulting with President Hácha and Prime Minister Beran, he left the same afternoon with Sidor for Bratislava. Meanwhile Beran had secured the ambitious Sidor for co-operation with Prague. On the evening of the same day a few of the chief members of Hlinka's National Unity party met at Bratislava and there was then a meeting of the Slovak Diet. After midnight Sidor announced that a successful agreement had been reached for the formation of a new Government. This Government was appointed on the next day, March 11. At its head was Karol Sidor, of whom Deputy Čavojský said in a broadcast speech on March 12: " Our Slovak nation fanatically believed in its great leader, Andrej Hlinka. Karol Sidor, to whom the Slovak people has now transmitted its affection and belief, is regarded as a pupil of Andrej Hlinka. The Slovak people clamoured for Karol Sidor."

It was certainly a success that with such comparative speed a new Slovak Government had been formed which had undertaken to combat treacherous separatism. There is not the slightest doubt that it would have achieved its purpose if the separatists had remained dependent upon their own resources alone. But they received help from Germany, and it was this which decided the issue.

On March 11 and 12 there was a regular wireless warfare raging between Bratislava and Vienna, from which centre provocative messages against Sidor's Government were broadcast by Durčanský and Murgaš. Both sides accused each other of having betrayed the Slovak nation. Durčanský alleged that Tiso's Government had been removed unconstitutionally by the Czechs and that it was therefore entitled to continue its functions. This was also the German official point of view, which was first enunciated by German propaganda and finally expressed by Hitler himself. In Slovakia the Hlinka Guards split up into two factions, comprising the adherents of Sidor and Murgaš respectively. The rebellious Guards were everywhere supported by the Germans in Slovakia, whose leader Karmasin declared at Bratislava on the evening of March 11: " Monseigneur Tiso's

Government is the only legal Government and the only Government recognised by the Germans in Slovakia: but the latter have nothing to fear, for if any steps were adopted against them, our great neighbour, the German Reich, would immediately intervene. The mission and the duty of the Germans in Slovakia is to join the Slovak autonomist movement in order to safeguard the free Slovak state. A common front of Slovaks and Germans must be formed." Karmasin was right in saying that the Germans in Slovakia, and together with them the Slovak separatists, who were now beginning to assert themselves, had nothing to fear as they were certain of help from Germany: although martial law had been proclaimed in Bratislava, they continued to demonstrate, and practically before the very eyes of the Government authorities responsible for public safety, a continuous supply of arms and bombs were sent to them from the German side of the Danube. Serious disturbances then occurred at Bratislava and elsewhere, and even when they did not assume any considerable proportions, German propaganda at once triumphantly declared them to be far more extensive than they really were.

While on March 10 the German Press and wireless were still exercising a certain restraint, from March 11 onwards they let loose the whole familiar gamut of German propaganda against the Czechs. They openly supported the Slovak rebels and began to allege, just as in the summer of 1938, that the Germans in the Czech territories were being harshly persecuted by the Czechs.

On the night of March 11–12 Seyss-Inquart invited Sidor to a meeting at Petržalka, which is situated on the other side of the Danube, opposite Bratislava. Sidor refused to leave Bratislava in order not to be taken prisoner by the Germans. Accordingly, Seyss-Inquart, together with Bürckel, proceeded to Bratislava to deliberate with him there. The meeting led to no results. Sidor was proof against promises and threats; having attained the rank of Prime Minister, he remained true to the terms of the Czecho-Slovak Constitution.

On March 12, however, the threats were considerably reinforced by the presence of German troops prepared to occupy Bratislava immediately. Sidor gave way. On the same day he appealed to the authorities in Prague, asking them to moderate the Czech military measures and to place the military detachments completely under Slovak control.

On March 13 it was announced that Tiso, the former President of the Slovak Government, which in Germany had been declared, in opposition to that of Sidor, as the only legal Government, had received an invitation from Hitler to proceed immediately to Berlin. Sidor was compelled to yield to German pressure. Tiso was released from custody and on the same day, accompanied by the German Consul-General at Bratislava, Daniehel, a Deputy of the Hlinka party, and Karmasin, he started for Vienna, from where he continued his journey to Berlin by aeroplane.

Thus on March 13 Hitler took the stage to decide the fate of Czecho-Slovakia. His conversation with Tiso, which took place on the same day after 6 p.m., was brief. Tiso simply received orders that on the next day the Slovak Diet was to proclaim " unanimously " the independence of Slovakia.

After the removal of Tiso's Government, the Slovak Diet had been prorogued until the end of March. Now, however, at Hitler's orders, President Hácha summoned it to meet at 10 a.m. on March 14. Tiso returned to Bratislava on the same night, March 13, for the purpose of rapidly making the final preparations for the treachery which had been arranged between Berlin and himself.

Meanwhile, that same evening saw the culmination of the campaign of terrorism and provocation which the Hlinka Guards and the Nazis, in close collaboration, had, during the last three days, continually provoked. On the evening of March 13, at Bratislava a number of infernal machines exploded and caused the death of several innocent persons.

It was amid this atmosphere of terrorism, within range of German rifles and cannon, trained on Bratislava from the other side of the Danube, that the Slovak Diet met in the forenoon of March 14 for a " free decision." From the preliminary discussion, it was obvious that many of the Deputies were opposed to the separation of Slovakia from Bohemia. It was therefore necessary to declare the meeting of the Diet as a secret one, whereupon Tiso announced that Hitler had demanded an immediate declaration of Slovak independence: if it were not

made, Slovakia would be immediately partitioned among her
neighbours. After this categoric communication, seconded by
Mach, the Deputies voted for Slovak independence. When, however, Tiso announced that Hitler also demanded that Slovakia
should ask him to give it the protection of the Reich, there were
still certain Deputies who opposed it. This demand was, nevertheless, also accepted. The separatist traitors then struck up the
anthem " *Hej Slováci*," but there were many Deputies who knew
that "independence," dictated by Berlin, was the grave of
Slovak freedom.

The first and the chief paragraph of the law which was thus
passed on the subject of Slovak independence ran as follows:
" The Slovak region is declared to be a separate and independent
Slovak state. The Diet of the Slovak region is transformed into
the legislative Diet of the Slovak state." At the same time the
Diet elected a new Government. The President was Mgr. Tiso,
Tuka was Vice-President and Durčanský, Minister of Foreign
Affairs. The leading positions were thus occupied by the chief
betrayers of the Slovak nation acting in the service of the
German Nazis. Sidor continued to be a member of the Government as Minister of the Interior, but he was at once deprived of
his office as commander-in-chief of the Hlinka Guards, and he
then went " on leave." The command of the Guard was entrusted to Mach, another leading traitor. His first order was that
all persons wishing to leave Slovakia should be deprived of all
their money and other valuables by the Hlinka Guard, who
would allow them to retain at the most the sum of 500 Czech
crowns. In this way the robbery of Czechs and Jews, who
naturally endeavoured to get out of the country as quickly as
possible, was organised publicly: in actual practice, the Hlinka
Guard took everything away from them.

On March 15, *Slovak* published what may be described as an
exultant ode on " The Unending Future of the Independent
Slovak State," in the course of which it took its farewell of the
Czechs thus: " The Czech nation has remained entirely by itself.
How the Czechs arrange their further state existence is their own
affair. Undeniably we must thank them for having helped us in
very many ways and we must also admit that without them
we should not have gained our freedom twenty years ago. This

is a historical fact and only an unjust man would wish to deny it."

The next few days showed that just as the Slovaks were not able to gain their liberty without the Czechs, they were also unable to maintain it without them.

3. *The Occupation of the Czech Territories.*

Meanwhile the final act of the tragedy drew near in the Czech territories also. Outwardly until almost the last moment, Germany maintained good relations with Prague as far as formal correctness was concerned. In the early days of March, the option agreement was prolonged for another three months. Before this, on February 18, an agreement had been reached with Hungary on the subject of rights of option, state citizenship and legal status of persons residing in the occupied territories, and on March 6, the final Protocol of the Magyar-Czecho-Slovak Commission was signed on the subject of the delimitation of frontiers; in accordance with this agreement about twenty communes were assigned to Hungary, while eight communes were returned to Czecho-Slovakia, the number of inhabitants affected by this exchange having been approximately the same on both sides, i.e. roughly about 15,000. By this adjustment a readiness to reach an agreement was manifested both on the Magyar and the Czecho-Slovak sides; already before this, the terroristic disturbances in the Magyar frontier district had practically ceased. The negotiations with Poland, too, which had been carried on since the end of February, concerning the right of option and other matters arising from the Polish annexation of Czecho-Slovak areas, were making progress in a better atmosphere. The official Polish policy, of course, continued to pursue its aim of a common frontier with Hungary. Prague was anxious to achieve good relations both with Poland and Hungary, and therefore endeavoured to stop the mischievous activities of the Ukrainian nationalists, as well as to moderate the fierce anti-Magyar utterances of the Slovak chauvinists. These signs—that attempts were being made to bring about peaceable relations with Poland and Hungary—produced the impression that the general course of events did not involve direct menace to Czecho-Slovakia.

The Ministry of Foreign Affairs at Prague under Dr. Chvalkovský continued to cherish remarkably optimistic illusions. It interpreted in a most favourable manner Hitler's reference to Czecho-Slovakia in his speech on January 30, 1939: " May Czecho-Slovakia also succeed in finding the way to internal peace and order which will exclude any return to the tendencies of the former President Beneš." Dr. Chvalkovský evidently imagined that it was enough to abuse Beneš, to remove all his adherents, to strengthen anti-Semitism and to fawn to Berlin in every possible way in order to gain Hitler's favour. He underestimated —or perhaps did not even heed—the reports which, from the end of February onwards, kept announcing the hostile intentions and preparations of Germany. The casual attitude of this smiling optimist was indeed incredible. As late as March 9, he allowed his praises to be sung in *Národní Listy*, as follows:

" Dr. Chvalkovský's new policy has put an energetic stop to the unfortunate methods of the old régime. . . . To-day at last a different atmosphere prevails in the Černín Palace. Our foreign policy is in the hands of men who are unburdened by morbid ambition and who do not live on the paid glory of legendary liberation; nor are they handicapped by the ill-fated ideologies and the professorial dilettantism and doctrinaire methods of the romantic ' realists.'[1] We are readjusting our relationship to our neighbours, and this includes not only the Germans, but also Magyars and Poles."

Such opinions as these were published at the moment when the first German military detachments had already been sent to the frontiers of Czecho-Slovakia and when the Slovak crisis was at its height. This merely made it easier for Berlin to conceal until the last moment its plan for the liquidation of Czecho-Slovakia. Berlin, of course, was very anxious that these intentions should not be prematurely disclosed with any degree of certainty. It is clear that only the Press and the wireless were allowed to intensify the tone of the warnings and then the threats addressed to Prague. As late as March 11, it was officially denied by Berlin that any hostile action was being prepared against Czecho-Slovakia. The foreign diplomats received information from the

---

[1] I.e. the followers of Masaryk and Beneš, who, under the guidance of democratic ideas, led the nation to freedom.

Wilhelmstrasse to the same effect at this juncture, though it was also emphasised that Berlin was dissatisfied with the attitude of Prague, not only towards the Slovaks, but also as regards the Germans in Czecho-Slovakia.

To the latter, Hitler assigned a similar task as had been prepared for the Slovaks in the plan for the destruction of Czecho-Slovakia. We have already pointed out that from January onwards and particularly in February the reckless agitation of the Nazis in Bohemia and Moravia was intensified. Though Kundt officially continued negotiations with the Prague Government, he was helping at the same time to spread discontent. Undue optimism was shown in Czech quarters at the news that, by an agreement between Berlin and Prague on February 24, the Czechs who came under German rule as a result of Munich would be exempt from military service in the German Army, just as the Germans living in Czecho-Slovakia would not have to serve in the Czecho-Slovak Army. In reality, this agreement meant nothing and in no way promoted an improvement in the relations between Germans and Czechs. At the beginning of March, Kundt went to Berlin; he was to have returned immediately to continue his negotiations with the Prague Government for the final settlement of the position of the German *Volksgruppe* in Czecho-Slovakia, but it was suddenly reported that he had fallen ill. From that time onwards Kundt's newspapers adopted an increasingly aggressive tone towards the Czechs, and his followers behaved in an increasingly provocative manner. As early as the beginning of March, they began to greet each other in public with the words " *Heil März!* " and altogether they made no attempt to conceal the fact that something serious had been arranged for March. Among the Czechs there was increasing alarm that possibly Brno, Jihlava, Moravská Ostrava and Plzeň would be occupied, but it was not believed that this would be the fate of the whole country.

On Sunday, March 12, the *Heldentag* was celebrated throughout Germany to honour the memories of fallen German heroes. Germans from Czecho-Slovakia were also to take part in the celebrations with banners, badges, and all the usual decorations which accompany Nazi festivities. The Czech authorities had arranged with them that side by side with the swastika banner the Czecho-Slovak state flag should also be displayed. The Czecho-Slovak authorities were also anxious that there should be no disturbances, and the Czecho-Slovak wireless and the whole of the Press called upon the Czech population to show due regard for the German celebrations and to refrain from any anti-German demonstrations. But the Nazis had received orders that they were to provoke disturbances at any cost, and paid agents were hired for this purpose. Berlin badly needed a pretext to intervene " for the protection of its German brothers." At a number of places on March 12, the Nazis did actually succeed in provoking serious disturbances, in spite of all measures adopted by the Czech police authorities and the almost unbelievable self-control showed by the Czech public. In the districts of Jihlava, Budějovice and Olomouc, the Nazis broke into the Czech schools and inflicted damage upon the premises and their contents. In several places they fired at the gendarmes, a number of whom were wounded. Violent demonstrations occurred also at Brno and in the Ostrava district, while in Prague there were minor brawls. Nevertheless, in spite of all the German efforts, none of these incidents assumed far-reaching proportions.

German propaganda, however, alleged that they had, and the German journalists in Prague telephoned to Germany accounts of disturbances which had never occurred. On the afternoon of March 12 a telephone message was sent from Berlin to Jihlava, stating " there are still too few disturbances." The Nazis behaved with unconcealed cynicism, and no longer even troubled to take into account the fact that the Czech authorities would tap their telephone conversations in which they arranged the staging of provocative acts and the invention of disturbances. The German wireless and Press proceeded on the same lines as in September, 1938: they gave a detailed account of a Czech reign of terror to which the defenceless Germans in the Czech territories were exposed, and they once more produced their whole stock of tales about the " Bolshevik " or " Hussite " hordes who had been equipped with the help of the Czech authorities and were ranging over Bohemia and Moravia. The German Press of March 13, contained such phrases as " monstrous Czech terrorism," " revolting acts of terrorism," " again Germans are the victims of their hatred and brutality " and " an orgy of Hussite insolence has taken possession of the Czechs overnight." *Die Zeit* alleged that in Prague the Legionaries and a part of the General Staff were preparing a *Putsch* to restore the Beneš régime. The *Völkischer Beobachter* wrote: " The bulk of the Czechs maintain the same mentality as before the collapse in September. The spirit of Beneš, supported by the organisations of the *Sokols* and the Legionaries, is again finding favour with the man in the street. . . . It is obvious to-day that the poison penetrated more deeply than was supposed, and that it infects the whole of the Czech body. The situation has become untenable." The *Börsen Zeitung* declared: " The new Czecho-Slovakia, too, has become a focus for widespread disorder. . . . The whole country is ablaze from Prague to Bratislava, from Plzeň to Chust. Moscow is already preparing to cook its soup on this fire. Prague is lapsing into chaos. All the nationalities, except the Czechs, are making ready to resist it with all their strength." The *Hamburger Fremdenblatt* asserted: " To-day the countries adjacent to the Reich must clearly realise that insults to our flag and ill-treatment of Germans, whoever they may be, have all the political weight of an affront levelled at a great Power conscious of the strength of its arms."

By this time there could be no further doubt of what this frenzied propaganda was leading to. " Germany has been directly provoked," stated the *Deutsche Allgemeine Zeitung* finally. In this way adequate reasons were obtained for justifying the need of intervention on the part of the Führer.

On March 13 official quarters in Berlin also threw aside the mask. On that afternoon it was stated at the Wilhelmstrasse that the Czechs had failed to keep to the spirit of the Munich Agreement, that in Prague there had been a marked change of attitude towards Germany after President Roosevelt's speech in Congress, that the situation was developing in a menacing manner for the Germans in Czecho-Slovakia, and that therefore Germany, unable to tolerate this state of affairs, would intervene in Bohemia to establish the order which the Prague Government was unable to maintain. It was not, however, until March 14 that the announcement was made in Berlin concerning the decision to " establish order " by the military occupation of the Czech territories.

From the moment when Hitler had summoned Tiso to him, no further doubts were entertained by the Prague Government, or even by the Ministry of Foreign Affairs, that Germany had decided upon drastic action against Czecho-Slovakia. But it was not yet known what form exactly this action would take. On the afternoon of March 13 President Hácha asked the German *Chargé d'Affaires*, Hencke, to call on him for an informative conversation. Hencke, however, was ordered by Ribbentrop not to go to President Hácha, who, he said, could inform Hencke in writing if he had anything to communicate to him. It was not until the following day, when Slovakia had already declared its independence, that Germany intervened against Prague with open brutality. In the meanwhile the German troops, various units of whom had been moved in the direction of Czecho-Slovakia ever since the beginning of March, were concentrated on all Czecho-Slovak frontiers. On March 14 they were in readiness for the command to march upon the Czech territories. All these military preparations, reports of which had been reaching the various European cities with increasing definiteness from March 6 onwards, had taken place without arousing any special attention in the rest of Europe. Actually, on March 12, important English and French newspapers were writing in a manner which conveyed the impression that Europe was not threatened by any further dangerous surprise. On that day, too, Flandin made a speech at Dijon in which he said: " The reports from London during the last few days are much more optimistic as regards the international situation. It is a fact that the prophets who have striven so hard, and who are still striving hard, to alarm French opinion see the lie given to each of their terrifying predictions." As late as March 14 Mr. Chamberlain stated in the House of Commons that the guarantee promised to Czecho-Slovakia held good only in case of an unprovoked attack, but that " no such aggression has yet taken place." Up to the last moment there were no signs that London or Paris felt particularly disturbed about the manner in which the situation was developing between Germany and Czecho-Slovakia. Nor did the Prague Government do anything to draw the attention of Europe to the threatening danger. Under these circumstances, Germany was able, quite undisturbed, to complete all the military preparations for dealing a sudden blow.

Shortly after midday on March 14 President Hácha was ordered to proceed immediately to Hitler. M. Beran presented to President Hácha the resignation of his Cabinet, but President Hácha refused to accept it and asked him to wait. In point of fact, Beran's gesture could change nothing in the situation. It could not even delay the final decision. President Hácha started off accompanied by Dr. Chvalkovský, Minister of Foreign Affairs, and reached Berlin that same night before eleven o'clock.

On arriving he was given all military honours due to the head of a state, but he also learned that Moravská Ostrava and Mistek had already been occupied by German troops. First of all there was a conference between Ribbentrop and Chvalkovský. After it Chvalkovský told Hácha that there was no need to fear anything disastrous and that he would do well to ask Hitler for protection. It was after 1 a.m. when Hitler received Hácha and Chvalkovský in the presence of Ribbentrop and Göring. The latter had, at Hitler's request, broken off his holiday in Italy and had returned to Berlin that evening. Hácha endeavoured to persuade Hitler that the Prague Government was anxious for the closest co-operation with the Reich, without any *arrière-pensée* or reservations, and he expressed the wish that the German Chancellor might protect and respect the independence of the Czech territories. Hitler, however, curtly informed him that he had decided upon the military occupation of the Czech territories, a proceeding which offered the sole guarantee for the establishment of order. Hácha was aghast. Chvalkovský had not mentioned this to him even as a possibility. He tried to dissuade Hitler from his purpose. This, of course, was useless. Göring stressed the fact that 800 aircraft were in readiness to bombard Prague if the Führer's decision were not immediately accepted. The conversation with Hitler lasted for less than three-quarters of an hour. Hácha and Chvalkovský then discussed the matter, partly between themselves, partly with Göring and Ribbentrop. Hácha saw that all his efforts would be completely useless. He got into touch with the Prague Government, which met at about 3 a.m., and took note of the fact that it was not possible to raise any opposition and that nothing could be done but surrender. Before 4 a.m., Hácha, with the others, was again received by Hitler, and at 3.55 a.m. the following declaration was signed by Hitler, Hácha, Ribbentrop and Chvalkovský:

" The Führer to-day, in the presence of the Reich Minister for Foreign Affairs, Herr von Ribbentrop, received the Czecho-Slovak President, Dr. Hácha, and the Czecho-Slovak Minister for Foreign Affairs, Dr. Chvalkovský, at their request in Berlin. At the meeting the serious situation which had arisen as a result of the events of the past week on what was hitherto Czecho-Slovak territory was closely and frankly examined. Both sides gave expression to their mutual conviction that the aim of all efforts in this part of Central Europe should be the safeguarding of calm, order and peace. The Czecho-Slovak President declared that in order to serve this purpose, and in order to secure final pacification, he placed the destiny of the Czech people and country with confidence in the hands of the Führer of the German Reich.

" The Führer accepted this declaration and expressed his determination to take the Czech people under the protection of the German Reich and to guarantee to it an autonomous development of its national life in accordance with its particular characteristics."

This was the end of the dismal farce, the object of which was to produce the impression that the constitutional representative of Czecho-Slovakia had, of his own free will, asked Germany to assume a protectorate over the Czech territories. It was, of course, clear to everybody that it was only the most blatant compulsion which had induced Hácha to put his signature to the agreement quoted above. Incidentally, it may be added that on March 15 Hitler issued the following proclamation to the German nation, in which he simply announced that he had decided upon the military occupation of Bohemia and Moravia:

" To the German people: After Germany, only a few months ago, was compelled to protest against the unbearable régime of terrorism in Czecho-Slovakia against those of our co-nationals living in areas inhabited chiefly by Germans, the same events again occurred to an ever-increasing extent during the past week.

" In an area where so many nationalities are living side by side this must lead to an unbearable situation. As a reaction against these renewed attacks on their freedom, national groups have separated from Prague. Thereby Czecho-Slovakia ceased to exist.

" Since Sunday, riots have occurred in many communities, with many Germans as victims. Hourly they cried for help for the persecuted, who steadily increased in number.

" From those German-language areas, which German magnanimity last autumn let Czecho-Slovakia retain, a stream of fugitives who had been deprived of their belongings and property, is beginning to flow into the Reich.

" Continuation of this condition must lead to the destruction of the last vestige of order in a territory in which Germany is vitally interested—nay, which even over a thousand years belonged to the German Reich.

" In order definitely to eliminate this menace to peace and order, and to create the prerequisites for the necessary new regulations in this area, I have decided, as from to-day, to allow German troops to march into Bohemia and Moravia.

" They will disarm the terrorist gangs and military forces who protect the gangs, and will thus protect the lives of all who are menaced and will secure a basis for the introduction of a new and fundamental settlement which will do justice to a thousand years of history and to the practical needs of the German and Czech peoples. " (*Signed*) ADOLF HITLER."

This proclamation publicly confirmed that it made no difference whether President Hácha and the Prague Government would or would not agree to the German protectorate. Hitler, backed by the strength of his troops, who were massed in readiness on the frontier, simply imposed his decision regarding the occupation of the Czech territories. In fact, this occupation was begun by the entry of German troops into Moravská Ostrava even before the arrival of Hácha in Berlin.

In the small hours of the morning of March 15 the German troops began to march into the Czech territories, and very early

in the day the Prague Government announced this appalling
news to the public, whom it urged with the utmost emphasis to
offer no resistance and to maintain order. It was plain that the
Government could do nothing but submit. Any attempt at
resistance would have involved a massacre.

It was a little after 9 a.m. when the first mechanised columns
of the German army began to reach Prague. The weather provided a dramatic background for this awful scene: an icy wind
was blowing and snow fell heavily. The distress and despair of
the Czechs were indescribable. Since Munich, a strict censorship
of the Czech Press had been introduced, and for this reason the
people did not know exactly what was happening in the world.
The German occupation affected them like a thunderbolt. When
they saw the German troops driving through the streets of
Prague, some broke down, while others raged in impotent anger.
The demonstrations were particularly violent on the Václavské
Náměstí. Heedless of the risk which they ran, the Czechs shouted
abuse at the German troops and spoke openly of revenge. The
troops were, of course, welcomed by the Germans in Prague, who
from the very outset behaved with the notorious insolence with
which the Czechs were familiar from the days before and during
the War. The indignation of the Czechs reached its climax when
they learned that after seven o'clock that evening, Hitler had
taken up his quarters in the Prague Hrad, where the Czech
Kings and Presidents had lived. Among all sections of the
people, without distinction of party or class, it was realised that
this act of Hitler's was deliberately intended as an additional
humiliation with which to increase the bitterness of defeat suffered by a defenceless people. The Czecho-Slovaks will not forget
this outrage to their feelings. They will also remember that Hitler
selected Konrad Henlein of all people to act as his Commissar in
Bohemia with the whole of the civil administration under his
charge (in Moravia this function was entrusted to Bürckel from
Vienna).

On March 16, Hitler signed at the Hrad the following decree
regarding the " protectorate over Bohemia and Moravia ":

" Bohemia and Moravia have for thousands of years belonged to the *Lebensraum* of the German people. Force and

unreason have arbitrarily torn them from their old historical setting. Above all, their incorporation in the artificial structure of Czecho-Slovakia created a breeding ground of constant unrest.

" Year by year there grew the danger that from this region there might emerge—as already once in the past—a terrible threat to European peace. For the Czecho-Slovak state and its rulers had failed to organise on a reasonable basis the communal life of the several nationality groups arbitrarily united within it. It had failed therefore to arouse and to preserve the interest of each group in the maintenance of the common state structure. It thus showed its innate incapacity to live and has now crumbled in actual fact.

" In this region, which for its own peace and safety as well as for the common weal and the general peace is of such decisive importance, the German Reich cannot tolerate continued disturbances. Sooner or later the Reich, as historically and geographically the Power most interested in that region, would have to bear the heaviest consequences. It is in accordance, therefore, with the principle of self-preservation that the Reich is resolved to intervene decisively, to re-establish the bases of a reasonable Central European order, and to take all measures which in consequence arise. For in its long historical past it has shown itself, through the greatness and the qualities of the German people, as being alone fitted to fulfil these tasks.

" Imbued with the sincere wish to serve the interests of the peoples living in this region, to secure the independent existence of the German and the Czech nations, and to further peace and social welfare, I therefore order, in the name of the German Reich, that the future communal life of these peoples be established on the following basis:

" *Terms of Protectorate*

" *Article I.* (1) The territories of the former Czecho-Slovak state occupied by the German troops in March, 1939, belong henceforth to the territory of the Great German Reich, and enter under its protection as the ' Protectorate of Bohemia and Moravia.'

" (2) In so far as the defence of the Reich demands it, the Führer and Reich Chancellor makes arrangements which diverge from this rule for isolated portions of territory.

" *Article II.* (1) The German inhabitants of the Protectorate become German nationals [*Staatsangehörige*] and, in accordance with the Reich Citizenship Law of September 15, 1935, Reich citizens [*Reichsbürger*]. The regulations for the protection of German blood and German honour therefore hold valid for them. They are subject to German jurisdiction.

" (2) The other inhabitants of Bohemia and Moravia become nationals [*Staatsangehörige*] of the Protectorate of Bohemia and Moravia.

" *Article III.* (1) The Protectorate of Bohemia and Moravia is autonomous and administers itself.

" (2) It exercises the prerogatives which fall to it within the framework of the Protectorate in accordance with the political, military, and economic importance of the Reich.

" (3) These prerogatives are exercised through its own organs and its own authorities, with its own officials.

" *Article IV.* The Head of the autonomous administration of the Protectorate of Bohemia and Moravia enjoys a protection and the rights of the head of a state. The head of the Protectorate must have the confidence of the Führer and the Reich Chancellor for the discharge of his office.

" *Article V.* (1) As the protector of Reich interests, the Führer and Chancellor appoints a ' Reich Protector in Bohemia and Moravia.' His seat of authority is Prague.

" (2) As the representative of the Führer and Reich Chancellor, and as the delegate of the Reich Government, the Reich Protector has the task of seeing that the lines of policy laid down by the Führer and Reich Chancellor are observed.

" (3) The members of the Government of the Protectorate are confirmed by the Reich Protector. This confirmation can be withdrawn.

" (4) The Reich Protector is authorised to inform himself about all measures taken by the Government of the Protectorate and to give advice. He can object to measures which are calculated to injure the Reich, and when delay seems dangerous can himself take measures necessary in the common interest.

" (5) The promulgation of laws, decrees, and other orders, as well as the execution of administrative measures and judicial decisions, is to be stopped when the Reich Protector objects to them.

" *Article VI.* (1) The foreign affairs of the Protectorate, and in particular the protection of State subjects abroad, are managed by the Reich. The Reich will direct foreign affairs in such a way as to consort with the general interest.

" (2) The Protectorate is to have a representative accredited to the Reich Government with the official title of ' Minister ' [*Gesandte*].

" *Article VII.* (1) The Reich provides for the military defence of the Protectorate.

" (2) In carrying out this protection the Reich keeps garrisons and military establishments in the Protectorate.

" (3) For the maintenance of internal security and order, the Protectorate can set up its own bodies. Their organisation, strength, number, and armament are determined by the Reich Government.

" *Article VIII.* The Reich takes direct charge of communications, as well as of the post and telephone system.

" *Article IX.* The Protectorate belongs to the Customs territory of the Reich and is subject to the Reich Customs authority.

" *Article X.* (1) Until further notice the crown will be legal tender along with the mark.

" (2) The Reich Government fixes the ratio of each money to the other.

" *Article XI.* (1) In so far as the common interest demands it, the Reich can promulgate orders applicable to the Protectorate.

" (2) In so far as there is a common need for it the Reich can take administrative branches into its own administration and set up the requisite Reich authorities.

" (3) The Reich Government can take measures necessary for the maintenance of law and order.

"*Article XII.* The law now in force in Bohemia and Moravia remains valid except in so far as it contradicts the spirit of the protection undertaken by the German Reich.

"*Article XIII.* The Reich Minister of the Interior promulgates, in agreement with the other competent Ministers, the legal and administrative rules necessary for the execution and amplification of this proclamation."

Thus Bohemia was deprived of its independence which had lasted for many centuries and which, from a juridical point of view, had not entirely disappeared even under Austria. Now it was delivered over, not only to the mercy, but also to the administration of Hitler's Germany. On March 18, Baron von Neurath was appointed Protector of Bohemia and Moravia, and at the same time the notoriously brutal Henlein leader, Karl Hermann Frank, was appointed State Secretary, and Freiherr von Burgsdorff became private secretary to the former. At the beginning of April General Frederici was entrusted with the military administration and one of his first duties was to liquidate the Czech Army. The authority of Baron von Neurath extended above that of President Hácha and the Prague Government; the latter continued in a formal manner to exercise its functions, although to all intents and purposes the actual power was transferred into German hands.

Hitler remained in Prague for one day only, March 16, and fortunately showed sufficient courage merely to exhibit himself on the balcony of the Hrad to the German children who had come to welcome him. On the afternoon of the same day he received President Hácha in special audience. (President Hácha had returned to Prague from Berlin on the previous day, but his train was so late that Hitler was already at the Hrad before his arrival.) Besides him, Hitler received only General Syrový, the Minister of National Defence, and the representatives of the Municipality of Prague, headed by Dr. Klapka, the Lord Mayor of Prague, who had entered into office at the end of February as successor to Dr. Peter Zenkl, an adherent of Dr. Beneš. The Cabinet headed by Beran was received only by Ribbentrop. On March 17, Hitler left for Olomouc and Brno, where he was welcomed by Bürckel, Governor of Vienna, and the

Vice-Governor Seyss-Inquart. He then proceeded to Vienna. Meanwhile the military occupation of the Czech territories had been completed; only in a few places had there been demonstrations of any gravity. The German Army was, of course, accompanied by the Gestapo, which immediately started on its task of arresting people and sending them off to hastily improvised concentration camps. The Gestapo made a special point of tracking down the *emigrés* from Germany who had still remained in Czecho-Slovakia, and also those Czechs who had been associated with Dr. Beneš. The Jews were seized with panic, and many of them committed suicide as early as March 15. There then arose a new problem of the *emigrés* from the Czech territories, who comprised, of course, not only the Jews, but also the Czecho-Slovak democrats. The German officers and troops behaved correctly, their aim being to get on well with the Czech people. Many of the soldiers wanted to know where the violent battles had occurred in which the Czech " Bolsheviks " had shed German blood. They were very surprised when they discovered that no such battles had taken place. When they had started on their march to the Czech regions, Hitler had made a special proclamation to them, in the course of which he had said: " In Bohemia and Moravia there is an intolerable reign of terror against the Germans." When they reached these areas, they had an opportunity of convincing themselves that their Leader was inaccurate. How deliberately the occupation had been prepared may be judged by the fact that from the very first day Nazi Commissars were assigned, not only to the public offices, but to all the newspapers, as well as to the social and cultural institutions, including even the libraries. As early as March 15 printed directions in German were issued to persons wishing to leave the country. German " thoroughness " was displayed in such details as this, but at the same time it revealed the fact that the occupation had been carefully prepared a long time beforehand. This had been done, of course, on the basis of the full reports which the Nazis from Bohemia and Moravia had sent regularly to Berlin. That is why the Germans were able so rapidly to occupy the public offices and institutions; that is why all persons in political or professional circles who had shown themselves troublesome or dangerous were able at once to be arrested or placed under observation; and that, too, is why the incoming Germans managed to establish themselves so promptly in the various important economic concerns and above all in the armament and export industries. All the economic wealth of the Czech territories (it should not be forgotten that Bohemia comprised 75 per cent. of all the economic resources of former Austria) were seized by Germany. From the very outset, too, the supplies of grain and the industrial commodities were " bought up " or simply confiscated—the Czech territories continued for some time to be the object of Nazi looting. And from the very first day huge quantities of war material and foodstuffs were systematically taken out of the country by instalments. Within two weeks, the Germans had transported from the country 48,000 machine guns (heavy and light); 1,500,000 rifles; 600,000,000 rounds of ammunition for machine guns and rifles; 2,500 guns (of different calibres), 4,500,000 rounds of ammunition for the artillery: as well as 600 tanks and 1,000 aeroplanes. All this material was simply seized, without any sort or kind of compensation.

The German occupation upset not only the constitutional and administrative order which had hitherto existed in the Munich Republic, but also the whole of the political organisation. At first complete confusion prevailed. Straightaway on March 15 a " Czech National Committee " was set up entirely of its own accord. It consisted mostly of Gajda's followers and of the *Vlajka* group, although it contained also several former Deputies belonging to other parties. At the same time Gajda, imagining that his chance had now come, rashly issued a proclamation to the people in which he forced himself upon them as their " leader." But the Germans perceived that it would be more expedient, at least in the early stages, if the political conduct of affairs were left in the hands of President Hácha and the Government of Beran (the Ministries dealing with foreign and military affairs had, of course, been immediately closed down).

President Hácha, it has not escaped notice, did everything to meet the wishes of the Nazis. He lacked the moral strength to oppose the ultimatum forced upon him in the night of March 14–15, and he then became an obedient implement of Nazi policy.

In the wireless message which he delivered on the evening of March 16, he went so far as to admit that, even in 1918, when the nation was liberated, he had felt doubtful " whether all the external and internal guarantees for a lasting character " of the freedom which had been secured were at hand. " What we regarded as a settlement which would last for ages," he said, "has proved to be only a brief episode in our national history." The Nazis were, of course, able to utilise so docile and adaptable a man for their own purposes, and they, therefore, preferred him to Gajda, who was an adventurer whom nobody among the Czech people took at all seriously; however, Gajda is being kept in reserve, in case he may be useful later on. On March 21, President Hácha nominated the Committee of National Trusteeship, comprising fifty members from various former political parties, including also the Social-Democrats and some from the Fascist groups. At the same time Parliament was dissolved. President Hácha himself became " Leader " of the National Trusteeship, and Adolf Hruby, an Agrarian, its Chairman. The latter declared: " The system of political parties is abolished. The Committee of the National Trusteeship is the sole representative of political life in Bohemia and Moravia." The new Committee was immediately inspired by a great ambition: it wished to act as substitute for Parliament. On March 25 it recommended to President Hácha that there should be " a political concentration of the nation in one totalitarian party," that the Committee of National Trusteeship should be invested with the authority of Parliament and other representative bodies, that all political parties and movements should be immediately dissolved, that anti-Semitic measures on the model of the Nürnberg laws should be introduced, that the duty to work should be made compulsory, etc. President Hácha was obliged to moderate this great zeal. He expressly refused to invest the National Trusteeship with parliamentary authority, and decided that it was entitled to deal with the political organisation of the people and to form " advisory bodies representing the various movements." The National Trusteeship became the sole political party allowed to exist and it was established on completely totalitarian lines. On April 1, " on the instructions of the leader of the nation," i.e. President Hácha, the two still existing parties which had been established after Munich, the party of National Unity and the National Labour Party were superseded. The Communist Party had been dissolved as far back as the autumn of 1938. While these parties presented no difficulties, Gajda had not yet been disposed of. It is true that on March 30 he had proclaimed the dissolution of the " Czech National Committees " which he had organised from the day of the occupation, and he called upon his followers to work with him in the National Trusteeship. But this co-operation was far from satisfactory.

From April 1 onwards the whole of the Czech Press was officially co-ordinated as the Press of the " National Trustee-ship "; in practice it is strictly controlled by the propaganda of Dr. Goebbels and simply publishes Czech versions of the German material supplied to it. On April 2 the Committee of the National Trusteeship issued a bombastic proclamation to the " Czechs," promising that it would build up the national life " on three fundamental pillars: (1) national community, (2) social justice in the class order, (3) morality and education in the national and Christian spirit." The destruction of state independence was in-separably bound up with the destruction of the democratic order upon which this independence had been constructed. Thus in a negative way it was confirmed that the independence of the Czecho-Slovak nation had been inseparably associated with the democratic idea and order.

With the liquidation of Czecho-Slovakia, the autonomous Carpathian Ukraine also became a thing of the past. As soon as the Slovak Diet had proclaimed the independence of Slovakia on March 14, Mgr. Vološin proclaimed also the independence of the Carpathian Ukraine and formed a new Government, in which he appointed as Foreign Minister Julian Revay, who at this moment was staying in Berlin. But on the same day the Magyar Government presented Prague with an ultimatum demanding the withdrawal of Czech troops from the Carpathian Ukraine within twelve hours. On the afternoon of the same day, Hun-garian troops crossed the frontier of the Carpathian Ukraine and approached Chust. Vološin telegraphed to Berlin for help, but did not receive it. He was compelled to escape into Rumania. His offer that the Carpathian Ukraine should be incorporated with Rumania was declined by Bucharest, which occupied some

Rumanian communes near the frontier but did nothing further.
Vološin then withdrew into Yugoslavia. On March 16, the
Hungarian Government proclaimed the annexation of the Carpathian Ukraine as follows: " Herewith we incorporate this land
in Hungary . . . and guarantee autonomy to our brother-nation,
the Ruthenians." There were a number of encounters, accompanied by bloodshed, between the Hungarian troops and the
Ukrainian *Sič*; the Ukrainians, however, were defeated. The
Czech soldiers had no reason to risk their lives for the cause of
the Greater Ukrainian Nationalists, who had hitherto served the
Germans. Little by little, they were taken back to the Czech
lands, as the conditions permitted. On March 17, the Hungarian
Government officially announced that the occupation of the
Carpathian Ukraine had been completed. Although local
struggles continued then and later, they made no change in the
prevailing conditions. After the liquidation of Czecho-Slovakia,
Germany was no longer so greatly interested in the maintenance
of an autonomous Carpathian Ukraine: from a strategic point of
view it was enough for the Germans to have complete control
over Bohemia and Moravia and for their troops to hold the main
positions in Slovakia. In this way Germany had direct access
to the Carpathians (against Poland), and at the same time was
more sure of Hungary than before. To-day, as before, there is
nothing to stop her from marching through Carpathian Ukraine
even though this territory has come under the sovereignty of
Hungary, for now that Germany has gained control of Slovakia,
Hungary does not present her with any serious obstacle. The
Ukrainians have now had ample opportunity of discovering
what they mean to the Germans: a somewhat primitive tool
which is scornfully cast aside as soon as it proves of no further
use.

Moreover, Slovak independence itself lasted actually only for
the one day on which it was proclaimed. As early as March 15,
Tiso sent the following telegram to Hitler:

" With strong confidence in you, the Führer and Chancellor
of the Greater German Reich, the Slovak state places itself
under your protection. The Slovak state asks you to undertake this protection."

On the next day Hitler replied:

" I confirm the receipt of your telegram of yesterday, and herewith undertake the protection of the Slovak state."

Thus, those who with the help of the Germans had done their utmost to drag Slovakia away from what was alleged to be its subservience to the Czechs, had by their own efforts merely made it a real vassal of Germany. Scarcely had they succeeded in putting into effect the war-cry " Away with the Czechs ! " than the gates of Slovakia were open wide for the arrival of the Germans. From March 16 onwards German troops continued to pour into Slovakia and to occupy all the strategic positions of any importance. It was not easy for Tiso's Government to explain to the Slovak people the arrival of the German troops. Šano Mach, in a wireless message on March 16, admitted that this circumstance had caused " considerable excitement " among the people. He expressed the assurance, however, that this did not mean an " occupation " of the Slovak territories, but protection against the Hungarian and Ukrainian troops and also against the Czech troops—to make sure that they would really leave the country. " The presence of the German troops," he declared, " guarantees complete security to the Slovak people." Murgaš, the commander of the Hlinka Guards, ordered those in charge of them to place themselves everywhere at the disposal of the German military leaders.

On March 23 a German-Slovak " protective agreement " was signed in Berlin. Under its terms, Germany made herself responsible for the integral character of the Slovak state. The German armed forces were entitled to set up military bases on the new Slovak territory and to convey commodities and foodstuffs to them without paying any duty. In the zone indicated, supreme military justice would be exercised by the German armed forces; German subjects would be submitted to German courts during the time they were occupied there with the establishment of the military bases. The Slovak Government would organise its army in close consultation with the German armed forces and would always pursue its foreign policy in close consultation with the German Government. This agreement is to remain in force for a period of twenty-five years.

Thus Slovakia, in a formal respect, also became subject to the power of Germany. Though it outwardly maintained a Government of its own, it was in reality completely under the sway of the Third Reich. The difference between the position of the Czech territories and Slovakia was merely one of external formality: there were German troops in both of them. Hitler rewarded the treachery of the Slovak separatists by allowing them to play at having an independent Government with ministries for foreign and military affairs. In other respects, he reserved to himself the right to make all decisions; for his military requirements, he immediately marked off a definite zone on Slovak territory and subordinated it directly to the German military and judicial authorities.

The Slovaks at once learned what reliance could be placed on Hitler's word. When on Sunday, March 20, the independence of Slovakia was celebrated throughout the country, Prime Minister Tiso made a speech in which he said that Hitler had declared to him: " I will act as a surety for the complete independence of Slovakia and guarantee its frontiers. . . . The historical frontiers of Slovakia are inviolable and will remain so for all time." But Hitler had obviously reserved to himself the right to decide where these " inviolable Slovak frontiers " ran. By that time a serious struggle had already started between Slovaks and Hungarians concerning the eastern frontiers of Slovakia. The Hungarians entered Eastern Slovakia from the Carpathian Ukraine on the pretext that these regions were inhabited by Ruthenians who were separated from the Carpathian Ukraine in 1919 by an artificial frontier which the Czechs had set up. The Slovaks did not acknowledge this point of view, and accordingly serious fighting ensued between the Hungarian troops and Slovak detachments. Aircraft also took part in these hostilities. The Slovaks appealed for help to their German Protector, but he hesitated, being unwilling to anger the Hungarians, who, for reasons of power politics, meant more to him for the time being than did the weak Slovaks. The Germans gave no assistance to the Slovaks, but merely urged them to reach an agreement with the Hungarians. This agreement, which was reached at the beginning of April, had to be paid for by Slovakia, which surrendered to Hungary roughly all those regions which were claimed by Budapest. And thus at the very outset of their " independence " the " liberated Slovaks " discovered to their cost that they too were only Hitler's plaything, to be used or discarded according to the requirements of his power interests.

In general, one can sum up by saying that everything which has happened since Munich has proved with tragic clarity certain facts of supreme importance for the present and for the future.

1. It is impossible to trace ethnographical frontiers in Czechoslovakia—or in any part whatever of Central Europe. After the decisions of Munich and Vienna, there were still national minorities in Czechoslovakia, whereas at the same time the minorities in Germany, Hungary and Poland had been increased. The rigid and unilateral application of the ethnic principle in these regions will always engender prodigious absurdities. Germany herself, who appealed to this principle to justify her claims concerning the Sudeten Germans, violated it immediately by annexing regions with a Czech majority or even purely Czech, while even Poland annexed considerably more Czechs than Poles. The principle which, in fact, Germany pursued at Munich and again in March, 1939, was not the right of peoples to dispose of themselves, but the advisability for " dynamic " nations to seize strategic vantage points. (*See* Appendices I and II.)

2. The destruction at Munich of the organic unity of Bohemia produced such considerable economic difficulties that Germany forced Prague to give many economic privileges to the annexed Sudeten regions; in reality, it was not the new frontier but the old historic frontier of Bohemia which remained—for Germany as for Czechoslovakia—the most convenient economic and Customs boundary between Germany and Czechoslovakia.

3. The annexation of the important German-Czech territories was purposely arranged in such a way that Czechoslovakia was deprived of all possibility of independent life, either militarily or economically. Inevitably Czechoslovakia became the vassal of Germany and even this was but the transition stage which led to complete subjection.

4. The experience of Munich and after Munich proved for the benefit of all small and isolated states that there is no such thing as friendly and loyal collaboration with the Third Reich. The

only independence which the Nazis respect is that which is militarily effective; what they seek from others is their complete submission to Nazi orders. With the best will in the world, the Beran Government, which consisted exclusively of men who had consistently advocated collaboration with the Third Reich, achieved nothing. The policy of Beneš, based on the conviction that there was no middle road between complete independence and complete submission, has been tragically justified by the whole of the Munich experience.

5. The federalisation of Czechoslovakia, demanded by the Slovak autonomists and encouraged by the Germans and Hungarians, led to the complete decomposition of the State for which not only the Czechs but the Slovaks also paid by subjection to foreign rule. The weakening of the Czechs delivered the Slovaks over to the cynical game of Germany and her neighbours, whose ultimate result justifies the conception of Czecho-Slovak unity which alone guarantees to each of them their liberty and independence. The solution of the so-called Slovak problem is not federation, but the decentralisation of administrative power. Equally, this is the only way to reach a workable and satisfactory solution of the German minority problem.

6. In the post-Munich Republic it was obvious that the country was further weakened by the suppression of democratic government. Czechoslovak democracy perished with Czechoslovak independence, since each was inextricably bound up with the other. Masaryk was proved to be right in his estimate that democracy was the only possible form of government for the Czechoslovak state. The existence of dictatorial forms of government, however, in all the neighbouring countries inevitably brought upon Czechoslovakia the dislike of its neighbours. The hatred of the Nazis and the aversion of the Hungarian and Polish gentry was for the risk entailed for their own forms of government by the prospect of an advanced and prosperous democracy at their gates.

7. The loss of Czechoslovak independence was due to the fact that the Czechs were, at the critical moment, left completely isolated before Germany. Every country in Europe, not excluding the Great Powers, would suffer the same fate if it was left completely single-handed to deal with the direct onslaught of an

80,000,000 Nazi Germany. It was this realisation, in the spring of 1939, which suddenly convinced even the British Government of the necessity for a policy of collective security and the creation of an anti-aggression front, which included, not only the small Powers which were directly menaced, but the Great Powers whose outlying defences they were suddenly realised to be. The great injustice to Czechoslovakia was that it paid the price which brought wisdom to the rest of Europe. The Czechs were the victims of an international policy which realised too late the necessity for a system of collective security if peace or freedom are to be preserved.

8. The destruction of Czechoslovakia changed sharply and abruptly the whole balance of forces between the European nations. This change has already reverberated throughout the entire world. The old dictum of Bismarck that the master of Bohemia was the master of Europe reappears in modern form and once more it is shown that the peoples of Europe cannot afford to disinterest themselves in the fate of the Czechoslovak people, which has been shown to change the face of Europe. Czechoslovakia, enslaved by Germany, increases the potential German military and economic strength to such an extent that the Germans are in a position to proceed with the realisation of their dream of a *Mitteleuropa* from Hamburg to Constantinople which all the rest of Europe combined could not equal in strength. There is not, and there cannot be, a free and justly balanced Europe without a free Czechoslovakia. The restoration of Czechoslovak independence is of vital interest, not only to the Czechoslovaks, but to all the nations of Europe if they want to live in freedom, justice and veritable peace.

4. International Crisis.

The forcible liquidation of Czechoslovakia caused world-wide alarm, although nothing was done to prevent it. Apparently, until the very last moment, nobody would believe that Germany would take possession of Czechoslovakia by military means. Of course, in September, 1938, Hitler had given a solemn assurance that after the inclusion of the Sudeten Germans in the Reich he would have no further territorial demands in Europe. On September 27 he stated publicly in the Sport Palace at Berlin:

" I assured Mr. Chamberlain, and I repeat this assurance
here, that once the Sudeten problem is settled, there will be
no further territorial problems in Europe, and I also assured
him that as soon as Czechoslovakia has settled the other problems . . . the Czech state will be of no further interest to me
and that I would, for my part, guarantee it. We want no more
Czechs within our frontiers."

It is true that purely Czech areas were included in the fifth
and sixth zones which Germany annexed, but no importance
was attached to this in Europe. Hitler's word was believed. After
Munich Chamberlain and Daladier emphasised that the guarantee which Great Britain and France offered Czechoslovakia
against unprovoked attack would ensure for it the possibility of
a free existence, even though reduced in size. The policy of
Munich met with approval in Great Britain and France because
it had saved peace for a lengthy period. Some people imagined
that whole generations would derive a benefit from this peace.

Six months had not yet elapsed when Hitler, disregarding the
solemn promises which he had made in September, 1938, tore up
the Munich Agreement. The thing which nobody wanted to believe until the very last moment, in spite of reports concerning
the movements of German troops towards the Czechoslovak
frontiers, became an accomplished fact: Hitler took possession
of the whole of Czechoslovakia. The whole world was thus able
to convince themselves of what the Czechoslovaks had previously—in vain—tried to convince them, namely that the Sudeten
Germans were not the real issue at all, but that they were being
used only as a means for destroying the independent Czechoslovak Republic, which formed an obstacle to Hitler's plans for
gaining possession of Central Europe and finally of all Europe.
Moreover, in April, 1939, it became plain to everyone that
Hitler's appetite for territory had not been satisfied even by the
seizure of Czecho-Slovakia, when, within a fortnight, he had
annexed Memel (March 22) and was openly threatening Poland.

The reaction throughout the world was considerable, certainly
more considerable than the Germans seem to have expected. In
a speech at Birmingham on March 17 the British Prime Minister
bitterly condemned Hitler's action and asked:

" Does not the question inevitably arise in our minds, if it is easy to discover good reasons for ignoring assurances so solemnly and so repeatedly given, what reliance can be placed upon any other assurance that comes from the same source ? "

In an important speech which Lord Halifax made in the House of Lords on March 20, he adopted an attitude of most determined opposition to Germany's forcible procedure.

" On all the evidence that is available to me, I find it impossible to believe that the sudden decision of certain Slovak leaders to break off from Prague, which was followed so closely by their appeal for protection to the German Reich was reached independently of outside influence. It is said that German intervention in Czecho-Slovakia was justified in the oppression of the German minority by the Czechs. Whatever may have been the truth about the treatment of 250,000 Germans, it is impossible for me to believe that that can ever be remedied by the subjugation of 8,000,000 Czechs.

" Actually the position of the German minority, which is about 250,000, would appear, since the Munich Agreement, to be one which might be termed of exceptional privilege. Notwithstanding the right of option which had been accorded by Article 7 of that Agreement, the members of the German minority were encouraged to remain in Czecho-Slovakia in order that they might form useful centres of German activity and propaganda, an advice to that effect was given to the minority by its leader. It was as a result of the German-Czecho-Slovak agreement for the mutual protection of minorities that the German Government obtained the legal right to take a direct interest in their minority in Czecho-Slovakia, and that minority at once obtained the right to set up separate organisations, and the Czecho-Slovak Government subsequently agreed that the German National-Socialist Party in Czecho-Slovakia should be given full liberty to pursue its activities in Bohemia and Moravia.

" It is difficult to avoid the conclusion that the bulk of incidents which occurred before the German invasion were deliberately provoked and that the effects were greatly magnified. It must, I think, be added in fairness that the

Czecho-Slovak authorities received orders to act and did act with great restraint in the face of that provocation.

" It is not necessary, I think, to say much upon the assertion that the Czecho-Slovak President really assented to the subjugation of his people. In view of the circumstances in which he came to Berlin and of the occupation of Czech territory which had already taken place, I think most sensible people must conclude that there is little pretence of negotiation and that it is more probable that the Czech representatives were presented with an ultimatum under the threat of violence and that they capitulated in order to save their people from the horrors of a swift and destructive aerial bombardment. . . .

"We have also taken occasion to protest against the changes effected in Czecho-Slovakia by German military action and have said that in our view those changes are devoid of any basis of legality.

" It is quite true that we have always recognised that for reasons of geography, if for no other, Germany must, from some points of view, be more interested in Czecho-Slovakia or South-Eastern Europe than we are ourselves.

" It was a natural field for the expansion of German trade, but, apart from the fact that changes in any part of Europe have produced profound effects elsewhere, the position is entirely changed when we are confronted with the arbitrary suppression of an independent sovereign state by armed force and by the violation of what I must regard as the elementary rules of international conduct. It is natural enough that in the light of these events the Government should be told that the policy of Munich was a tragic mistake. . . .

" German action in Czechoslovakia has been furthered by new methods. The world has lately seen more than one new departure in the field of international technique—wars without declaration of war, pressure exercised under threat of immediate employment of force, intervention in the internal struggles of other states. Countries are now faced with the encouragement of separatism, not in the interests of separatist or minority elements, but in the material interests of Germany. The ill-treatment of German minorities in foreign countries, which, it is true, may sometimes perhaps have arisen from natural causes, but which also may be the subject and result of provocation from outside, is used as a pretext for intervention. These methods are simple and with growing experience quite unmistakable. Have we any assurance that they will not be employed elsewhere ?

" Every country which is Germany's neighbour is now uncertain of the morrow, and every country which values its national identity and sovereignty stands warned against the danger from within inspired from without.

" It is not possible as yet fully to appraise the consequences of the German action. History records many attempts to impose a domination upon Europe. But all those attempts have sooner or later terminated in disaster for those who made them. (Cheers.) It has never in the long run proved possible to stamp out the spirit of free peoples. If history is any guide the German people may yet regret the action that has been taken in their name against the people of Czecho-Slovakia.

" Twenty years ago the people of Czecho-Slovakia recovered their liberties with the support and encouragement of the greater part of the world. They have now been deprived of them by violence. In the course of their long history this will not be the first time that this tenacious, valiant and industrious people have lost their independence, but they have never lost that which is the foundation of independence— the love of liberty. (Hear, hear.)

" Meanwhile, just as after the last War the world watched the emergence of the Czech nation, so it will watch to-day their efforts to preserve intact their cultural identity, and, more important, their spiritual freedom under the last and most cruel blow of which they have been the victims." (Cheers.)

France, also, found herself forced to reconsider the Munich policy. The French Prime Minister, Monsieur Daladier, declared on March 19:

" The Munich Agreement ? Destroyed. The joint declaration of Franco-German co-operation ? Infringed both in letter and spirit. All this has disappeared at the same time as there disappeared from the map of Europe, in spite of the most solemn commitments undertaken, a country about which I shall not say much, for it would be useless to do so. But I believe that the painful feelings by which we are overwhelmed at the sight of these tragic events will be realised by the Senate, which shares them."

Though these speeches by leading British and French statesmen were exceptionally strong, public opinion reacted in an even more violent manner. There was a unanimous refusal to recognise the forcible occupation of Czecho-Slovakia. The indignation was particularly marked in the United States of America. Ex-President Beneš (who was at the University of Chicago at the time), immediately after the German occupation, sent telegrams of protest to Roosevelt, Chamberlain, Daladier and Litvinov, as well as to the League of Nations, urging them " to refuse to recognise this crime and to assume the consequences which to-day's tragic situation in Europe and in the world urgently requires."

As early as March 16 it became known that the United States had refused to recognise the annexation of Czecho-Slovakia. Mr. Sumner Welles, Under-Secretary of State, declared:

" The Government of the United States has on frequent occasions stated its conviction that only through international support of a programme of order based upon law can world peace be assured. This Government, founded upon and dedicated to the principles of human liberty and of democracy, cannot refrain from making known this country's condemnation of the acts which have resulted in the temporary extinguishment of a free and independent people with whom, from the day when the Republic of Czechoslovakia attained its independence, the people of the United States have maintained especially close and friendly relations. . . . It is manifest that acts of wanton lawlessness and of arbitrary force are threatening world peace and the very structure of modern civilisation."

The Four Great Powers, Great Britain, France, United States and Soviet Russia, then adopted the same attitude. When the German Government, in its notes on March 16 and 17, notified to them the agreement concluded between Hitler and Hácha on the night of March 14–15, they replied that they did not recognise the annexation of Czecho-Slovakia. In its note of March 18, the French Government uttered a " categorical protest " and added with emphasis:

" The French Government consider, in fact, that the Reich Government's action against Czecho-Slovakia constitutes a flagrant violation of the letter and the spirit of the Agreement signed in Munich on September 29, 1938.

" The circumstances in which the agreement of March 15 was imposed on the heads of the Czecho-Slovak Republic cannot be regarded by the French Government as constituting *de jure* the state of affairs registered in this Agreement.

" The French Ambassador has the honour to inform the German Foreign Minister that the French Government cannot in these circumstances recognise the legitimacy of the new situation created in Czecho-Slovakia by the action of the Reich."

The British Government, too, sent a note of protest on March 18. With regard to this, Mr. Chamberlain said in the House of Commons on March 20:

" His Majesty's Ambassador in Berlin was instructed on March 17 to inform the German Government that His Majesty's Government desired to make it plain to them that they could not but regard the events of the past few days as a complete repudiation of the Munich Agreement and a denial of the spirit in which the negotiators of that Agreement bound themselves to co-operate for a peaceful settlement. Sir Nevile Henderson was also instructed to say that His Majesty's Government must take this occasion to protest against the changes effected in Czecho-Slovakia by German military action, which are, in their opinion, devoid of any basis of legality. . . .

" His Majesty's Government will require to give full consideration, in concert with other Governments, to all the consequences of German action against Czecho-Slovakia before any statement can be made on the question of recognition."
(Hear, hear.)

On March 19 the Soviet Government replied to Germany in a detailed note containing this declaration:

" The Soviet Government does not consider it possible to pass the above-mentioned Notes [the German Notes of March 16 and 17] in silence and thus create a false impression of its allegedly indifferent attitude to Czecho-Slovak events, and therefore finds it necessary, in answer to the above Notes, to express its real attitude to the aforesaid events.

" 1. The political and historical conceptions expounded in the introductory part of the German ordinance [announcing the establishment of the Protectorate] as grounds and justification for it [the German action], and in particular the references to the existence of the Czecho-Slovak state as a source of constant unrest and menace to European peace, to the lack of vitality of the Czecho-Slovak state and to the resulting necessity for particular care on the part of the German Empire—cannot be considered as correct and corresponding to the facts known to the whole world.

" In actual fact, after the first World War, the Czechoslovak Republic has been one of the few European states where internal tranquillity and a peaceable foreign policy were really secured.

" 2. The Soviet Government is not aware of any state constitution that entitles the head of a state to abolish its independent existence as a state without the consent of his people.

" It is difficult to admit that any people would voluntarily agree to the destruction of their independence and to their inclusion in another state, still less a people that for hundreds of years fought for their independence and for twenty years maintained their independent existence.

" In signing in Berlin the Act of March 15, Dr. Hácha, President of Czecho-Slovakia, had no authority from his people for doing so, and acted in manifest contradiction with Articles 64 and 65 of the Czecho-Slovak Constitution.

" Consequently, the aforesaid Act cannot be considered legally valid.

" 3. The principle of self-determination of nations, not infrequently referred to by the German Government, presupposes the free expression of the will of the people, which cannot be replaced by the signatures of one or two individuals, however high the positions they may occupy.

" In the present case there was no expression of the will of the Czech people, even in the form of such plebiscites as took place, for example, in determining the fate of Upper Silesia and the Saar region.

" 4. In the absence of any expression of the will of the Czech people, the occupation of the Czech provinces by German troops and the subsequent actions of the German Government cannot but be considered as arbitrary, violent and aggressive.

" 5. The above remarks also refer in their entirety to the change in the status of Slovakia, subordinating the latter to the German Empire, which was not justified by any expression of the will of the Slovak people.

" 6. The actions of the German Government served as a signal for the gross invasion of Carpatho-Ukraine [Ruthenia] by Hungarian troops and for the violation of the elementary rights of its population.

" 7. In view of the above, the Soviet Government cannot recognise the inclusion of the Czech provinces and also, in one form or other, of Slovakia in the German Empire to be legitimate and in conformity with the generally accepted standards of international law and justice or the principle of self-determination of nations.

" 8. In the opinion of the Soviet Government, the actions of the German Government, far from eliminating any danger to universal peace, have on the contrary created and enhanced such danger, violated political stability in Central Europe, increased the elements of alarm already previously created in Europe, and dealt a fresh blow to the feeling of security of the peoples."

Finally, the United States Government declared in its Note of March 21:

" The Government of the United States has observed that the provinces referred to are now under the *de facto* administration of the German authorities. The Government of the United States does not recognise that any legal basis exists for the status so indicated.

" The views of this Government with regard to the situation above referred to, as well as with regard to the related facts, were made known on March 17. I enclose herewith for the information of your Government a copy of the statement in which these views were expressed."

The statement was made by Mr. Welles, and read: " This Government, founded upon and dedicated to the principles of human liberty and of democracy, cannot refrain from making known this country's condemnation of the acts which have resulted in the temporary extinguishment of a free and independent people. . . ."

The refusal of these four Great Powers to recognise the German annexation of Czecho-Slovakia was not only of great importance as regards international politics, but also in its practical consequences to the Czecho-Slovaks themselves. The Czecho-Slovak Legations accredited to the Governments of these Great Powers refused to hand over their premises to the German Government, which claimed them, and they still continue to act as the officially recognised Czecho-Slovak representatives. In other countries, too, such as Poland, the existing Czecho-Slovak representatives have refused to submit to the authority of Germany. The continued existence of these Legations means that Czecho-Slovak independence has been maintained in a political and juridical respect throughout the world.

In Germany various attempts were made to justify the occupation of Czecho-Slovakia, but they failed in their object. Least of all did they succeed in their attempt to show that the occupation had taken place on the basis of an agreement reached with President Hácha. It was obvious to everyone that what had been done was an act of violence which could in no way be justified unless the arbitrary and brutal power of Germany were to be acknowledged as an international law. In the above-mentioned speech, Lord Halifax pointed out that even before the agreement had been reached, the German troops had already occupied Czech districts, and he rightly emphasised the fact that Hitler had done something which was at complete variance with the principles to which he had hitherto appealed and in the name of which he had in September secured the incorporation of the Sudeten Germans. The Nazis, who had dropped all pretence of aiming at the principle of self-determination, could only declare that the Czech territories are what they describe as " areas vital to Germany," but this is an utterly imperialistic conception; in accordance with it the " areas vital to the German nation " can be arbitrarily extended as far as German power will suffice to annex them. While, for various reasons, it had not been possible to convince the world of the real basis and meaning of the Munich Agreement, which turned Czechoslovakia into a vassal state of Germany and provided Pan-Germanism with an open road for the formation of a German *Mitteleuropa*, the forcible occupation of Czecho-Slovakia made it clear to everybody that not only the smaller nations of Central Europe, but the whole of Europe and, indeed, other continents as well, are most seriously threatened by the danger of the hegemony of the Third Reich united with the aggressive dictatorships of Italy and Japan.

The first effects of this recognition were displayed in the change of British policy towards Poland. At the end of March Poland was promised assistance by the British Government if her independence were threatened. From March 15 onwards the policy of the Western Powers began to reveal a change involving a return to the principles of collective security. This is one of the most significant vindications—unfortunately, it is far too late—of the policy pursued by independent Czechoslovakia until Munich.

The Czechoslovaks accepted Munich only under the overwhelming pressure of the Great Powers, and they accepted it with a solemn protest. They will never become reconciled with the subjection of their country to the brutal domination of Germany. President Hácha had no right, even of an externally formal character, to surrender the independence of Czecho-Slovakia. His action can be excused by the circumstance that he acted, not of his own free will, but under irresistible pressure. Whatever may be done by him or any other of the political figures who are tolerated in leading positions in the Czech and Slovak territorities through the indulgence of the German Protector (whom they have to obey unconditionally in every detail), their actions have not the slightest binding power upon the Czechoslovak nation. They cannot have any such power, because this nation, supervised as it is with the aid of German rifles, has no opportunity to express its opinions freely. Its true attitude was revealed by the Nazis themselves when their Press declared in March that the Czech nation had not changed even after Munich. In this the Nazis are right. How could it undergo a sudden change in its opinions, so unfavourable to the Nazis, now that it is itself directly exposed to Nazi despotism and violence ?

It is a falsification of history when Nazi propaganda declares that the addition of the Czech territories to the Reich renews a state of affairs which lasted for whole centuries. This statement continues to be wrong when uttered by Czechs who are answerable to the German Protector. It is true that in the Middle Ages the Czech Kingdom formed part of the " Holy Roman Empire of the German Nation," but it occupied there a position, not only involving freedom and equality of rights, but, in contrast to the territories of other imperial electoral princes, it enjoyed an altogether exceptional and privileged status by which it greatly differed from the other imperial lands. The Czech kings were more than once Roman-German emperors as well, and it was mainly from their title as Czech kings that the Hapsburgs acquired the rank of emperors. In any case, no comparison at all can be made between the Mediæval German Empire, comprising a completely free league of several more or less independent states, ecclesiastical principalities and cities, with the present-day Third Reich, which has abolished the last remnants of the federative order of the German territories, and which in all respects is administered by a principle of the most rigid totalitarianism. It is a complete distortion of historical facts when now Berlin proclaims, and Prague, in its subjection, parrot-like repeats, that the present position of the Czech territories renews the century-old tradition of the German-Czech relationship. On the contrary, this is the first time in history that the Czech territories were annexed by Germany. Moreover, the Third Reich has taken possession of Slovakia also, although the latter country never had anything whatever in common with the Holy Roman Empire. The fact is that the Nazis have no other justification for occupying Czechoslovakia than sheer numerical superiority and their own aggressive inclinations.

They have succeeded in destroying any free expression of the real will and true opinions of the Czechoslovak people. But they will never succeed in stifling their faith and overcoming their determination to recover their freedom.

Edward Beneš, the legitimate representative of the Czech nation, spoke on its behalf immediately after the Germans had seized his country. He is entitled to speak in this capacity, not only because until October, 1938, he was President of the Czecho-slovak Republic, and previously, from 1918 to 1935, its Foreign Minister, but above all because, as Masaryk's chief fellow-worker, he conducted the struggle of the nation for its freedom and unification, and he then, more than anybody else, helped it to build up and secure its renewed independence. He at once raised his voice against the " great international crime " in the tele-grams of protest which, as before mentioned, he sent to the leading statesmen of the four Great Powers and also to the League of Nations.

On March 18, at the University of Chicago, he made an appeal to the American people, in which he declared:

" In this tragic moment of European history I am address-ing this appeal to the American people.

" There is to-day in Central Europe a nation of Czechs and Slovaks whose territory has been violently invaded. Might has occupied a free country and subjugated a free people. A most brutal crime is perpetrated against this people. They have suddenly been robbed of everything they hold most dear and this crime has been committed as part of a carefully prepared programme—just as a common criminal plans for the robbery of an individual. The crime is committed within the framework of invasion by several hundred thousand soldiers, with hundreds of aeroplanes and tanks and military motor cars. And this tragedy occurs—this invasion comes—in time of peace and without provocation or excuse. . . .

" Five months ago, during the so-called September crisis, the Czechoslovak nation was asked to make the sacrifice of territory, and pressure was put upon my people not to fight for their freedom, integrity and independence, in order to save the world from war. The appeal was made to that little people to sacrifice themselves for the peace of the world. That little people did it. And that little people received the promise of the integrity of the remnant of its national territory and of the security of its national state. That little people, having made these sacrifices under pressure of the decisions at Munich, accepted, because the four Great Powers at Munich signed an obligation to guarantee the new state. . . .

" For twenty years I have worked for peace, for real peace. But to-day there is no peace in Europe. What is considered a state of peace is but a terrible illusion, an illusion which will one day take its toll in the enormous sacrifice of all the nations of the world. Because there is war already ! Yes, there is war to-day in Europe; but there is war on one side only, and while one party makes war, the other can merely look on.

" And again I say to the world that everybody must understand that there will be no peace, there will be no respite, there will be no order until the crimes that have been committed in Europe are wiped out, until there is again respect for the given word, until the idea of honesty—personal honesty and state honesty—is re-established, until the principles of the individual and international liberty are secured, and until real courage takes command and requires that brute force must stop.

" Don't forget that it is not only Europe that is involved, not only Central, South, and Eastern European nations, the French nation, the British nation, the Scandinavian nations, the people of the United States, but the whole world that is in danger, not only from war, but from the destruction of every high concept of human morality, by the demolition of every fine concept of liberty, by the disintegration of every concept of honesty and decency. That is the danger to-day. A society which continues to tolerate such a state of things will be destroyed and will disappear.

" I place before the world court of public opinion these facts and in at last stating clearly what I mean and what I feel, I continue to be a believer in the ideals of liberty and in the simple concept of human honesty and dignity. I know that in the history of mankind brute force has always fallen after every such brutal and terrible misuse of power. The man who in modern history has been taken as a symbol of brute force, Napoleon, has declared: ' There are in the world two powers— the Sword and the Spirit. The Spirit has always vanquished the Sword.' In this statement I agree with the words of Napoleon.

" I declare that the independence of Czechoslovakia was not crushed; it continues, it lives, it exists. And I solemnly declare that those who have perpetrated this crime against the Czechoslovak nation and against all mankind are guilty before God and will be punished.

" During the last months, and especially in the period that preceded and followed the September crisis, I have many times been attacked personally. I have never answered. I never shall answer. But until my last breath I shall continue the fight for the freedom of my people and for their rights, and I am sure that my nation will emerge from this struggle as it has done many times before in its history, as brave and as proud as she has been throughout the past, and having always with her the sympathy and the recognition and the love of all decent people in the world. And there is no more fitting place for me to make this declaration than in this free country of Washington and Lincoln.

" So I must end with an appeal to the American people. I would beg that they do not permit such conceptions and ideas as are now trying to dominate Europe to be tolerated *in this free country*. Because in the approaching battle for the victory of the Spirit against the Sword, the United States has a very great role to play. Be ready for that fight and be strong—O people of Democracy !

" To all right-thinking men and women everywhere I give the motto of my beloved nation—' *Truth prevails.*' "

Other Czechoslovak representatives abroad—above all, MM. Masaryk and Osuský, made similar declarations.

The Czechoslovaks, animated as they are by belief in the victory of the spirit over the sword, will unceasingly struggle for the restoration of an independent and democratic Czechoslovakia. They will carry on this struggle in common with all democrats and anti-Nazis of all nationalities, German included, with whom they lived closely associated in the free homeland which they shared with them. And they cherish the hope that in this struggle of theirs for a righteous cause they will be supported by all who desire a righteous establishment of a Europe of free nations in which alone lasting peace can be ensured.

CHAPTER VIII

Europe at the Crossroads

THE Germans and Italians are perfectly correct in maintaining that the Versailles system was overthrown at Munich. Not that everything which had been created by the victory of the Western democracies was destroyed; but the whole system on which post-war Europe was built up ceased to exist. The ruins of the League of Nations, which was the symbol, if not of all the aspects, at least of the most important tendencies of world politics after the war, themselves prove more plainly than anything else that the order established in 1919 is on the eve of extinction. The balance of power in Europe, in the maintenance of which an independent Czechoslovakia was the decisive factor, has been radically disturbed. To-day it turns in favour of the Third Reich and the new Italian Empire.

Nor is it only the relations between states which have been changed; the very foundations of those ideas and ideals on which the Peace of 1919–20 was built have been removed. The basic idea was the idea of world democracy, for which Great Britain, France and the United States of America had fought and still preserved. This ideal found its world-wide expression in the League of Nations and the International Court at The Hague. Its effect was apparent also in the domain of domestic politics. It found expression in the internal affairs of the great majority of the countries of Europe, not only in the west, but in Germany, Poland, the Danube Basin and the Balkans. Even in Soviet Russia, after the first violence of the Bolshevik revolution had died down, an approach was made towards democratic ideas. This period has now passed.

The victorious progress of German National Socialism, seconded by Italian Fascism, threatens not only the international order set up by the victory of 1918, but also the democratic principle which was its basis. The rule of law, respect for the rights and freedom of the individual are giving way to a system where force, violence and the oppression of the weak by the strong are the rule. Might is right in a world where the strongest rules. The advocates of Pan-Germanism, whose most masterful prophet is Hitler himself, inculcate this doctrine into every sphere of life, in the relations between individuals and between states. The Munich Agreement not only opened the way for the territorial advance of Pan-Germanism, but created the moral and psychological conditions for its rapid penetration.

In analysing the causes which led to the Munich Agreement, inevitably the question of responsibility arises. As a Czechoslovak citizen, I shall confine myself to examining the responsibility of Czechoslovakia.

1. *Czechoslovak Responsibility for the Munich Agreement.*

(a) *Czechoslovak Minority Policy.* It has often been said that Czechoslovakia, by her refusal to solve the Sudeten-German problem, brought, or at least helped to bring, the catastrophe upon herself. Some people even go so far as to seek the root of the cause in the Peace Treaties which placed the Sudeten Germans within the Czechoslovak frontiers. All those who have studied the problem at all will know, however, that the question whether the historic frontier dividing Germany and Bohemia should be maintained, or whether the Sudeten Germans should not in fact be transferred to Germany, never in fact arose. It was a matter simply of confirming an actual state of affairs and not of creating a new one; the Sudeten Germans had never formed part of Germany, but had, on the contrary, always formed an integral part of Bohemia. For this reason, therefore, after long deliberation based on extensive information (at Munich decisions were taken without detailed information and after a few hours discussion), the delegates to the Peace Conference decided that it was impossible to apply rigorously in Central Europe the principle of national self-determination on account of the intermingling of national groups, and the necessity also to take into consideration economic, geographical and strategic factors. All these reasons convinced the competent Committees of the Peace Conference that the most reasonable solution was to maintain intact the former frontiers of Germany and Bohemia. The representatives of the Great Powers would not even listen to the proposal put forward by the Czechoslovak delegate, M. Beneš. Beneš, who was then Czechoslovak Foreign Minister, proposed that, in return for certain German concessions,

Czechoslovakia should cede to Germany certain districts on the north and west of Bohemia which were inhabited almost exclusively by a German-speaking population. This rectification of the German-Czech frontier would have reduced the German minority in Czechoslovakia by about 800,000 so that the number remaining would not have been many more than 2,000,000. Though this arrangement would probably have simplified the problem, it would not, of course, have been disposed of entirely.

When the Peace Conference realised the impossibility of establishing homogeneous national states in Central Europe, it decided to concern itself with the protection of minorities, and the League of Nations was charged with the realisation of this principle. The only legal obligation which Czechoslovakia undertook was that arising from its signature of the Treaty of St. Germain on September 10, 1919, a part of which was devoted to the protection of minorities. From a formal, juristic point of view, the famous Memorandum on the treatment of the Sudeten-German minority which the Czechoslovak Delegation submitted to the Conference on May 20, 1919, was not binding on the new state. It did, however, put a moral obligation on the Czechoslovak Government, and its author, Beneš (to quote his own words), "took very seriously" the promises made in this Memorandum. Together with President Masaryk, he made constant efforts to see that the minority policy of the Czechoslovak Republic conformed to the principles which he had laid down.

It is entirely false to suppose that the Memorandum promised a federal or autonomous régime to the Sudeten Germans. In so far as the question of the Swiss model arose (" the régime shall be similar to that of Switzerland ") the intention was that the régime should be as liberal and tolerant towards all minorities as is the Swiss. Furthermore, certain necessary reservations were made: " The intentions of the Czechoslovak Government are to create . . . a sort of Switzerland, *taking into account, naturally, the special conditions of Bohemia.*"

It is possible however, to reproach the minority policy of Czechoslovakia with having often been inspired by a narrow and provincial nationalism which compromised the best intentions of the Government and the political leaders. This narrow-minded nationalism, which ignored both the principle of national justice and the necessity for good relations with Germany, was consistently opposed by Masaryk, Beneš and their followers. This did not prevent them from being the object of the special hatred of Hitler and the Nazis. In fact, the Nazis, who constantly proclaimed their concern for their co-nationals in Czechoslovakia, deliberately sought the support of the most narrow and Chauvinist Czech political parties in their efforts to destroy the democratic Republic of Masaryk and Beneš.

But whatever may have been the faults—and we do not deny them—of the Czechoslovak minority policy no impartial observer could deny the following facts:

1. The régime accorded to the national minorities in Czechoslovakia, not only fulfilled all the obligations of the Treaty of St. Germain concerning the protection of minorities, but considerably exceeded those obligations by granting greater rights to the minorities than those laid down by Treaty. From the point of view of international law, it is impossible to raise any complaints on this score against the Czechoslovak state. Moreover, the Czechoslovak Government always declared itself ready to carry out all decisions and all recommendations formulated by the League of Nations.

2. In spite of its faults, the Czechoslovak minority régime was on the whole exceedingly liberal and tolerant. From 1926 onwards, when certain German parties entered the Government, close collaboration was established between the Czechs and Germans. This progress was arrested by the victory of Hitler in Germany, though, even after 1933, an understanding between the Czechs and Germans was not out of the question. It was only after the two Western Powers encouraged the triumph of Henleinism and of Nazism that every effort to reach an agreement was doomed to fail.

3. No other state in Europe treated its national minorities more liberally or more justly than Czechoslovakia. No comparison can be made between Czechoslovakia and Belgium and Switzerland, since neither of the two latter countries had " minorities " in the sense in which they existed in Czechoslovakia.

To reproach Czechoslovakia with having pursued an unjust minority policy is either to confess complete ignorance of the facts or to prove bad faith. Certain critics, however, put forward a more specific complaint. According to these, we were reproached for not having reached an agreement with the Sudeten German Party of Konrad Henlein. In fact, it was precisely in believing that an understanding of this sort was possible, that the Great Powers made their fatal mistake. The Henlein party was simply an instrument in the hands of the Pan-Germans of the Third Reich. They were far more dependent on the decisions of Berlin than are the Communists on the decisions of Moscow. In spite of the disagreement of certain Henleinists (whose fate recalls the fate of Hugenberg's *Deutschnationale*), the Nazification of the party took place very rapidly and proved fatal to all understanding. Henleinism was simply the form of National Socialism which was considered suitable for the Sudeten Germans and for the conditions of a Parliamentary democracy. " Agreement," as we have over and over again pointed out, was possible only if the method of Munich was applied—that is, on the basis of handing over everything which they demanded. If Czechoslovakia wanted to maintain her independence, agreement with the Henleinists was completely out of the question, because the final aim of this party was simply to bring the Czechs under German domination. The Czech Agrarians who thought they could " pacify " the Henleinists and win the favour of Berlin by admitting the Henlein leaders into the Government were making a fatal mistake. In fact, they would simply have introduced the Trojan Horse into the town of Prague and permitted the Germans to install German supremacy behind the Czechoslovak ramparts. An agreement with the Henlein party would, as we have shown, have made Czechoslovakia, by her own action, the vassal of Germany. Though we have not avoided the most complete and brutal domination by Germany, it was not we who admitted the enemy within our fortifications. This is important for the future.

In the Introduction I have mentioned two criticisms which were levelled at Czechoslovak policy so far as the conversations with the Henlein party were concerned in the months immediately preceding the September catastrophe. The first was that we should have submitted a far-reaching scheme of local autonomy and carried it out, if necessary, without the co-operation of the Henlein party. This criticism, in my opinion, is just, but I have shown why it was difficult to do this. The second was that we should categorically have refused any sort of negotiation with the Henlein party. Unfortunately, this attitude, though justified by the impossibility of reaching agreement, would have been difficult, if not impossible, in the circumstances. Neither in England nor in France would this attitude have been approved and its adoption would only have assisted the work of German propaganda in presenting Czechoslovakia as the real threat to world peace. We had, therefore, at least to attempt to negotiate, and we hoped the fact that it was we who in every deadlock gave way and made concessions would ultimately convince the Western Powers that goodwill was not lacking on our side, but that we were faced with the demands of a revolutionary Pan-German movement which concerned Europe as a whole and which Europe as a whole alone could stem.

It worked out otherwise. As General Faucher said: " The Sudeten-German problem arose because Czechoslovakia had been abandoned. So long as nobody doubted that there were forces in Europe which could come to the aid of Czechoslovakia and maintain the order of the Peace Treaties, there was no question of Sudeten-German secession."

(b) *Czechoslovakia and Germany.* Czechoslovakia has also been reproached for her failure to establish friendly relations with Germany—paradoxically enough, this criticism has often been made by French nationalists. Czechoslovak foreign policy was from the beginning of the Czechoslovak state under the direction of Dr. Beneš, first as Foreign Minister and, after 1935, as Presi-of the Republic. Though his influence was supreme, Dr. Beneš disposed of no dictatorial powers, and his policy was necessarily limited by the exigencies of the internal and external situation. Even a slight acquaintance with Czechoslovak foreign policy reveals that Beneš, in his relations with Germany, always tried to conform to those principles which he himself laid down in his first speech to the Czechoslovak Parliament on September 30, 1919 (Dr. Beneš had just returned to Prague after his four years' work in Paris during the War had been crowned with success):

" As far as our future relations with Germany are concerned, they are a *vital problem* for our young republic, and we must therefore study this question with extreme care and the utmost caution. Present-day Germany is an unfinished product; it will be fully occupied by its internal crises for some years to come. It will certainly soon try to have its say in world affairs, but for a long time will be unable to force its will upon even a state much less powerful than is, for example, the Czechoslovak Republic. It is in our interest to pursue a loyal and proper policy towards Germany, and thereby early to establish a tradition in our relationship; but we can never allow ourselves to become an instrument in the hands of our neighbour, and consequently to lose our liberty, our political, diplomatic and military importance."

After the war, the relations between Germany and Czechoslovakia took, on the whole, a favourable turn. There was no direct hostility between the two countries and no appreciable tension. Berlin understood quite well that Czechoslovakia should seek support in a Franco-Czech alliance, and even the Little Entente appeared to no one as an alliance directed against Germany. A satisfactory solution of all the questions which arose directly between the two countries was easily found. Dr. Beneš has himself described in detail the relations between the two countries during this period.[1]

" The Treaty of Versailles gave Czechoslovakia—in addition to general clauses allowing certain rights to all the signatories of the treaty—two important advantages affecting Czechoslovakia alone: the sequestration of German property and the internationalisation of the Elbe and Oder, with a free zone in Hamburg and Stettin.

" As has already been remarked, Prague renounced the first of these rights as early as 1921, immediately after the amount of the reparations was fixed. In 1925 Prague spontaneously took a second step: the Government sent Dr. Krofta—now Minister of Foreign Affairs—to Berlin with an offer of direct agreement regarding both rivers and the zone in Hamburg, adding that if the Berlin Government would make an offer

[1] *Germany and Czechoslovakia*, pp. 65–6. Orbis, Prague.

securing for Prague the rights on the Elbe and in Hamburg which are essential and economically indispensable for it, Prague would renounce the rights granted it in these questions by the Treaty of Versailles. This was made subject only to the consent of the Allies, i.e. of the International Elbe Committee. Berlin accepted the offer gratefully and the agreement was concluded, so that when the river clauses of the Versailles Treaty were recently annulled, the former position between Czechoslovakia and Germany was not affected. We quote this merely as a document of Prague's behaviour and as characteristic of the spirit in which Prague's policy towards Berlin was conceived.

" Let us recall another episode equally characteristic of the situation between Berlin and Prague at that time. Prague consistently supported Briand's policy of *rapprochement*, and when, on Germany's joining the League of Nations, the well-known difficulties in connection with a permanent seat on the Council of the League of Nations for Brazil and Spain arose, and there was a danger of dissolution and of the withdrawal of Germany as well, then Dr. Beneš placed his seat on the Council at the disposal of the Great Powers with the aim that, prompt satisfaction being granted to the others, the permanent seat for Germany could be immediately established and consequently the whole policy of agreement with Germany saved. At that time there were also long discussions at Geneva between Dr. Beneš on the one hand and Reich Chancellor Luther, Stresemann and Schubert, the Secretary of State, on the other; the German politicians spoke highly of Prague's policy of reconciliation, discussed the further development of the relations between the two neighbouring states with the Czechoslovak delegate, and a period of relations ensued which were considered by both parties to be friendly. When Stresemann first participated in a session of the Council of the League of Nations as Germany's delegate on the Council, he gave expression to this fact in a public speech full of praise for Czechoslovakia.

" The relations between Prague and Berlin in the succeeding years, 1926 and 1927, were governed by the same spirit. Czechoslovakia considered her Locarno Pact with Germany, even though the Rhine Pact did not affect her directly, to be the main and definite basis of her relations with Germany, the foundation on which future construction would take place and which would certainly lead to that system of collective security which, in the scope of the League of Nations and European equilibrium, has been and will remain the final aim of Czechoslovak policy.

"Later, in the years 1927 and 1928, when the economic and financial problem of Austria became once more acute, and at the same time the question of disarmament was first discussed, Dr. Beneš procured an invitation from the Berlin Government for an official visit to Berlin, in order that an exchange of opinions could take place between Prague and Berlin regarding these questions. Dr. Beneš visited Berlin in April, 1928, on his return journey from London, had important political discussions with Reich Chancellor Marx, the President of the Reichsbank, Schacht, Reichswirtschafts-minister Curtius and Schubert (Stresemann was at that time already seriously ill and died soon afterwards) regarding Central European questions, German-Czechoslovak economic co-operation, the Austrian problem and the progress of disarmament work at Geneva. The negotiations were sincere, cordial, friendly, even when Dr. Beneš at that time openly and loyally stated in Berlin what resistance would be raised in Europe to any attempt by Germany at an *Anchluss* with Austria. The friendly relations between Berlin and Prague were only improved by this visit."

From every point of view, the relations between Germany and Czechoslovakia were considerably better than those between Germany and Poland. If the former never resulted in close and friendly collaboration, this was above all due to the failure of France and Germany to reach a real understanding. Germany often reproached Czechoslovakia with being a vassal state of France and the " French watchdog in Central Europe." This reproach was, of course, made chiefly by the German nationalists and later by the Nazis. The real aim of Beneš, and his greatest ambition, was in fact to achieve an understanding and even close collaboration between Germany and France.

It was natural that, in the absence of this collaboration, Czechoslovakia should feel herself more closely attached to France; this was determined not only by her sincere and profound sympathy with Western civilisation, but by the necessity to safeguard her national independence. Many of the more reasonable German politicians understood very well the need of a small Power to seek some sort of support in a larger Power, rather than remain isolated at the side of a neighbour much stronger than itself. During the Briand-Stresemann period, Beneš did his utmost to encourage the cordiality of Franco-German relations, which seemed to be growing. Thus the Treaty of Locarno, which was the symbol of this policy, contained not only the Rhineland Pact, but an Arbitration Treaty between Germany and Czechoslovakia, to which, though confirmed by Germany as late as March, 1938, the Czechoslovak Government was prevented from appealing during the September crisis by the British and French Ministers in Prague, who were " instructed to point out to the Czechoslovak Government that there was no hope of a peaceful solution on this basis."[1]

The first serious tension which arose between the two countries was in the spring of 1931, when Curtius and Schober tried to arrange a Customs union between Germany and Austria, which was nothing more nor less than a rudimentary attempt at the *Anschluss*. In this question, the policy adopted by Czechoslovakia was also that adopted by France and Italy; in collaboration with these two countries, Czechoslovakia did its utmost to prevent the realisation of this Austro-German plan. The question of the *Anschluss* was not the unique concern of Germany and Czechoslovakia; it was a European problem. During the war, in laying the foundations of the future Czechoslovak state, Masaryk and Beneš counted with the possibility of union between Germany and German Austria. They were both convinced that Czechoslovakia could perfectly well exist as an independent Power even if Germany stretched as far as the Hungarian frontier. When, however, the Peace Conference decided against the *Anschluss*, Czechoslovakia certainly had no reason to oppose a decision which could but be favourable to her interests. In collaboration with France, Czechoslovakia resisted

---

[1] Chamberlain, speech in the House of Commons, September 28, 1938.

all attempts to bring the *Anschluss* about. We were convinced that Austria was perfectly capable of leading an independent existence—a conviction strongly supported later by the Austrian Chancellors, Dolfuss and Schuschnigg.

In this question, as in all questions which concerned the Danube Basin, Czechoslovakia opposed German imperialist expansion and all attempts to establish German hegemony in Central Europe. In taking up an attitude frankly hostile to the German *Drang nach Osten*, Czechoslovakia was protecting not only her own interests, but those of the whole of Europe—of Western, Central and Eastern Europe alike. She recognised the legitimate efforts of Germany to establish close economic relations with the Danubian countries, but only on condition that Germany did not exploit her economic position to establish her political supremacy. Czechoslovak policy was based first and foremost on the principle: the Danubian Basin for the Danubian peoples. In the name of this principle, Czechoslovakia was bound to oppose all attempts at unilateral interference— whether this came from Germany or from other Great Powers.

Each time trouble arose it was due, not so much to direct differences between Germany and Czechoslovakia, as to the general tension which still existed between Germany and the rest of Europe, and particularly between Germany and France. Yet even during the first few years of the Hitler régime, the relations between Germany and Czechoslovakia were by no means those of hostile Powers. However, the tension inevitably increased and became more and more menacing in character till, finally, in 1938, the crisis broke. It was inevitable that the moment Germany recommenced her pan-German policy of expansion in Central and Eastern Europe she should be brought up against the Czechoslovak state, which was the keystone to the entire post-War edifice of Central and Eastern Europe. Until Czechoslovak independence had been destroyed, there was no question either of the establishment of a Pan-German *Mitteleuropa* nor of the realisation of the German plans for the Ukraine. Czechoslovakia was a very serious obstacle in Germany's way, not only because of her strong military and economic position, but because she was a country with a healthy and well-balanced social system, a culture not inferior to that of Western Europe and an ardently patriotic population, of whom all social classes were prepared to make the greatest sacrifices for the national cause. From the military point of view, Czechoslovakia was all the more dangerous to Germany because it extended a Slav promontory into the heart of German territory.

Even at the end of the last century, when the Czechs were under Austrian domination, the German historian, Mommsen, the apostle of Pan-Germanism, declared that " the hard heads of the Czechs must be broken." In our own day, Ewald Banse, the military expert of National Socialism, never ceased to advocate the complete crushing of Czechoslovakia. It was in this spirit that Markomannus, in his book, *Brennpunkt Böhmen,* published in 1935, wrote:

> " In case of war, the Czech promontory would represent so great a danger for Germany that the best solution would be to smash it completely like a huge nut. It should be surrounded and attacked simultaneously from all sides. But in the centre of this nut is the Czech spirit, which is as hard as stone and has at its disposal a large army, furnished with the most up-to-date equipment."

It was clear that the Third Reich, whose Führer consistently demands the expansion of the German *Lebensraum,* had sooner or later to attempt to smash this promontory. This intention would not have been any different had the Czech-Soviet Pact not existed. The destruction of the independence of Czechoslovakia became necessary for Germany the moment German policy decided on eastward expansion.

In these circumstances, it was obviously foolish to believe that an understanding could be reached between Nazi Germany and an independent Czechoslovakia. Every understanding must necessarily be a compromise, and both the interested parties must necessarily desire to reach an agreed solution. Hitler had no intention of reaching a permanent understanding with Czechoslovakia; he intended, demanded and achieved the complete submission of Czechoslovakia and its relegation to the position of a German vassal. Czechoslovakia, for her part, made every effort to secure a *modus vivendi,* which she desired as much for her own sake as for that of Britain and France. Several times it seemed as if a satisfactory arrangement had been reached. So long as the Third Reich felt insecure or found itself in a difficult situation, its representatives pretended to desire improved relations with Czechoslovakia. Every time an opportunity seemed to present itself for a Czech-German understanding, Beneš tried to seize it. Although he knew perfectly well that there could be only a temporary improvement, he was nevertheless not going to lay himself open to the charge of preventing an understanding between Germany and the Western Powers. Sincerely and assiduously, he did everything in his power to prevent Czechoslovakia from becoming a weight, either on Britain or on France, which could embarrass them in the conduct of their European policies. At the same time, it was expected that the Western Powers, in their turn, would realise the importance of Czechoslovakia, not only in the defence of French security, but in the maintenance of France's position as a Great Power. This is why the Czechoslovak Government, in all the negotiations which took place between Prague and Berlin for the establishment of closer relations, always insisted that any arrangement which was made, must be made in close agreement with the French Government, that under no conditions could such an arrangement destroy the French system of alliances, which guaranteed the security of Czechoslovakia as of France, and that it should in no way infringe upon the loyalty of Czechoslovakia to her obligations under the League of Nations. Once this principle had been accepted, Czechoslovakia was ready to satisfy to a large extent the claims of the Sudeten-German minority, to avoid everything which could give rise to a hostile impression in Germany and to begin a period of close co-operation with Germany. But the fundamental condition of such a policy was that it should in no way infringe upon the independence of Czechoslovakia. It was exactly this condition which blocked the ambitions of the Third Reich. Nazi Germany wished to conclude with Czechoslovakia a bilateral pact which, by excluding the Czechoslovak allies, would have put the country at the mercy of the Third Reich. The German Government never openly or formally demanded that Czechoslovakia should denounce her alliances with France or Russia, but it was understood that, after the signing of a German-Czech bilateral agreement, these alliances would come gradually and automatically to an end. By this means Czechoslovakia would herself have prepared her complete isolation, the only consequence of which would have been complete and merited submission to the Third Reich.

(c) *Should We have Pursued a Policy Similar to that of Colonel Beck ?* Czechoslovak policy could be reproached with having made the great mistake of trusting too far in certain allies, and above all in France, who abandoned her at the very height of the crisis. Would it not have been better to seek an agreement with Germany without so much consideration for France and Russia ? In fact, certain Czechoslovak politicians, chiefly in Agrarian and banking circles, did advocate this policy and gave as an example Colonel Beck, Foreign Minister of Poland. But, paradoxical as it may seem, it is just the Munich Agreement which has, in fact, proved that the only policy open to us was, in fact, that pursued by Beneš and Krofta.

It was, of course, quite possible to adopt the methods of Colonel Beck. We also could have signed a bilateral pact of non-aggression with Germany and maintained formally our alliances with France and Russia. But the results would have been those of the Munich Agreement. Czechoslovakia would have been reduced to the role of a German vassal; the Sudeten-German districts, if not formally incorporated in Germany, would have been administered—as the whole country would have been administered—by methods and by elements completely Nazi in outlook. Germany would gradually have accentuated its pressure until all ties with France and with Russia would have been entirely severed. Czechoslovakia would thus voluntarily have courted its own complete isolation and would have placed itself of its own free will in the position which it enjoyed after Munich. It also would have had to pay the price of the occupation of the whole country if it had attempted the slightest show of resistance. Nazi Germany, as the events of March, 1939, have proved, would never have tolerated the independent existence of Czechoslovakia a day longer than was necessary. Even a country economically crippled, geographically mutilated, deprived of its fortifications, with its democratic political system completely subordinated and the men who, in all spheres of life, had been the closest collaborators of Beneš and Masaryk expelled from power—even such a country still appeared to the great German Reich so dangerous an enemy that total extinction alone brought security. What, therefore, does anyone propose could have been the price of our continued independence ?

We might perhaps have delayed for a certain time the fulfilment of German plans, but catastrophe could not have been far off. The fact that Poland has not suffered the same fate proves nothing. Poland delayed the inevitable challenge, but when it came—as it did immediately after the occupation of Czecho-Slovakia in March—Poland found security, not in the policy of Colonel Beck, but in a rapid and startling return to the policy which Czechoslovakia had consistently pursued—the policy of collective security and alliance with the two Western Powers.

The position of Poland rapidly deteriorated after the dismemberment of Czechoslovakia, and even in the autumn of 1938 she found herself obliged to seek the tactical support of Soviet Russia in resisting the attempt by Germany to stir up the Ukrainian minority against the Polish Government. Poland had undoubtedly hoped that the disappearance of Czechoslovakia would secure for Poland and Hungary a common frontier and thus facilitate the creation of a " neutral *bloc* " from the Baltic to the Black Sea, which would prevent a German-Russian war from being fought on the territory lying between these two Powers and would secure the neutrality of Eastern Europe in the event of a German attack on the West.

The vanity of these hopes was revealed as we have seen above, within a few days of Poland achieving the long-desired common frontier with Hungary. This frontier was established in what was Sub-Carpathian Ruthenia, but was clearly achieved only because Germany did not enforce the veto which she had declared some months previously. Poland found herself at the side of a Hungary whose loyalty to Poland could no longer be trusted should Poland have need of military assistance. At the same time, Poland found herself threatened simultaneously from Slovakia, on her southern frontier, from Danzig, East Prussia and Memel on the north, and divided by Germany in the north-east by the small Vilna corridor of Lithuania, who had already been forced to give way to Germany under threat of force. If, in this almost desperate military and strategic situation, Poland found support from Britain and France, no one could attribute this to the policy or the foresight of Colonel Beck.

Germany, on the other hand, had every reason to congratulate herself on the results of the treaty which she had concluded with Poland in January, 1934. Unhampered in any way by adherence to the letter or spirit of a treaty after it has outlived its usefulness to the Third Reich, German diplomacy can nevertheless welcome the immense advantages she derived from five years of Polish-German friendship. The Polish-German Treaty of January, 1934, was the first breach in the system of collective security which was alone capable of restraining the immense dynamic forces of the dictatorships and forcing them to adapt their foreign policy to the needs and methods of other European countries. By deliberately making this breach, Pilsudski and Beck effectively aided the expansion of Nazi Pan-Germanism. But this expansion will not halt at the frontiers of Poland. The Third Reich can no more tolerate an independent Poland than it tolerated an independent Czechoslovakia. It was not difficult to foresee and we did not hesitate to foretell, that once Germany had weakened Czechoslovakia, she would force her to enter the German orbit. Colonel Beck miscalculated the situation fatally when he imagined that a humiliated Czechoslovakia would be allowed to turn to Poland for support. The Poles will one day realise that Masaryk was right when he said: " Without a free Poland, Czechoslovakia cannot be free. Without a free Czechoslovakia, Poland will lose its independence."

From whatever angle, therefore, one approaches this question, one comes always to the same conclusion: in trying to buy favours from Nazi Germany, Czechoslovakia would have been reduced to the role of a vassal state. As it was, Beneš was unable to save his country from this fate only because Czechoslovakia was abandoned by France and delivered over to Germany by the two Western Powers. But he succeeded in saving what is the most precious of a country's possessions—the honour of the Czechoslovak people and their unshakable faith in the

resurrection of their country. If we had tried to win favours from
Germany, ignoring our allies and our friends, we might have
saved the appearance of our former independence while in fact
submitting voluntarily to the domination of the Nazis. But we
would have demoralised our people and we would have lost for
ever the moral right to reclaim our freedom when the face of
Europe is changed. As it is, having remained faithful to the
policy of Masaryk, represented by Beneš, to the very last moment
and in spite of the terrible catastrophe which came upon us, we
have won an inestimable advantage. We proved that we were
ready to fight not only for our own liberty, but for the liberty of
the whole of Europe; we proved that, though abandoned by
all our friends, we neither broke faith nor gave in, until the very
last minute when we were sure that Britain and France knew
what they were doing and had taken the entire responsibility
upon themselves. We did not submit of our own free will. Servitude was brutally imposed upon us. But our conscience is clear,
and the nation of Masaryk, though crushed by violence, in
saving its honour, preserves an undying hope for the future.

(d) *Czechoslovak Policy in Central Europe.* Czechoslovak policy
has been reproached for its failure to reach an understanding
with Poland. In the spring of 1938, a French Cabinet Minister
gave me to understand that we should be willing to sacrifice
Těšín (Teschen) in return for Polish friendship. But the cession
of territory inhabited by a Czech majority, and playing a vitally
important part in the economic life of the country, would have
been a sacrifice accepted only with the greatest difficulty by
Czechoslovak public opinion. Moreover, this sacrifice would have
been as vain as it was dangerous. At that moment it was impossible to win Polish friendship, since Poland could not risk expos-
ing herself openly against Germany. Furthermore, a precedent
would have been created which the Germans and Hungarians
would not have hesitated to exploit. The demands of the Henlein
party would immediately have been raised and the most which
could have been achieved was the stopping of the violent Polish
Press campaign which was directed against Czechoslovakia.
Except for this, Poland would certainly have continued to
manœuvre between Germany and Russia. The assistance which

Poland would have given Czechoslovakia would have been more than problematic, whereas Czechoslovakia would have run the risk of seriously compromising her alliance with Russia. Yet, in the event of a European conflagration, it is certainly Russia and not Poland who will play a decisive part in Eastern Europe.

But even if Poland had consented to a Polish-Czech *rapprochement*, she alone would have profited from it, since she would have accepted the reinforcement it gave her without in any way changing the policy which she inaugurated in January, 1934, with her treaty with Germany. On the other hand, Czechoslovakia, by allying herself with Poland would have taken on all the risks and disadvantages of Polish policy and all the inevitable effects on her relations with Russia and Germany. In vain Czechoslovakia tried to find a friendly solution to all the quarrels which Colonel Beck provoked after the signing of his pact with Germany. The Polish Foreign Minister asked no more than that German attention should be distracted away from Poland and German expansion directed towards the Danubian Basin.

Several times the Czechoslovak Government suggested that some solution should be found to the question of the Polish minority in Těšín. This minority was not a big one—even according to Polish figures, it numbered only 100,000—and the Prague Government suggested that it should be solved either by direct negotiation, according to the Polish-Czech Arbitration Treaty of 1936, or by arbitration or by mediation of the League of Nations. Several times Beneš proposed a pact of " eternal friendship " between Poland and Czechoslovakia which would permit the complete demilitarisation of the Polish-Czech frontiers, but he never once had a reply. Beneš wanted to sign a Polish-Czech treaty before he concluded the Czech-Soviet Pact, in order that the latter should not even have the appearance of an anti-Polish alliance.

If Czechoslovakia did not seek a military alliance with Poland, this was because she did not want to undertake any commitments towards a state which had so many unsettled disputes to resolve, both with Germany and with Russia. For her part, Poland never showed the slightest desire to help Czechoslovakia to defend the difficult position which she occupied in the Danube Basin. As proof of this, we have only to draw attention to the fact that

Poland never ratified the Treaty of Trianon and always sought a *rapprochement* with Hungary, even when the latter, in pursuance of its revisionist ambitions, was violently attacking Czechoslovakia.

There was a complete incompatibility of view between Poland and Czechoslovakia. Czechoslovakia would certainly never have taken part in a hostile action directed against Poland,[1] and would certainly have come to the assistance of Poland if the latter had been attacked by Germany. Poland, on the other hand, always displayed either complete indifference towards Czechoslovakia or a condescending hostility which was, to say the least, ready to bring Czechoslovakia, with all her military force and economic wealth, under Polish domination. The official foreign policy of Poland encouraged Germany in her hostility towards Czechoslovakia and it must, unfortunately, be admitted, that the idea of the partition of Czechoslovakia was suggested by certain Polish politicians even before it had been decided upon by Germany. Poland carries a very grave responsibility for the tragic fate which was imposed on Czechoslovakia. Furthermore, the manner in which Poland, profiting from the misfortune of her neighbour in order to despoil her, seized upon Těšín in October, 1938, will go down in history. Never would Poland have dared to proceed in so brutal a manner had Czechoslovakia not been abandoned by France and Britain.

Though there is little to reproach Czechoslovakia in her policy towards Poland, there are certain criticisms to be made concerning Czechoslovak activities in the Danube Basin. Probably much more could have been done in this area than was done, and Czechoslovakia should undoubtedly have taken the initiative in seeking a *rapprochement* with Hungary, especially during the last two years which preceded the catastrophe. Such efforts would probably have been counteracted by German and Italian intervention and would certainly have met with a certain reserve occasioned by the antipathy of the Hungarian ruling classes for the Czechoslovak democracy. But, on the other hand, Hungary was beginning to be afraid of the growing influence of Germany

---

[1] According to the terms of her treaty, Czechoslovakia was obliged to come to the assistance of Russia only in the event of a direct Polish attack and only after France had intervened.

in the Danube Basin; this fear was confirmed after the annexation of Austria by Germany. For this reason, in certain Hungarian economic and political quarters, it was at last realised that a *rapprochement* with Czechoslovakia would be in Hungary's interest. The Czechoslovak Government failed to make the best of this more favourable disposition towards it.

It is true that the official Czechoslovak policy can be defended on the score that these Czechophil tendencies had yet to prove themselves sincere. Above all, Prague, in making an experiment whose results were far from certain, risked alienating both Belgrade and Bucharest, thus destroying the solidarity of the Little Entente. It was, above all, Rumania who refused to make concessions to Hungary by granting a more liberal régime to the Hungarian minorities in the Little Entente states. Fairly satisfactory conversations were started between Prague and Budapest, especially after the Geneva meeting of their respective Foreign Ministers, Krofta and Kanya, in September, 1937. But these conversations could not reach a satisfactory conclusion on account of the negative attitude adopted by Bucharest.

When the conference of the Little Entente, held at Bled in August, 1938, resulted in an agreement which recognised Hungarian equality of rights in the matter of armaments and a mutual pact of non-aggression, the question of the minorities was not mentioned except in the most general terms. Although formerly Hungarian complaints had been addressed chiefly to Rumania, whereas the Hungarian minority in Czechoslovakia was recognised to have far better treatment than in either of the other succession states, in the summer of 1938, Hungary, encouraged by the success of the Henlein party, started to direct its chief attacks against Czechoslovakia and to demand far more important concessions in this country than in either Rumania or Yugoslavia. In this way, Hungary also tried to undermine the solidarity of the Little Entente. Czechoslovakia did not reap the fruit of her loyal and consistent attitude towards the other countries of the Little Entente. Yugoslavia, under the Stojadinovitch Government, interpreted its obligations towards Prague and Budapest in a wholly arbitrary fashion.

In spite of all the difficulties, Czechoslovakia consistently tried, through the whole of the post-War period, to organise the closest collaboration possible between the Danubian states. It was far from easy. Hungary, under the directions of an ancient and very nationalist aristocracy, allowed itself to be inspired by the idea of revenge; all her efforts were directed toward frontier revision and the restoration of pre-War Hungary. Austria oscillated perpetually between the idea of the *Anschluss* and that of the restoration of the Hapsburgs; it was only after Hitler came to power in Germany that the two last Chancellors of the Austrian Republic defended the idea of an Austria which they considered capable of independent existence. In all the succession states without exception, excessive nationalism was all the rage: in a narrow and provincial spirit, each state watched its neighbour jealously lest its own sovereignty should be challenged, while at the same time insufficiently respecting the sovereignty of others. All three states strove towards economic self-sufficiency although close collaboration, above all in the economic sphere, was the indispensable condition of the welfare of each. Often these autarchic tendencies took on a wholly senseless and impossible form; for instance, in both Austria and Czechoslovakia, agriculture was deliberately increased at the expense of old and well-established industries, although corn could have been imported from the Agrarian countries of the Danube Basin. These, on the other hand, created artificial industries although it would have been far more advantageous to them to buy good-quality manufactures from Austria and Czechoslovakia at a reasonable price. The political predominance in each one of these countries was contrary to the economic structure: in Czechoslovakia, an essentially industrialised country, it was the Agrarians who had a strong political predominance; in the agricultural countries—Rumania, Yugoslavia and Bulgaria—political power was chiefly in the hands of industrialists and financiers; whereas in Hungary, where the immense majority of the population consists of peasants, the country is still governed by large landed proprietors. Under such conditions all attempts to organise close economic collaboration met with immense obstacles. One of the most serious of these obstacles was the attitude adopted by Germany and Italy, both of whom tried to exploit the jealousies and rivalries of these small countries for their own ends.

All constructive plans, of which the most complete was that elaborated by M. Tardieu in 1932, met with strong resistance from Germany and Italy. The efforts of Masaryk, Beneš and Hodža to reconstruct the Danube Basin on the basis of a collaboration between small, independent countries were not sufficient by themselves to unite all the divergent forces. The sole concrete result which they achieved was the creation of the Little Entente. It would be wrong to underestimate the work of these three states—Czechoslovakia, Rumania and Yugoslavia: without them, the Danube Basin would undoubtedly have become the scene of complete anarchy in the post-War years and the cockpit of the rival ambitions of the Great Powers and the intrigues of revisionists and legitimists. If, little by little, the new order was established in the Danube Basin, the revisionist aims of Hungary were moderated, and Austria herself sought a *rapprochement* with the Danubian states and above all with Czechoslovakia, this was almost entirely due to the Little Entente. This group of states could have been the basis of the total reconstruction of the Danube Basin— this was the aim of its creators. All these possibilities were destroyed by the Munich Agreement which has handed to Germany the opportunity of organising the Danube Basin within the sphere of a German *Mitteleuropa*.

(*e*) *Czechoslovak Policy in Eastern Europe.* Czechoslovak's policy of alliance with Soviet Russia has also been severely criticised. It was maintained that by this alliance Czechoslovakia exposed the whole of Europe to the danger of " Bolshevisation " and irritated the German Führer to such an extent that all agreement with Germany became entirely out of the question. Those who put forward this thesis usually forgot that it was France who originated the policy of alliance with Russia, and that it was M. Laval himself who drew up the agreement and prided himself on his achievement. The Czech-Soviet Pact was, moreover, entirely dependent on the Franco-Soviet Pact for its implementation. According to a specific clause, it was to come into action in a general conflict only after France had already intervened either on the side of Russia or of Czechoslovakia. Furthermore, the application of the treaty was even then not automatic, but had first to be submitted to a series of formalities before the League of Nations. This necessarily meant a certain control on the part of world public opinion and, above all, the possibility of Great Britain bringing important influence to bear at Geneva. The Czech-Soviet alliance was, from every point of view, a purely defensive alliance. Of course, it is true that the Nazis regard as a " provocation " all defensive organisations whose aim is to resist the aggressive intentions of the Nazis, but it is unfortunate that this somewhat peculiar interpretation should have been widely accepted, and those who defended themselves should have been regarded as a danger to the peace of Europe. It would seem that Germany has very quickly forgotten the period when she herself threatened Europe with " Bolshevisation " by allying herself with Russia. It should not be forgotten that the Treaties of Rapallo and Berlin, whose aim was to establish Russo-German co-operation, were both prolonged by the Nazi Government in 1933 and have never, up to date, been denounced.

The contention put about by German propaganda that Czechoslovakia itself was " Bolshevised " has already been exposed in its true colours. It is interesting, however, in retrospect, to note the testimony of General Faucher, given to a French conservative newspaper, L'Époque:

" What truth is there in the story that Czechoslovakia is the bulwark of Communism ? There was, of course, a Communist Party, but this party had no influence whatever on policy. In spite of frequent attempts on the part of the Communists, not even a Popular Front was ever established. The real truth is that the Czechoslovak Government realised that it was absolutely necessary for Czechoslovakia to be able to get supplies from Russia in the event of war with Germany. This was mere common sense. From a French point of view, this policy of resistance to Communism within the country and of collaboration with the Communist state outside the country was wholly logical, and could not but have been approved. I want to draw your attention to the complete falsehood of the campaigns whose intention was to prove the Bolshevisation of Czechoslovakia. From time to time the

German newspapers published lists of Soviet officers who were supposed to be attached to the staffs and to the units of the Czechoslovak Army. Mark you—they gave even the names of these officers. I am in a position to tell you that these lists were wholly imaginary, as were the so-called mutinies of non-existent Soviet detachments within the Czechoslovak Army. Unfortunately, German propaganda, which consisted of a perpetual flow of lies, succeeded in confusing foreign opinion."

In spite of the fact that their influence on the policy of the country was insignificant, although they were perpetually exposed to persecution on the part of the Government, which showed them much less indulgence than it showed to the Henlein Nazis, the Czechoslovak Communists gave proof of real patriotism and a most moving spirit of self-sacrifice. The Republic knew that it could count absolutely on the Communists, both Czechoslovak and Sudeten German, the day they were called upon for the defence of their country.

In its foreign policy, Czechoslovakia always favoured a collaboration between Soviet Russia and Europe. As in the case of Germany, within the limits of our power, we tried to bring about a *rapprochement* between Soviet Russia and the rest of Europe. There is no reason to hide the fact that M. Beneš took a very active part in the conversations which preceded the entry of Soviet Russia into the League of Nations. Beneš was always convinced that this practical collaboration would diminish the points of difference between Russia and the rest of the world, and in this way lead to a more favourable atmosphere and general European appeasement.

We were never afraid of the so-called "Bolshevik danger" because a sensible and far-reaching social policy had established our social system on a sound basis. The real danger was the "Nazi danger," and as the threat of German expansion increased, the necessity for close collaboration between Soviet Russia and the Western Great Powers became more and more apparent. This was the sole effective method of resisting this danger, and at the height of every crisis this necessity is revealed. After Godesberg, when the September crisis reached its

most dangerous point, Paris and London immediately turned to
Russia, and the Foreign Office communiqué of September 26,
1938, threatened Germany with an Anglo-Franco-Russian
coalition. Six months later when Germany seized what remained
of Czechoslovakia and occupied Memel, contacts with the Soviet
Government were immediately renewed. Too late for our own
protection, but not too late for the cause of European freedom
with which our own is still bound up, the policy which Czechoslovakia had followed was proved to be the right one, though
the practical means of carrying it out had been seriously curtailed at Munich. Nothing, perhaps, proves more clearly the
efficacity of this policy than the violent opposition which Nazi
Germany has always opposed to each attempt at co-operation
between Russia and the Western Powers. The Nazis are well
aware that this co-operation means the end of the expansionist policy of the Third Reich. If Soviet Russia had really
been as militarily weak and insignificant as Nazi propaganda
maintained in order to minimise in the eyes of the public the
value of the Franco-Soviet Pact, such immense and costly
efforts would hardly have been made by the Nazis to prevent all
co-operation between Eastern and Western Europe. The Führer
has realised all along, and perhaps better than any statesman in
Western Europe, the immense importance of this co-operation.
It was for this reason that, ever since the occupation of the
Rhineland, Hitler consistently attacked the French alliance
with Russia, while appearing to ignore the French alliances with
Poland and Czechoslovakia, which were practically identical
with it. For this same reason, he violently opposed the Czech-
Soviet Pact. The future will prove how right Hitler has been and
how costly it will be for Europe that the vital Czechoslovak
bridge which united Eastern and Western Europe was destroyed
at Munich.

(*f*) *The Crisis of the Alliance with the Western Democracies.*
One last question, perhaps the most important, remains to be
answered. Surely the whole foundation of Czechoslovak foreign
policy was removed when France, who was the corner-stone of
the whole Czechoslovak system of alliances and security, abandoned her ally at the exact moment when, according to her
treaty obligations and her own self-interest, she should have

come to the aid of her ally? Was it not the basis of this policy which was itself faulty and hence the whole construction rotten which was built upon it ? Certain critics have even gone so far as to maintain that the mistakes which Beneš made and which led up to the catastrophe were inherent in his democratic ideology to which he subordinated everything else, even the interests of the State. In the pursuit of an ideological policy, they maintained, Beneš relied on the Western democracies, and for this reason refused to come to terms with Nazi Germany and Fascist Italy; and at the same time he increased the tension between Czechoslovakia and these two countries by emphasising unceasingly his friendship for the Bolsheviks of Moscow.

The answer is quite simple: In so far as Czechoslovakia wished to remain an independent state, she had no choice but to rely in the first place on France and in the second on Russia. If ever she wishes to regain her independence, she will be able to do so only in preserving the friendship of one or other of these two countries. A small country, situated by the side of a strong neighbour, if it wants to maintain its independence, must inevitably base its security on the friendship of a Great Power. Whatever the organisation of Europe in the future, this principle must always hold good. For Czechoslovakia, there are only two possible alternatives: either she submits to a Germany eight times as strong as herself or she guards her independence by allying herself to those whose interest it also is to see her free and independent. This policy does not necessarily mean an hostile attitude towards Germany; it is simply a means of self-defence towards a neighbour considerably stronger than herself. It was in this way that the democrats of Weimar Germany interpreted the Czech alliances; with the result that relations between a democratic Germany and a democratic Czechoslovakia were perfectly good, though the relations between that Germany and Poland were as consistently bad.

If Czechoslovakia sought first and foremost the friendship of France, it was not only because her relations with that country were based on a centuries-old tradition, nor because, during the War and at the Peace Conference, France did more than any other country for the liberation of the Czechoslovak people, but first and foremost it was because France, being the direct neighbour of Germany, had more than any other Great Power a positive interest in the maintenance of the independence of that country which was the corner stone of the Danube Basin. The democratic ideal which these two countries defended in common was not the only, nor even the decisive, reason for their alliance. The foundation of the alliance existed in the geopolitical, historical and strategic position of the two countries. It was just because it was a matter of political and strategic realities, accepted and emphasised in France as well as in Czechoslovakia, that the defection of France in September, 1938, was impossible to foresee. For this reason, in spite of our doubts, it was difficult to admit that France, in abandoning us, was not betraying herself. That which was at stake was not exclusively Czechoslovak interests, but, and for the same reasons, the interests of France.

The events of September, 1938, can only be explained in the light of the serious internal crisis which was dividing France. Whenever a country is on the eve of important social changes or in the process of bringing those changes about, it is bound to be preoccupied with its internal difficulties to the point of losing all interest in the problems of foreign policy which are based on unchanging geopolitical factors. There results a complete disorientation, general confusion of mind, reason gives place to passion, the interests of class and of caste take precedence over the national interest. It is inevitable at such times that cynical elements succeed, by a clever manipulation of the facts, in stifling the voice of those who put the national interest above everything else. Nazi and Fascist propaganda knew well how to profit from the state of mind then existing in France. Much play was made with the argument of the Bolshevik danger, and this argument never ceased to produce the required effect both in England and in France. In both countries it was assiduously pointed out that Communism would be the sole victor in a war.

The tragedy of Czechoslovakia consisted in the fact that, just at the moment when we needed the assistance of the Western democracies, they were passing through a profound crisis which obscured their judgment and prevented them from acting in their own national interests. Czechoslovak foreign policy was powerless to prevent this crisis or the fatal consequences which it brought in its train. Czechoslovakia was the immediate victim of the crisis, but the future will prove that the Western Powers will themselves suffer the consequences of the sacrifice which they imposed on their ally, by delivering her into the hands of their own enemy.

One might perhaps reproach Czechoslovakia that she did not foresee the consequences of this crisis. From the moment she realised that she could no longer count on the support of the Western Powers, would she not have done better immediately to change her entire policy and thus try to avoid the threatening catastrophe ? It is far easier to criticise this policy than to indicate what should have been the alternative. We have shown above why a *rapprochement* with Germany would have entailed just those consequences which resulted from Munich with the important difference that we would have lost our honour with our independence. As for a *rapprochement* with Italy, the examples of Hungary and Austria, who placed themselves under the protection of Italy, was hardly encouraging. Austria had already been annexed by Germany and Hungary was little more than a satellite of the Third Reich. A *rapprochement* with Poland would have cost, not only the cession of Těšín, but would immediately have provoked Germany as well as aroused the suspicions of Russia; besides which, nobody has ever suggested that Poland would be a surer ally than France, nor could anyone maintain that she was stronger and more capable of defending the security and independence of Czechoslovakia. If Czechoslovakia had relied entirely upon an alliance with Russia without at the same time co-operating with the Western Powers, she would immediately have been denounced as bulwark of Communism in Central Europe and would at the same time have been torn with internal dissensions on account of this unilateral alliance. This also could but have invited German aggression.

The whole history of Czechoslovakia proves that this country is closely bound to the West. It was only by relying on the Western Powers that she could have hoped to maintain her independence. The day this support was withdrawn catastrophe was inevitable. It would be naïve to reproach Masaryk and Beneš for this disaster, for to do so would be to ignore the geographical situation of Czechoslovakia which always played a decisive part in determining the main lines of her foreign policy. To reproach Masaryk and Beneš for their " Western orientation," with its complement—co-operation with Russia (which by its revolution is Westernising itself)—would be to reproach them for having fought to conquer and maintain national independence and freedom for their country. Whatever other possibilities may be discussed, inevitably one is forced to the conclusion that there are only two alternatives: submission to Germany or independence in alliance with France and Russia.

For Czechoslovakia there was no possibility of neutrality. Nowadays neutrality is becoming more and more difficult even for countries situated on the outer fringes of Europe. For a country which, like Czechoslovakia, is situated at the very crossroad, it is completely out of the question. Neutrality meant inevitably that Czechoslovakia would become the instrument of German expansion.

Can one reproach Masaryk and Beneš with having pursued an ideological policy ? If it is true that identity of political principles, without being a decisive factor, did at least help to consolidate the Franco-Czech alliance, ideological differences between Czechoslovakia and Russia did certainly prevent that complete intimacy of collaboration which was desirable from the point of view strictly of national interests. If Masaryk and Beneš, as convinced democrats, found it difficult to have any great sympathy with the totalitarian states, they did at least attempt to establish correct relations between their country and Germany and Italy. They always hoped that Nazi Germany and Fascist Italy would be forced by pacific means to adapt themselves to the needs of the rest of Europe, if only they found themselves confronted with a strong coalition whenever they contemplated armed aggression.

As for Czechoslovakia, her entire history, the structure of her country both internally and in relation to Europe, demanded a democratic régime which alone was capable of balancing all the diverse social and national forces within the country. A totalitarian régime on the Fascist model would necessarily have been socially reactionary and, from the point of view of the minorities, not only reactionary but Chauvinist. The principles of democracy, both in internal and foreign policy, were the only ones which ensured the vital interests of the state, the only ones which were at all realist and the only ones which guaranteed the security and independence of the state. It was their very efficacy which drew upon them the violent hatred of Hitler for Beneš and his whole régime, in spite of the fact that it was the school of Beneš and Masaryk which, more than any other group of politicians, always defended a just and generous policy towards the German minority.

The aim of Nazi policy being to destroy Czechoslovakia, their chief hatred was directed inevitably against the person of Beneš, who pursued the sole policy capable of preventing that destruction. The moment the Munich Agreement was signed, all the efforts of the Germans were directed to the destruction of the " Beneš régime "—that is, to the elimination of all elements which could be suspected of a strong aversion to the predominance of Nazism or a consequent plan for the preservation of Czechoslovak independence.

M. Krofta finished the short study he wrote about Beneš in 1934 (*Beneš and the Foreign Policy of Czechoslovakia*) with the following words:

" I am convinced that the general line which this policy follows does not contradict in any way the ideals or the sentiments of the great majority of the people of this country, and I am convinced that it fulfils completely the interests of the state. Without previous experience and in a field of European politics hitherto completely unmapped, Beneš laid down, with unerring instinct and indefatigable energy, the path which Czecholovak foreign policy must always follow, whatever the conditions in which the country may be placed."

This statement was not refuted, but confirmed, by the Munich Agreement and its consequences in March, 1939. If the Czechoslovak people is ever to shake off the servitude imposed upon it by the Third Reich and regain its freedom and its independence, the path it must again tread is the path laid down by Masaryk and Beneš.

2. *Hegemony of the Third Reich or European Federation?*

(*a*) *The Importance of Czechoslovakia for Europe.* Masaryk always insisted that the " Czech problem " was a European problem. By this formula he hoped, on the one hand, to prevent his people from falling into a narrow provincialism by opening before them the wide horizon of Europe as a whole; on the other, he wished to remind the rest of Europe that it could not be indifferent to the fate of the Czechoslovak nation. The reason for this lay in their geographical situation in the very heart of Europe and at the crossroads, where meet all the conflicting interests, tendencies and aspirations of the Continent. The fate of a great number of European countries will always depend on the fate of Czechoslovakia; their position in Europe will depend in a large measure on whether Czechoslovakia is free or whether it is subjected to Germany.

The importance of Czechoslovakia far exceeds the extent of its resources. It derives from the at once exposed and dominating position which Czechoslovakia holds on the north-west of the Danube Basin, and from the hilly Czech massif, which cuts right into the German flank and presents the strongest bastion barring the way to the Danube Basin, the Balkans and the Black Sea. In this respect, the importance of Czechoslovakia is greater than that of former Austria. It is true that Germany, by the annexation of Austria, became the direct neighbour of Italy, Hungary and Yugoslavia, and thus considerably increased the pressure on these countries. But if Germany were to realise her plan for a German *Mitteleuropa* which should include the whole of the Danube Basin and the Balkans, she had first to destroy the Czechoslovak rampart. Pan-Germans, both of to-day and of yesterday, never ceased to underline the necessity for " cracking the Czech nut " and smashing the Czech block. Nor would a German *Mitteleuropa* affect only the peoples of Central and South-Eastern Europe. It would directly impinge upon the situation of Eastern and Western Europe. It would give Germany such a superiority of strength over all other European nations that once German hegemony was established in Europe, its predominance in other continents would only be a matter of time.

We have already drawn attention to the fact that the moment Munich was signed and the declaration of Germany's " last territorial demand " committed to paper, it was clear that Germany intended to increase her territory in Eastern Europe.

It was no longer clear, however, that this was the exclusive intention of Germany. The passage was recalled in *Mein Kampf*, in which Hitler wrote that, before expansion was embarked upon in Eastern Europe, France must be liquidated in order that the German rear should be protected from intervention by the Western Powers. After Munich, there was more prospect of neutralising the small Powers of Central and Eastern Europe in the event of an attack on the West than there was of neutralising the Western Powers while this expansion took place and slowly sapped their position in Europe and the world. The Munich policy had not even succeeded in increasing the tension between Germany and Russia. If it, nevertheless, continued, tactical manœuvres on both sides secured a temporary truce rather than a further deterioration of their relations. Though it was certain in the September crisis that Russia would, from the outset, have come in immediately on the side of Britain and France, six months later there was a certain apprehension on this subject. Even should the Third Reich go to war in order to create an " Independent Ukraine," it is exceedingly doubtful whether this war, in which Japan would certainly participate, could remain localised. If it should do so and the war should end in the victory of Germany, it is difficult to see how Britain and France would be able to resist the immense German superiority and the desire of the Third Reich to dominate the world. The future will show that Britain and France will be unable to disinterest themselves in Central and Eastern Europe without suffering the fatal consequences of this policy. Six months after the attempt to do so at Munich, that exact policy has directly involved Great Britain in a guarantee for the independence of three countries, each of which is far and away weaker, militarily, economically and strategically, than Czechoslovakia.

The destruction of the Czechoslovak rampart weakened, not only France, but Britain. German pressure was suddenly and alarmingly accentuated, not only in Prague, in Budapest, Belgrade, Bucharest, and Sofia, but in Ankara too. The Anglo-Turkish Agreement, though of utmost importance, lost some of its value through the occupation of Prague. The direct road from Berlin to Bagdad passes through Prague. The famous

Berlin-Bagdad plan with its variant—Berlin-Cairo—has regained all its old reality now that the Czech fortress, which blocked the path, has been taken. At the same time, the road has been planned which will lead from the Ukrainian Piedmont of Sub-Carpathian Ruthenia via Kiev, Odessa and Trapezunt into Asia Minor. Immense economic and political pressure is being put on Rumania, the gateway to the Black Sea.

Though official quarters in London deliberately ignored these dangers, to-day it is painfully apparent that an independent Czechoslovakia served also as one of the many fortresses which protected the world interests of Great Britain. Furthermore, the ensuing weakness of France, whose frontiers are those on which Britain also must base her security, is a direct handicap to Britain's position in the world. The fate of all European countries is too closely bound up together for countries to be able totally to ignore the fate of their fellows.

It is interesting in this respect to recall certain periods in our history which prove as fatally as recent events that Europe cannot afford to be indifferent to the fate of our country.

It was thus in the thirteenth century that the destruction of the great Czech Empire of Premysl Otokar II allowed the Hapsburgs to extend their power to such an extent that they tried to bring about a " Universal Monarchy " which would dominate the whole of Europe.

At the beginning of the fifteenth century, it was the Hussite revolution which, to a large extent, decided the course of events in Europe, and which started the great movement for emancipation which saw its zenith in the French Revolution. When, in 1526, the Hapsburgs were elected Kings of Bohemia, they gained a position exceedingly favourable to the progressive development of their kingdom, which lasted more than four centuries, and secured right up to the beginning of the nineteenth century German predominance in Central Europe. The defeat of the Czechs at the Battle of the White Mountain in 1620 precipitated Europe in a war which lasted for more than thirty years and which finally assured the supremacy of the Hapsburgs in Europe.

The situation which the Battle of the White Mountain brought about in Europe resembles to a quite extraordinary degree the present European constellation. The Hapsburgs, bent on a policy of expansion and attempting the domination of Europe by installing a universal Catholic monarchy, found themselves in conflict with those countries which stood for the freedom of the individual both in religion and politics. Masters of Spain and of Central Europe, they rallied to their cause the Catholic Church, the Catholics of Germany and of Poland, while against them were the Protestants—Czech, Austrian, Hungarian, Dutch and German, with the exception of the Prince-Elector of Saxony, who sympathised with the Hapsburgs. France, although Catholic, wanted to stop Hapsburg expansion, which already threatened her on the Rhine and from the Pyrenees. Henry IV sought allies everywhere and did not hesitate to ally himself with Protestant England and Protestant states of other countries. Under French auspices, the Protestant princes of Germany formed the " Protestant Union " in 1608, and it was French agents who stirred up the Czech and Hungarian Protestants to rebellion, promising them French aid against the Hapsburgs. But Henry IV was unable to realise his plan. In 1610, just at the moment when he was preparing war with the aid of a strong coalition of France, England and the Protestants of Holland and of Central Europe, he was assassinated. Immediately violent dissension arose between the Queen Mother and the Protestants of La Rochelle, and France passed through a profound internal crisis. This was the reason why, in 1618, when the rebellion broke out in Bohemia which was to be the signal for a general campaign against the Hapsburgs, France, in spite of her former promises of assistance and her vital interest in the cause which the Czechs were also defending, nevertheless abandoned them to their fate. The Czechs were unable to secure even the help of the Protestant Court of England. James I was in the middle of trying to marry his children in Spain in order that he should become the heir of a world dynasty, and he had no thought for anything else. The French Government hoped that the rebellion in the Czech districts, with which the Hungarians under the influence of Gabriel Betlen, Duke of Transylvania, associated themselves, would weaken the Hapsburgs. But for the most part, the French Government inclined rather to the view of the French Ambassador in Vienna, Baugy, who

considered that France had as much to fear from " a strengthening of the heretics in Bohemia and Hungary as from the growing
influence of the House of Hapsburg." As for the King of England,
his fear of seeing royal prerogative weakened by the victory of
the Third Estate was considerably stronger than his Protestant
fervour. Although in England, as in France, there were determined supporters of a policy of intervention in favour of the
Czechs, the Governments of the two countries refused to give
any assistance. The French Government even prevented the
German Protestants from going to the assistance of the Czechs,
saying, word for word, " that a first-class war might be the
result." In spite of the considerable success of the Czech rebellion, which, if England and France had adopted a less passive
attitude, would certainly have brought about the defeat of the
Hapsburgs, the two Western Powers held aloof. The analogy
can be pursued even further: French diplomacy, authorised by
the King of France, was the instigator of the famous Treaty of
Ulm, signed on July 3, 1620, according to which the Catholic
and Protestant princes of Germany gave mutual undertakings
no longer to fight each other. This treaty secured a " peace "
whose consequence was that the Catholic League of Germany,
under the direction of Maximilian of Bavaria, having nothing
more to fear from the Protestant Union, was able to concentrate
all its efforts against the Czechs and give effective support to the
Hapsburgs, whose empire was on the point of collapsing. The
Ulm Agreement, concluded under the auspices of France, was
the direct cause of the Czech defeat: the Battle of the White
Mountain was won by Maximilian of Bavaria. If this battle
meant a terrible defeat for the Czechs which deprived them both
of their religious freedom and of their political independence, it
was also a defeat for France. The work of Henry IV was
destroyed. The Hapsburgs not only were saved, but were
strengthened more than ever to threaten France from the
Rhine and the Pyrenees. Peace was saved only for a very short
time. From 1625 onwards, France was forced to intervene in all
sorts of ways; first by giving financial aid to the Danes and
Swedes, and afterwards by active intervention in the war itself.
In spite of the French efforts, the Peace of Westphalia, signed
after thirty years of war had left Europe a field of ruins, was no

more than a valueless compromise. The supremacy of the Hapsburgs over a large part of Europe was not shaken, and by their
side grew up a new state, the Kingdom of Prussia, destined to be
one of the most dangerous enemies of France. France was forced
to continue the struggle until the first half of the eighteenth
century in order to put an end to the hegemony of the House of
Hapsburg. The King of England also proved to have made a
serious mistake in yielding to the fear which the freedom of the
Third Estate caused in him; shortly afterwards, the Kingdom
of England was in the throes of civil war.

The analogy between the events which we have just described
and those which we experienced in September, 1938, is startlingly
close: the Hapsburgs, with their aim of establishing a universal
monarchy, represented for the Europe of those times the same
danger which Hitler with his Pan-German ambitions represents
to-day. We find the same hesitations on the part of the French
and English Governments before the danger of a general war;
the same hope that the enemy would be weakened by trouble
in Central Europe; the same hope that the conflict would be
localised; the same apprehension lest the " heretics " should be
strengthened (the Protestants were the " Bolsheviks " of that
day). The Agreement of Ulm was a copy of the Munich Agreement. In one as in the other, the Czechs were sacrificed—in
spite of the promises of assistance which had been given them
and the encouragement they had had to resist the Hapsburgs
in the seventeenth and the Germans in the twentieth centuries.
Peace was saved as little in 1618 as it was in 1938, although in
each case the Czechs were handed over to the mercy of the
enemy. All that one can hope for is that the consequences of
Munich will not be as terrible or as lasting as those of Ulm.
Finally, in 1618 as in 1938, the Czechs stood for progress and
liberty; in each case, this cause met with a terrible defeat. After
the Battle of the White Mountain, the Czechs regained their
independence; after Munich, they will regain it also.

(b) *Masaryk and Pan-Germanism.* To-day, as in the seventeenth century, it is not exclusively the fate of the Czechs which
is at stake, but the fate of Europe as a whole. After the Munich
Agreement, which brought neither peace nor even a respite to

the world, one question and one question only is in the minds of all those who realise the gravity of the present moment for the future history of the world. Will Europe accept the domination of Nazism or will it pull itself together to avoid this danger and to organise itself on the basis of freedom and justice ?

Up to a certain point, we find ourselves in a situation analogous to that which existed before the World War of 1914–18. Then, as now, the real question was would Europe allow itself to become the prey of Pan-Germanism or would it prove itself capable of organising itself freely ? Twenty years after that terrible War, exactly the same issue is at stake, though the War resulted in the wholesale defeat of Pan-Germanism. History will record that those who won the War failed to draw the lesson of their victory. To-day Hitler has restored Pan-Germanism; he has given it a dynamic force which it has never before possessed, and has opened before it the prospect of a new victory.

Masaryk was one of the very few statesmen who have closely followed the Pan-German movement and he often expressed his astonishment that the British and French should take so little interest in a problem so serious for themselves. Even after the experience of the War, these two countries did not take any greater interest in the danger which this movement represented. If they had done so, the British would have realised earlier that Nazism was simply a new form, though infinitely more powerful, of the old Pan-Germanism. What Masaryk wrote during the War about the ideas and ambitions of the Kaiser could be applied word for word to the tendencies of the Third Reich. It will suffice only to give a few quotations from his book, *The New Europe*, written in 1917–18:

" The political push of the Pan-German movement is directed at three points of the compass: west, south and east; against France and England, against Italy and the Balkans, and against Russia. The thrust against Italy, especially since the formation of the Triple Alliance, was disguised in friendship. Against France, too, after the annexation of Alsace-Lorraine, more moderate claims were made, and the bitterness was due more to the French *revanche* politics; yet many Pan-Germanists threatened to break France for good and all.

Others looked upon France as a *quantité négligible*, believing that she was now small [40 millions against 68], and that she would in the near future be relatively still smaller and that, like all Romance nations, she had degenerated and played out her role. In this connection, the Pan-Germanists were always pointing to Belgium and Holland [East India colonies]; their plans covering the Belgian coasts of the English Channel, for it is nearer to Germany than the coast of Northern France, and, in addition, the Flemings as well as the Dutch were claimed as Teutonic peoples. There is an extensive Pan-Germanist literature about Antwerp and its economic significance for the Germans.

" But in the forefront of the discussions and plans were England and Russia. The industrial expansion, the building of a great fleet to rule the oceans, colonial politics in Africa and latterly also in Australia and Asia, and the avowed plan of Berlin-Baghdad, directed Germany against England. . . . The Pan-Germanists are divided; a part is looking upon Russia as the most dangerous enemy of the Germans the others upon England; antagonism against Russia is found chiefly among the Baltic Germans, like Schiemann, Rohrbach and others [to-day we can add Alfred Rosenberg]; the adversaries of England are Count Reventlow and his adherents. . . .

" The opponents of Russia point to Russia's size and its tremendous population in the near future, drawing the conclusion that Russia is the true enemy of Germany. England, they argue, is separated from Germany by the sea, has no common frontier, is small in Europe, and its other parts are scattered throughout the world without practical centralisation; its true strength is in the Navy; it cannot therefore threaten Germany, because Germany will have a fleet to oppose that of England. . . .

" The Germans vindicate the right to their aggressive Pan-German policy in several ways; in the main it is the right of the stronger which they advocate. The Germans fear hunger. They point to the rapid growth of their population. . . . And so Germany must weaken Russia, and, as far as possible, occupy Russian territory for its own increasing population. In the west, Germany needs Antwerp; she needs the district of Briey; in general, she needs territory, bread, raw materials, ports. With a brutal naïveté the Pan-Germans forget that other nations also need bread. ' Necessity knows no law,' declares Bethmann-Hollweg as the foundations of Pan-Germanistic jurisprudence.

" The strategical argument is of the same quality: the geographical situation of Germany, enclosed by hostile nations on three sides, demands a rectification of the frontiers, and therefore again the annexation of non-German territory. . . . In general, not merely geography, but even geology and other sciences are used in Pan-Germany to decide questions of right; territory similar from the geographical point of view to German territory belongs to the Germans. . . .

" The Germans, so runs the Pan-German argument, are the best soldiers in the world; Prussian militarism is exemplary; the German is a born soldier. Militarism and war, moreover, as has been proved by Moltke, are the God-given social order, and therefore the Germans are entitled to hegemony. . . . Nietzsche gave to the Germans the principal and the only commandment—the will to power, the will to strength, the will to victory.

" The Germans, by virtue of their *Kultur*, have the right— nay, even the duty—of ruling the world. The Germans are, in fact, the *Herrenvolk*, the only and absolute *Herrenvolk*. Germany, so we read literally, will be the saviours of Europe and of mankind.

" The Germans, by their Pan-Germanistic plans, utilise their historical development. Prussia in 1871, after uniting the Germans, proceeded with the erection of the German Mediæval Empire, the Empire of Charlemagne, the continuation of the Roman Empire; Prussia created the political concept of Central Europe. The Prussian-German imperialism and militarism are the culmination of the Roman world idea; Berlin is the fourth Rome—after Rome, Byzantium, Moscow. . . .

" The Pan-Germans, it is plain, believe in materialism, force and technique; neither Schiller nor Herder nor Kant, but Hegel, Feuerbach, Büchner [*Kraft und Stoff*], Nietzsche, Schopenhauer and Hartmann become the spiritual leaders of

Prussianised Germany. This materialism harmonised very easily with that national and racial mysticism which the Pan-Germans derived from the Frenchman Gobineau, from Nietzsche, Schopenhauer, Hartmann and others; Lagarde even prescribed for the Germans their higher religion, and William believes in his own and his grandfather's Messiahship [the same is not less true of Hitler]. . . .

" The Pan-Germans uphold and spread hostility and hatred against neighbouring nations, especially the Slavs; and the Czechs, above all, because of their special world situation, are a thorn in the eyes of the Germans. In Pan-Germanistic literature, the Czechs, equally with the Poles, are threatened with extermination and forcible Germanisation; people still remember the exhortation of Mommsen, that the Germans should break the hard skulls of the Czechs, and Lagarde and the other leaders of Pan-Germanism speak in an equally brutal manner. The Pan-Germanists turn history and sociology into zoology and mechanics—that is, in harmony with their tactics of frightfulness, as practised in this war. . . .

" The Pan-Germans in Germany and Austria did not forget the Ukraine, encouraging the Ukrainians to play an anti-Russian part. For example, in 1917, Professor Jaffe wrote: ' The permanent Russian danger may be abolished in any case only by the formation of an Ukrainian State, and thereby our doubts regarding the Polish question will be solved.' . . .

" Russia now took on a different significance for Germany; the weakening of Russia and the annexation of the Russian south-west (fertile soil—coal—Black Sea), became the new German policy, and the policy of the present war. The annexation of western Russian Governments, the juggling with the Baltic Provinces, with Poland and the Ukraine, all that is the result of aiming at the organisation of a German Central Europe and domination in Asia and Africa. Berlin-Bagdad was broadened to Berlin-Warsaw-Kiev-Odessa. The East, Russia and the zone of small nations would mean far more to Germany than parts of the West (Belgium, Alsace-Lorraine or parts of France). Controlling the East, Germany would be enabled to conquer the West. Europe and humanity need an independent and strong Russia.

" The day the Germans are masters of Eastern Europe, they will have no difficulty in settling accounts with France, England, and eventually with the United States of America."

(c) *Hitlerian Pan-Germanism.* This is the analysis and criticism which Masaryk made of Pan-Germanism in the form which it took before and during the War of 1914–18. No better analysis could be made of the post-War Pan-Germanism which is represented by Hitler and the Nazis. All the main ideas, all the fundamental tendencies of the Pan-Germanism of before and during the War are to be found, often word for word, in National Socialism, both in its doctrine and in its practice. It is all the more surprising, therefore, that almost no attention has been paid to this phenomenon. It is true that before the War, Pan-Germanism was regarded as a theory held by certain crank professors and fanatical intellectuals whose influence on actual German policy was thought to be slight. But the War and, above all, the German war aims which became apparent in the anti-British, anti-French programme of the Kaiser, in the Treaties of Brest-Litovsk and Bucharest and the plan for a Customs union between Germany-Austria and Hungary as in Naumann's plan for a German *Mitteleuropa*, revealed that the practical policy of Germany was in complete agreement with the theories of the crank professors. To-day, again, there is another attempt to distinguish between the propaganda period of Herr Hitler and the political aims of the German Chancellor. According to this interpretation, the " exaggerations " of *Mein Kampf* and the programme of the Nazis should not be taken literally. In fact, in spite of certain modifications of a purely tactical nature whose aim is primarily to confuse the enemy, Hitler's programme rests as he outlined it in 1923. The year 1938 is the proof.

Hitlerism, like the old Pan-Germanism, stresses the idea of racial purity, but what was formerly a more or less theoretical programme is now being brutally carried into practice. For the Nazis, the Jews are the most inferior of all races, a poison in the blood of the Aryans, but they regard other nations also with scarcely less disfavour, hating in particular the Slavs and the French. Hitler makes a distinction between *kulturschöpferische* and *kulturtragende* races—the former, creative races, are represented by the Nordic races, more especially by the Germans, among whom the National Socialists are an élite; while the latter are represented by all those other races who have ruined the purity of their blood by intermarriage with other races, notably the Slavs and the French. But even the English are regarded as having sinned against the principle of racial purity, as is proved by the " commercial utilitarianism." The Jews, in a special category, represent the negation and disruption of culture.[1]

The Nazi Pan-Germans, like their predecessors, proclaim the necessity of increasing the space available for the German nation, using the same arguments in support of their claims. " *Blut und Boden* " (blood and land) is the war-cry of the Nazis, and when they speak of land, it is of land in the east of Europe that they are thinking. That does not mean, of course, that they would not move also against the west, and indeed Hitler is always conscious of the fact that, in order to guarantee his expansion towards the east, he must destroy France, the mortal enemy of the German nation. Immediately after the annexation of the Austrians and the Sudeten Germans, Hitler began to cry out for more space for the Germans, regardless of the fact that, when he annexed the Sudeten-German territories, he had assured Mr. Chamberlain that that was his last territorial claim in Europe. Dr. Goebbels, speaking in Berlin on December 15, 1938, declared:

" In Germany nearly 140 people live on every square kilometre of land. It is no fault of the Germans that their territories are so crowded. . . . Although their territories have been increased, they are not yet sufficient for the German nation."

On January 24, 1939, Bernhardt Kohler, head of the Economic Committee of the German National Socialist Party, explained:

" The Germans are the greatest people in Europe. The German Reich is the greatest Empire in Europe. The German national economy is the strongest in Europe; therefore it wishes to have the greatest influence there."

He went on to say that the National Socialists would have three main obstacles to overcome: the domination of Jewish capital,

---

[1] The logical conclusion of this view is that reached by the German writer, Hermann Gauch: " The only existing differentiation is between Nordic man, on the one hand, and animals as a whole, including all non-Nordic human beings or sub-men."

their lost population and their lack of space in which to live. Two days before this, on January 22, Dr. Ley, leader of the Labour Front, expressed himself at Nürnberg in even more definite terms:

" We are to-day the strongest nation in the world, but we do not yet possess absolute liberty. We have yet to overcome our last drawback, our lack of space. We have too little space; we are choking, with 140 Germans to every square kilometre. . . . But we shall break through this last barrier, for we are a nation of 80 millions."

Herr Hitler, in his speech to the Reichstag on January 30, 1939, repeated these arguments as follows:

" The Reich numbers 80 million people—that is to say, more than 135 per square kilometre. Therefore it must have colonies," and the Chancellor of the Reich made an official claim for these with all the necessary firmness. Pursuing his familiar tactics, he tried, at the same time, to calm down England and France by assuring them that there need be no armed conflict over the question of colonies, and that Germany has no territorial claims against them beyond the restitution of her former colonial possessions.

In the same speech, however, he said quite definitely: " The riches of the world must either be divided up by force, in which case they will be re-divided from time to time by force, or their division will be carried out amicably, in which case common sense should see that equality of opportunity is secured."

England and France are thus challenged to give back to Germany her colonies without resort to war, otherwise Germany will be forced to try to expand her territories by every means, including that of war. Herr Hitler, however, in the speech which has been quoted, gave an assurance that " there is not a single German, and more especially not a single National Socialist, who entertains the slightest intention of making difficulties for the British Empire." And yet, as early as December, 1938, Germany had already informed Britain that she intended to add to the strength of the German Navy by building new submarines and cruisers.

It may seem that Hitler's colonial ambitions are in conflict with his original intentions. In his book, *Mein Kampf,* he bitterly criticised the Germany of William II for having embarked on colonial conquests instead of persisting in the *Drang nach Osten*, and for having thus made an enemy of England. Yet he is himself now making colonial claims. To a certain extent he is obliged to do this, because he cannot control at will the dynamic expansion of Pan-Germanism, which aims not only at the domination of Central and Eastern Europe, but also at establishing German hegemony over the whole of Europe and finally over the whole world. Hitler, of course, has not abandoned his idea of coming to an agreement—even a temporary one—with Britain; he hopes therefore that the re-distribution of colonies may be carried out in such a way that England will suffer little. The losses should fall on others, more especially on France. In the mind of a Nazi, however, any agreement with Britain should be designed to render her innocuous to Germany, and therefore he aims at weakening the British position by destroying France and by obtaining colonies as strategic points to be held in hand against possible British intervention. Hitler came to an " agreement " with Mussolini also, but the solidarity of the Berlin-Rome Axis was not assured until Germany had squeezed Italy out of Central Europe and had deflected her expansionist ambitions against France, and incidentally against Britain also, in the Mediterranean. Italy is not an equal, but a junior partner in the Axis. England, in the view of the Nazis, should be reduced to a similar position. Herr Hitler's colonial demands, therefore, only appear to be in conflict with his programme; in fact, they in no way weaken his resolution to enfeeble the West to such a degree that the hegemony of German *Mitteleuropa* shall be guaranteed in the East.

The aims of the old Pan-Germanism and of the Nazi Pan-Germanism are absolutely identical, but there is a fundamental difference between the two movements which should not be overlooked: whereas the Pan-Germanism of pre-War days and of the War period affected the minds and imaginations only of the political ruling classes of imperial Germany, the Army, the diplomatic service and the professional classes, National Socialism, which is essentially a mass movement, has introduced Pan-German ideas to the masses and has fired the imagination of young people of every class. The old Pan-Germanism was simply imperialist—Nazi Pan-Germanism is not only imperialist, but also revolutionary, and is therefore much more dangerous. It is an indication of the contradictions of our times that Conservatives have considered the National Socialists and the Fascists as " the defenders and saviours " of the existing order against Communism, while the National Socialists and the Fascists have learned from the Bolsheviks that they must revolutionise the masses; hence their movement has all the characteristics of " the revolt of the masses " which is described so well by Ortega y Gasset. They have adopted, especially in their economic and social policy, a system of State capitalism, and are thus much closer to the Bolsheviks than they are to the Liberal capitalists. National Socialism is in every way a movement of political and social revolution. Its foreign policy is one of dynamic expansionism. It fights, not only against " Jewish Marxism," but also against " Jewish capitalism." It removed from power not only the Socialists and the democrats, but also the Neuraths, Schachts, Fritzsches, Becks and all other exponents of German Conservatism, whether in the economic field, in the Army, in the Civil Service or in the Foreign Office. Neurath and General Fritzsch were replaced (Neurath has now been removed to the Protectorate of Bohemia and Moravia) early in 1938, and early in 1939 Dr. Schacht was deprived of his decisive influence upon the economic affairs of Germany; at the same time, the transfer by decree of responsibility for military training to the S.A. and S.S. substantially increased the influence of the Nazis in the German Reichswehr. Herr von Ribbentrop is an extreme representative of the dynamism of Nazi foreign policy. During the Czechoslovak crisis, it was he who drove the Chancellor to take the most extreme steps, bringing the Reich to the verge of a war in which it would have been completely isolated. The more completely Germany becomes Nazified internally, the more she is forced on to achieve the fulfilment of her Pan-German aims. The two things cannot be dissociated from each other. Hitler's successes abroad are always followed by the reinforcement and extension of National Socialism inside Germany. The insatiability of German dynamic expansionism was strikingly shown after the annexation of Austria and of the Sudeten-German territories: the enlargement of the Reich by no means satisfied Nazi expansionism, but, on the contrary, became the starting-point for new demands for an increase of " living space." As there are so many Germans in the Reich—over 80 millions already—they must have new territories, in order that they may not choke in their present " cramped space." Such arguments make a considerable impression on the popular masses, who are experiencing increased economic and social poverty—as was admitted by Hitler in his speech of January 30, 1939—and do not understand that this is directly due to the economic and financial policy necessitated by the vast scale of German rearmament. German propaganda makes no secret of this increasing poverty of the masses, but tries to exploit it for political reasons by attributing it to the lack of living space of the German people. This lack is again attributed not to the wrong policy pursued by the Nazis, but to the selfishness of the other nations, who stole the German colonies and are now deliberately encircling Germany itself and challenging its right to live. Thus the German working classes, angry at the reduction of their standard of living, are encouraged to direct this anger against foreign countries and to see in the Nazi plans of foreign conquest pleasant dreams of the new space over which Germany will spread and where those Germans who are suffering from poverty, crowded 135–140 to the square kilometre, will all be well off. At the same time the youth of the nation is stirred to wild enthusiasm by the prospect of a world dominated by the *kulturschöpferische*, German people, which has been called upon and chosen to rule over all other peoples, which are inherently inferior to itself.

(d) *The Three Weapons of National Socialism.* The National Socialists have considerably increased the force of Pan-Germanism by gaining for it the support of the popular masses, who are inspired with the revolutionary spirit of the unpossessing against those who have too much. Mussolini's differentiation between the proletarian and the super-saturated nations has become very useful for this propaganda, and has carried into the international field, the strength of revolutionary sentiment. The pupils have surpassed their revolutionary masters in other directions also—for instance, in the tactics which they employ against their victims. They are constantly and diligently striving to bring about the disintegration of other nations from within, making use for this purpose of three weapons: anti-Semitism, anti-Bolshevism and national minorities. It is true that the brutal persecution of the Jews is arousing strong anti-German feeling throughout the world, especially in the Anglo-Saxon countries; but this has, nevertheless, done little harm to the Third Reich, except perhaps in so far as its relations with the United States are concerned; whereas it is true, also, that the Nazis have succeeded in reviving or sometimes in introducing anti-Semitic feelings in other countries, even in certain countries of Western Europe. In the Central European States, Nazi anti-Jewish laws and practices are quite openly imitated; this is happening in Poland, Rumania, Hungary, Slovakia and the Carpatho-Ukraine, and even the Czechs were being forced after Munich towards an anti-Semitic régime. Anti-Semitism is spreading even in Serbia, where it never existed before, and in Bulgaria, and symptoms of it are becoming evident even in Turkey. It is well known that anti-Semitism is being disseminated in Alsace-Lorraine, where the inhabitants are being stirred up against " Jew-ridden " France, and even in Paris anti-Semitic feeling is becoming stronger. By means of this anti-Semitism, the Nazis aim, not only at stirring up internal discontent, but also in arousing those base and barbarous instincts which confuse the reason and dull the sense of justice and right and the respect for humanity. It is thus made difficult to fight an ideological battle against the barbarism of the Nazis, since even those who are threatened by it are themselves becoming barbarians. The anti-Semites in every nation are being drawn over to the side of the Nazi anti-Semites. The Nazis present themselves before the world as the saviours of European civilisation, but, by their anti-Semitism, they are thrusting Europe backwards into barbarism, organised in a manner such as did not exist even in the Middle Ages. How can these Nazis save European civilisation when, with their neo-paganism, they are fighting against Christianity—whether Catholic or Protestant—which is the foundation stone of that civilisation ?

The anti-Bolshevik slogan is an even more effective weapon for disintegrating nations internally, and there is no doubt that it has been used with great success, especially in the democratic countries. It also, as has already been shown, played a disastrous role in the Czechoslovak crisis: the horror of war was reinforced by the spectre that after another war the whole of Europe would be Bolshevised. By the skilful use of this slogan, social tension is maintained everywhere in an acute state and people are misled into mistaking democracy for Communism. There are to-day in every democratic country three principal political divisions: the Fascists, the Communists and the democrats. The last of these are numerically the most powerful, but as they are composed of people ranging from democratic Conservatives to democratic Socialists, they are without the unified doctrine and united political determination which are possessed by the Fascists and by the Communists, who are constantly penetrating into their ranks. In this matter of ideological penetration, there is no doubt that Fascist propaganda is achieving more obvious and more marked success than is that of the Communists. Marxism, by stressing the principle of class war, is attractive as a rule only to the working classes, and more especially to those of the town, having little appeal for the agricultural workers and to the lower middle classes. The progressive " proletarianisation " of the middle classes on the Continent has not lead to its joining the workers' proletariat, but, on the contrary, has tended to put it in opposition to the workers, and has thus facilitated its conversion to Fascism and National Socialism. If it had not been for the proletarianisation of the middle classes, leading to their increased anxiety before their constantly falling standard of life, and if it had not been for their external social superiority over the working classes, neither Fascism nor National Socialism could ever have become a mass movement. The middle classes, both in the towns and in the countryside, are always the main basis of a Fascist movement, and because they are on the whole conservative in their outlook, they readily adopt the traditional well-known nationalist slogan, especially if anti-foreign sentiment is emphasised—or its variation, anti-Semitism, for the Jew is regarded by the middle classes as a " foreign element." The capitalist and *bourgeois* classes are always afraid lest there should take place in their own countries what happened in Russia. It is true, of course, that the Soviet experiment has not yet succeeded in introducing the Communist system—that is admitted even by the leading Soviet authorities, who add, of course, that they are on the way towards it—but, nevertheless, Russia is administered on State-capitalist collective principles, which are in conflict with those of Liberal capitalism, and its political rulers are certainly representatives of the working classes and peasants. The régime in Russia, in spite of its shortcomings and mistakes, has maintained itself now for more than twenty years, and, even if the Communist International did not exist, this fact in itself represents a threat to the capitalist system, inasmuch as it suggests the possibility that some alternative system may work successfully.

This question, which is no longer merely theoretical, but now quite practical, is worrying both the capitalist and the working class—for different reasons, of course, for in the first it inspires fear and in the second it inspires hope. Fascism and Nazism have declared war against Bolshevism. The capitalist classes accept the help which they offer them, but they must pay dearly for it, for Fascism and Nazism are totalitarian movements, and, just as they impose the dictatorship of the State in all cultural and political affairs, so they impose it also in economic affairs. Everything must be subordinated to the State and harnessed to the service of a militarised economy. It is true that Liberal capitalism is finished, but the Nazis speak about it as " Jewish capitalism " or play up to the dislike of the middle classes for big financiers by calling it " big capitalism." Private profits earned in free competition are becoming smaller in Germany, for the State thrusts its insatiable hands into the pockets of the rich capitalists—but it does so to the other classes as well, not only by levying taxes, rates and " voluntary " loans, but also by means of various " voluntary " gifts and subscriptions. Liberal capitalism has been replaced in Germany, however, by State capitalism, which permits the capitalist and *bourgeois* classes, despite all their losses and restrictions, to maintain their socially privileged positions. It even makes their position more advantageous and more influential, since it worsens the position of the working classes, who are subjected to strict discipline and obedience, and are organised in trade unions which are administered in a totalitarian manner and have only the name in common with the trade union movement which raised the position of the workers in the last quarter of the nineteenth and first quarter of the twentieth centuries. The corporative system which the Nazis are creating serves as an effective check to the social and political rise of the worker. Under these circumstances, it is not surprising that the Nazis meet with success in their anti-Bolshevik propaganda among certain classes abroad. Yet this propaganda is damaging, not only to the Communists and Socialists, but to the whole democratic system, for, since the entire political, social and moral structure of the nations concerned depends on their internal solidarity, the moment this becomes lessened they are nationally weakened as regards external dangers. This is precisely the aim of the German Nazis and the Italian Fascists—to disrupt from within the national solidarity of the Western democracies and thus to weaken as much as possible their defensive power. Anti-Bolshevism is being used as an effective and, alas ! a successful weapon against the democracies, and has already done much to facilitate the progress of Nazi-Fascist aggression.

The policy of the Nazis with regard to National minorities also serves towards this end; the promotion of national discord is, as the Czechoslovak experience has shown, one of the most useful instruments for disrupting the states of Central and Eastern Europe from within. The Nazis are naturally concerned in the first place with the German minorities, who are looked after by several special organisations, such as the Deutscher Volksbund im Auslande, and have a first-class Institute in Stuttgart. According to National Socialist ideas, Hitler is the Führer not only of the Germans in the Third Reich, but also of every German in the world, wherever he may be—in Europe, in America or in any other continent; and it is the duty of every German to follow on all occasions the orders and requirements of German National Socialism. All Germans living abroad are regarded as mere cells of Nazi Pan-Germanism, and are carefully organised everywhere; where the laws and temper of the country in which they live necessitate it, this organisation takes the form of a cultural or sporting society.

There are over 20 million Germans living abroad. The

following statistics, quoted from German sources, and treating as " Germans " all those who speak the German language or a dialect of it, appeared in the *Daily Herald* last November:

Switzerland	.. ..	2,900,000	Belgium ..	.. ..	50,000
France ..	.. ..	1,634,000	Lichtenstein	.. ..	10,000
Poland ..	.. ..	1,245,000	U.S.A. ..	.. ..	12,000,000
Russia ..	.. ..	1,185,000	Brazil ..	.. ..	750,000
Rumania ..	.. ..	800,000	Chile ..	.. ..	720,000
Yugoslavia	.. ..	740,000	Argentine ..	.. ..	200,000
Hungary ..	.. ..	385,000	Australia ..	.. ..	100,000
Danzig ..	.. ..	348,000	Africa ..	.. ..	78,000
Luxembourg	.. ..	250,000	Canada ..	.. ..	50,000
The Baltic States	..	248,000	Small States of Latin		
Italy ..	.. ..	235,000	America	.. ..	28,000
Denmark ..	.. ..	77,000	To which should be added—		
			Czechoslovakia	.. ..	380,000

I have already described how Germany uses her minorities for exerting pressure on the Governments of all the Central European states, by asking for special rights and even privileges for them. This was seen particularly clearly in the post-Munich Czecho-Slovakia, where the exceptional privileges extorted from the Czechoslovak Government were, as Ribbentrop openly said to Chvalkovský, intended by Germany to be used for exerting pressure in Poland, Hungary, Rumania and Yugoslavia, so that those countries should also grant similar privileges to their respective German minorities. Germany can use similar tactics against any other state, whether in the West or in the East, and is already showing a great interest in her nationals in America, where some states have been obliged, since Munich, to take preventive measures against the increasingly provocative behaviour of the Nazis.

German propaganda can be used to stir up other, non-German minorities in various states, and has already started stirring up the Ukrainians. Minority discontent is a far-reaching weapon, for there is, in fact, no state in Europe without minorities, Britain has her Irish and France her Alsatians. This was pointed out by the Czech Press in an article published in *České Slovo* of October 13, 1938:

GERMANY:	Czechs (110,000 before Munich and 750,000 more after Munich) ..	860,000
	Croats	75,000
	Jews	692,000
	Dutch	82,000
	Italians	23,000
	Poles	680,000
	Wends	65,000
	Russians	20,000
	Other nationalities ..	155,000
DANZIG:	Poles	15,000
	Jews	9,000
	Other nationalities ..	5,000 (i.e. 7 per cent. minorities)
BELGIUM:	French and Walloons ..	3,480,000
	Flemings	4,200,000
	Germans	115,000
	Other nationalities ..	165,000 (i.e. 3·3 per cent. minorities, if we exclude the Flemings, who are often counted as a minority)
ENGLAND:	Irish	1,100,000
	Welsh	600,000
	Jews	300,000
	Others	265,000 (i.e. 4·8 per cent. minorities)
BULGARIA:	Jews	50,000
	Gypsies	110,000
	Turks	550,000
	Others	150,000 (i.e. 13·8 per cent. minorities)
DENMARK:	Germans	80,000
	Others	90,000 (i.e. 4·5 per cent. minorities)
ESTONIA:	Germans	16,000
	Russians	94,000
	Others	90,000 (i.e. 11·9 per cent. minorities)
FINLAND:	Swedes	400,000
	Others	50,000 (i.e. 11·8 per cent. minorities)
FRANCE:	Italians	1,300,000
	Spaniards	650,000
	Bretons	1,000,000
	Germans	1,750,000
	Flemings	250,000
	Slavs	530,000
	Basques	170,000
	Jews	200,000
	Others	535,000 (i.e. 15·1 per cent. minorities)
GREECE:	Slavs	90,000
	Jews	80,000
	Turks	100,000
	Others	218,000 (i.e. 7·1 per cent. minorities)
ITALY:	Germans	260,000
	Yugoslavs	450,000
	Jews	50,000
	Others	219,000 (i.e. 2·4 per cent. minorities)

YUGOSLAVIA:	Czechoslovaks ..	..	160,000
	Rumanians ..	..	285,000
	Albanians ..	..	520,000
	Germans ..	..	610,000
	Hungarians ..	..	560,000
	Jews	..	80,000
	Others	..	290,000 (i.e. 18·5 per cent. minorities, if we do not take into account the problem between the Croats, Slovenes and Serbs)
LITHUANIA:	Russians ..	..	236,000
	Germans ..	..	63,000
	Jews	..	93,000
	Others	..	89,000 (i.e. 24·4 per cent. minorities)
LATVIA:	Russians ..	..	150,000
	Germans ..	..	110,000
	Jews	..	160,000
	Others	..	32,000 (i.e. 17·9 per cent. minorities)
HOLLAND:	Flemings ..	..	1,000,000
	Germans ..	..	100,000
	Jews	..	135,000
	Others	..	97,000 (i.e. 15·6 per cent. minorities)
NORWAY:	Lapps	..	37,000
	Others	..	23,000 (i.e. 2·1 per cent. minorities)
POLAND:	Ukrainians ..	..	4,700,000
	Russians ..	..	1,220,000
	Germans ..	..	1,150,000
	Jews	..	3,050,000
	Others	..	350,000 (i.e. 30·6 per cent. minorities. This percentage was increased after Munich by—
	Czechs	..	123,000)
PORTUGAL:	Various ..	..	40,000 (i.e. 0·6 per cent. minorities)
RUMANIA:	Germans ..	..	810,000
	Ukrainians ..	..	520,000
	Russians ..	..	250,000
	Bulgarians ..	..	410,000
	Hungarians ..	..	1,480,000
	Jews	..	880,000
	Gypsies ..	..	200,000
	Turks	..	180,000
	Others	..	250,000 (i.e. 25·7 per cent. minorities)
SWEDEN:	Finns	..	37,000
	Others	..	58,000 (i.e. 1·5 per cent. minorities)
SWITZERLAND:	Germans ..	..	2,926,000 (i.e. 70 per cent. of the total)
	French	..	886,000 (i.e. 21·2 per cent. of the total)
	Italians ..	..	260,000 (i.e. 6·2 per cent. of the total)
	Rhetoromans ..	..	45,000 (i.e. 1·1 per cent. of the total)
	Jews	..	25,000 (i.e. 0·6 per cent. of the total)
	Others	..	40,000 (i.e. 0·9 per cent. of the total)
SPAIN:	Basques ..	..	45,000
	Others	..	100,000 (i.e. 2·3 per cent. minorities)

HUNGARY:	Germans	..	..	650,000
	Slovaks	..	..	160,000
	Jews ..	..	..	570,000
	Others ..	..	..	140,000 (i.e. 16·9 per cent. minorities, but the percentage increased after Vienna by—
	Slovaks	..	..	289,000; there will now be altogether 450,000 Slovaks)
	Ruthenes	..	..	39,000

The foregoing statistics are probably not strictly accurate but that is of no importance in connection with my present object, which is to show that there are national minorities practically everywhere, and that it is therefore possible to create a minority problem, if desired, almost anywhere in the world. I remember that when, in 1932, I was speaking with one of the National Socialist leaders in Cologne, he told me perfectly seriously that the minorities in France numbered 14 millions (he included among these even the Provençeaux), and that he was convinced that France would be obliged to grant autonomy to the Alsatians, Lorrainers, Basques, Bretons and Italians. I recall this merely to show that even at that time the National Socialists entertained plans for disintegrating their rival states by means of real or artificially created minorities. Fascist Italy has already used the principle of nationality as an argument in favour of her expansionist intentions against France, by appealing to the Italians in Tunis, Corsica, Nice and even in South-West France —wherever, in fact, they may be settled. If the Communist parties, as sections of the Third International, are regarded as being dangerously disruptive elements in the body of the nations to which they belong, it should not be forgotten that expansive Pan-Germanism is making use of German, and if necessary, of other, minorities as instruments for the internal dislocation of all states. In spite of the apparent national homogeneity of the Western countries, Germany is prepared to make use of this weapon even against Switzerland, France, Belgium or Denmark, while the Nazis claim the whole of Holland as being a branch of the German race. The Nazis have cleverly invented the idea of form-ing *Volksgruppen*. They claim for all minorities the right to form autonomous organisations, the so-called *Volksgruppe*, to include all the representatives of their respective nationalities. These *Volksgruppe* should have cultural autonomy at least, but also, if possible, political autonomy, and the state in which they live would have to deal with the *Volksgruppe* in all questions regarding the " national life " of the minority which it represents. (Its members could deal with the state authorities solely through the medium of the *Volksgruppe*.) The whole structure may appear quite innocent, and merely an effective means of safeguarding the minorities, but in reality it makes it more easy for the Nazis to establish absolute control over the German minorities, for each of whom the *Volksgruppe* would be directed in a totalitarian way by its Henlein (in Memel his name is Dr. Neumann; in Hungary, Dr. Basch; in Bohemia, Herr Kundt; in Slovakia, Herr Karmasin, and so on), and indirectly over the other minorities, as is actually being done with regard to the Ukrainians. Since under modern conditions there is no question which cannot be considered as concerning the " national life " of a minority, the state authorities would have to " come to terms " with the representative of the *Volksgruppe*, who could, of course, in the name of the " defence of the minority," exercise his right of veto against any measure of which the Germans disapproved. The organisation of the minorities into these *Volksgruppen* leads simply to the formation of foreign elements within the framework of the state, if not actually to the formation of small states within the state and ultimately to the disintegration of the whole country. The principle of nationality and of self-determination of nations, were fundamentally democratic ideas. In this connection, as in many others, the Nazis and Fascists are making use of democratic instruments and ideas to the detriment of democracies.

Enough has been said above to show how much more dangerous is Pan-Germanism as practised by the Nazis than that of their predecessors. The aim of both is the same, however: German hegemony in Europe and elsewhere, especially in the Near East and in the Americas. The means applied to that end have been carried to an extraordinary pitch of perfection.

(*e*) *Conflict between Germany and Europe.* During the Great War the world was faced with a terribly real danger of Pan-German domination; now, only twenty years later, it is once more in the same situation. Then the world was threatened by Prussian militarism, which hated democracy and despised humanitarian ideals. To-day the whole of our Western civilisation, based on the traditions of Greece and Rome, of Christianity and of the French Revolution, is menaced by plebeian National Socialism. Prussian militarism, with its worship of power and violence, has been enormously reinforced by the dynamic revolutionary ardour of the German people, who are stirred into, and permanently maintained in, a state of hysteria. The great problem of Germany's relations with the rest of Europe has again come to the fore, this time with such force and urgency as never before in the history of European civilisation. It is a relationship which, beginning more or less in the period of Luther, has for centuries developed along lines of increasing conflict, and of which T. G. Masaryk wrote in his *Making of a State*.

" In the Middle Ages, German thought and culture formed part of those of Europe; but in more modern times they were increasingly differentiated and isolated. The Prussian state, which the Reformation strengthened, was aggressive from the outset and dominated Germany. The idea of the State, the so-called ' Statism,' prevailed also in Western Europe, though there the State became an organ of Parliament and of public opinion. In Germany, on the contrary, the monarchical State was literally deified, and its absolute power generally recognised. Indeed it was not until the end of the World War that the King of Prussia, in his capacity as German Emperor, decided in favour of the parliamentarisation of Germany. Prussia and Germany were really an organised Cæsarism. . . . The Prussian officer, the soldier, became the German criterion for the organisation of society and, indeed, of the world. The soldier and war were regular institutions.

" Nor did the Reformation, classical humanism, science, art and philosophy prevail over theocracy in Germany as they prevailed in the West; for the German people accepted the Reformation only in part, and the German Lutheran Reformation adapted itself to Catholicism. Thus there arose a sort of Cæsaro-Papism, albeit distinct from the Russian Cæsaro-Papism. In course of time, Pan-German Imperialism took the place of Lessing's, Herder's, Goethe's, Kant's and Schiller's humanitarian ideals, which were derived from secular and Western evolution and from participation in it.

" The catchword ' Berlin-Baghdad ' represented an endeavour to secure mastery over Europe, and thus, eventually, over Asia and Africa also—an endeavour which, in itself, expresses an ideal of the ancient world. Germany cherished and sought to realise, even geographically, the ideal of the Roman Empire. The Western ideal tends, on the contrary, to organise the whole of mankind and, above all, to link Europe with America and with other continents. In the World War they were thus linked. . . .

" Not only in politics, philosophy, science and art, but even in theology this Prussianism expressed itself. As soon as the leading men and classes in a nation begin to rely on might and violence, the wells of sympathy dry up. People lose interest in knowing the feelings and thoughts of their neighbours, since the mechanism of the State, the word of command, the fist, suffice for all purposes of intercourse. They cease to think freely and their learning becomes barren of living ideas.

" This is the explanation of the great errors and faults of German history and in German thought before and during the war. Bismarck, with his overbearing treatment of those about him, is the type of the domineering Prussian."

What is to be the solution of this tragic problem ? Several attempts have already been made to come to some compromise and to establish a tolerable *modus vivendi*. It was to this end that the statesmen of Europe gave Czechoslovakia to Germany, but this did not solve the problem nor even relieve the tension. Now, there are only two possibilities: either National Socialism will be victorious and will enforce its hegemony upon the world or it will be destroyed.

National Socialism is exclusively German; its strange, purely German and inimitable mysticism makes it impossible for other nations to become " Nazified " in the strict sense of the word. They may be or become Fascist, Communist or democratic, for Fascism, Communism and democracy are creeds which, in the appropriate social and political conditions, are practicable every-where—or at least everywhere within the sphere of our Western civilisation. But National Socialism, being exclusively German, stands or falls by its mystic doctrine that the Germans are a superior and chosen nation, representing the flower of the Nordic race; for that reason the only relationship between them and the nations among whom they live which could satisfy the Nazis is one based on the hegemony of the former over the latter. Herr Hitler's Pan-Germanism, as opposed to that of Wilhelm II, does not advocate the Germanisation of other nations, because it does not want to spoil the purity of the German blood. It is for this reason that it lays even greater stress on the importance of establishing German hegemony over the other nations, as a right ensuing from the racial superiority of the German nation.

To anyone who realises the inherent consequences of the Nazi doctrine and policy, it is evident that either Europe must submit to the hegemony of the Third Reich or Germany must submit to Europe and become culturally and socially a member of the European community. This does not mean, necessarily, that the existing irreconcilable conflict must result in war; it is possible to imagine the Munich method being applied again and again, country after country capitulating without a struggle before the Reich until the German plan is fulfilled; or, alternatively, one can imagine the threatened countries uniting against the common menace and forming themselves into a great coalition, based essentially on an alliance of Great Britain, France, the Soviet Union and the United States. Against the overwhelming superiority which such a coalition would represent, the Nazis might not dare to risk a war, and their régime would sooner or later collapse under the strain of its cumulative internal tension, which could no longer find external relief. Neither of these alternatives is impossible, but, as time goes on, they both become less probable. All the available evidence seems to indicate that the effect of Munich has been to increase the danger of war. The policy of making increasing concessions to the dynamic dictatorships can never reduce that danger and can at best only postpone the outbreak of war—at the cost of increasing the strength of the dictatorship.

(f) *Hitler or Masaryk*. The vital dilemma cannot be evaded:
Europe must either become unified under the hegemony of the
German Dictator, a fate which even the Dictator of Italy would
be unable to escape, or it must rid itself of this tyranny and
unify in a federation of free and independent nations, all obedient
to the humanitarian ideals of freedom, right, equality and justice.
Europe must create itself according either to Hitler's conception
or to that of Masaryk. Just as the anlysis of Pan-Germanism
made by Masaryk during the World War remains true to-day, so
also his constructive proposals, made at the same time, for a new
Europe have in no way become out-of-date.

The basis upon which, even while one-half of the world was
destroying the other in war, he proposed to found the new
Europe was that of a humanitarian democracy which would
recognise and respect the freedom and independence, not only of
men and women, but also of nations, both great and small !

" It is a question," he wrote, " of recognising the importance
of human individuality, regardless of material differences
between individuals. That is the real significance at the root
of this great humanitarian movement, which characterises the
new era, and which finds expression in Socialism, democracy
and nationalism. Modern humanitarianism [humanism] recognises the rights of the weak, because therein lies the significance
of all efforts for progress and for the recognition of human
dignity; the strong will always help themselves unaided—the
defence of the weak and small, whether they be individuals,
corporations, classes, nations or states, that is the task of the
new era. Everywhere the weak and oppressed, and those who
are exploited, are uniting—association is the great programme
of our time: federation, the free federation of small nations and
states, will be the application of this principle, assuring an
effective organisation of humanity. . . .

" The real federation of nations will come only when the
nations are free and will unite of their own free will. It is towards this that the development of Europe is tending. . . .
The free and the freed nations will organise themselves according to their needs in bigger units and the whole Continent will
thus become organised. If federations of smaller nations come

into existence, they will be federations freely founded to meet the real needs of the nations within them, not for the furtherance of dynastic and imperialist aims. Federation without freedom is impossible.

" The principle of nationality is not incompatible with internationalism. The European nations, in proportion as they become separate entities, are striving after the close coordination of their economy and communications and are generally coming closer to each other, both technically and culturally; but individualisation and centralisation gain a deeper spiritual value from the interchange of ideas and of culture, from the knowledge of foreign languages, and from translations. Europe, humanity, unite ! . . .

" Germany is both strong and weak on account of her systematic, constant organisation, organisation of organisations, super-organisation—but her aim, the domination of all other nations, is morally bad. The Prussian system has been scientifically thought out and represents a force, and the Germans therefore feel themselves a *Herrenvolk* [a ruling nation]; but a little more or a little less culture (and after all that is only a superficial one) does not give them the right to dominate other nations which develop in their own way. Different nations are on different levels of culture; it is not written that they must all be educated at the same speed and to the same extent; it is sufficient if they honestly strive after their moral and rational perfection and progress. Europe should be united and unified, but that does not mean that it must be standardised. On the contrary, development aims at diversity, at individualisation.

" A Pan-German Central Europe, with all its political consequences, is a great scheme; it is also an attempt at the organisation of Europe and of humanity, but this organisation is supposed to be brought into being dynastically, by absolutism, by militarism, by the domination of the other nations by the chosen German nation. The organisation of Europe and humanity according to the programme of the Allies[1] is a larger programme, a pan-human programme, which would be brought about democratically and without militarism through the

[1] These words were written during the World War in 1918.

self-determination of nations. Pan-Germanism is geographically and culturally a narrower and baser programme: Pan-Germanism aspires to unify the Old World of Europe, Asia and Africa. But besides the Old World there has developed a New World—America—and the programme of the Allies advocates the organisation of the Old World and the New, a direct organisation of the whole of humanity."

I repeat with emphasis, because I am convinced of it, that in spite of the numerous changes which have taken place since the World War, Masaryk's programme, formulated in 1917–18, remains valid even to-day in its main ideas and directives. This is simply because it is the only constructive programme upon which it would be possible to build up a free Europe and a real pacific organisation of the world.

The Nazi programme of Pan-German domination is not merely a threat to the independence of individual nations, planning to reduce them to mere vassals of the Third Reich. Its realisation would threaten the whole of our civilisation, built upon a synthesis of the ideas of the classical world, of Christianity and of the French Revolution. Nazism wants to destroy, not only Socialism and Communism, but even Christianity and democracy, which are based on humanitarian philosophy. It persecutes Jews, democrats, Socialists and Communists—and also Catholics and Protestants, for Teutonic neo-paganism, with its mystic conception of " blood and land " taken from the old barbarians, is the real religion of the National Socialists. It does not recognise the laws which are generally valid, and has abolished Roman Law, which is more or less accepted throughout the sphere of Western civilisation, replacing it with " German law," founded on the ideas of force and the supremacy of the German nation. Even physics and mathematics must be German ![1] Nazism is the negation of European culture; it is the sinister revolt of the Germanic myth against general humanity.

Among the leading statesmen, it is only President Roosevelt who is conscious of this danger, and because he judges it correctly he does not console himself by thinking of the distance between America and Germany. He is trying to awaken American

[1] " Occidental mathematics is an expression of the Nordic fighting spirit."— Dr. Geck.

democracy in time to its danger; and, realising quite clearly that
after the fall of European democracy it would be America's turn,
he is already offering encouragement to all who want to defend
themselves against the expansionism of the aggressive dictatorships. In his message to Congress on January 4, 1939, he said:

" Everywhere around us threats of *new* military and
economic aggressions arise. Storms coming from abroad
menace directly three institutions which are as indispensable
to the Americans to-day as in the past.

" The first is religion. It is the source of the other two,
democracy and international good faith. Religion teaches
man the bonds which unite him with God, and gives the
individual a sense of his own dignity, and teaches him to
respect himself by respecting his neighbours.

" Democracy—the practice of government by all—is a
convention between free men to respect the rights and
liberties of others.

" International good faith, sister of democracy, is born of
the will of men belonging to the civilised nations to respect
the rights and the liberties of men belonging to other nations.

" In modern civilisation these three institutions—religion,
democracy and international good faith—are complementary
to each other.

" Where the freedom of religion has been attacked, the
attack has come from sources hostile to democracy. Wherever
democracy has been destroyed, liberty of conscience has
disappeared. Wherever religion and democracy have vanished,
good faith and moderation in international affairs have
opened the way for unbounded ambition and brute force.

" There comes a time when men must prepare to defend
themselves—not only their homes, but also the principles of
religion and humanity on which are founded their Churches,
the government and their civilisation.

" The defence of religion, of democracy and of international
good faith are phases of the same struggle. In order to save
one, we must decide now to save the others. We know what
would happen to us in the United States if the new phil-
osophies of force dominated the other continents and invaded

ours. Just like the other nations, we cannot allow ourselves to be surrounded by enemies of our faith and of our humanity."

President Roosevelt finished this great speech which was a fiery appeal for the organisation of defence against the aggressive dictatorships, with the following warning:

" I prophesied once that this generation had an engagement with Destiny. My prophecy is coming true: we have received much, but more is still required of us."

The question upon which the future of humanity for a whole century depends is the following: will Europe or, more precisely, will France and England, capitulate before the domination of the united aggressive dictatorships of Germany and Italy, or will it recover itself for a firm resistance of some sort? Will Munich be the beginning of a general capitulation or of the recovery of the Western democracies?

It is not yet too late. Germany's power was, it is true, very much increased after the fall of Czechoslovakia; and the position of Italy, in relation to France, has also been considerably improved. These are the fatal consequences of the Munich capitulation, as well as of the unfortunate and, especially for France, very wrong policy of " non-intervention " in Spain. The power-political potential of Germany and Italy is undoubtedly increased, and their strategic position is certainly improved, both in Central Europe and in the Mediterranean. But, nevertheless, it is still possible to organise against them a defensive front, which would certainly enjoy a superiority over them. To-day, of course, much more even than before Munich, Britain and France are dependent on the co-operation of the United States and Russia, if they want effectively to resist the Berlin-Rome Axis. Without the help of these two Great Powers, they would find it difficult to defend themselves. It must not be forgotten that to-day Germany alone has 80 million inhabitants and Italy 43 million, while France and Great Britain together have only 87 million. In the event of a conflict between these rival groups of Great Powers, if Russia were to remain neutral, Japan would attack, not her, but the British Empire. Furthermore, the neutrality of Russia would inevitably lead to the neutrality of all the states from the Baltic to the Ægean Sea, which are even now being terrorised by Germany, after the fall of the Czechoslovak bastion. The uniting of the two Western Great Powers with Russia is from every point of view a matter of vital necessity to them, if they do not want to surrender to the hegemony of the Berlin-Rome Axis. Similarly, they need the material, political and moral support of the United States, not only in order to obtain armaments, war materials and food-stuffs, but also if they are to resist Japan.

Signs of the internal recovery of the Western Great Powers are apparent. In Britain, where the resistance against the Munich capitulation was at the time and is now increasingly strong, and where very serious preparations for defence are being made, there is ample evidence of growing disgust with the policy pursued by the dictatorships. The moral forces of British democracy are still strong, and it is only neces-sary that they should be mobilised and " dynamised." But even in France a change is taking place, although slowly and with some hesitation. In many quarters it is believed that France is in the last stages of decadence, and that therefore she is almost resigned to surrender, of her own will, her position as a Great Power and her traditional civilising mission in the world. This is, however, a superficial view, suitable, no doubt, for purposes of Nazi propaganda, which persists in disseminating stupid Pan-German theories about " degenerate and decadent France." No. France is not in a state of decadence, but only in a state of social and political regeneration—a process which is always very painful and difficult, and accompanied by dangerous convulsions. The sources of the creative power of this splendid nation, which by its great Revolution inaugurated a new era for humanity, an era which is only in the first stages of its evolution, are still active. In spite of the bitter and deep disappointment which was inflicted on us Czechoslovaks by the French policy in September, 1938, our faith in France is not weakened. To lose faith in France would mean to lose faith in Europe and in humanity. I do not doubt for a single moment that the French nation, revivified and strengthened by the progress of its common people, will recover again, to carry on in the world its creative mission.

Fortunately, it is not only the Western democracies who suffer from internal crises, but Nazi Germany and Fascist Italy as well. If these crises cannot manifest themselves so freely in the dictatorships as in the democracies, it does not necessarily mean that they do not exist. The " unanimous " approval of the Führer which is obtained in all the pseudo-plebiscite elections held in the Third Reich, cannot deceive anyone; plebiscites are well-known tricks of the tyrants. Napoleon III was in this connection, as in many others, the teacher of Mussolini and Hitler. The constant economic and financial difficulties of the two dictatorships are well known, and Hitler's public confession of Germany's critical economic situation in his speech of January 30, 1939, has already been described. It is easy to suppress by force any opposition or resistance among people who are helpless, but force, which is the only means by which tyrants can maintain their power, brings them also to their grave—that is the lesson of the history of all tyrannies.

The history of political and social progress is full of paradoxical changes. The World War, which caused revolutionary changes in the social structure of every nation, made urgent the problem of the " fourth estate " (the workers). The Bolshevik Revolution could be a clear indication to the whole world that, after the liberation of the " third estate " (the middle classes), which was realised in the nineteenth century, there has come, in the twentieth century, the turn of the " fourth estate." The grave mistakes made by the Communists and the Nazis are largely responsible for the fact that this question has not yet fully been understood and that incorrect, or even impossible, solutions are being sought. Masaryk, already forty years ago, in his *Social Question*, criticised the one-sidedness of the materialist conception of Marxism, and reproached it especially for its over-estimation of the power of the State, which Marx adopted from Hegel.[1] But Masaryk, nevertheless, declared: " Because I do not agree with Marx, I am not blind to the fact that workers are oppressed. . . . We must open the path for social justice." In other words, even if the whole of Marxist doctrine and policy were absolutely incorrect, this would not dispose of the political

---

[1] Hegel's deification of the State and his idea of its omnipotence were, of course, adopted by the Fascists and the Nazis also.

and social problem of the " fourth estate," which also must obtain real (not merely formal) political equality and its fair share in the direction of society. Political democracy must be completed by economic democracy; the " fourth estate " must be ranked as an equal and as an economically free member of the social community. It is understandable that, just as there was resistance against the equalisation and political progress of the " third estate," there should now be resistance against the liberation of the " fourth estate." Fascism and National Socialism originated to some extent as attempts to check the movement for the liberation of the " fourth estate," but in spite of that, or, more correctly, because of that, they are constantly being obliged to take it into consideration. Since the needs of modern production make it impossible to crush the workers into an unorganised, amorphous mob, which could become very easily anarchised, the Fascists find it necessary to create for them various organisations, corporations and institutions. It is true that these organisations are directed in an authoritarian manner and are carefully watched, yet because of them, and in spite of their compulsory character, the industrial workers, and to a large extent also the agricultural workers, maintain their class consciousness and their sense of class solidarity. The very fact that they are differentiated from other economic and social classes contributes to this effect. This is a social fact of great importance,[1] but even more important, perhaps, is the fact that the totalitarian régimes are inevitably led towards the " nationalisation " and " collectivisation " of their economy. The political and social influence of the " capitalists " still persist, it is true, to a smaller or greater extent, but the control of economy is more and more being concentrated in the hands of the State. During the World War, also, it was found necessary to submit economy to State control, and it cannot be disputed that the measures of " nationalisation " which all the states were forced to introduce in their economy during the last war greatly strengthened the tendency towards Socialism after the war. A very similar situation is now being obtained in the totalitarian dictatorships, which, because of

[1] For only thus it is possible to explain that, in spite of all the vigilance of the police, illegal anti-Fascist activity can develop continuously among the German and Italian workers.

their expansionist aspirations, have organised their entire economy " on a war footing," and have therefore also " nationalised " it. By doing this, whether they like it or not, they have furthered the present tendencies towards " socialisation," and thus, instead of crushing and destroying the Socialism which they so hate, they are themselves providing the conditions of economic organisation required for its development. Hitler's party has, as a matter of fact, maintained its original name of the German National Socialist Workers' Party !

National Socialism is really a revolutionary mass movement. Never since the Reformation has the German nation experienced such an acute, revolutionary unrest as that into which it has been plunged by National Socialism. Hitler has set in motion the revolutionary forces of the German people. Hitherto he has managed to control them—thanks to the success of his adventures abroad, for which he is indebted to those who have been so passive and so ready to make concessions—according to his needs and desires, but if anything should happen to shake his reputation of omnipotence, the revolutionary forces which he has aroused in the German people will turn against him. The defeat of the Kaiser's Germany led to the Weimar Republic, but the German Revolution of November, 1918, was of a purely political character, and the advent of the Weimar Republic did not touch, on the whole, the economic and social positions of the ruling class of the old régime; so it was with their help that Hitler came to power. The defeat of Nazism would lead in Germany to a great revolution, the political and economic conditions for which have been prepared by the Nazi régime itself.

Such a revolution in Germany is indispensable if the German nation is to re-enter the cultural community of Europe, from which, especially by its Nazism, it has excluded itself. Only after the destruction of Nazism will Europe be able to organise itself freely and to found, on the basis of a free federation of its nations, the structure of a real and lasting peace. Such a federation, so urgently necessary if Europe is to be saved from self-destruction, would be incomplete without the German nation, and therefore the situation would not be improved by a war, which could lead only to the defeat of Germany. If Europe is to be saved, the German nation also must be saved. It is not only the other European nations, but above all the German nation, which must be liberated from the yoke of Nazi oppression. The other nations would do best to help the Germans to bring the Nazi régime to the ground. It would not be sufficient, however, merely to do that, for it is essential that National Socialism shall be overcome, not only politically, but also spiritually and morally, otherwise there will be a repetition of what happened in Germany and elsewhere in Europe after the World War. A great revolution of the German nation is necessary, not only for the salvation of Europe, but also for the salvation of Germany, and that revolution must not only wipe out the Nazi régime, but must re-convert the Germans to Europeanism. Our slogan, and that of the German nation, must therefore be: Not against Germany, but against the Third Reich; not against the German nation, but against National Socialism.

There is no doubt that the pan-German tendency, which, as a matter of fact, started as far back as the eighteenth century, has a majority hold on the German people. For too long a time they have been brought up to the cult of force, to a love of purely material strength, to militarism, to the adoration of State omnipotence, to *Kulturträger*-ing haughtiness and contempt for other nations, expresssed as the idea of the superiority of the German race. Even the German Socialists were not immune to the militarist and violent tendencies which have predominated for so long in Germany. This was correctly diagnosed even before the World War by Charles Andler, who, after Masaryk, was the best authority on Pan-Germanism. It is because these tendencies have become deeply rooted in the German character by centuries of teaching that it will be possible to eradicate them only by a far-reaching social and spiritual revolution.[1] German revolution could not overcome Nazism and Pan-Germanism, with their immoral belief that might is right, merely by bringing about a

---

[1] " The revolution must be also a spiritual and a moral one," wrote Masaryk, for otherwise the German revolutionaries would run the risk of which Masaryk warned us when he wrote about the Russian revolutionaries: " They removed the Czar, but did not overcome Czarism." Masaryk was convinced, however, that Russia would have a great political influence in Europe (having already exercised a cultural influence through Pushkin, Turgenev, Tolstoi, Dostoievsky and Gorki), if she would carry out her revolution thoroughly, " making it a revolution of the head and the heart."

political upheaval and a change of the socio-economic system. Such a change is necessary, it is true, but the revolution would stop half-way if it did not consciously link up with the famous tradition of German humanism and if it did not strive after spiritual co-operation and co-ordination with the other European nations in the spirit of Leibnitz, Lessing and Goethe. Kant and Herder—not Fichte, Hegel or Feuerbach; Schiller and Goethe—not Nietzsche or Treitschke; Thomas and Heinrich Mann, F. W. Foerster, Kurt Hiller—not Alfred Rosenberg, Hans Günther or Ewald Banse !

Only in this way will it be possible to bridge the gulf which to-day so tragically divides Germany from the rest of the world. The liberation from the menace of Nazi domination is indissolubly linked with the revolutionary renaissance of the German nation from Bismarckism and Hitlerism to the Europeanism of Goethe and the humanism of Leibnitz and Lessing. Many Germans themselves are very clearly aware of this.

In September, 1937, at the graveside of Masaryk, President Beneš swore, in the name of the whole Czechoslovak nation, that we would remain faithful to the legacy of our President-Liberator. His work of liberation was not ended with his death. The desire for freedom and justice and faith that one day they will again direct our fate and reverse the terrible humiliation, which we neither caused nor still less deserved, animates us all. The defeat of free Czechoslovakia in September, 1938, was a defeat for the whole of free Europe. An important round was lost, but the fight has not yet been decided—that fight which is going on between Nazism, which aims at the mastery of Europe, and democracy, which aims at a free federation of independent European nations.

When Nazism falls—and there is no doubt that it will fall—it is natural that again, as always, the question of the future of Czechoslovakia will arise. Munich has shown that the face of Europe is changed when the fate of Czechoslovakia is changed. During the World War, Masaryk wrote: " I do not pretend that the liberation of Bohemia is the most vital question of the war, but I can say without exaggeration that the aims, proclaimed by the Allies, cannot be achieved without the liberation of Bohemia." In the same sense, I say to-day that I do not pretend that the crux of the great struggle between the Third Reich and the rest of the world is the Czechoslovak question, but it is no exaggeration to say that there is not, and will not be, a free and peaceful Europe, until independence and freedom are restored to the Czechoslovak nation.

Even in the darkness of the Third Reich, that nation firmly believes that the victory will not rest finally with powers of evil and violence. The motto of the first Czechoslovak Republic, " *Pravda vítězí* " (" Truth prevails ") continues to inspire belief.

The day will come when the truth will triumph, and Europe will be transformed according to the conceptions of Masaryk. Its form will, of course, not correspond precisely with the form that Europe took after the World War—at that time also many things were not done as Masaryk would have wished.

But this time Europe will have to unite in a free federation of independent nations. This inevitably results from the extraordinary technical progress, the economic necessity for an effective organisation of production and consumption and the intensification of the exchange of the spiritual values, not only between nations, but between continents. The world has become smaller and therefore it must unify itself. Nationalist autocracy, both economic and spiritual, has been made out-of-date by the progress of humanity and is already to-day a painful anachronism. Nationalism is justifiable only as a conscious and positive love of one's nation, free of all hatred towards other nations, and on the contrary, completed by sympathy with other nations and by collaboration with them. The salvation of Europe demands the conscious and deliberate defeat of biological, racial and Chauvinist nationalism by a conscious and deliberate cultivation of international collaboration; this can be achieved only by some form of federal union between the European nations. Such a reorganisation would also facilitate the return of Germany into the European community—a Germany of course which will be spiritually and socially reborn after an internal revolution.

The federation must be a voluntary one, springing essentially from the will and from the well-understood necessities of the respective European nations. It will have to be based, therefore, on the collaboration of nations externally independent and

internally free. This means that Europe must be also ideologically
united by a common creed and the common recognition of
certain main ideas and principles. The political reconciliation
and unification of the European nations is inconceivable, so
long as they are divided by deep differences of opinion. The
foundation—the only foundation—of a European federation must
be social democracy, which unites the principles of freedom and
of the inalienable rights of the individual with those of economic
and social justice, and guarantees real equality for the " fourth-
estate."

As Masaryk also recommended, it would be useful, if the
European federation were based on small regional units, and if
there could be especially close collaboration between the nations
of certain geographical areas. This would be particularly necessary in Central and Eastern Europe, in the belt of small nations
which stretches from the Baltic to the Black Sea, to the Ægean
and Adriatic Seas. After the War of 1914–18 the federative
tendencies of these nations were clearly evident, but were only
partially realised in the pacts of the Little Entente, and of the
Balkan and Baltic Ententes. All that was left undone in spite of
the efforts of Masaryk and Beneš after the War of 1914–18 will
have to be done when Europe is next re-organised. The principal
ambition of the Czechoslovak nation will be to bring about, in
accordance with Masaryk's conception, the federation of all
Danubian nations, which would naturally include also the
Hungarians. The Danubian federation will fundamentally
increase the security and the independence of these nations,
giving them greater possibilities of protecting themselves by
closer mutual collaboration against the interventions and
pressure of neighbouring Great Powers.

Just as the French Revolution led ultimately to France
respecting the freedom and rights of other nations, especially
those which were weaker than herself, so Russian policy was
affected in the same way by the Russian Revolution. Revolutionary Russia made an end of the imperialism of the Czars,
which had made use, when necessary, of Pan-Slav[1] slogans.
Revolutionary Russia, like President Wilson himself, demanded

---

[1] In actual fact the Czarist policy was very little Slav; it regarded with scorn
the smaller Slav nations and oppressed them.

the self-determination of nations and itself realised it by transforming the Czar's centralist Empire into a federation of autonomous nations, a Union of Soviet Socialist Republics. Whatever reproaches it may be possible to level at Soviet policy, not even its bitterest opponents could say that it has ever tried to destroy the independence of any neighbouring state, great or small. Respect for other nations and for the independence of their governments and the rejection of all imperialist ambitions for hegemony over other independent states are among the positive and permanent results of the Russian Revolution. The Central European states have never been threatened as regards their existence or independence by the Soviet Union, and it is certain that they never will be threatened.

It is to be hoped that the Germany of the future will develop its international relations along similar lines and that eventually it also will realise that the greatness of a great nation is not to be judged by the efforts which it makes to dominate other nations. The same is to be hoped of the future Italy. Under such circumstances were a federated Europe not immediately to be formed, successful co-operation between the federated Danubian states and the neighbouring Great Powers would be possible. This would, of course, be complemented by similar co-operation with the Western democracies, not only on account of the traditional cultural bonds which exist with them, but also for the sake of the no less traditional maintenance of the balance of power.

The creation of a Danubian federation and the development on a more satsifactory basis of the relationship of this part of the world with the European Great Powers will be facilitated by a new arrangement of frontiers. There is no doubt that in the next European crisis the existing frontiers in Central and Eastern Europe will be changed, and it is doubtful if any state will be left untouched by such changes. It is certain that an attempt will be made to arrange that in each state there shall be the smallest possible number of national minorities or that their numbers should reciprocally balance. It is certain, however, that national minorities will, nevertheless, remain in most, if not all, of the states, owing to the considerable intermingling of nationalities in Central and Eastern Europe, and the difficulties of mass exchanges of population. The frontiers of states will have to be determined, not on the Munich principle, but with regard to geographical, economic and certainly also strategic considerations. Thus the principle of self-determination will be somewhat limited in its application, just as any other principle is liable to be limited in practice, in order to avoid absurdities. For, without a reasonable limitation, freedom becomes anarchy, and equality of rights becomes a merely levelling down, which can be maintained only by means of an enforced dictatorship, which suppresses all freedom. Practical limitations of different social ideas and principles are directed by the simple requirements of the common life of the members of the society and of its effective reorganisation. So far as the states of the future Danubian federation are concerned, they can come to an agreement about a minority régime, and special organs of this federation might be entrusted with the task of ensuring its observation; thus these countries would effectively complete and assure by their own arrangement of the minority question its general settlement, which would be introduced for the entire European federation. In order that this minority régime should really be fulfilled and observed, it will be necessary that common principles of justice and freedom should be recognised everywhere; for otherwise no practical co-operation would be possible.

The community of ideas, is, of course, the fundamental requirement for a free federation of independent European nations. The community of ideas does not mean ideological uniformity, but voluntary acceptance of certain simple principles of humanitarian democracy which are designed to ensure common duties—and the prevention of the exploitation of man by man, of class by class, or of nation by nation. The practical realisation of these principles will be, of course, in the hands of the various nations, and will naturally differ according to their particular needs, geographical situation, social structure, cultural level and historical tradition. Thus, for example, to-day there already exists a community of ideas and culture between Britain and France, in spite of the fact that the French and English democracies differ greatly from each other, each preserving its particular national characteristics. European federation does not mean a standardisation and levelling suppression of national individuality, but, on the contrary, its free development by means of effective organisation of mutual collaboration. This would also facilitate the co-operation of Europe with America, Asia and other parts of the world. It is certain that the League of Nations will be re-organised, and it would be most useful if this could be done on a federative basis. The federative principle is the most suitable principle for organised co-operation between nations: it limits any exaggerated tendencies towards national sovereignty and exclusivity, as well as those towards super-national and super-State centralism.

If human civilisation is to be saved, the efforts of its best and most courageous minds must aim at the realisation of humanitarian ideals of freedom, right and social justice. It is for this reason in particular that some form of conflict with the aggressively expanding and power-politically insatiable Third Reich is almost inevitable. Such a conflict, if it comes, will have to be a fight to the finish, for an evil is not suppressed if a half-evil is tolerated. Masaryk, the great humanist and pacifist, did not hesitate to proclaim during the war:

" The democratic organisation of Europe on the basis of the self-determination of nations requires a decisive victory of the Allies; without defeat, the Prussian Germany and Prussified Austria-Hungary will not become democratic, they will not allow a democratic organisation of Eastern Europe and will hinder the desirable progress of the whole of Europe."

Masaryk was afraid of what might happen if the divisions of a defeated Imperial Army should return to the German towns after the war with their standards blowing in the wind—the reality that the Kaiser's Prussian militarism and Bismarck's entire system were defeated was concealed from the German people. In the same way, the total annihilation of warlike and brutal Nazism, which seeks to dominate the whole world, has again become the necessity of our time. The duty is first and foremost on the German people itself, but lest it prove too heavy for them alone to bear it, to organise defence against such a great and terrible danger is not only morally admissible, but is the duty of every decent man, of every nation which recognises freedom and justice to be the greatest values of humanity. To those who are afraid of war, we answer in the words of Masaryk: "War is not the worst, and certainly not the only evil. To live in dishonesty and slavery is worse."

Europe is at a fatal crossroad. Nazism is threatening, not only the external and internal freedom of small Danubian nations, but also that of the great nations of the whole of Europe, not excepting the Italian. The future development of Europe—indeed of the whole world—will depend upon whether the great nations will allow Nazism to continue its march of aggression, or whether they will resist it. This dilemma cannot be escaped. To-day, more than ever before in history, the words of the German humanist poet Schiller have a tragic significance for Europe:

> *Und setzt Ihr nicht das Leben ein,*
> *Wie wird euch das Leben gewonnen sein.*

(a) *The German Occupation.* It was decided at Munich that four marked zones should be occupied by the German Army between October 1 and 7, while a fifth zone was to be delimited by an International Commission composed of the representatives of the four Great Powers and of Czechoslovakia. The International Commission started work on October 1, but it was evident from the very first that it was the Germans who would really decide everything. In vain the Czechoslovak delegates asked their British and French colleagues for help or support. No word was raised in their defence, except by Signor Attolico, the Italian delegate, who alone showed a certain sympathy with their arguments. By October 5 the Commission had completed the delimitation of the fifth zone, having in reality merely accepted the German proposals. These, made with a total disregard not only for Czech interests but even for the scruples from time to time expressed by Mr. Chamberlain during his visits to Herr Hitler, met with no sort of resistance from the International Commission. The surrender of most of the Czechoslovak fortifications had rendered Czechoslovakia incapable of physical resistance, and so far as Britain and France were concerned, the Germans now knew they could do as they liked.

The Berlin decisions of October 5 represented in fact nothing but the terms which were brutally dictated by the Germans, and were even contrary to the stipulation of the Munich Agreement that " the remaining territory of preponderantly German character will be ascertained by the aforesaid International Commission forthwith and be occupied by German troops on the 10th of October." It was stipulated that the further territory to be transferred in this manner should be " of preponderantly German character," and it is clear that those who drafted the Agreement had thought on purely ethnological lines, for Paragraph 6 of that Agreement states: " This Commission will also be entitled to recommend to the Four Powers . . . in certain exceptional cases, minor modifications in the strictly ethnographical determination of the zones which are to be transferred without plebiscite." The International Commission paid no attention, however, to the principle laid down at Munich. It simply accepted the German thesis that, for the delimitation of the territory of preponderantly German character, the Census figures for 1930 could not be used, since it must be done on a basis of the situation in 1918, and that therefore the Census figures for 1910 must be used. It is generally known, however, that the Census of 1910 was carried out by the Austrian officials of the day with the sole intention of proving that there were more Germans than in actual fact there were in Austria. Nationality was recorded, not according to the mother-tongue, but according to the language most commonly used in daily life, because the Czechs who lived in the mixed districts used the German language in their daily life and could thus be recorded as Germans. Even Mr. Wickham Steed, who was living at that time in Vienna, has mentioned that in this way he also was recorded as a German ! The acceptance of this basis meant, therefore, the acceptance of the effects of the policy of germanisation to which the Czechs in Austria had been subjected for many centuries. In addition, it revealed an incredible disregard for the profound social changes which had taken place during the previous thirty years.

Nor was this all. Even the 1910 Census was disregarded when it proved inconvenient to the Germans. Many parishes which had had a Czech majority or which had been entirely Czech in 1910 were transferred wholesale to Germany. In short, the decisions of the so-called Berlin International Commission roughly fulfilled the demands of the Godesberg ultimatum, which both France and Great Britain had considered unacceptable ! The Czechoslovak statistical expert, A. Boháč, has described in detail the negotiations of the Berlin International Commission. This will be found in *Národnostní obzor*, Vol. ix, January 31, 1939.

It would take too long to describe in detail the many cases of injustice inflicted by the Munich frontier. Some of these injustices (relating to Bohemia alone) have been exposed in the *Central European Observer*, December 16, 1938, but what was done in the neighbourhood of the town of Plzeň (Pilsen) is perhaps worthy of special note here:

The parishes of Litice, Dobřany, Čišice, Robčice and Lhota had an aggregate population of 5,982 Czechs and 3,773 Germans in 1930, and some of these parishes had been predominantly Czech, even according to the Census of 1910. They formed, moreover, an unbroken Czech area, within which there was only a single German village. These parishes were nevertheless occupied by the Germans after Munich, merely in order that the frontier might be brought as close as possible to Plzeň.

There were cases also of no less conspicuous injustice in the delimitation of the frontiers of Moravia–Silesia. One can find no justification, for instance, for the occupation of the railway junction at Břeclav and the adjacent parishes of Hlohovec, Chorv. Nová Ves and Poštorná, which even in 1910 had only 6,421 Germans as compared with 11,186 Czechs in their aggregate populations, a proportion which had changed to 18,120 Czechs and only 1,808 Germans by 1930. It is obvious that this occupation was decided upon simply in order to deprive Czechoslovakia of an important railway junction.

The district of *Zábřeh* is another whose inclusion after Munich within the occupied area was impossible to justify, for, apart from the fact that it has a population of 42,094 Czechs and only 26,017 Germans, it was closely linked up with the Czech portion of the *Šumperk* district, consisting of fourteen parishes, with 11,440 Czech inhabitants. The district is also linked up with the Czech district of *Žamberk* by a belt of purely Czech parishes in the *Lanškroun* area. Its real importance is due, however, to the fact that through it runs the main railway line from Prague to Moravia and thence to Slovakia. The excuse that this territory was assigned to Germany as compensation for the retention in Czechoslovakia of the German-speaking enclave round *Jihlava* (*Iglau*) cannot be considered as valid, for the nineteen predominantly German parishes round Jihlava have only 16,490 German inhabitants, a number for which more than ample compensation had already been made by the sacrifice of several predominantly Czech parishes in the districts of *Most* (*Brüx*) and *Duchcov* (*Dux*). A contributory reason for this striking case of injustice to 42,094 Czechs which gave Germany a hold over the main Czech railway line may have been the desire to link up the German districts of *Svitavy* and *Moravská Třebová*, which have 48,980 German and only 5,948 Czech inhabitants, with the German territory in Northern Moravia. But the injustice to Czechoslovakia could have been obviated by arranging for an exchange of populations.

Further cases of complete and almost incomprehensible disregard for the actual racial composition of the population occurred
in the delimitation of the frontier of the *Hranice* district. Seven
parishes (Spalov, Lubomě̌r, Heltímov, Jindřichov, Partutovice,
Střítez and Vysoká), which had been predominantly Czech even
in 1910, and whose aggregate population at the time consisted of
4,027 Czechs and a mere 115 Germans, were assigned to Germany
without any justification. Even more scandalous cases of similar
injustice were the occupation by the Germans of forty-one predominantly Czech parishes adjacent to one another (over 40,000
Czechs to 1,500 Germans) in the districts of *Nový Jičín*, *Příbor*
and *Bílovec* and of sixty-three predominantly Czech parishes
(56,480 Czechs to 2,915 Germans) in the districts of *Klimkovice*
and *Opava* (*Troppau*)). In both these last cases there would
have been no difficulty in arriving at a more equitable decision if
there had been a genuine desire that justice should be observed.
One can hardly be surprised at such decisions, when " justice "
was stretched to give sanction for the occupation of the *Hlučín*
district, which was indicated by the statistics of the Germans
themselves as being Moravian, and of thirty-five neighbouring
parishes, which were inhabited by 47,311 Czechs and 2,519
Germans.

The most obvious of many similar cases of disregard for the
nationality principle, which the Germans themselves were
claiming as their justification, that occurred in Southern
Moravia was that of the parish of Moravský Krumlov and four
other parishes adjacent to it, which had an aggregate population
of 3,047 Czechs and only 349 Germans. These parishes were
assigned to Germany, despite their predominantly Czech
character and despite the fact that they constituted an artificial
and awkward German salient in the heart of the Munich
Czechoslovakia.

All in all, the Berlin decisions made by the International
Commission incorporated in Germany 315 parishes which were
shown as predominantly Czech by the census of 1930, and of
these no fewer than 251 had been predominantly Czech even in
1910. These numbers refer only to parishes contiguous with the
main Czech territories, and do not include those predominantly
Czech parishes, which formed enclaves in predominantly German

districts, such as *Most* (*Brüx*) and *Duchcov* (*Dux*). Some sixty of such enclaves were, of course, also occupied by the Germans, and represented to Czechoslovakia a loss of population which offset completely the loss which Germany considered herself to have suffered through not obtaining certain German enclaves, such as that round *Jihlava* (*Iglau*).

With the final delimitation of the fifth zone, Germany gained 10,906 square miles of territory and not only 2,806,638 Germans, but also 719,127 Czechs. On the other hand, in the 19,197 square miles of territory which remained Czech there were still some 250,000 Germans, in addition to the 6,476,987 Czechs. The Czechs who were handed over to Germany by the Four Powers in September, 1938—almost three-quarters of a million— represented, however, more than a tenth of the total number of Czechs, while the quarter of a million Germans who remained in Czechoslovakia were a body barely one-eighth the size of the population of the Sudeten territories and represented not even 1 per 1,000 of the population of the Reich. In spite of this German annexation of non-German peoples in October, 1938, its logical consequence—the annexation of the whole Czech nation—came apparently as a shock to the Western Powers, who had deliberately put their hand to the agreement which placed one-tenth of the Czech people under German rule.

It will be seen, therefore, that the idea of a settlement based on the ethnographic principle had hardly been proposed before it was flagrantly abandoned in favour of a settlement dictated by Germany in direct contradiction to the principle to which the Nazis had appealed. After that it can occasion little surprise that no consideration should have been paid to the possibility of assuring the new Czechoslovakia an independent economic existence. On the contrary, the terms imposed at the command of Berlin were designed to place Czechoslovakia even economically at the mercy of Germany. The new frontiers were deliberately drawn in such a way as to dislocate entirely the Czechoslovak system of communications, based on the double-track railway lines which run from Western Bohemia, through Prague, Česká Třebová, Brno and Bratislava, to Szob, on the Danubian frontier with Hungary, and from Česká Třebová, through Olomouc, Přerov, Moravská Ostrava, Žilina and Košice, to

Halmei on the Rumanian frontier. As a result of the German occupation, the line Prague–Bohumín was cut in three places and the line Prague–Bratislava in one place, in addition to which the direct line between Moravská Ostrava and Žilina was cut by the Polish occupation. As a result of this, express railway communication between Bohemia, Moravia, Slovakia and Ruthenia was completely interrupted in the second Czechoslovak Republic. In the last two of these provinces the disaster originated by the German occupation was intensified by the Hungarian occupation before it was consummated by the German " protectectorates " over Bohemia, Moravia and Slovakia in March, and the Hungarian occupation of Ruthenia. The only communications which remained intact after Munich were the less important, single-track lines. Various other lines in other parts of Czechoslovakia were dislocated in different ways, such as by the separation of the railway stations from the towns whose name they bore. Boiler houses and other installations were cut off from the transport centres on which they were completely dependent, and in this way the economic life of the second Czechoslovak Republic was completely upset.

In Western Bohemia, for instance, the industrial and cultural centre of Plzeň suffered greatly owing to the interruption of certain lines which converged there. This town was deprived of its direct railway communication with the neighbouring districts of Klatovy and Domažlice, with the result that large numbers of people from those districts were no longer able, as before, to go to work in the factories there. Many students who attended its various educational establishments were also no longer able to reach the town of Plzeň.

Further examples were the town of Dvůr Králové on the Elbe, an important textile centre, and Moravská Ostrava, the most important centre of the iron industry in Czechoslovakia. The former, having been deprived of every means of communication by rail with the outside world, was, for a time, despite the substitution of bus services for its lost railway lines, almost inaccessible, owing to the bad state of the roads. The latter, with a population of over 200,000, was cut off from its sources of raw materials in the occupied districts of Hlučín and Opava, and had to depend for its communication on the secondary railway line through Frydlant and Krásno and Bečvou, which is, of course, an inadequate substitute for the double-tracked main lines to Přerov and, through Bohumín, to Žilina, which were interrupted.

The loss of the coal-mining area in Northern Bohemia, including the hard-coal mines at Trutnov, as well as of the greater part of the mines at Plzeň, Moravská Ostrava and Karvinná, was a catastrophe for the whole economy of the Czechoslovak state, for it dealt a direct and deadly blow to railways and to the power supply for industries, which were designed for use with home-produced fuel.

The frontier changes seriously harmed also many local enterprises, such as, for example, the electrical generating station at Ervěnice, which continued to supply the town of Prague after Munich had placed it in Germany. Other large generating stations, such as that at Poříčí, near Trutnov, which supplies numerous power-distributing stations in Eastern Bohemia, and the hydro-electric stations at Vranov and Bílá Třemešná, which supply the whole of the surrounding area, also found after Munich an international frontier between them and their consumers. The dams at Vranov and Bílá Třemešná formed reservoirs which supplied water to Brno, the capital of Moravia, which also found itself separated by a frontier from its water supply (as well as, incidentally, from most of the sources of its food supplies in Southern Moravia !). The brutal and callous occupation of Czecho-Slovakia in March, 1939, was a profound shock to the whole of civilised opinion. Yet even a cursory examination of the Munich terms reveals that Germany was but completing the work of the four statesmen at Munich.

In fact one need only look at an ethnographical map of the districts with which the International Commission dealt to realise immediately that the revised frontiers of Czechoslovakia did not represent a line between the territory which was more than half and that which was less than half Czech in character. The frontier dictated by Germany in October, 1938, like that dictated in March, 1939, was determined by a different principle than that of nationality. Those responsible for the determination of the new frontiers appeared to have been well-informed and skilful in the application of that principle, for the occupation of Ervěnice, already mentioned above, provided Germany with an excellent means of exerting pressure on Prague, while the occupation of Vranov and Bílá Třemešná exposed Brno to a similar possible exertion of pressure should she have cared to use it. In fact, Nazi Germany, already bored with the comparatively slow method of exacting obedience by threats, preferred in March simply to take, rather than be given, what she wanted.

As has already been stated above, Czechoslovakia received a catastrophic blow through the occupation by Germany and Poland of her coal-mining areas—according to the German statistics, she lost 66 per cent. of her coal and 80 per cent. of her lignite. In addition to these, she lost:

				per cent.
Iron and steel industry	..	..	..	.. 70
Textile industry	..	..	..	.. 80
Railway-carriage works	..	..	..	.. 75
Cement industry	..	..	..	.. 80
Porcelain industry	..	..	..	.. 90
Glass industry	..	..	..	.. 86
Chemical industry	..	..	..	.. 86
Newstype industry	..	..	..	.. 90
Timber	..	..	..	.. 40
Electric power supplies	..	..	..	.. 70

She lost also her Žatec (Saaz) hops, upon which the brewing of Plzeň (Pilsen) beer entirely depended, and all the watering places of Western Bohemia, Karlovy Vary (Karlsbad), Marianské Lázně (Marienbad), Františkovy Lázně (Franzensbad), Teplice-Šanov (Teplitz-Schönau) and Jáchymov (St. Joachimsthal), the last-named, of course, being one of the world-sources of radium. From being a highly-developed exporting country, with an industrial potential which rivalled that of the Great Powers, she found herself suddenly reduced to being a mainly agricultural state, with such industry as remained to her economically dependent upon the goodwill of Germany. Only three miles lay between the important industrial town of Plzeň, with the Škoda armaments works, and Germany, who was thus in a position to control her armaments industry. The new

frontiers were decided in accordance with the strategic requirements of Germany, as was clearly indicated by the creation of
German salients which would otherwise have been quite absurd,
so that Prague alone of Czechoslovakia's larger cities was out of
range of German heavy artillery. In this way Germany secured,
with the assent of the entire world, a frontier which she could,
without asking leave of anyone or meeting with any resistance,
simply wipe out at a moment's notice.

Needless to say, the Berlin decision caused horror throughout
Czechoslovakia. I will not attempt to describe the heart-rending
scenes which occurred in the predominantly or purely Czech
towns and villages assigned to Germany. Suffice to say with
emphasis that this terrible injustice, against which there was no
possibility of appeal, will never—literally never—be forgotten
by the Czechs !

The Czechoslovak Government, convinced at last by the
attitude adopted by the British and French representatives on
the International Commission that it would be useless to ask for
help from Britain or France, resorted to direct negotiation with
Germany, in the hope of obtaining some alleviation of the
conditions imposed upon them.

On October 13 the International Commission decided that the
plebiscite provided for in the Munich Agreement should not be
held. As a matter of fact, the Berlin decision rendered a plebiscite
unnecessary, for, since Germany had already obtained, roughly
speaking, all that she wanted, it would have been held only in
districts purely or mainly Czech. The abandonment of the
plebiscite could not, therefore, be considered seriously as a
concession by Germany. At the same time the International
Commission " took note of " the agreement which had in the
meanwhile been concluded privately between the German and
Czechoslovak representatives that " discussions, on a basis of
the principles already laid down, regarding the final revision
and delimitation of the frontier should be commenced forthwith," and that " in accordance with Article 7 of the Munich
Agreement, a German-Czechoslovak Commission should be set
up to determine the details of the right of option." With this
the activities of the International Commission may be said, for
all practical purposes, to have ended: from first to last this

Commission had done nothing but " take note of " whatever Germany chose to dictate.

The final delimitation of the German-Czechoslovak frontier was effected by a protocol, signed in Berlin on November 20 by the representatives of the two countries (and of which the International Commission duly " took note " on the following day !). At the same time they concluded a Treaty regarding national citizenship, the option and the protection of minorities. Hope that the dictated decision of October 5 would be softened was cruelly disappointed. Germany did give back to the Czechs some fifty villages and parishes, but at the same time she occupied a hundred and twenty new ones, with a total population of about 40,000, of whom more than three-quarters were Czechs. What was felt most bitterly by the Czechs was the loss of Chodsko, whose inhabitants, the *Psohlavci*, had been for centuries past the faithful watchmen on the Šumava border (Böhmerwald). The final frontier adjustments showed more clearly than ever before that Germany's aims were purely strategic. The German proposal accepted on November 20 represented a sort of compromise between the views of the Berlin Government and the demands of the Henlein radicals. These asked for the annexation of Moravská Ostrava (Mährisch Ostrau), Jihlava (Iglau), Olomouc (Olmütz), Brno (Brünn), etc. In March, 1939, they were satisfied to the full: the whole of Bohemia and Moravia was annexed. In the autumn of 1938 they had to be content with what Germany wanted mainly for strategic reasons. Thus in November, 1938, purely Czech districts round Domažlice, Dubá and Jilemnice and the German island round Brodek in Moravia and some other mixed communities were occupied. The occupation was completed on November 24, and was announced on that day by the Czechoslovak broadcasting station in the following terms:

" We have to-day painfully traversed a difficult crossroad. . . . This day of a sad farewell to those Czechs who are annexed by Germany will not be a day of hopelessness, but a day in which we will search our national spirit to its very depths, in order that, on both sides of the frontiers, we may draw new strength for the future which lies before us."

The net result of the operation performed upon our country

against our will by the Four Powers was that Germany occupied
territories in which there were (according to the 1930 Census)
2,800,000 Germans and 726,000 Czechs. There still remained in
Bohemia and Moravia 269,000 Germans. In order to do " justice " to Germany, in accordance with the principle of " self-
determination of the peoples," it was decided to hand over to
her 10 per cent. of the entire Czech population. Before that, it
had been considered a terrible injustice that 4 per cent. of the
German race should be included within the Czechoslovak
borders. Yet these 4 per cent., living under a democratic régime,
enjoyed more human, cultural and civic rights than did the
remaining 96 per cent., who were dominated by the Nazi
dictatorship. " Justice " had been done to Germany, not at
the expense merely of the 10 per cent. of the Czechs who had
been sacrificed, but of the whole Czechoslovak nation, which,
having been placed at the mercy of the Third Reich, experienced
what that mercy meant six months later. Nor should British
and French democrats forget, moreover, that they handed
over also to the brutality of the Nazis a million anti-Nazis
among the Sudeten Germans. If the previous régime had
not satisfied the ideal requirements of justice, that which
replaced it at Munich, with the approval, and even the help, of
the official representatives of the Western Powers, was one of
blatant injustice, which brutally denied the rights of man.
To-day, as a direct result, that régime, which for terrible brutality
the world has scarcely seen the like, has engulfed the whole
Czechoslovak nation, and the last free Germans in Central
Europe. Those democrats in France and Britain who were so
solicitous for the " oppressed " Sudeten Germans should consult
their consciences about the results of their solicitude.

(b) *The Polish Occupation.* Czechoslovakia was, of course,
mutilated not only by Germany. Poland and Hungary also each
asked for their share. Every attempt made by the Czechoslovak
Government after the crisis of Berchtesgaden to come to an
agreement with Poland proved unsuccessful. Directly it became
apparent that Czechoslovakia was being abandoned by the
Western Powers, the Polish Government hastened to take
immediate advantage of her distress.

On September 30 Prague received from Warsaw a peremptory Note demanding the immediate surrender of the *Těšín* district. The Czechoslovak Government yielded at once and agreed on October 1 to accede to this demand. The actual occupation of the district ensued very rapidly, the Poles sometimes entering the surrendered territories sooner than had been agreed, and was more or less completed by October 10. This hasty occupation caused indescribable suffering to the Czechs of Těšín, many of whom were immediately expelled from their homes.

This occupation represented one of the more flagrant cases of disregard for the ethnographical principle—at the expense, of course, of Czechoslovakia. Taking advantage of Czechoslovakia's inability to resist, Poland seized all or most of the territory in four districts, three of which unquestionably contained more Czechs than Poles, while even in the fourth, *Jablunkov*, the Czechs represented 31 per cent. of the population. In *Bohumín* the Poles represented a mere 10 per cent. of the population, as compared with the 74 per cent. of Czechs; in *Fryštát*, 34 per cent. as compared with 60 per cent. Czech; and in *Český Těšín*, 42 per cent. as compared with 46 per cent. Czech—the remaining percentages being, in each case, Germans. In this way Poland occupied territories in which there were only 76,000 Poles, as compared with 123,000 Czechs (56 per cent. of total population) and 20,000 Germans. Even the census which was carried out after November 2 by the Polish Government failed to show, as had been hoped, a majority of Poles in this territory, for the official Census Report issued on January 9, 1939, showed the population of the Těšín district to consist of 92,648 Poles, 6,591 Germans and 67,245 Czechs (to whom one should add some 20,000 Czechs who were ejected into the new Czechoslovakia by the Poles).

The figures quoted above show quite clearly how the principle of nationality professed by the Great Powers was ignored in practice. In the settlement with Poland, just as in that with Germany, no regard was paid to local economic needs; for example, the coal-mining and industrial district of Ostrava-Karvinná, which essentially constituted one economic unit, was nevertheless partitioned without regard to its future. Poland simply occupied whatever territories she fancied, robbing Czechoslovakia of the greater part of the Ostrava-Karvinná coal basin, together with the iron works at Třinec, and most of the blast-furnaces at Ostrava-Těšín, which depended upon it. Poland derived little economic benefit from the occupation of these mines, for she already, although the output of her mines was one-third lower than it had been in 1913, produced more than enough coal to satisfy her internal requirements and has found it impossible to increase her exports. The effect will be disastrous, however, on the mining industry of the Ostrava-Karvinná coal-basin, which under Czech management had enormously increased its output. The sudden loss of capital to the value of several millions of crowns invested in that highly industrialised area was a terrible loss for the second Czechoslovak Republic.

The Poles were not even satisfied with the cession of this territory, but started immediately to persecute the Czechs who lived there. Thousands were mercilessly expelled,[1] especially those who happened to occupy any kind of official position, and the Czech schools were immediately closed. It is not only what they took, but also the manner in which they took it, which caused a feeling of considerable bitterness against the Poles which will not easily be erased. Their brutal behaviour roused animosity among Germans as well as Czechs, for both races alike were subjected to persecution. Demonstrations and bloody revolts were not infrequent after Munich, and even now, months after the occupation, the situation is far from calm, especially in the Ostrava-Těšín district, where the clash of nationalities and of social classes is most marked.

Later on, Poland extorted from us two " rectifications " of the Slovak frontier to the North of Čadca in the western part of the Javoriny massif and in the northern slopes of the High Tatra Mountains. This came as a shock to the supporters of Hlinka's Slovak Catholic Party, which had by then come into power, for they had been encouraged by the leaders, and especially by the deputy Karol Sidor, to look to the Poles even more than to the Czechs. It was a further shock to them when Poland subsequently vigorously supported the Hungarian claims against them and strove hard to establish a common frontier with

[1] Within less than three weeks of the Polish occupation, more than 10,000 refugees sought shelter in Czechoslovakia.

Hungary at their expense—a frontier established in March by the Hungarian occupation of Ruthenia.

(c) *The Hungarian Occupation.* The third act in the ruthless partition of Czechoslovakia was performed by Hungary. After Munich, the attitude of Budapest towards Prague, which had up to that moment been not altogether unfriendly, underwent a change, and Hungary, supported in the background by Italy, joined Poland in the scramble to grab as much of Czechoslovak territory as possible. Negotiations between Czechoslovakia and Hungary were begun at Komárno on October 9, the Czechoslovak delegation being headed by representatives of Slovakia and Sub-Carpathian Ruthenia, which had now become autonomous. Czechoslovakia, as a sign of goodwill, immediately evacuated the frontier station of Slovenské Nové Město and the town of Šahy, which were occupied by Hungarian troops on the following day. The Hungarian delegation presented extravagant claims for the surrender of Bratislava, Nitra, Košice and Užhorod and demanded that a plebiscite should be held throughout the whole of the rest of Slovakia and Sub-Carpathian Ruthenia. Following the precedent established by the Berlin decision of October 5, the Hungarians based their demands on the Census figures of 1910, which were notoriously in their favour. Yet even on this basis the number of Slovaks to be sacrificed to Hungary was 400,000, who, together with 80,000 Ruthenes, would have swelled the Slovak-Ruthene minority in Hungary to nearly 800,000, none of whom enjoy national rights. The surrender of the territories which they claimed—territories rich in vineyards and corn-fields—would have meant the cutting of nearly all the lines of communication by rail or road between Western and Eastern Slovakia and between Eastern Slovakia and Sub-Carpathian Ruthenia, just as the communications in Bohemia had been cut by the Germans. The counter-proposal of the Slovak-Ruthene delegation was the transfer of territory with 400,000 inhabitants, of whom 330,000 were Magyars, and which might therefore rightly be termed " predominantly Magyar ": this transfer would have left 400,000 Slovaks and Ruthenes in Hungary, and would have left only 300,000 Magyars in Czechoslovakia. The counter-proposal was rejected by the Hungarian delegation, and on October 12 the negotiations were broken off. In accordance with the Munich Agreement, Hungary then appealed to the Four Powers for a decision. Germany and Italy, however, were anxious that an agreement should be reached between the disputants. On October 19 the Slovak Ministers, Tiso and Durčanský, and the Ruthenian Minister, Bačinský, proceeded to Munich, where on October 19 and 20 they had two meetings with Herr von Ribbentrop. Simultaneously the Slovak Catholic Deputy, Sidor, proceeded to Warsaw, where he had an interview with Count Szembek, Under-Secretary of State for Foreign Affairs, on October 19. On the same day also the Polish Foreign Minister, Colonel Beck, had a conversation at Galata with M. Comnen, the Foreign Minister of Rumania, and tried to obtain the consent of Rumania to the establishment of a common frontier between Poland and Hungary. A stern diplomatic struggle ensued regarding the future of Sub-Carpathian Ruthenia, which the Poles desired to partition between Poland and Hungary (Rumania perhaps also receiving a share) in order that Poland might satisfy her desire for a common frontier with Hungary.

The arguments advanced in favour of such an arrangement varied according to the circumstances. The Western Powers were told that it would create a barrier against German expansion in Central and Eastern Europe, while Germany was told that it would further the establishment of an anti-Soviet *bloc*. Poland and Hungary both tried to strengthen their arguments by provoking frontier incidents which were intended to indicate that the local population wished to be annexed to Hungary or Poland, as the case might be. The Hungarians managed to obtain support for their claims from the Ruthenian Deputy, Fencík, and from Brody, Prime Minister of Sub-Carpathian Ruthenia. On October 29, after he had declared that the Slovaks and Ruthenes wanted a plebiscite, the latter was charged with high treason and deprived of his functions. Brody's statement led to an outbreak of mass demonstrations of protest against both Poland and Hungary. Germany, on the other hand, regarding Sub-Carpathian Ruthenia as a suitable jumping-off place for her expansion eastwards against Poland, the Soviet Union and—which is often forgotten—against Rumania, was therefore anxious for its maintenance as an independent, autonomous part of Czechoslovakia. For this reason, and until Slovakia had come completely under German control, the Germans opposed the annexation of Sub-Carpathian Ruthenia by Hungary. Italy, on the other hand, would have been glad to see a common frontier established between Hungary and Poland.

Colonel Beck met with no success in Rumania. The Rumanians were naturally anxious that Hungary should not expand over Sub-Carpathian Ruthenia, since this would add force to Hungarian revisionist claims in Transylvania. Therefore, the Rumanians adopted an attitude of loyalty to their alliance with Czechoslovakia.

The direct negotiations between Prague and Budapest, conducted through the normal diplomatic channels by means of Notes on October 24, 26 and 27, proved fruitless, so both parties agreed to submit their dispute to arbitration by Germany and Italy. The Western Powers were completely ignored, which was another indication of the realities of the post-Munich international situation: Germany and Italy considered themselves the only Powers with a right to decide in the Danubian Basin.

Germany and Italy reached a common decision, which was announced in the Belvedere Castle in Vienna at 7 p.m. on November 2 by Herr von Ribbentrop and Count Ciano to the Foreign Ministers of Czechoslovakia and Hungary in the following terms:

" 1. The territories which must be ceded to Hungary by Czechoslovakia are indicated on the attached map. A Hungaro-Czechoslovak Commission will carry out the delimitation of the frontiers.

2. The evacuation of these territories by Czechoslovakia, and their occupation by Hungary, will commence on November 5, 1938, and will be completed on November 10, 1938. The stages of evacuation and occupation, as well as all the other formal matters, will be determined by a Hungaro-Czechoslovak Commission.

" 3. The Czechoslovak Government will see to it that the ceded territories are left in their normal state.

" 4. Questions of detail raised by the cession of these territories, and particularly those regarding the nationality of their inhabitants and their right of option, will be settled by a Hungaro-Czechoslovak Commission.

" 5. A Hungaro-Czechoslovak Commission will also draw up detailed provisions for the protection of those persons of Magyar race who remain in Czechoslovakia and of those persons of non-Magyar race who are in the ceded territories. This Commission will take particular care that the ethnical group of Magyars in Bratislava shall enjoy the same status as other ethnical groups in that city.

" 6. In so far as the cession of these territories may create economic difficulties as regards communications in the regions which Czechoslovakia will retain, the Government of the Kingdom of Hungary will do all that is within its power, in agreement with the Czechoslovak Government, to eliminate such difficulties and inconveniences.

" 7. In any case where the application of these decisions may cause difficulties or doubts, the Hungarian and Czechoslovak Governments will come to some agreement with each other directly. Should such agreement not be found possible, they will submit the question to the German and Italian Governments, who will decide them definitely."

The arbitrators at Vienna admittedly saved Sub-Carpathian Ruthenia and rejected—for the time being—the Polish-Hungarian plan of a common frontier, but, on the other hand, it imposed on Czechoslovakia a burden of further extraordinarily heavy sacrifices. Bratislava was saved, though, in actual fact, it was completely under the thumb of Germany, since the occupation of Petržalka and Děvín brought even the Munich frontier very close to that city—but Košice (63 per cent. Slovak, 16 per cent. Magyar), the capital of Eastern Slovakia, and Užhorod (41 per cent. Ruthene, 18 per cent. Hungarian), the capital of Sub-Carpathian Ruthenia, were handed over to Hungary, together with the whole of Southern Slovakia along the Danube, with its supplies of grain, and the fertile southern parts of Sub-Carpathian Ruthenia. Furthermore, the interruption of the main

railway line connecting the western parts of Slovakia with
Eastern Slovakia and Sub-Carpathian Ruthenia had completely
dislocated the system of communications in both of the last-
named provinces.

Again, as in settlements with Germany and Poland, the
ethnological principle was flagrantly defied. The following
examples of the Vienna arbitration is quoted from the Prague
review, *L'Europe Centrale*, of November 12, 1938:

" 1. In the district of *Galanta*, the northern frontier has
been drawn in such a way as to cede to Hungary eight predominantly Slovak parishes, most of which are immediately
adjacent to Slovak territory south of Sereda. In these parishes
live 5,968 Slovaks and only 416 Magyars.

" 2. An even more striking and more incomprehensible
infringement of the ethnic principle is found in the frontier
which runs through the districts of *Nové Zámky* and *Vráble*.
There an extensive region, comprising sixteen Slovak parishes
in Nové Zámky and sixteen in Vráble, as well as the Slovak
towns of *Šurány*, *Slovenský Meder* and *Vráble*, have been
annexed by Hungary. This region contains some 51,000
Slovak inhabitants, as compared with less than 3,000 Magyars,
while the majority of its principal towns also are predominantly Slovak; examples of this are:

	Total population	Slovaks	Hungarians
Vráble	3,347	2,931	140
Slovenský Meder ..	4,407	4,084	262
Šurány	6,388	5,811	218

" 3. At the outskirts of *Modrý Kámen*, Hungary has
annexed a series of parishes which stretch right down to her
former frontier at *Balažské Dármoty*, from which extend the
Slovak parishes which were already previously in Hungary.
These parishes, seven in number, contain some 2,000 inhabitants, of whom 690 are Magyars.

" 4. Near the town of *Lučenec*—which, according to the
1930 Census, had 8,725 Slovak and 4,007 Magyar inhabitants,
although the Census of 1910 recorded it as having a Magyar

majority—Hungary has annexed a circular area comprising four parishes with a mere 800 Hungarian inhabitants, as compared with almost 3,000 Slovaks.

" 5. Hungary has received also the southern portion of the district of *Revúca*, with the town of *Jelšava* and five predominantly Czech parishes, a compact region containing some 4,000 Slovaks, but only 294 Magyars. It is attempted to justify this annexation on the ground that, at least on paper, the existence of a Slovak majority in Jelšava only dates from the end of the Great War.

" 6. The neighbourhood of *Košice* provides another and a particularly blatant example of injustice. The Hungarians were obdurate in insisting that they should have the town of Košice, which, according to the latest Czechoslovak Census, had 42,245 Slovaks, as compared with 11,504 Magyar inhabitants, and which under the Czechoslovak régime had become one of the principle centres of Slovak national life in Eastern Slovakia. The Hungarians based their claim on the allegation that twenty-eight years ago the town had had a Magyar majority. In any case, the extensive area which stretches between Košice and the former Hungarian frontier had always been predominantly Slovak and remains so. Out of the fifty-eight parishes in this district, no fewer than fifty-four are shown to be predominantly Slovak, their aggregate population consisting of 30,918 Slovaks, to 1,024 Magyars. By winning the argument about this region, Hungary annexed, in addition to a vast area stretching southwards from Košice to her former frontiers, the 73,000 Slovaks who live there.

" 7. At the extreme eastern end of the new frontier, Hungary has been given the region of *Trebišov*, extending right down to the former frontier, in which there are fourteen almost completely Slovak parishes, with 8,387 Slovaks to 558 Magyars.

" When one takes into account all the changes resulting from this revision of the frontier, it is seen that, out of the 778 parishes, formerly in Slovakia, which have been allocated to Hungary, no fewer than 178—that is to say, almost a quarter of them—are predominantly Slovak.

" The territories allocated to Hungary total 3,980 square

miles in area and have a total population consisting of 853,670 composed as follows:

272,145 Slovaks.
503,980 Magyars.
8,947 Germans.
26,157 Jews.
1,825 Ruthenes.
14,617 Various Races.
26,005 Foreigners.

The Slovaks, therefore, constitute almost one-third of the population of the territories annexed by Hungary. Moreover, the compact Slovak regions which have been indicated above, containing altogether more than 150,000 Slovaks, could easily have been left in their own country if the delimitation of the new frontier between Slovakia and Hungary had really been carried out in accordance with the principle of ethnic justice. Even if that had been done, however, 120,000 Slovaks would nevertheless have been incorporated into Hungary, thus increasing the Slovak minority there to a quarter of a million. Under such conditions, the number of Maygars who would have remained in Czechoslovakia would not have been materially increased, for it would have added only 18,000 to the number (93,000) who have been left there in any case by the Vienna decision. It may be added that even this concession would have meant that the Slovak minority in Hungary would be very much greater than the Magyar minority in Slovakia."

As regards Sub-Carpathian Ruthenia, the province was deprived of its two principal towns, Užhorod and Mukačevo, and of the whole of its fertile territory, retaining, in fact, only the mountainous region in the north. By this transaction, Hungary acquired 87,000 Magyars, 37,000 Ruthenes, 1,700 Czechs and Slovaks, 26,000 Jews and 5,000 Germans.

Dr. Tiso, Prime Minister of Slovakia, in a mournful speech which was broadcast by wireless after the announcement of Vienna decisions, deplored the fact that Hungary would contain within her new borders a Slovak minority representing no less than 20 per cent. of the population, as compared with 6 per cent., which was the proportion of the Magyar minority in Slovakia as a result of the Treaty of Trianon. " We can do nothing but bow our heads and go on with our work, but no one can prevent us from declaring to the world that great injustice has been done to the Slovak people." Tiso added, by way of consolation, that Herr von Ribbentrop had tried to reconcile him to that injustice by the argument that: " Munich saved the Slovaks from the catastrophe of a total dismemberment of their country. If it had not been for the Munich Agreement, all those interested would have fallen upon you and torn you to pieces. For what you are receiving to-day, therefore, you must thank the Munich Agreement." In actual fact, though, thanks to Munich both Slovakia and Sub-Carpathian Ruthenia were hopelessly mutilated in such a way that they soon became the docile instruments of the German policy of domination. Thus the farce of the Slovak Protectorate was played out in March, 1939, in order to bring the Czechs finally to heel.

Those people in the Western countries who considered the Treaty of Trianon to have been unfair to Hungary may be edified by the study of this attempt to rectify that " injustice." Whereas formerly 6 per cent. of the Hungarian nation was incorporated in a democratic Republic; after Munich one-fifth of the Slovaks were exposed once more to the Magyarising policy of reactionary Hungarian rulers. To-day those Slovaks who are not directly under instructions from the Nazis in Berlin receive those instructions from their Hungarian rulers.

This decision by German and Italian arbitration at Vienna, which struck such a fatal blow at Czechoslovakia, did not, however, " appease " the Poles and the Hungarians. In the territories ceded to Hungary the Slovak population was mercilessly persecuted on racial grounds. On December 25, the Hungarian police fired upon a crowd of Slovaks coming from Mass, merely because they had wanted Mass to be read and the hymns to be sung in the Slovak language. Marie Kokošová, aged seventeen, was shot dead, and seven persons were seriously wounded. Slovaks were again fired upon on January 6, 1939, in the parish of Čechy (Szehi), three persons being seriously wounded, one of whom, Kateřina Mihalíková, subsequently died of her injuries.

Poland and Hungary were dissatisfied that they had failed to obtain a common frontier. Polish and Hungarian marauding bands began to provoke, by incessant attacks, a series of bloody " incidents " along the new frontiers of Slovakia and Sub-Carpathian Ruthenia. This was done with the object of maintaining such a state of unrest and tension as would convince the world that no real " appeasement " was possible until Hungary had obtained the whole of the last-named province.

Between November 2, the date on which the Vienna decisions were announced, and the end of 1938, the Hungarian terrorists carried out no fewer than nineteen armed raids which were officially investigated and reported on by the Czechoslovak Government. The following report was issued:

" 1. On November 3, 1938, that is to say, two days after the Vienna decisions, Hungarian terrorists attacked Czechoslovak military detachments near Kosino, firing on them with automatic pistols and machine guns and throwing hand-grenades. One Czechoslovak non-commissioned officer was killed and five men were wounded.

" 2. On the same date, two bands of Hungarian soldiers, armed with heavy machine guns, carried out an attack on Czechoslovak units near Královu Chlumec.

" 3. On the night of November 4, Hungarian terrorists again attacked Czechoslovak units near Kosino, wounding three men.

" 4. On November 5, a third attack was made in the same district.

" 5. On November 6, several further attacks were carried out by Hungarian terrorists near Kosino, one Czechoslovak soldier being wounded.

" 6. During the night of November 11, a Czechoslovak sentry was attacked while on duty in Vinice.

" 7. On November 17, a group of Hungarian terrorists attacked a Czechoslovak guard-post near Strabičov. On this occasion a Czechoslovak revenue collector was mortally wounded, and one Czechoslovak soldier was reported missing.

" 8. On the same date, a police sergeant was attacked and wounded by a hand-grenade near Nižní Koropce.

" 9. On November 21, terrorists fired with automatic rifles and machine guns on a Czechoslovak sentry near Malý Davídkov.

" 10. On November 22, two Czechoslovak revenue officers were ambushed and made prisoners near Salanky.

" 11. On November 28, a Czechoslovak guard-post near Goronda was attacked by Hungarian terrorists, one Czechoslovak soldier being wounded.

" 12. On December 6, one Czechoslovak gendarme was attacked from behind and killed by Hungarian terrorists at the demarcation line near Horany.

" 13. On December 7, a group of Hungarian terrorists, firing with machine guns and throwing hand-grenades, made an attack on a Czechoslovak emergency patrol near Dovhé (i.e. at the same place where occurred later the " incident " of January 8 mentioned later, with regard to which the Czechoslovak *Chargé d'Affaires* in Budapest made a formal complaint). Only one soldier was wounded on the Czechoslovak side, but the Hungarians suffered several casualties.

" 14. On December 10, firing was repeated near Dovhé.

" 15. On December 13, a Czechoslovak military guard-post was attacked by Hungarian terrorists near Vrbovec. One Czechoslovak soldier wounded.

" 16. On December 21, a Czechoslovak patrol was attacked by Hungarian terrorists near Redvanky.

" 17. During the night of December 22, a Czechoslovak police patrol was attacked by Hungarian terrorists near Romočevice.

" 18. On December 24, a Czechoslovak patrol was attacked from two sides near Baranice.

" 19. On December 30, Hungarian terrorists attacked a small house near the frontier where they wanted, according to the report of the owner of the house, to ambush the Czechoslovak patrol. While returning, they opened fire and threw hand-grenades."

These armed raids were continued into the new year, and on January 7 and 8 ,1939, in the parish of Dovhé, south of Užhorod, firing went on for a longer period and several people were seriously wounded. On January 10, again, somewhere between sixty and eighty Hungarian terrorists attacked with hand-grenades a Czechoslovak frontier patrol at Berrinkoše, between Dravce and Seredná.

Meanwhile the persecution by the Hungarians of the Slovaks in the occupied territories led to violent incidents of another nature. On January 10, 1939, Slovak refugees from Šurany, Komjatice and other Slovak parishes attacked the editorial offices of the Hungarian daily paper, *Esti Ujság*, in Bratislava, though actually there were no casualties. On the Hungarian side of the frontier, however, very serious repression was carried out by the authorities on January 6, 1939, at Roznezov, near the town of Mukačevo, firing being continued for several hours.

Eventually, on January 12, 1939, the Czecho-Slovak and Hungarian Governments mutually agreed to the creation of a " neutral zone " which no armed persons should be allowed to enter.

Numerous " incidents " of a type similar to those already described were provoked also by Polish terrorists, especially along the northern frontier of Sub-Carpathian Ruthenia. In the Těšín district, moreover, there was, for a considerable period, a state of profound unrest, of which both the Czechoslovak and the Polish Governments had constant reason to complain to each other. In fact, the dictates of the Four Powers at Munich let loose all the forces of unrest and disorder, not only throughout the whole of Central Europe, but further afield. Munich ushered in an era of increasing local disturbance and international tension.

(*d*) *Czechoslovakia's Losses.* If we summarise all the results of Munich so far as Czechoslovakia's territorial losses are concerned, it is shown that the shares in the loot taken by Germany, Poland and Hungary with the assent of the entire world were as follows (1930 statistics):

Germany gained, as a result of the Berlin and Munich decisions, 28,000 km.² of territory, with 3,615,833 inhabitants, of whom 2,806,638 are Germans and 719,127 are Czechs. To this last figure must be added a further 40,000 people (including some 30,000 Czechs), who were transferred to Germany in accordance with the protocols of November 20, fixing the final frontier.

Poland gained in the Těšín district 895 km.^{2} of territory, with 228,000 inhabitants, of whom 123,000 are Czechs, 77,000 Poles and 20,000 Germans, and in Northern Slovakia 167 km.^{2} of territory, with 9,000 Czechoslovaks.

Hungary obtained from Slovakia 10,309 km.^{2} of territory, with 853,670 inhabitants, of whom 272,145 are Slovaks, 503,980 Hungarians, 8,947 Germans, 26,151 Jews, 1,825 Ruthenes, 14,617 other nationalities and 26,005 foreigners. In Sub-Carpathian Ruthenia, 1,586 km.^{2} of territory, with 181,609 inhabitants, of whom 17,247 are Czechs or Slovaks, 36,735 Ruthenes, 86,681 Magyars, 4,908 Germans and 25,883 Jews.

See map of Racial Injustice of the Munich Frontier on page 511.

MAP SHOWING RACIAL INJUSTICE OF THE MUNICH FRONTIER

Original Czechoslovak frontiers.

Frontiers introduced after the Munich Agreement (line of demarcation fixing the limits of the areas occupied by German troops).

Black patches—areas containing more than 50 per cent. of Germans or Magyars.

INDEX

INDEX

LIST OF THE DOCUMENTS IN THIS BOOK

[1] Mr. Newton was knighted in the New Year's Honours, 1939, for his services in helping to bring about the Munich Agreement. His present title, therefore, is Sir Basil Newton.